尾田栄一郎

These days, even toothbrushes are technologically advanced. The ultrasound toothbrush is said to rotate 30,000 times per minute, so I tried counting. And it's true—I counted 30,000 rotations.

And now, let's begin volume 41!!

-Eiichiro Oda, 2006

E iichiro Oda began his manga career at the age of 17, when his one-shot cowboy manga **Wanted!** won second place in the coveted Tezuka manga awards. Oda went on to work as an assistant to some of the biggest manga artists in the industry, including Nobuhiro Watsuki, before winning the Hop Step Award for new artists. His pirate adventure **One Piece**, which debuted in **Weekly Shonen Jump** in 1997, quickly became one of the most popular manga in Japan.

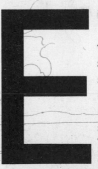

ONE PIECE VOL. 41
WATER SEVEN PART 10

SHONEN JUMP Manga Edition

STORY AND ART BY EIICHIRO ODA

English Adaptation/Megan Bates
Translation/JN Productions
Touch-up Art & Lettering/Elena Diaz
Design/Fawn Lau
Supervising Editor/Yuki Murashige
Editor/Alexis Kirsch

VP, Production/Alvin Lu
VP, Sales & Product Marketing/Gonzalo Ferreyra
VP, Creative/Linda Espinosa
Publisher/Hyoe Narita

Printed in the U.S.A.

Published by VIZ Media, LLC
P.O. Box 77010
San Francisco, CA 94107

10 9 8 7 6 5 4 3 2 1
First printing, April 2010

www.viz.com

PARENTAL ADVISORY
ONE PIECE is rated T for Teen and is recommended for ages 13 and up. This volume contains fantasy violence and tobacco usage.

RATED T FOR TEEN

ratings.viz.com

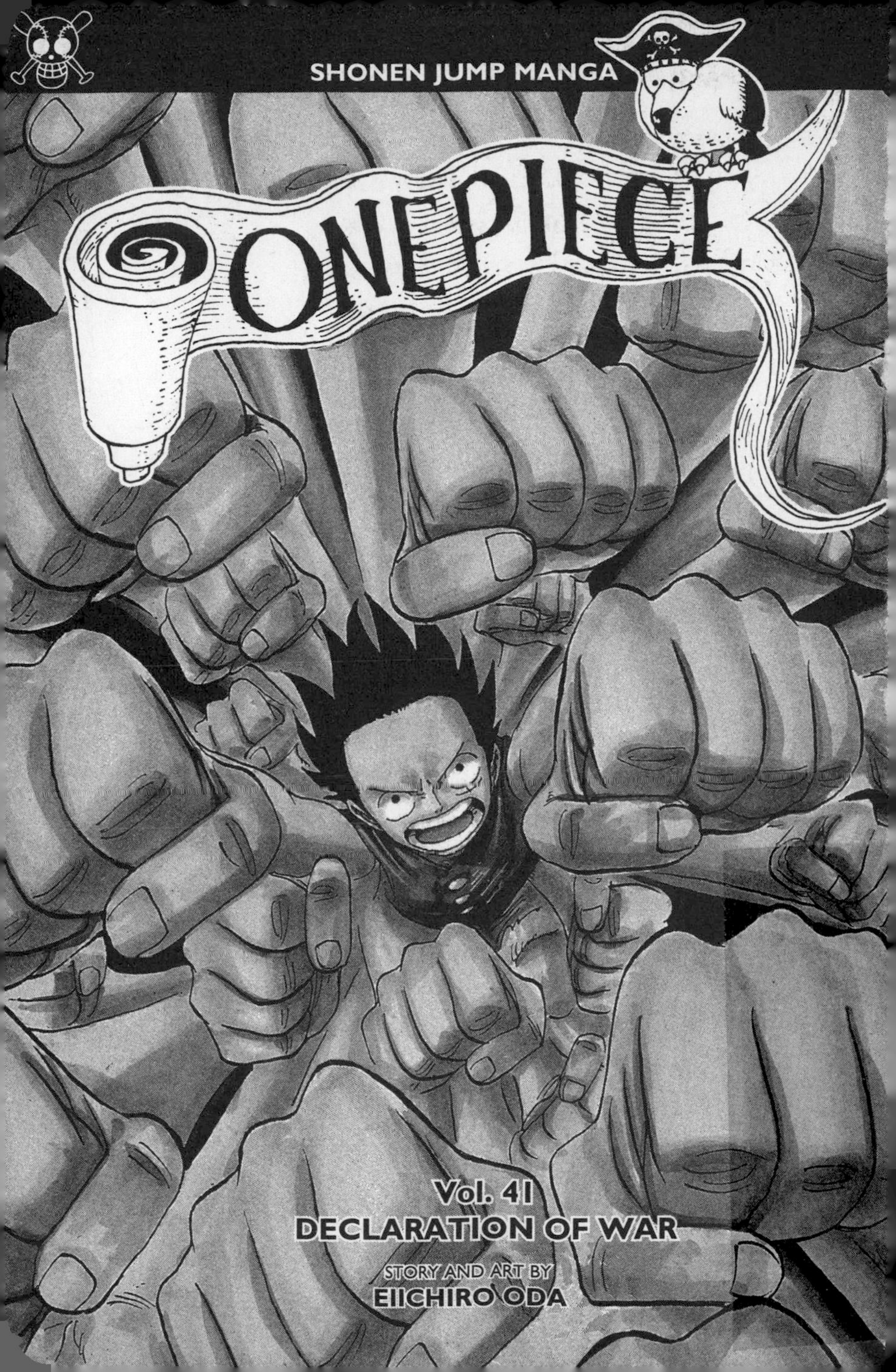

SHONEN JUMP MANGA

ONE PIECE

Vol. 41
DECLARATION OF WAR

STORY AND ART BY
EIICHIRO ODA

Cipher Pol No. 9

An undercover intelligence agency under the direct supervision of the World Government. They have been granted the right to kill uncooperative citizens.

Director
Spandam

Rob Lucci & Hattori

Kaku

Jabra

Blueno

Kumadori

Fukurô

Kalifa

Formerly the beautiful secretary of Tom's Workers. Now station-master of Shift Station.

Kokoro

The Straw Hats

Boundlessly optimistic and able to stretch like rubber, he is determined to become King of the Pirates.

Monkey D. Luffy

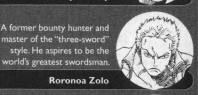

A former bounty hunter and master of the "three-sword" style. He aspires to be the world's greatest swordsman.

Roronoa Zolo

A thief who specializes in robbing pirates. Nami hates pirates, but Luffy convinced her to be his navigator.

Nami

The bighearted cook (and ladies' man) whose dream is to find the legendary sea, the "All Blue."

Sanji

A blue-nosed man-reindeer and the ship's doctor.

Tony Tony Chopper

A mysterious woman in search of the Ponegliff on which true history is recorded.

Nico Robin

Usopp's good friend, a superhero who's come to save Luffy and company... or at least that's what he says.

Sniper King

THE STORY OF ONE PIECE

Volume 41

Monkey D. Luffy started out as just a kid with a dream—to become the greatest pirate in history! Stirred by the tales of pirate "Red-Haired" Shanks, Luffy vowed to become a pirate himself. That was before the enchanted Devil Fruit gave Luffy the power to stretch like rubber, at the cost of being unable to swim—a serious handicap for an aspiring sea dog. Undeterred, Luffy set out to sea and recruited some crewmates—master swordsman Zolo; treasure-hunting thief Nami; lying sharpshooter Usopp; the high-kicking chef Sanji; Chopper, the walkin' talkin' reindeer doctor; and the mysterious archaeologist Robin.

Having successfully plunged into the Grand Line, Luffy and friends arrived at Water Seven, where the best shipwrights in the world gather. The crew planned to hire shipwrights to repair the *Merry Go*, but she was beyond repair, and after much agonizing, Luffy decided to leave *Merry* behind and get a new ship. Usopp furiously opposed Luffy in this decision and left the crew. On top of that, Robin also unexpectedly departed. These fractures rocked the Straw Hat pirates, and no one knew what would become of them.

The government group CP9 attacked the mayor of Water Seven in order to steal his blueprints of the ancient weapon Pluton. However, it became clear that the blueprints were actually in the possession of a criminal named Franky, and CP9 arrested both Franky and Usopp, who was with him at the time. After abducting Robin, the only person who could reactivate that ancient weapon, they boarded the sea train and headed toward Enies Lobby, known as "judicial island," with Sanji as a secret stowaway. Luffy and crew, plus the Franky Family and the shipbuilders of Galley-La, follow them to the island. Going solo, Luffy infiltrates the island and defeats the 10,000-strong Navy troops, only to confront Blueno. With his renewed strength and resolve, Luffy defeats Blueno and gets within sight of the tower where Robin is being held prisoner. Zolo and the others are about to join up with him, but will Robin ever return to her crewmates?

The Franky Family

Professional ship dismantlers, they moonlight as bounty hunters.

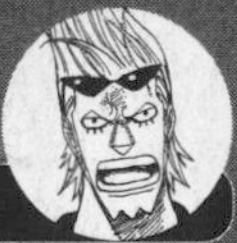

The master builder and an apprentice of Tom, the legendary shipwright.

Franky (Cutty Flam)

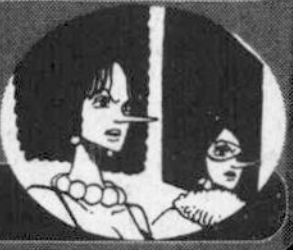

The Square Sisters

Kiwi & Mozu

Galley-La Company

A top shipbuilding company. They are purveyors to the World Government.

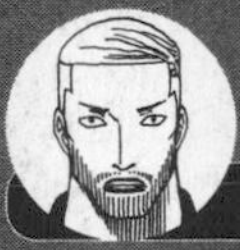

Mayor of Water Seven and president of Galley-La Company. Also one of Tom's apprentices.

Iceberg

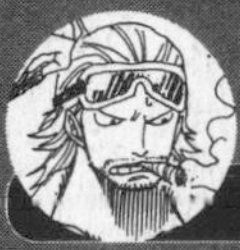

Rigging and Mast Foreman

Paulie

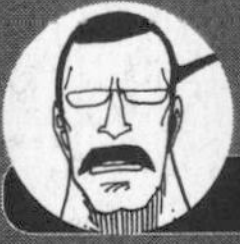

Pitch, Blacksmithing and Block-and-Tackle Foreman

Peepley Lulu

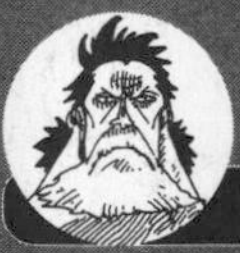

Cabinetry, Caulking and Flag-Making Foreman

Tilestone

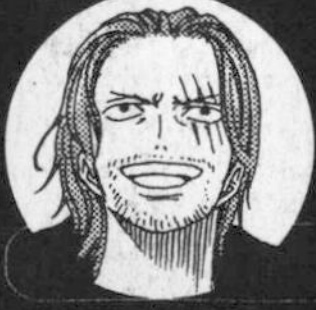

A pirate that Luffy idolizes. Shanks gave Luffy his trademark straw hat.

"Red-Haired" Shanks

Vol. 41
Declaration of War

CONTENTS

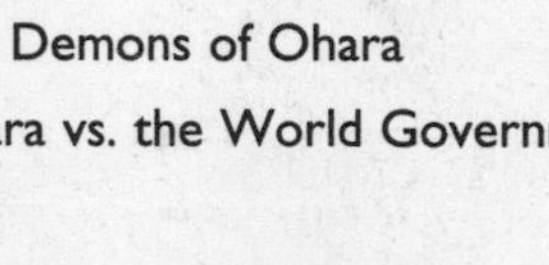

Chapter 389: RESPONSE

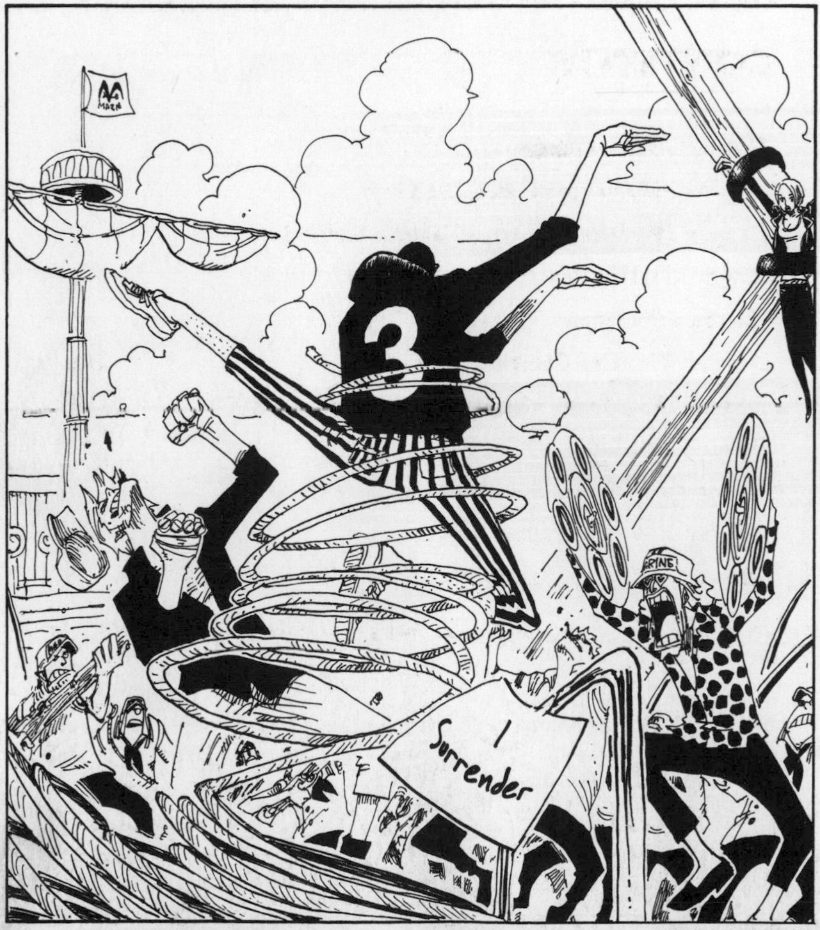

MARIN
MARINE
I Surrender

MS. GOLDEN WEEK'S PLAN, A BAROQUE REUNION, VOL. 23:
"EXPLOSION!! THE FAKE MR. 3'S OH, COME MY WAY KARATE"

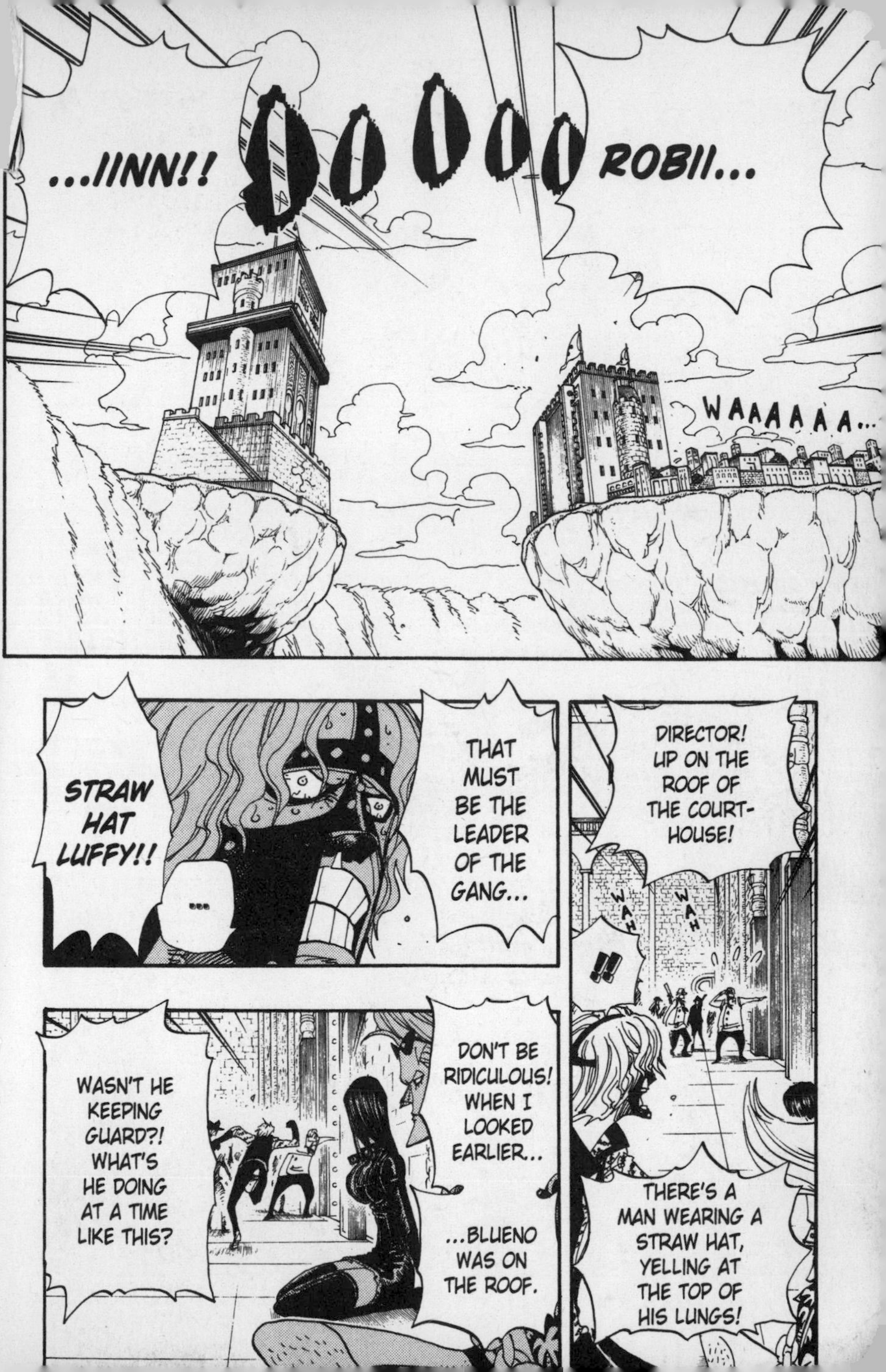
ROBII...
OOOOO
...IINN!!
WAAAAAA...
DIRECTOR! UP ON THE ROOF OF THE COURT-HOUSE!
WAH
WAH
!!
THERE'S A MAN WEARING A STRAW HAT, YELLING AT THE TOP OF HIS LUNGS!
THAT MUST BE THE LEADER OF THE GANG...
STRAW HAT LUFFY!!
...
DON'T BE RIDICULOUS! WHEN I LOOKED EARLIER...
...BLUENO WAS ON THE ROOF.
WASN'T HE KEEPING GUARD?! WHAT'S HE DOING AT A TIME LIKE THIS?

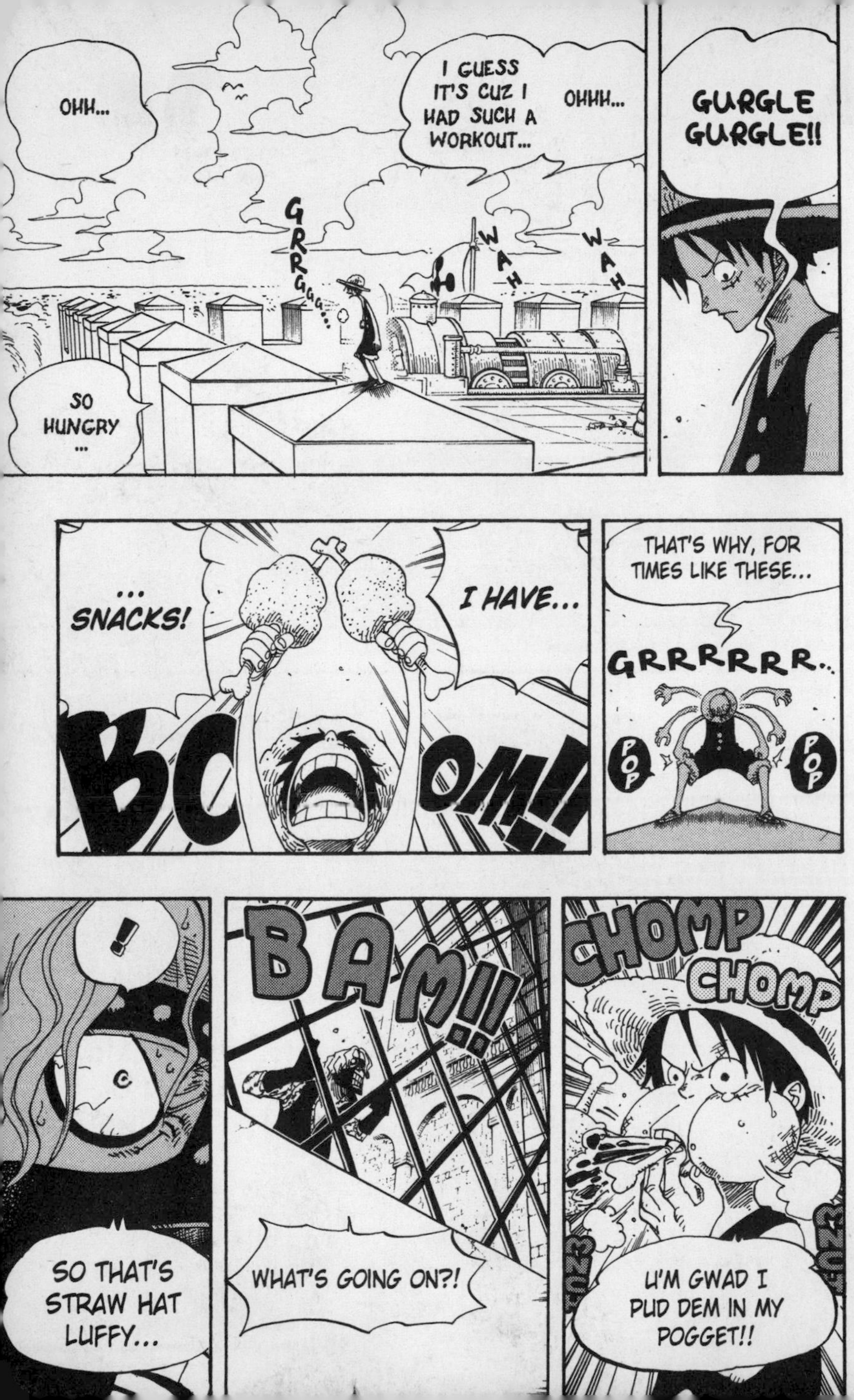
GURGLE GURGLE!!
OHHH...
I GUESS IT'S CUZ I HAD SUCH A WORKOUT...
OHH...
WAH
WAH
GRRRGGG...
SO HUNGRY ...
THAT'S WHY, FOR TIMES LIKE THESE...
GRRRRRRR..
POP
POP
I HAVE...
... SNACKS!
BOOM!!
CHOMP
CHOMP
U'M GWAD I PUD DEM IN MY POGGET!!
BAM!!
WHAT'S GOING ON?!
!
SO THAT'S STRAW HAT LUFFY...

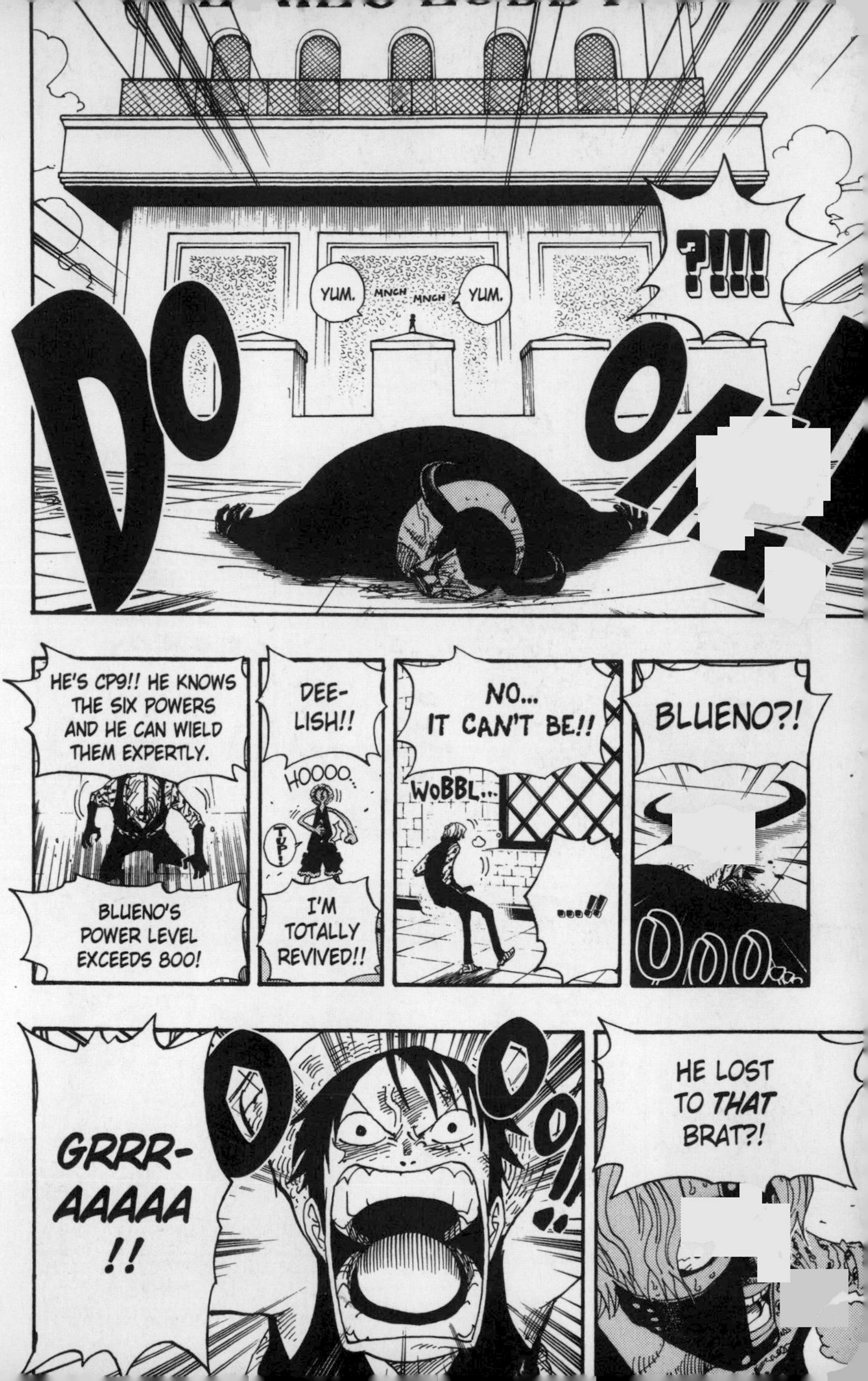
?!!!
YUM.
MNCH MNCH
YUM.
BLUENO?!
NO... IT CAN'T BE!!
WoBBL...
...!!
DEE-LISH!!
HOOOO...
I'M TOTALLY REVIVED!!
HE'S CP9!! HE KNOWS THE SIX POWERS AND HE CAN WIELD THEM EXPERTLY.
BLUENO'S POWER LEVEL EXCEEDS 800!
HE LOST TO *THAT* BRAT?!
GRRR-AAAAA!!

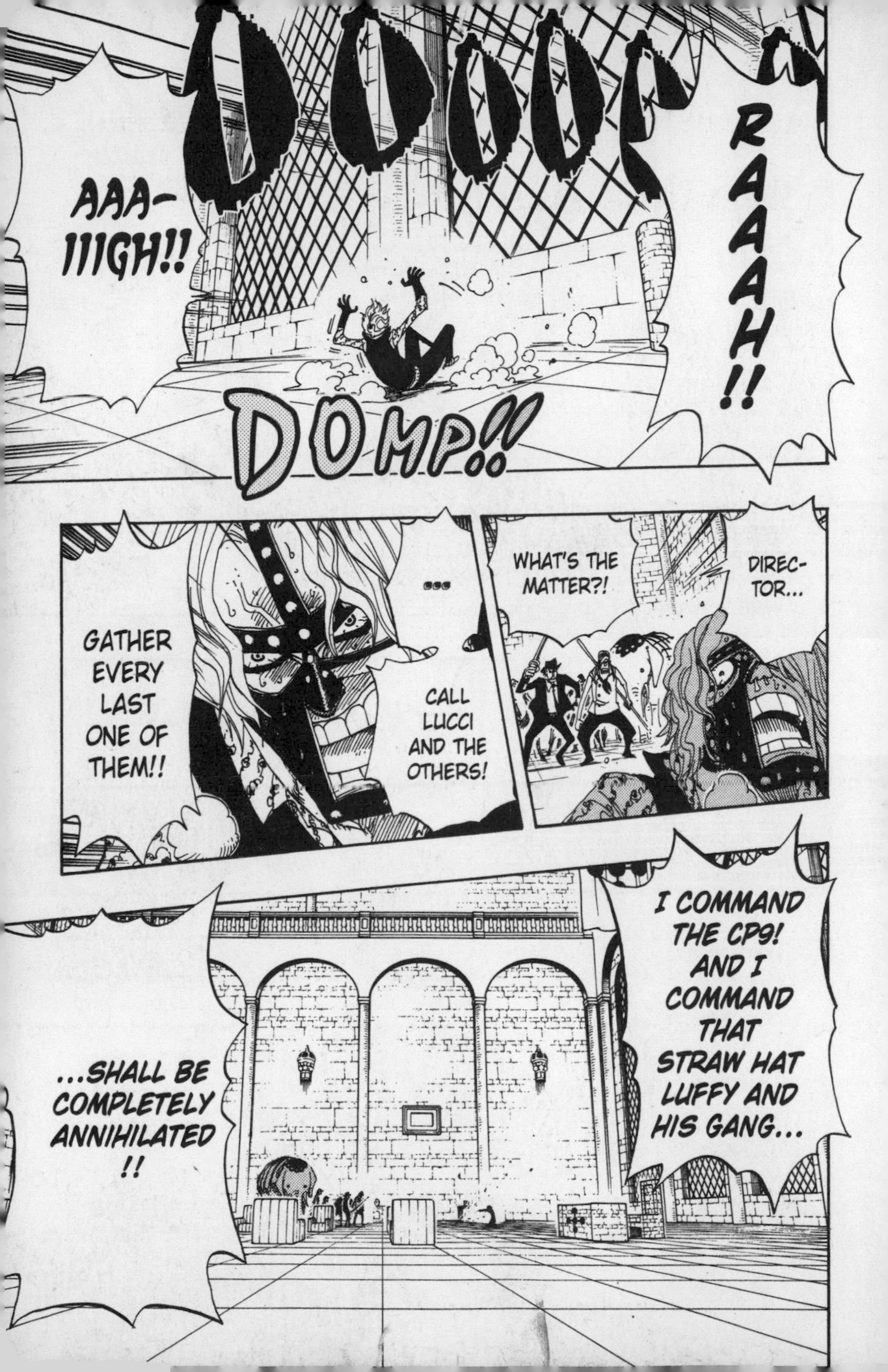
RAAAAH!!
AAA-IIIGH!!
DOMP!!
DIREC-TOR...
WHAT'S THE MATTER?!
...
CALL LUCCI AND THE OTHERS!
GATHER EVERY LAST ONE OF THEM!!
I COMMAND THE CP9! AND I COMMAND THAT STRAW HAT LUFFY AND HIS GANG...
...SHALL BE COMPLETELY ANNIHILATED!!

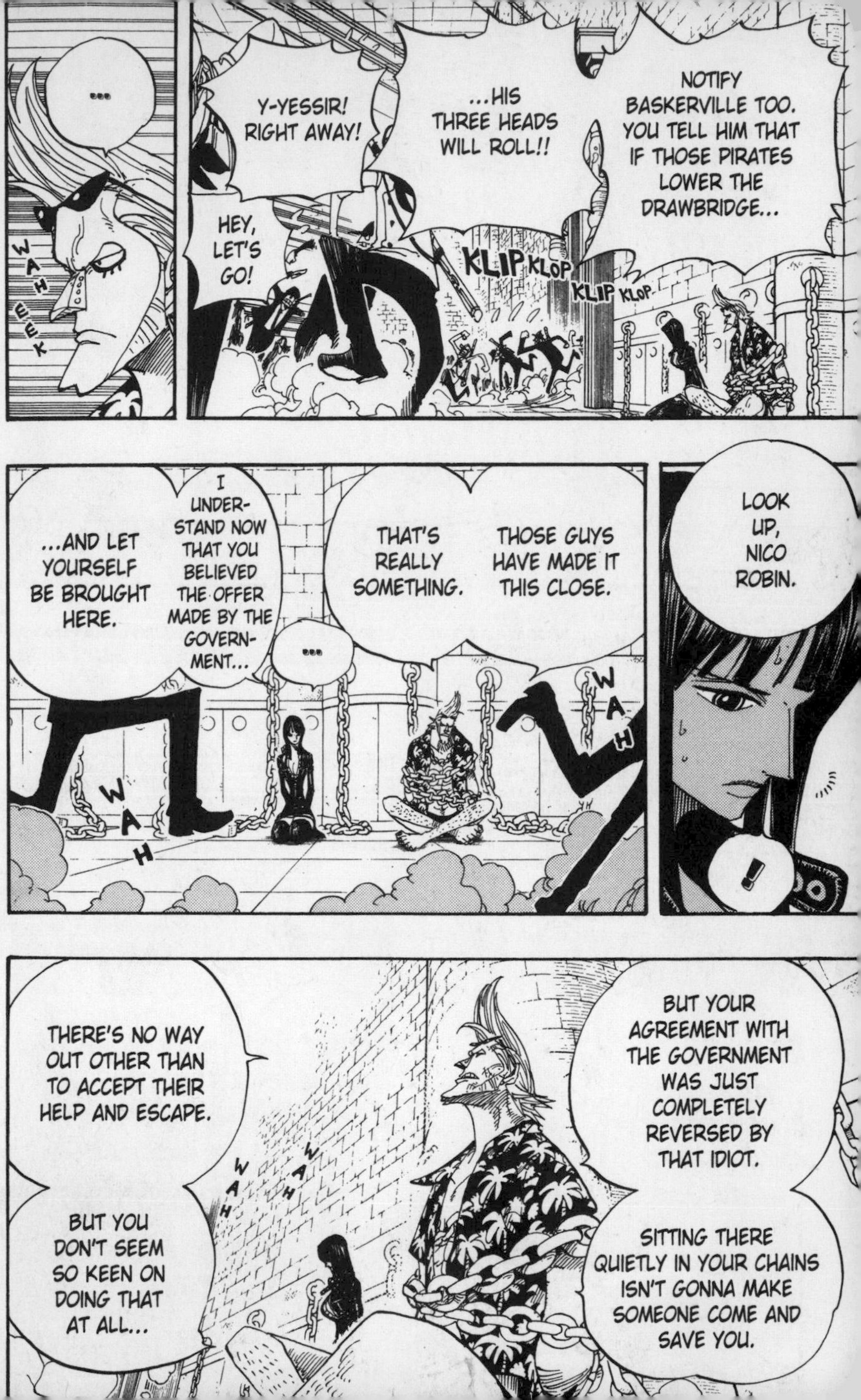
NOTIFY BASKERVILLE TOO. YOU TELL HIM THAT IF THOSE PIRATES LOWER THE DRAWBRIDGE...
...HIS THREE HEADS WILL ROLL!!
Y-YESSIR! RIGHT AWAY!
HEY, LET'S GO!
KLIP KLOP
KLIP KLOP
...
WAHEEK
LOOK UP, NICO ROBIN.
!
THOSE GUYS HAVE MADE IT THIS CLOSE.
THAT'S REALLY SOMETHING.
WAH
I UNDERSTAND NOW THAT YOU BELIEVED THE OFFER MADE BY THE GOVERNMENT...
...
...AND LET YOURSELF BE BROUGHT HERE.
WAH
BUT YOUR AGREEMENT WITH THE GOVERNMENT WAS JUST COMPLETELY REVERSED BY THAT IDIOT.
SITTING THERE QUIETLY IN YOUR CHAINS ISN'T GONNA MAKE SOMEONE COME AND SAVE YOU.
WAH
WAH
THERE'S NO WAY OUT OTHER THAN TO ACCEPT THEIR HELP AND ESCAPE.
BUT YOU DON'T SEEM SO KEEN ON DOING THAT AT ALL...

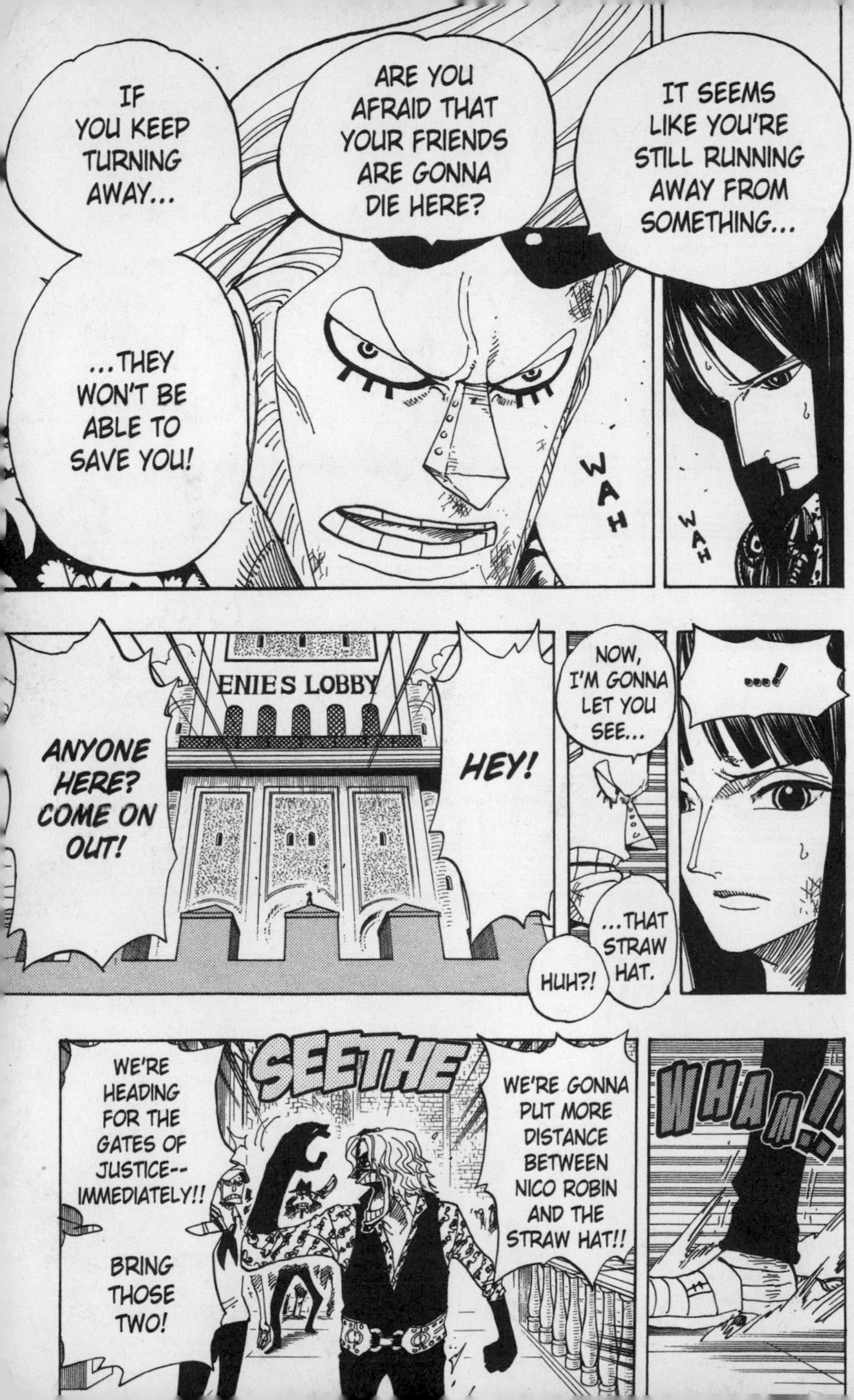
IT SEEMS LIKE YOU'RE STILL RUNNING AWAY FROM SOMETHING...
WAH
ARE YOU AFRAID THAT YOUR FRIENDS ARE GONNA DIE HERE?
IF YOU KEEP TURNING AWAY...
...THEY WON'T BE ABLE TO SAVE YOU!
WAH
...!
NOW, I'M GONNA LET YOU SEE...
...THAT STRAW HAT.
HUH?!
HEY!
ENIES LOBBY
ANYONE HERE? COME ON OUT!
WHAM!!
WE'RE GONNA PUT MORE DISTANCE BETWEEN NICO ROBIN AND THE STRAW HAT!!
SEETHE
WE'RE HEADING FOR THE GATES OF JUSTICE-- IMMEDIATELY!!
BRING THOSE TWO!

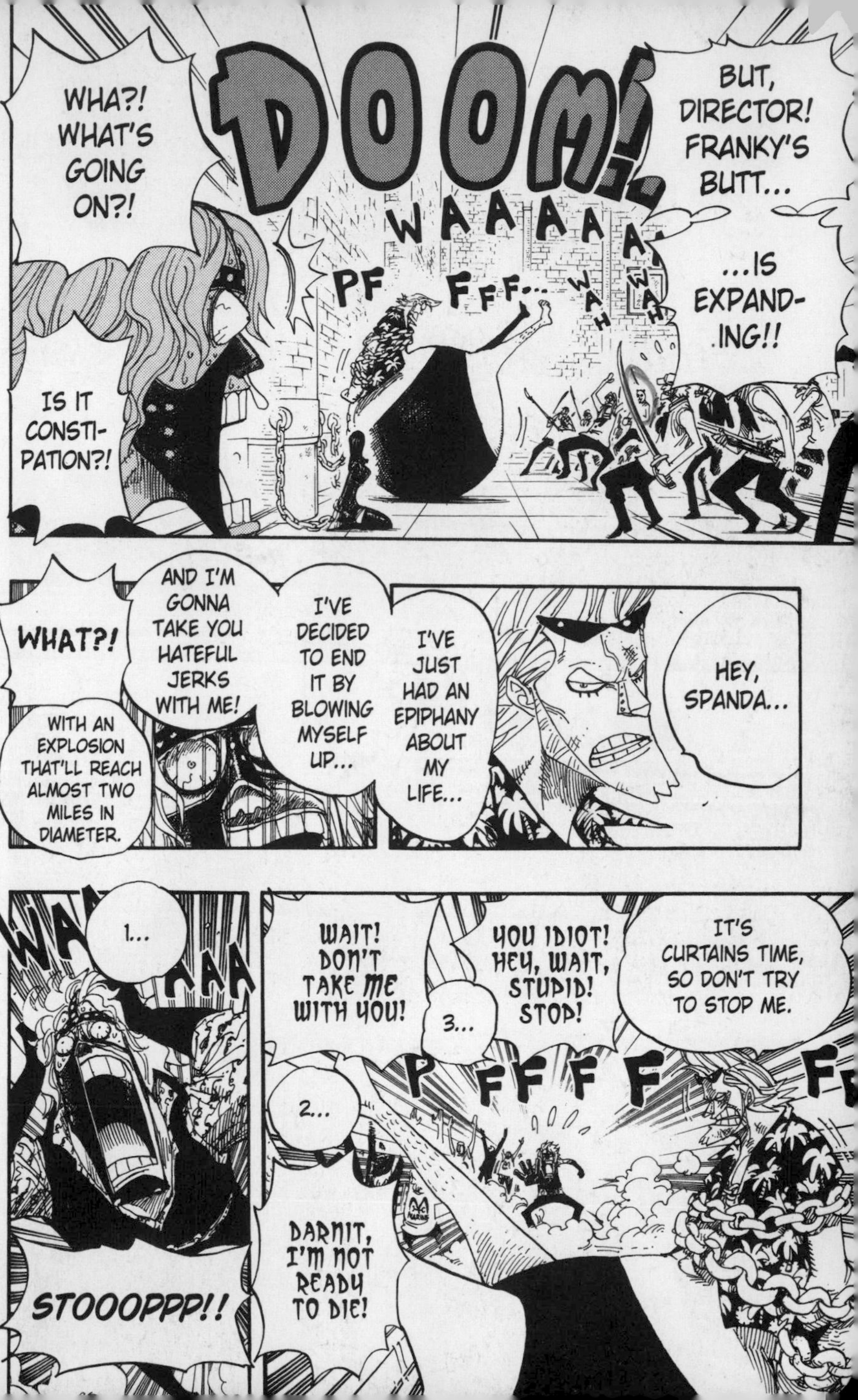
BUT, DIRECTOR! FRANKY'S BUTT...
...IS EXPAND-ING!!
DOOM!
WAAAAA
WAH WAH
PF FFF...
WHA?! WHAT'S GOING ON?!
IS IT CONSTI-PATION?!
HEY, SPANDA...
I'VE JUST HAD AN EPIPHANY ABOUT MY LIFE...
I'VE DECIDED TO END IT BY BLOWING MYSELF UP...
AND I'M GONNA TAKE YOU HATEFUL JERKS WITH ME!
WHAT?!
WITH AN EXPLOSION THAT'LL REACH ALMOST TWO MILES IN DIAMETER.
IT'S CURTAINS TIME, SO DON'T TRY TO STOP ME.
YOU IDIOT! HEY, WAIT, STUPID! STOP!
3...
WAIT! DON'T TAKE ME WITH YOU!
PFFFF
2...
DARNIT, I'M NOT READY TO DIE!
1...
WAAAA
STOOOPPP!!

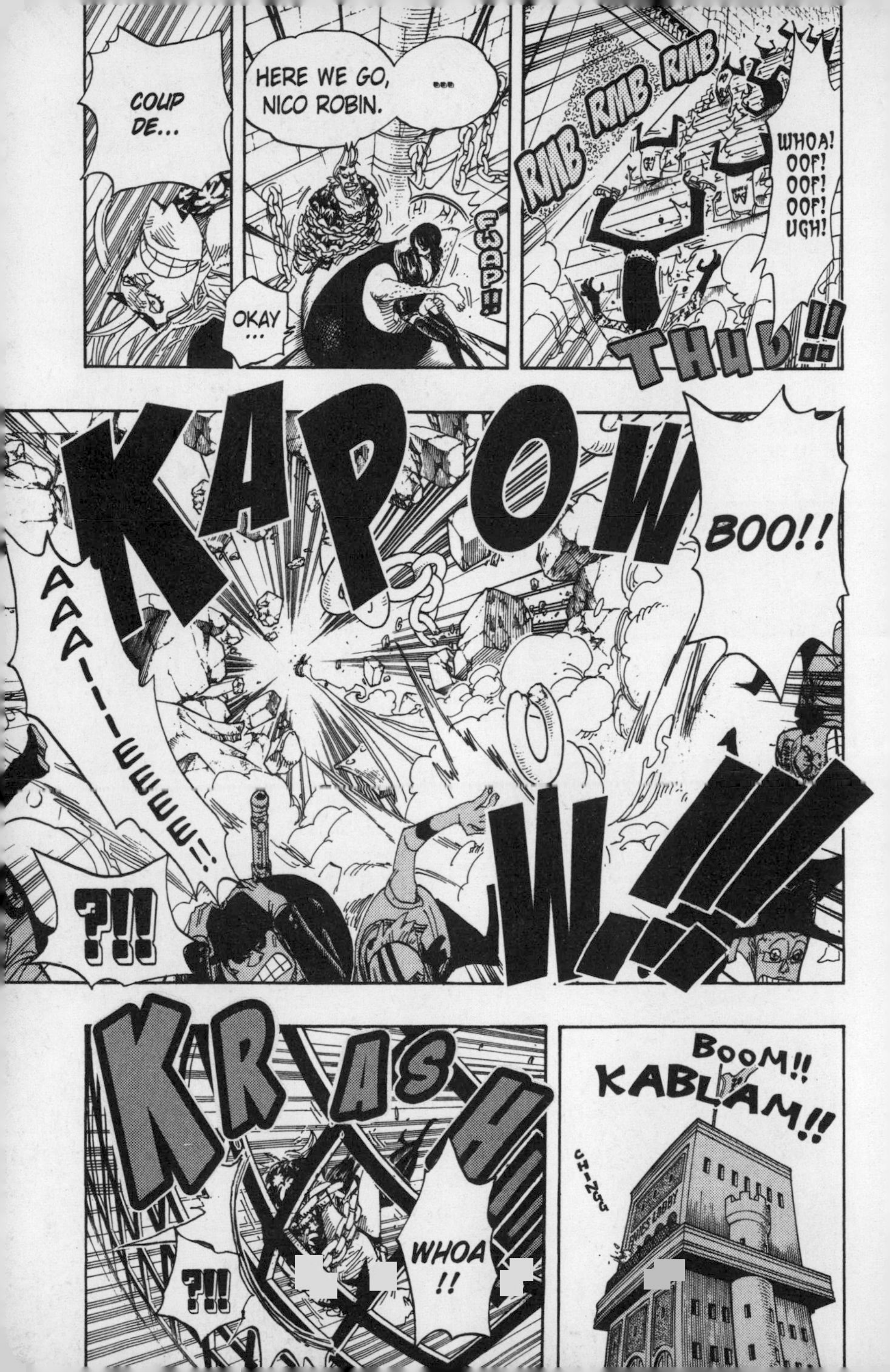
RMB RMB RMB
WHOA! OOF! OOF! OOF! UGH!
THUD!!
HERE WE GO, NICO ROBIN.
...
FWAP!!
OKAY ...
COUP DE...
KAPOW
BOO!!
AAAIIIEEEEE!!
W...!!!
?!!
BOOM!!
KABLAM!!
CHING
KRASH
WHOA !!
?!!

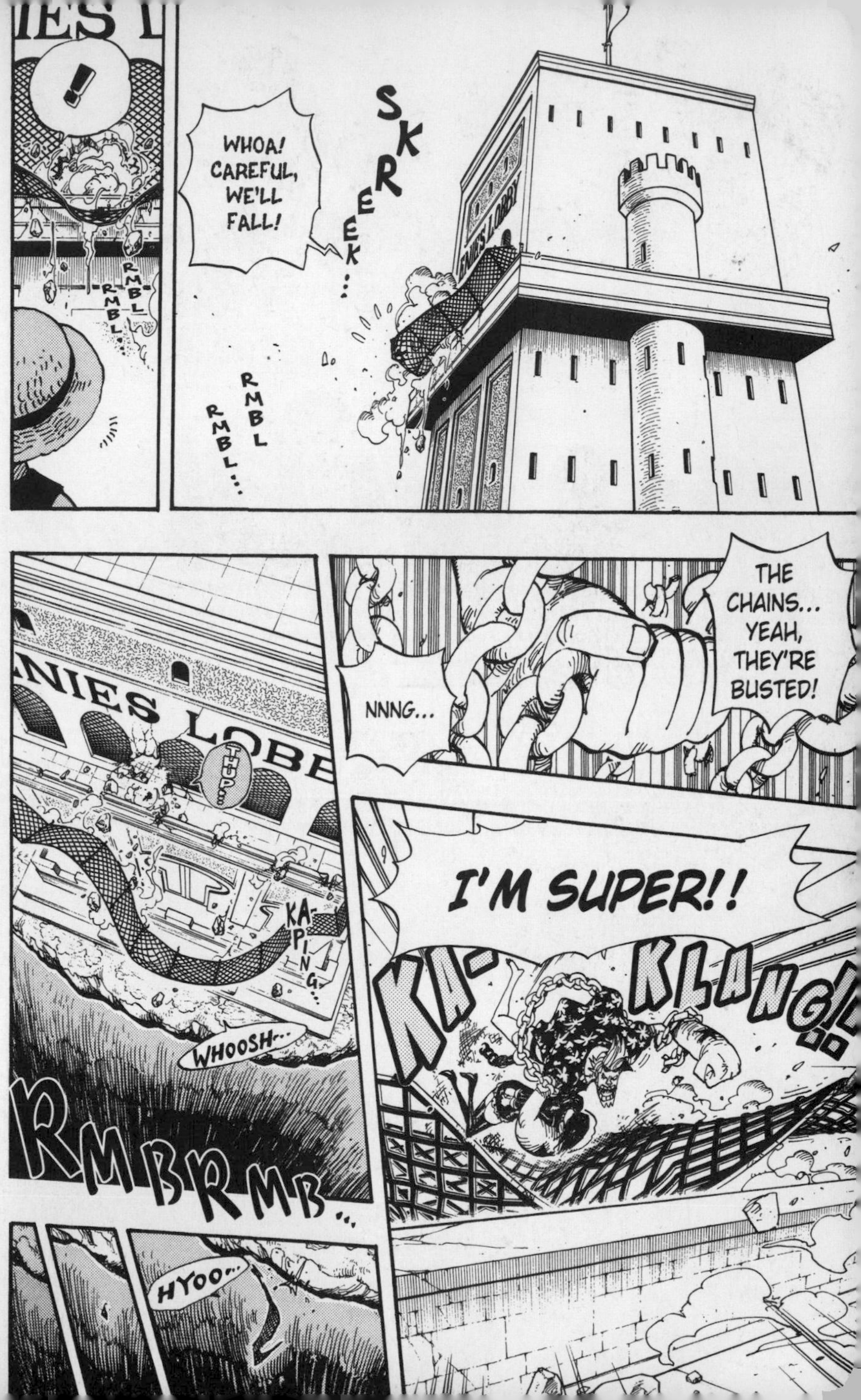
WHOA! CAREFUL, WE'LL FALL!
SKREEK!!
RMBL RMBL...
!
RMBL RMBL
THE CHAINS... YEAH, THEY'RE BUSTED!
NNNG...
I'M SUPER!!
KA-KLANG!!
THUP!!
KA-PING...
WHOOSH...
RMBRMB...
HYOO...

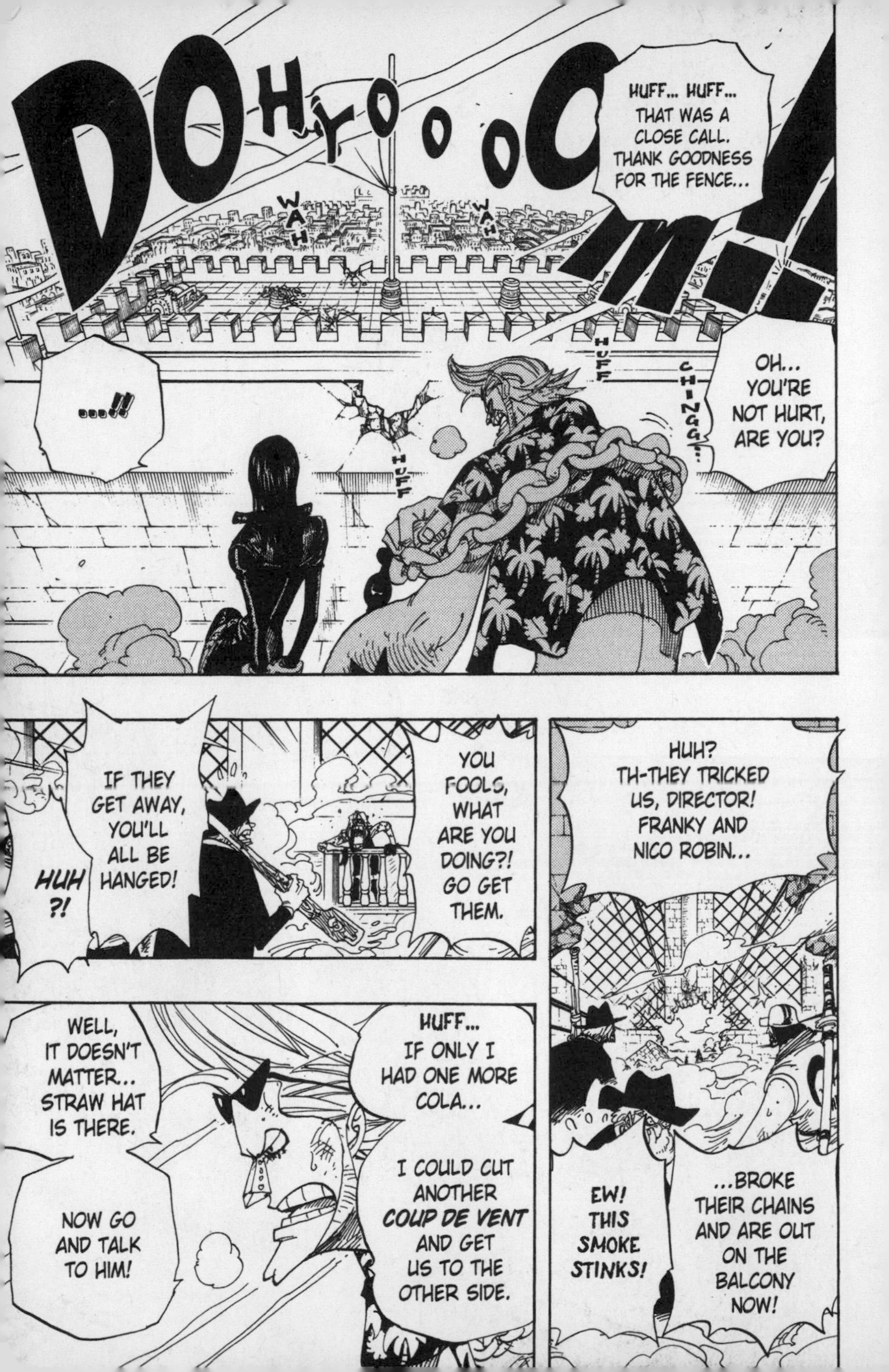
DOHYOOOOM
WAH
WAH
HUFF... HUFF... THAT WAS A CLOSE CALL. THANK GOODNESS FOR THE FENCE...
OH... YOU'RE NOT HURT, ARE YOU?
HUFF
CHINGG...
HUFF
...!!
HUH? TH-THEY TRICKED US, DIRECTOR! FRANKY AND NICO ROBIN...
...BROKE THEIR CHAINS AND ARE OUT ON THE BALCONY NOW!
EW! THIS SMOKE STINKS!
YOU FOOLS, WHAT ARE YOU DOING?! GO GET THEM.
IF THEY GET AWAY, YOU'LL ALL BE HANGED!
HUH ?!
HUFF... IF ONLY I HAD ONE MORE COLA...
I COULD CUT ANOTHER COUP DE VENT AND GET US TO THE OTHER SIDE.
WELL, IT DOESN'T MATTER... STRAW HAT IS THERE.
NOW GO AND TALK TO HIM!

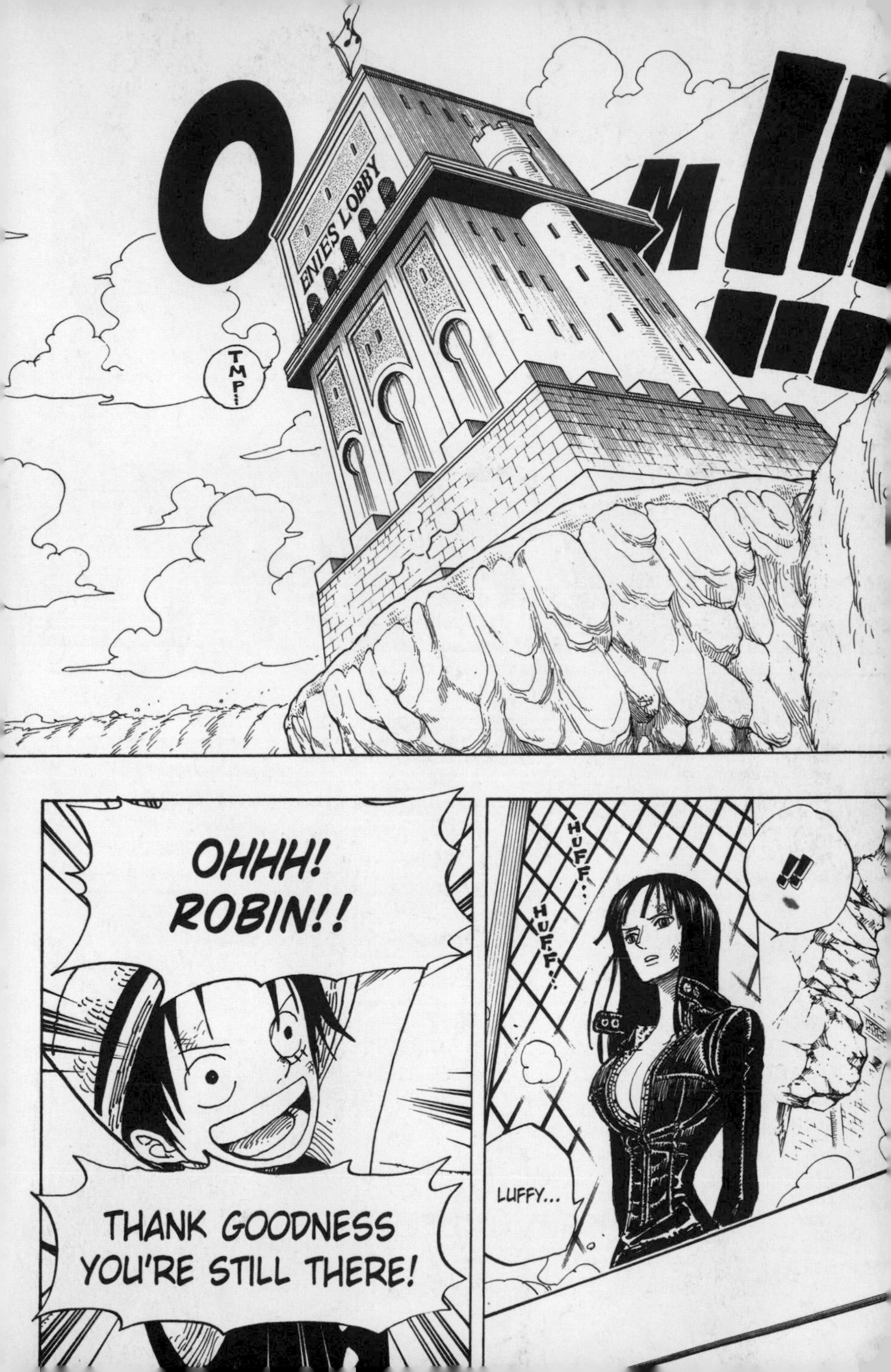
OM!!!
TMP...
!!
HUFF...
HUFF...
LUFFY...
OHHH! ROBIN!!
THANK GOODNESS YOU'RE STILL THERE!

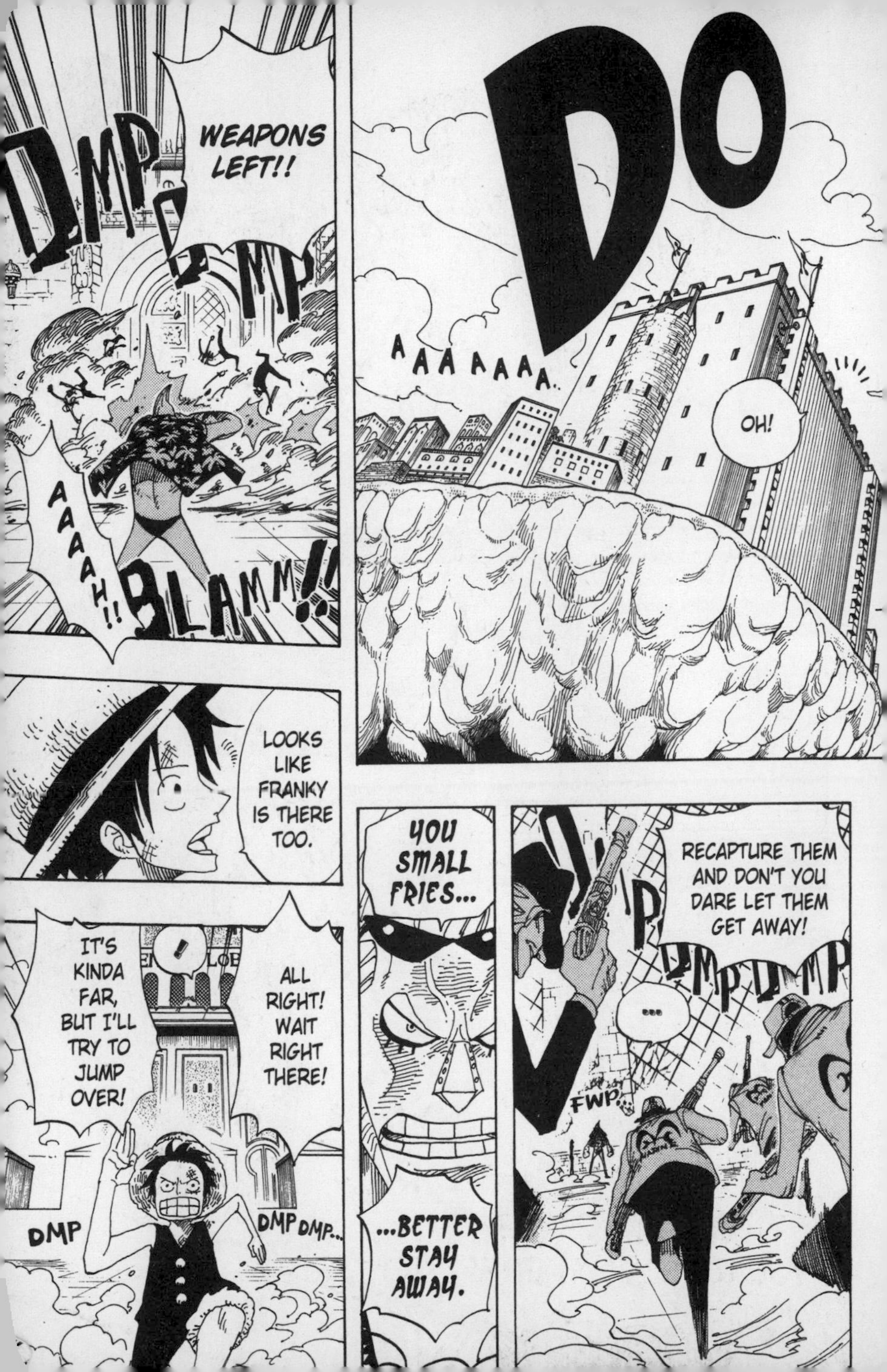
DO
AAAAAAA..
OH!
DMP DMP DMP
WEAPONS LEFT!!
AAAAH!!
BLAMM!!
LOOKS LIKE FRANKY IS THERE TOO.
RECAPTURE THEM AND DON'T YOU DARE LET THEM GET AWAY!
...
DMP DMP DMP
FWP..
YOU SMALL FRIES...
...BETTER STAY AWAY.
ALL RIGHT! WAIT RIGHT THERE!
IT'S KINDA FAR, BUT I'LL TRY TO JUMP OVER!
!
DMP
DMP DMP...

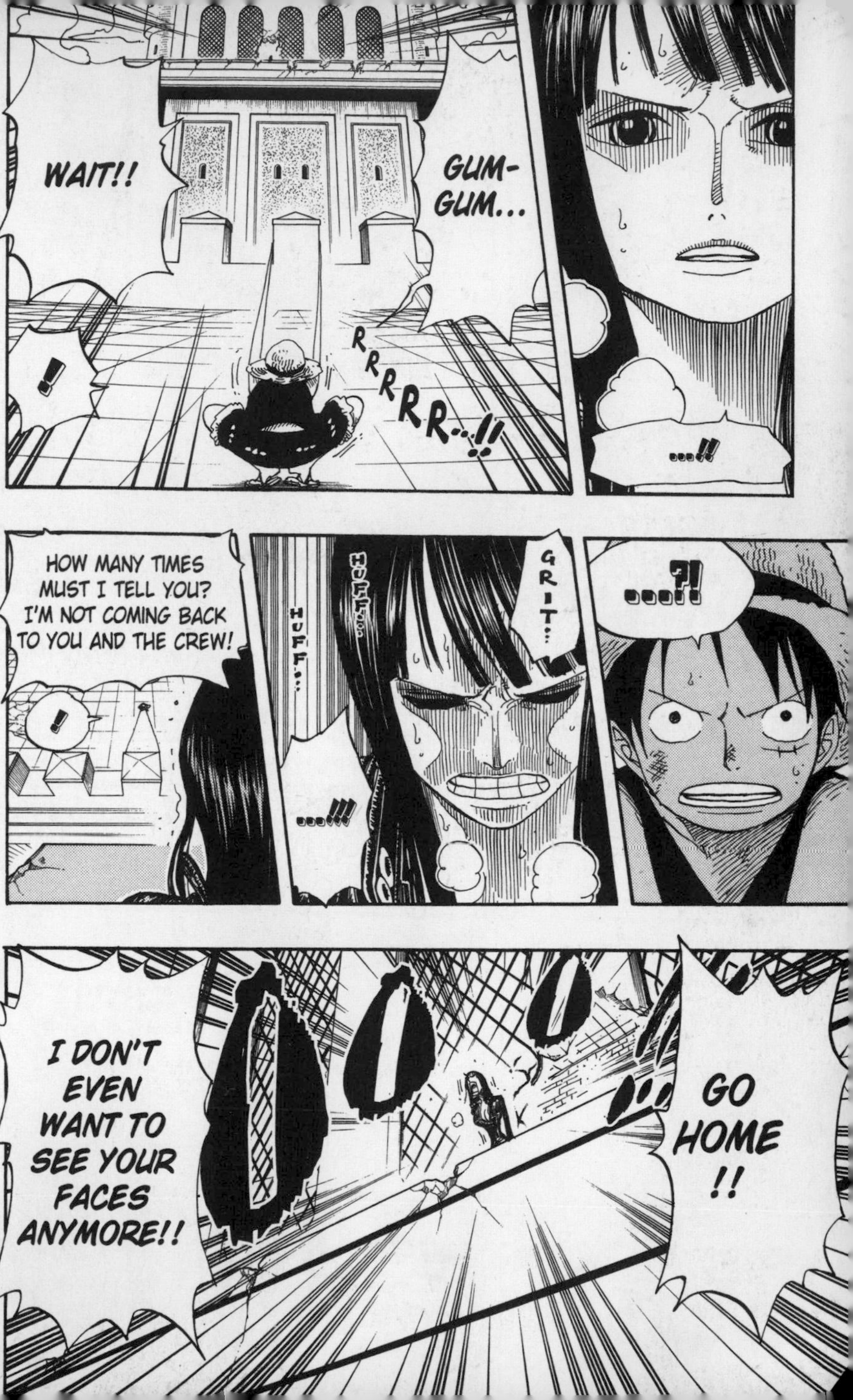
...!!
GUM-GUM...
WAIT!!
RRRRRR...!!
!
...?!
GRIT..
HUFF..
HUFF..
...!!!
HOW MANY TIMES MUST I TELL YOU? I'M NOT COMING BACK TO YOU AND THE CREW!
!
GO HOME!!
I DON'T EVEN WANT TO SEE YOUR FACES ANYMORE!!

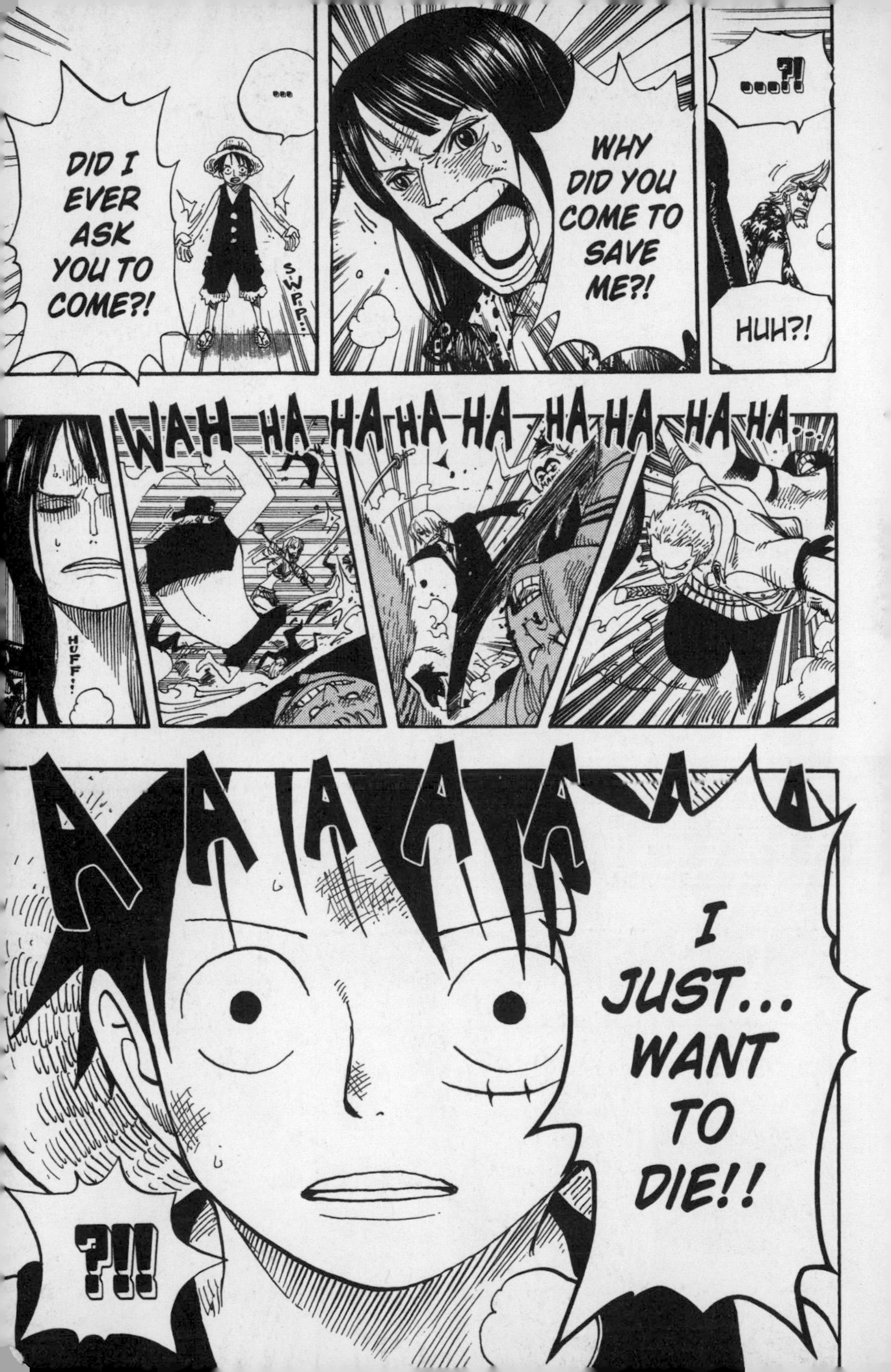

...?!
HUH?!
WHY DID YOU COME TO SAVE ME?!
...
SWPP...
DID I EVER ASK YOU TO COME?!
WAH HA HA HA HA HA HA HA HA...
HUFF...
AAAAAAAA
I JUST... WANT TO DIE!!
?!!

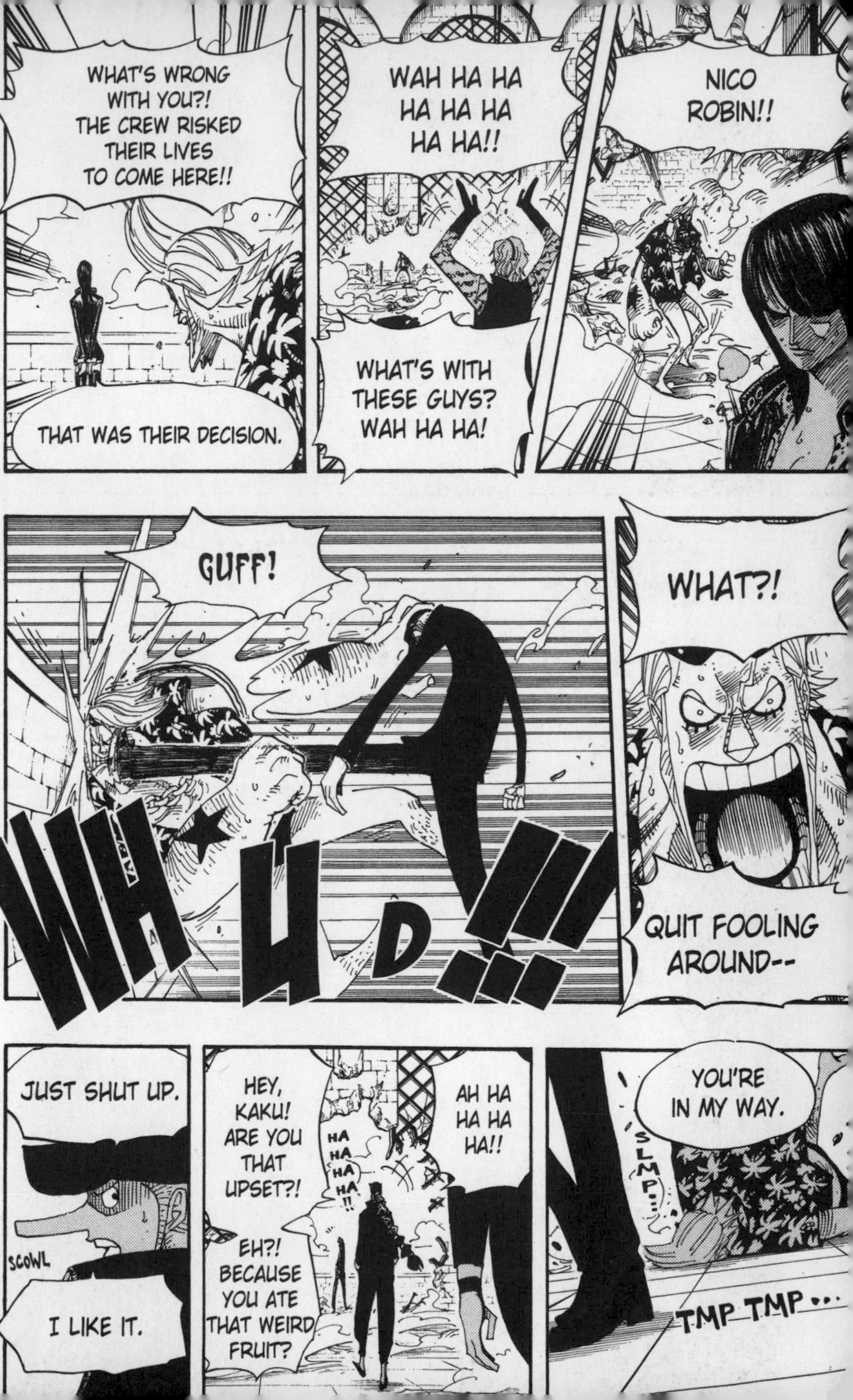
NICO ROBIN!!
WAH HA HA HA HA HA HA HA!!
WHAT'S WITH THESE GUYS? WAH HA HA!
WHAT'S WRONG WITH YOU?! THE CREW RISKED THEIR LIVES TO COME HERE!!
THAT WAS THEIR DECISION.
WHAT?!
QUIT FOOLING AROUND--
GUFF!
WHUD...!!!
YOU'RE IN MY WAY.
SLMP...
TMP TMP...
AH HA HA HA HA!!
HEY, KAKU! ARE YOU THAT UPSET?!
HA HA HA HA!!
EH?! BECAUSE YOU ATE THAT WEIRD FRUIT?
JUST SHUT UP.
SCOWL
I LIKE IT.

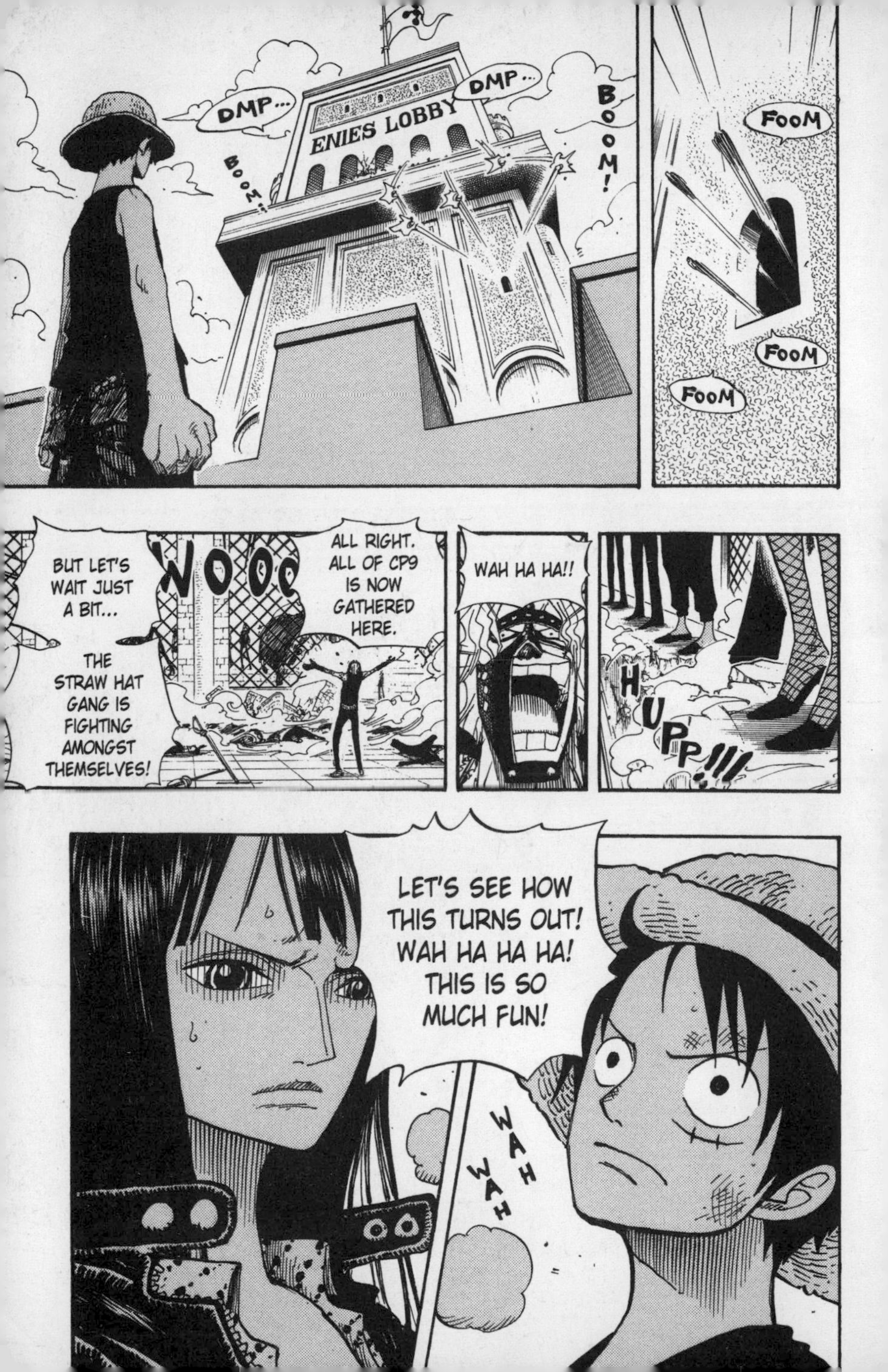
FOOM
FOOM
FOOM
BOOM!
DMP...
ENIES LOBBY
DMP...
BOOM!!
HUPP!!!!
WAH HA HA!!
ALL RIGHT. ALL OF CP9 IS NOW GATHERED HERE.
BUT LET'S WAIT JUST A BIT...
THE STRAW HAT GANG IS FIGHTING AMONGST THEMSELVES!
LET'S SEE HOW THIS TURNS OUT! WAH HA HA HA! THIS IS SO MUCH FUN!
WAH WAH

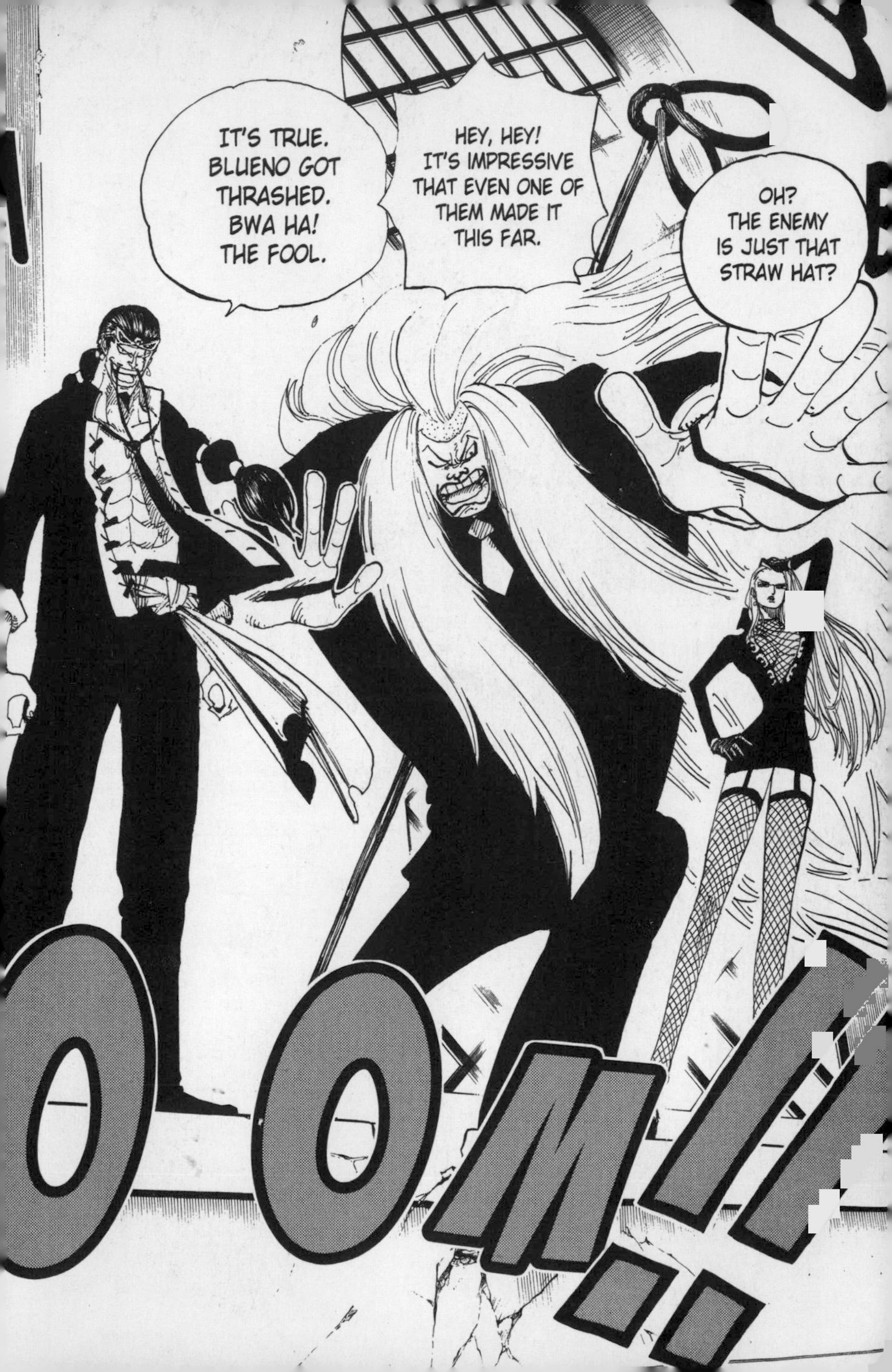
OH? THE ENEMY IS JUST THAT STRAW HAT?
HEY, HEY! IT'S IMPRESSIVE THAT EVEN ONE OF THEM MADE IT THIS FAR.
IT'S TRUE. BLUENO GOT THRASHED. BWA HA! THE FOOL.
OOM!!

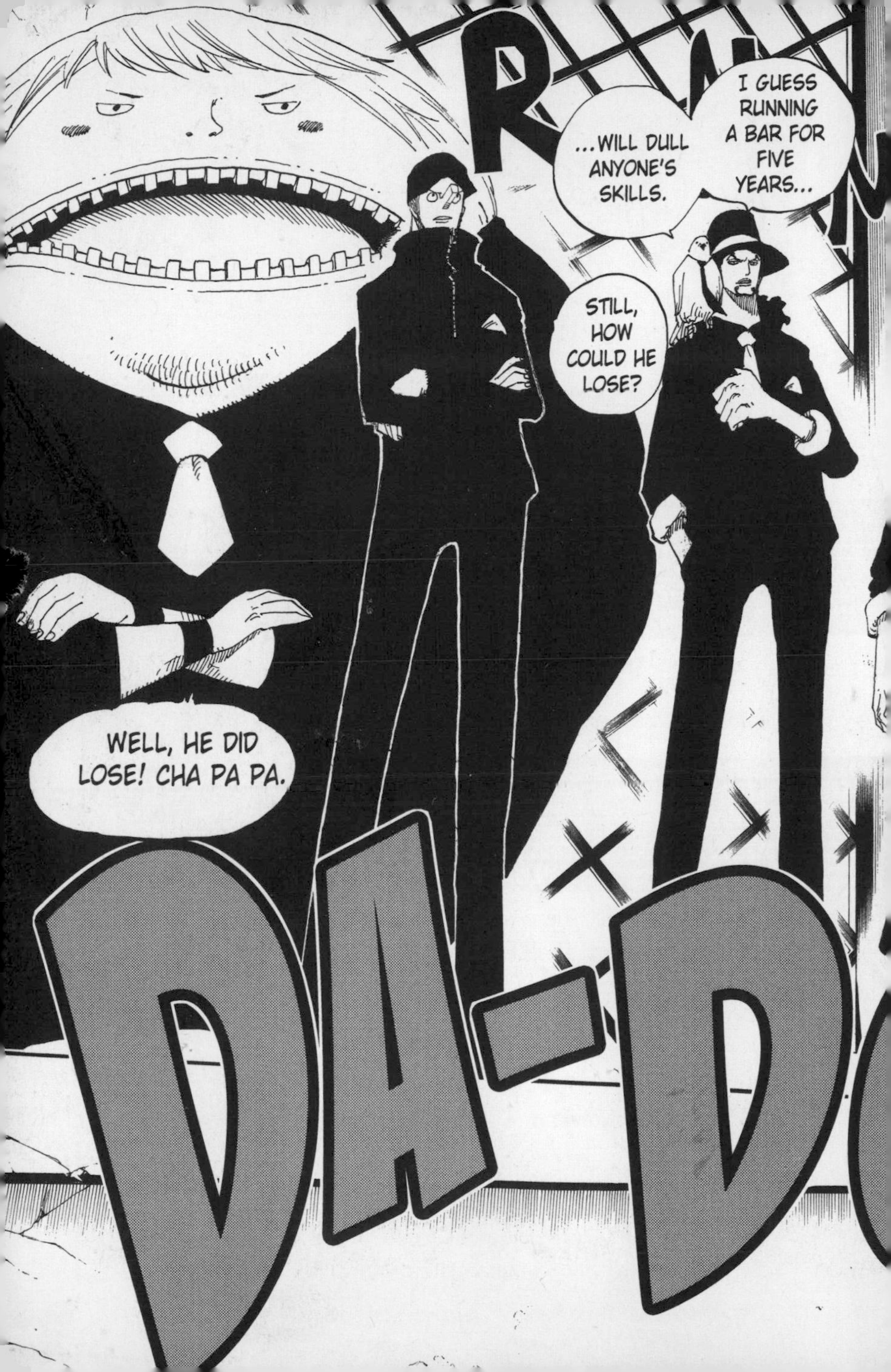
I GUESS RUNNING A BAR FOR FIVE YEARS...
...WILL DULL ANYONE'S SKILLS.
STILL, HOW COULD HE LOSE?
WELL, HE DID LOSE! CHA PA PA.
DA-D

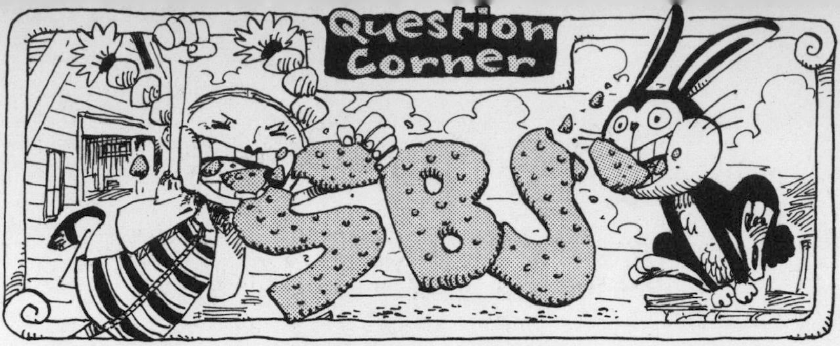
Question Corner
SBS

Reader: Yo, Oda Sensei, Happy New Year!! Looking forward to the next one. I have a very simple question. Since there are foreign versions of *One Piece*, shouldn't it be said in English? So I will:

"**Let's begin The Question Corner!!**"

There. Now I'll be able to pass my English test!

--Nanpou

Oda: Oh! How global of you. Yes, The Question Corner should span the world, right?! The thought that this corner is also translated in the foreign versions gives me the chills. (DOOM!!)

Q: Oda, can you make this guy one of the Seven Warlords of the Sea?

--Hikaru-kun

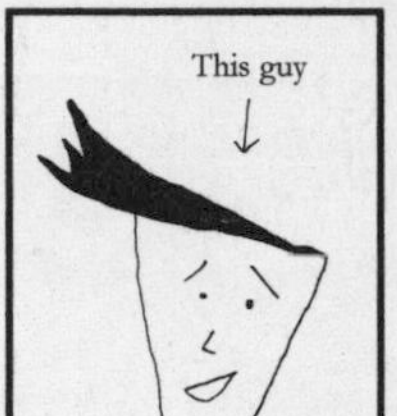
This guy

A: No.

Q: Oda Sensei, In the first panel of page 61 in vol. 40, the watchdog on the right of the Guard Dog Unit seems to be speaking to the watchdog next to him. What's the story? If this is the case, please ask Chopper about it.

--Right Baskerville

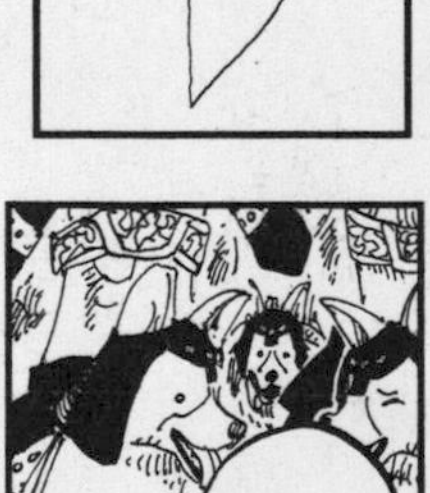
WOOF!!

A: I wonder what they're talking about. Chopper!

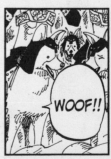

Chopper: This is what they're saying. Left dog: "Jabra of CP9 was dumped by the waitress, Gatharine."
Right dog: "No kidding? (laugh)"

A: It seems this rumor is the hot topic in town.

Chapter 390:
ACCEPTING THE CHALLENGE

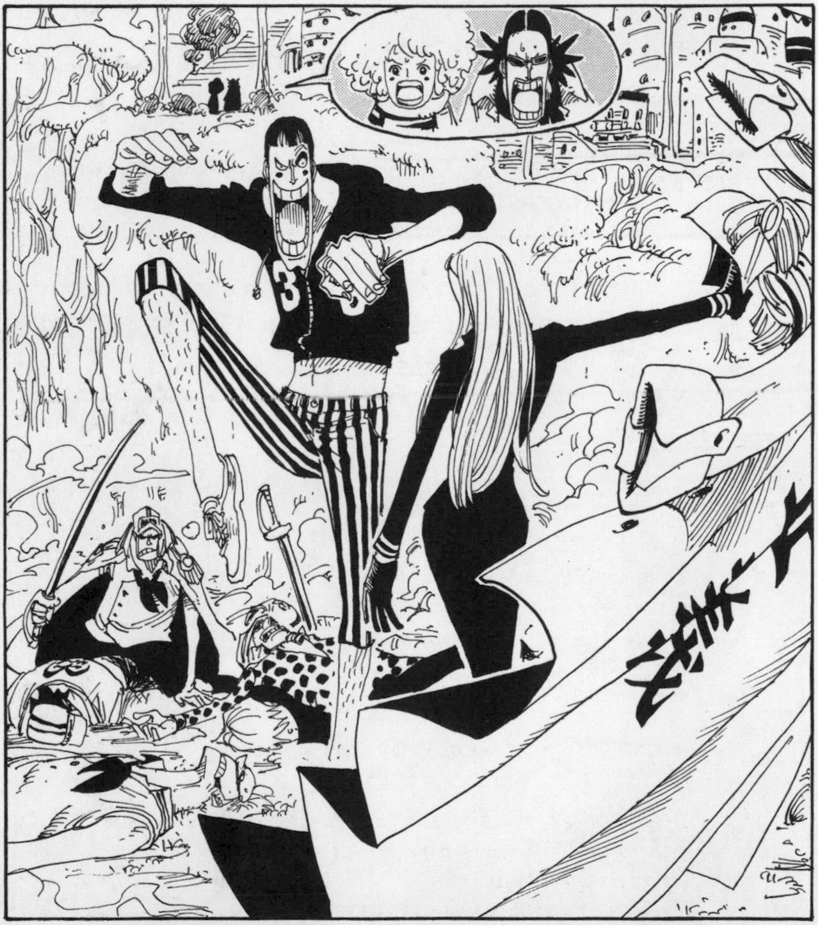

MS. GOLDEN WEEK'S PLAN, A BAROQUE REUNION, VOL. 24:
"THE DESTINED SHOWDOWN!! MR. 2 VS. BLACK CAGE HINA"

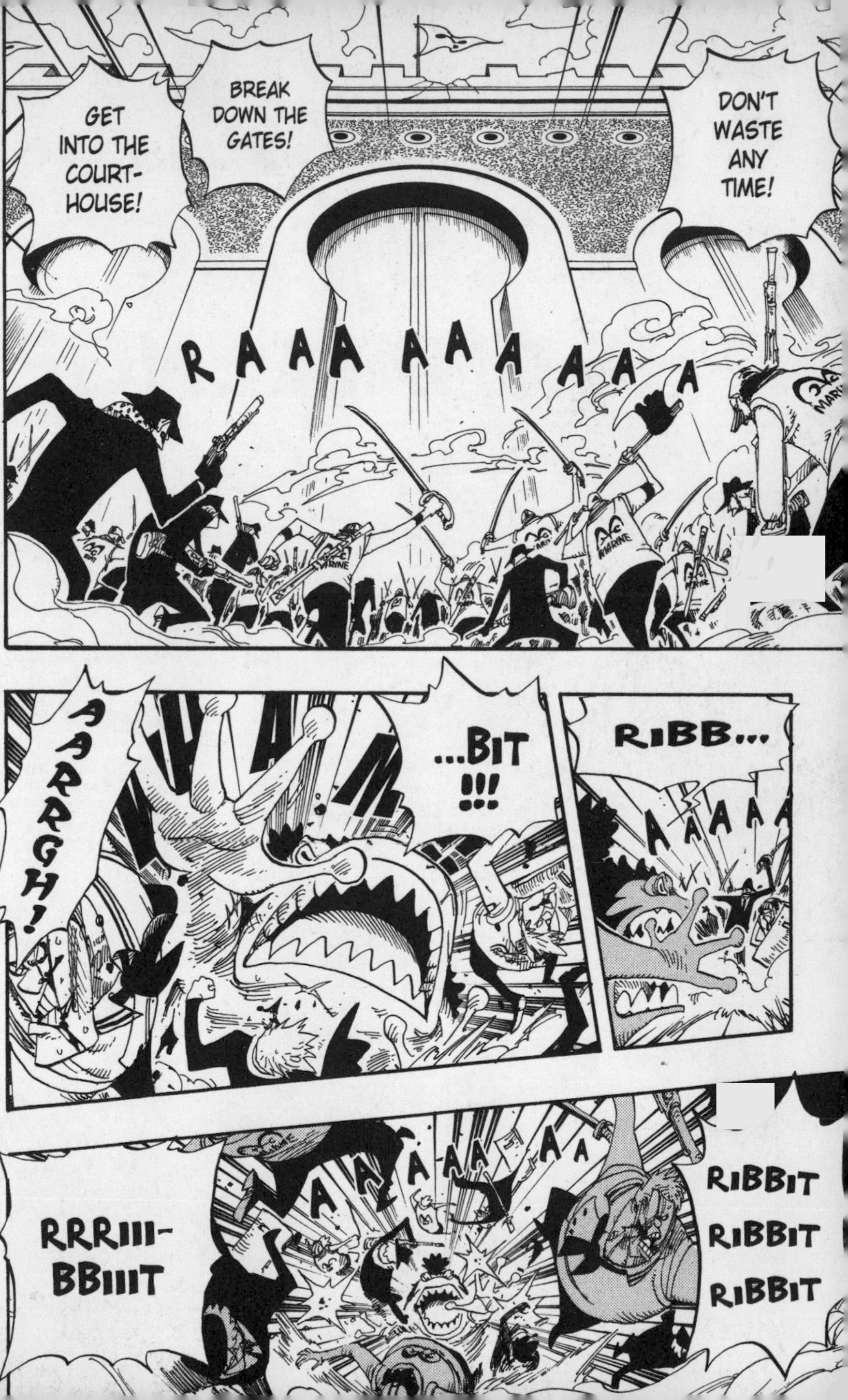
DON'T WASTE ANY TIME!
BREAK DOWN THE GATES!
GET INTO THE COURT-HOUSE!
RAAAAAAAAA
RIBB...
AAAAA
...BIT !!!
AARRGH!
RIBBIT
RIBBIT
RIBBIT
AAAAAAAA
RRRIII-BBIIIT

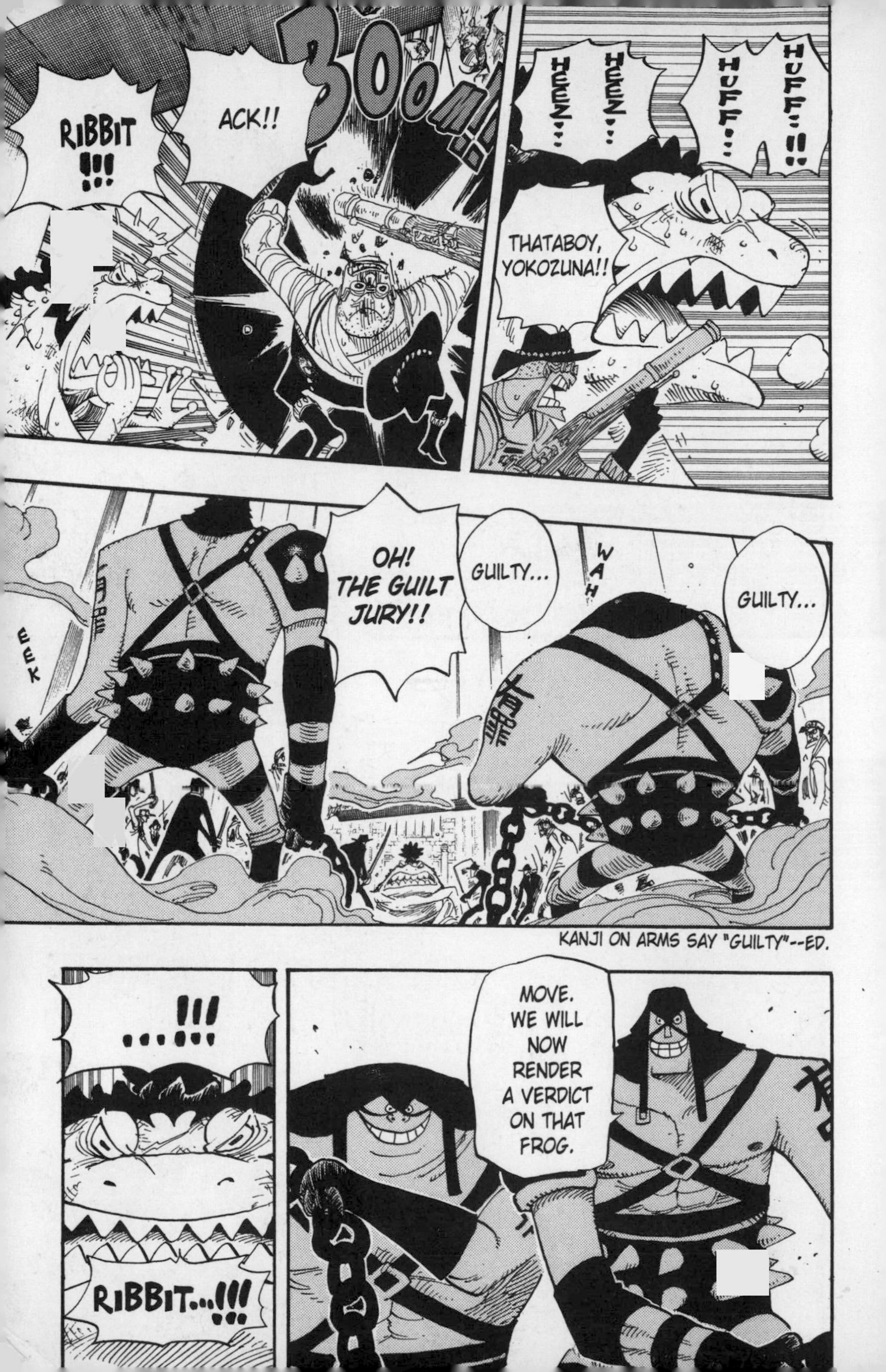
HUFF...!!
HUFF...
HEEZ...
HEEZ...
THATABOY, YOKOZUNA!!
ACK!!
RIBBIT!!!
GUILTY...
WAH
GUILTY...
OH! THE GUILT JURY!!
EEK
KANJI ON ARMS SAY "GUILTY"--ED.
MOVE. WE WILL NOW RENDER A VERDICT ON THAT FROG.
...!!!
RIBBIT...!!!

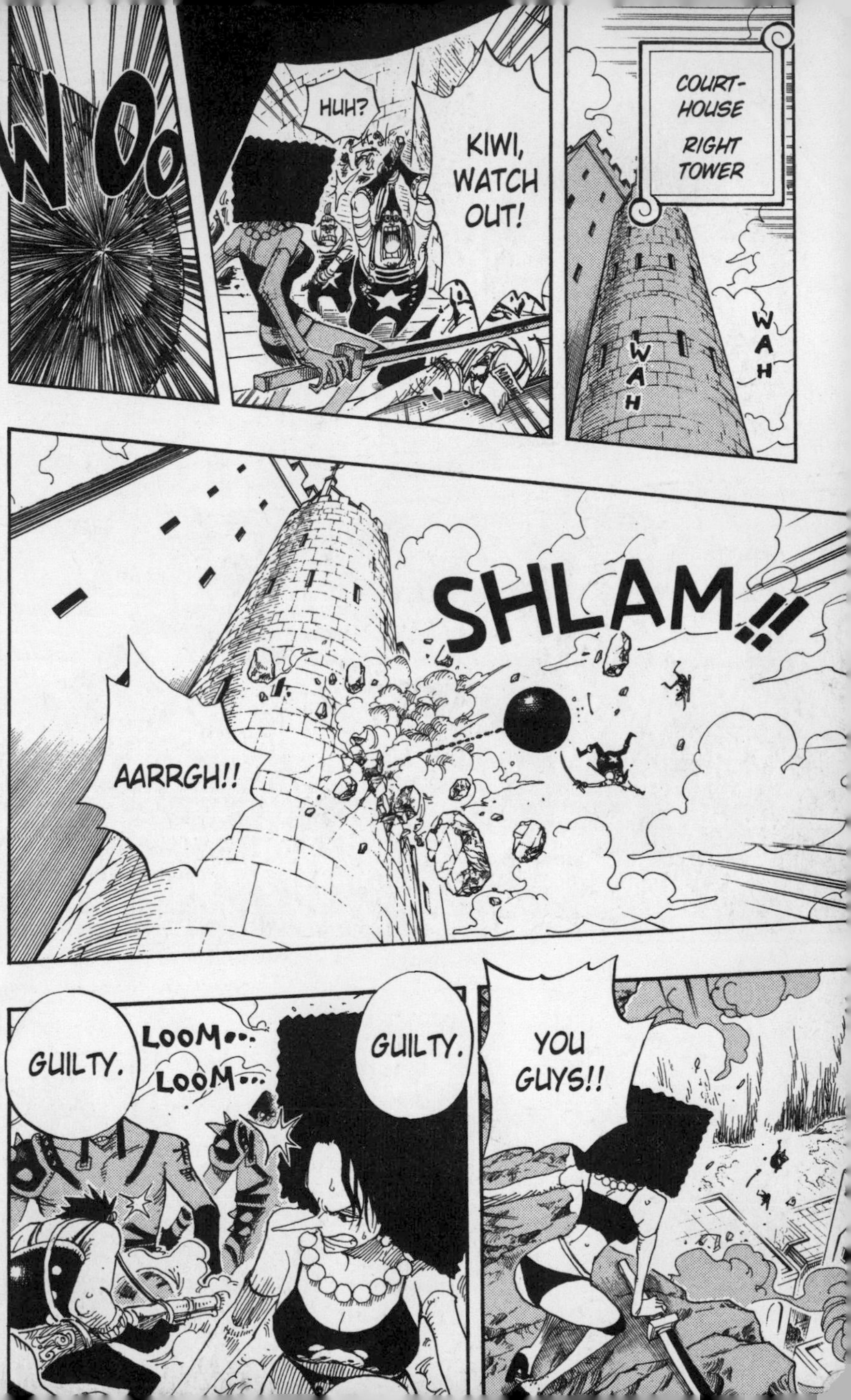
COURT-HOUSE RIGHT TOWER
WAH
WAH
KIWI, WATCH OUT!
HUH?
WOO
SHLAM!!
AARRGH!!
YOU GUYS!!
GUILTY.
LOOM... LOOM...
GUILTY.

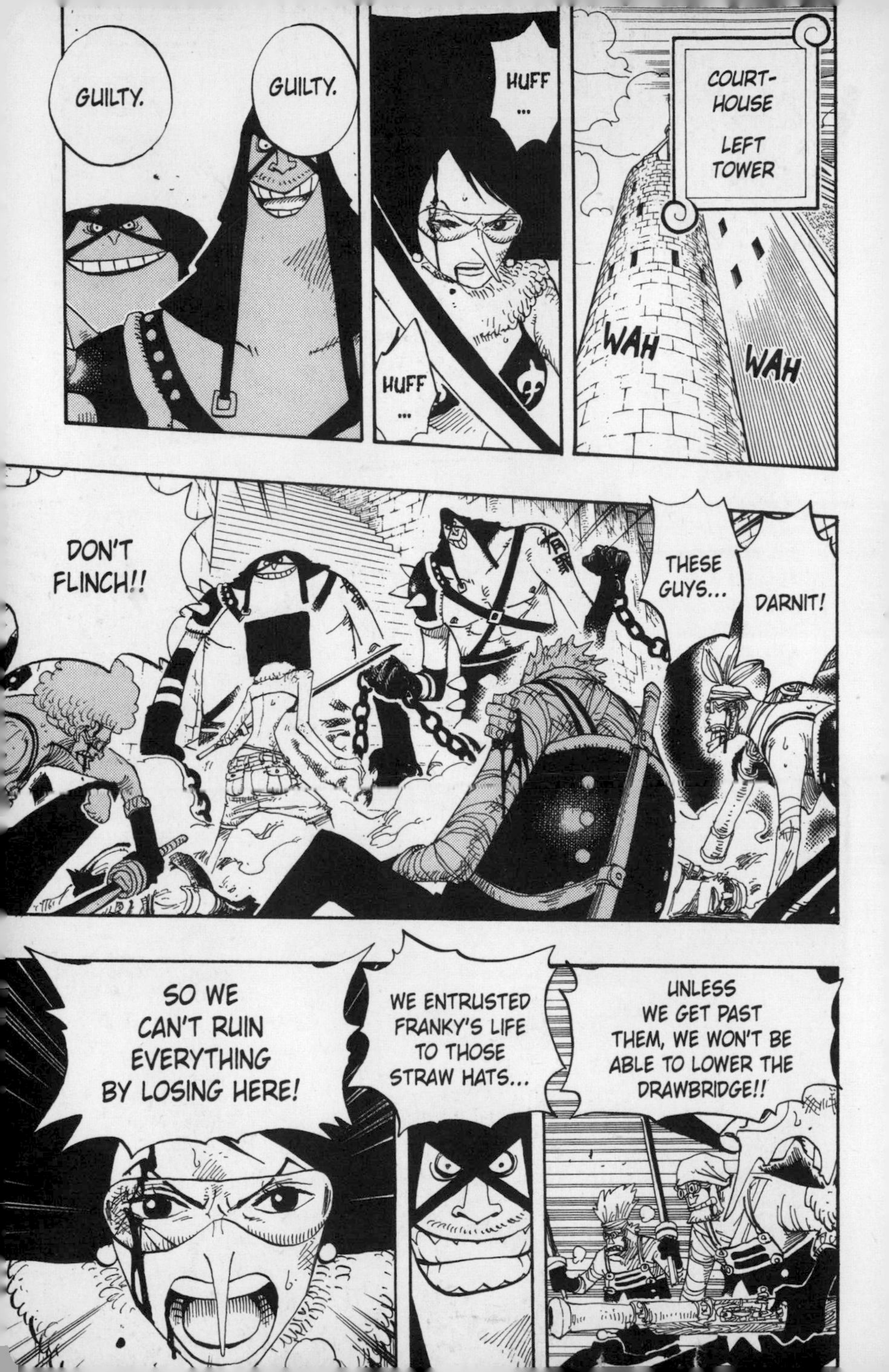
COURT-HOUSE
LEFT TOWER
WAH
WAH
HUFF ...
HUFF ...
GUILTY.
GUILTY.
DARNIT!
THESE GUYS...
DON'T FLINCH!!
UNLESS WE GET PAST THEM, WE WON'T BE ABLE TO LOWER THE DRAWBRIDGE!!
WE ENTRUSTED FRANKY'S LIFE TO THOSE STRAW HATS...
SO WE CAN'T RUIN EVERYTHING BY LOSING HERE!

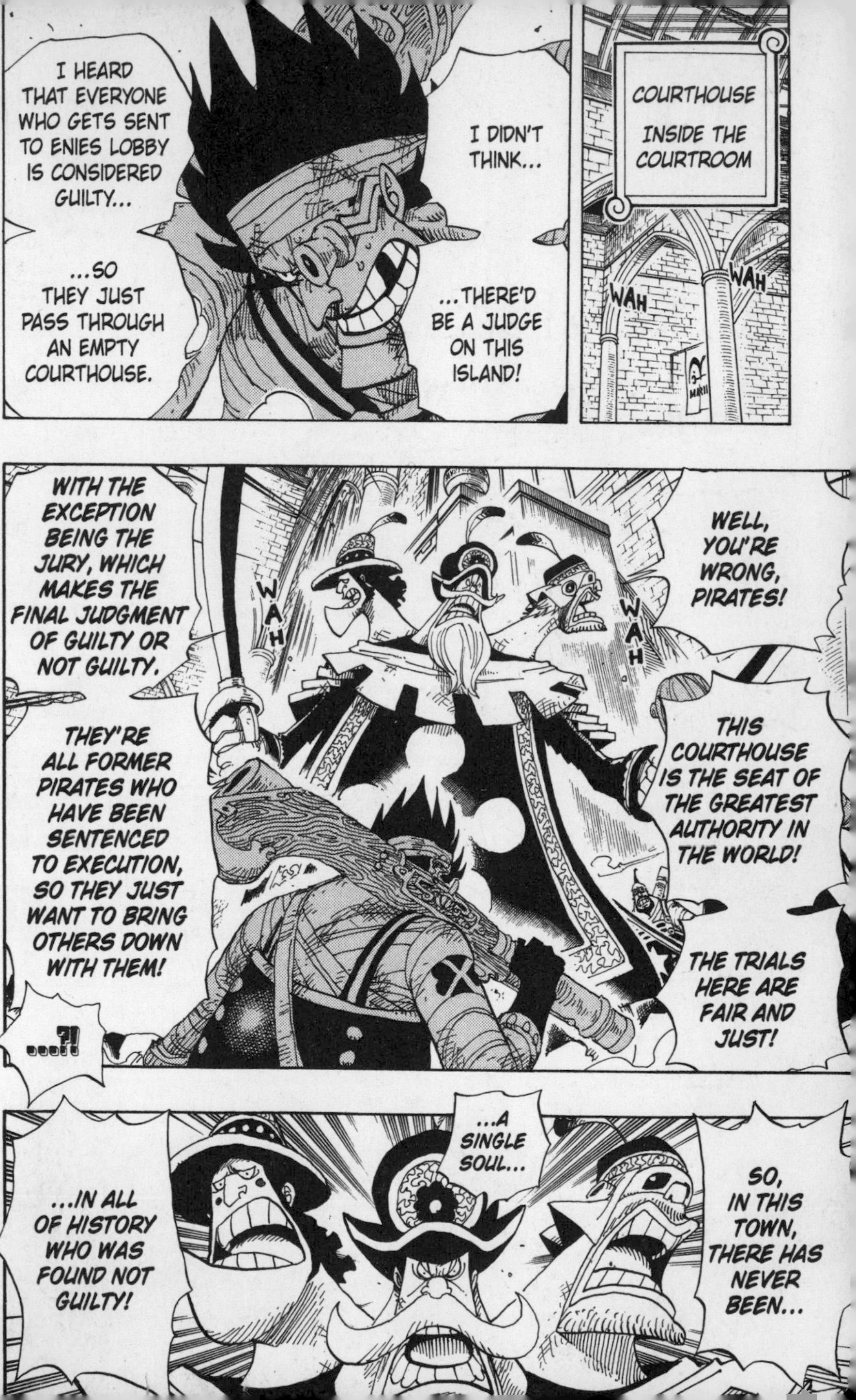
COURTHOUSE
INSIDE THE COURTROOM
WAH
WAH
I HEARD THAT EVERYONE WHO GETS SENT TO ENIES LOBBY IS CONSIDERED GUILTY...
...SO THEY JUST PASS THROUGH AN EMPTY COURTHOUSE.
I DIDN'T THINK...
...THERE'D BE A JUDGE ON THIS ISLAND!
WELL, YOU'RE WRONG, PIRATES!
WAH
WAH
THIS COURTHOUSE IS THE SEAT OF THE GREATEST AUTHORITY IN THE WORLD!
THE TRIALS HERE ARE FAIR AND JUST!
WITH THE EXCEPTION BEING THE JURY, WHICH MAKES THE FINAL JUDGMENT OF GUILTY OR NOT GUILTY.
THEY'RE ALL FORMER PIRATES WHO HAVE BEEN SENTENCED TO EXECUTION, SO THEY JUST WANT TO BRING OTHERS DOWN WITH THEM!
...?!
SO, IN THIS TOWN, THERE HAS NEVER BEEN...
...A SINGLE SOUL...
...IN ALL OF HISTORY WHO WAS FOUND NOT GUILTY!

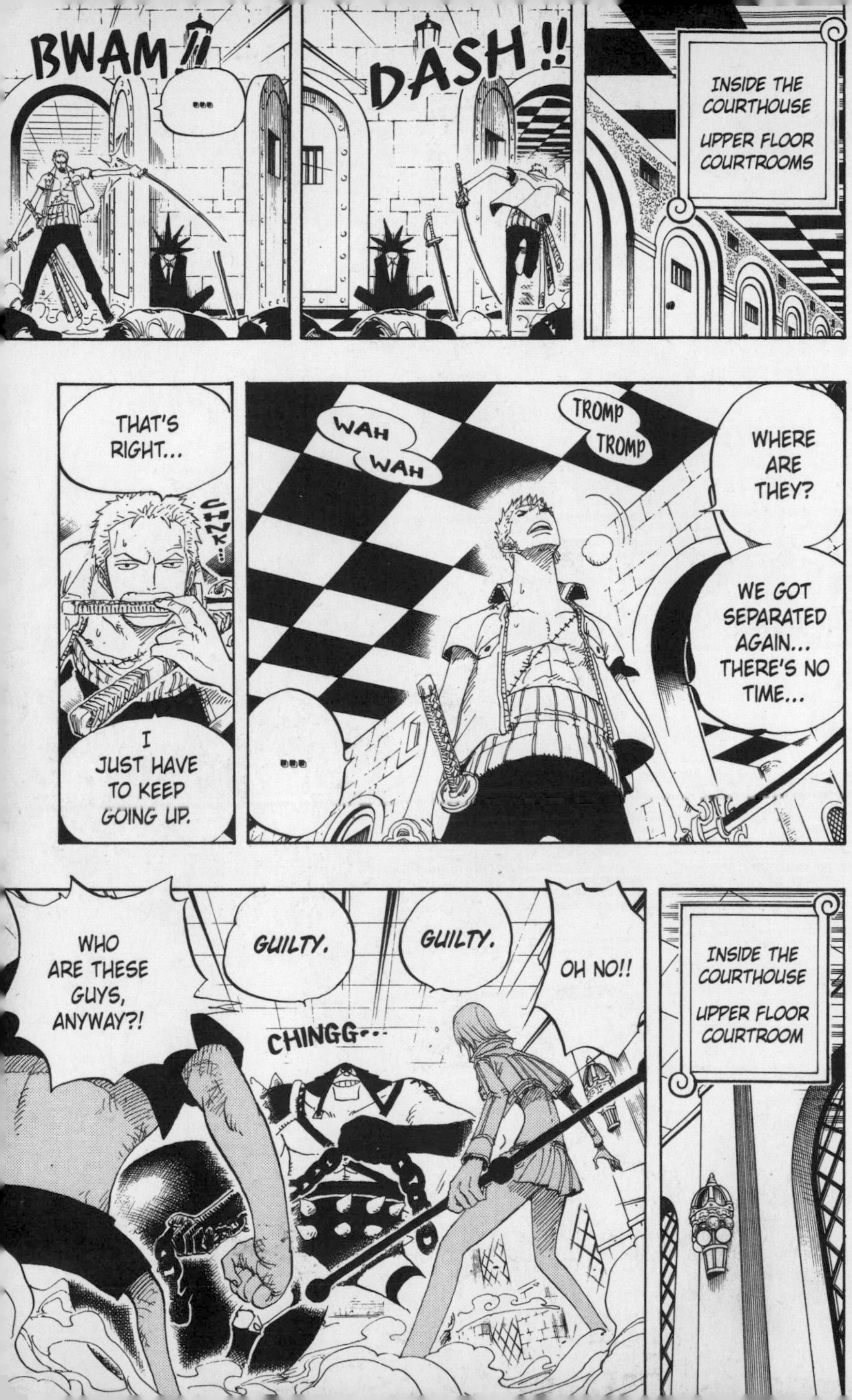
INSIDE THE COURTHOUSE
UPPER FLOOR COURTROOMS
DASH!!
BWAM!!
...
WHERE ARE THEY?
WE GOT SEPARATED AGAIN... THERE'S NO TIME...
TROMP TROMP
WAH WAH
...
THAT'S RIGHT...
CHNK...
I JUST HAVE TO KEEP GOING UP.
INSIDE THE COURTHOUSE
UPPER FLOOR COURTROOM
OH NO!!
GUILTY.
GUILTY.
CHINGG...
WHO ARE THESE GUYS, ANYWAY?!

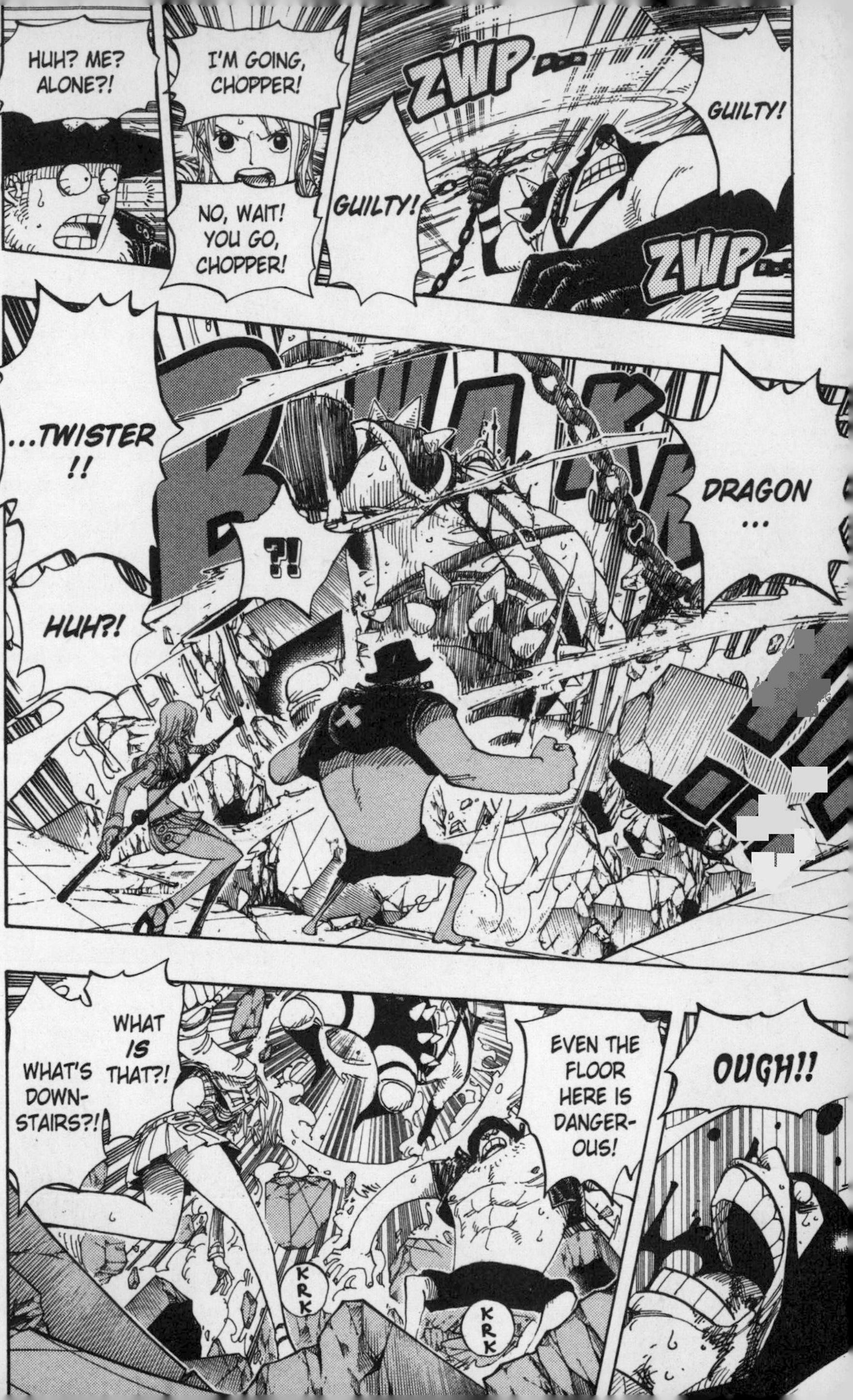
GUILTY!
ZWP
GUILTY!
ZWP
I'M GOING, CHOPPER!
NO, WAIT! YOU GO, CHOPPER!
HUH? ME? ALONE?!
DRAGON ...
...TWISTER !!
?!
HUH?!
OUGH!!
EVEN THE FLOOR HERE IS DANGER-OUS!
KRK
WHAT IS THAT?!
WHAT'S DOWN-STAIRS?!
KRK

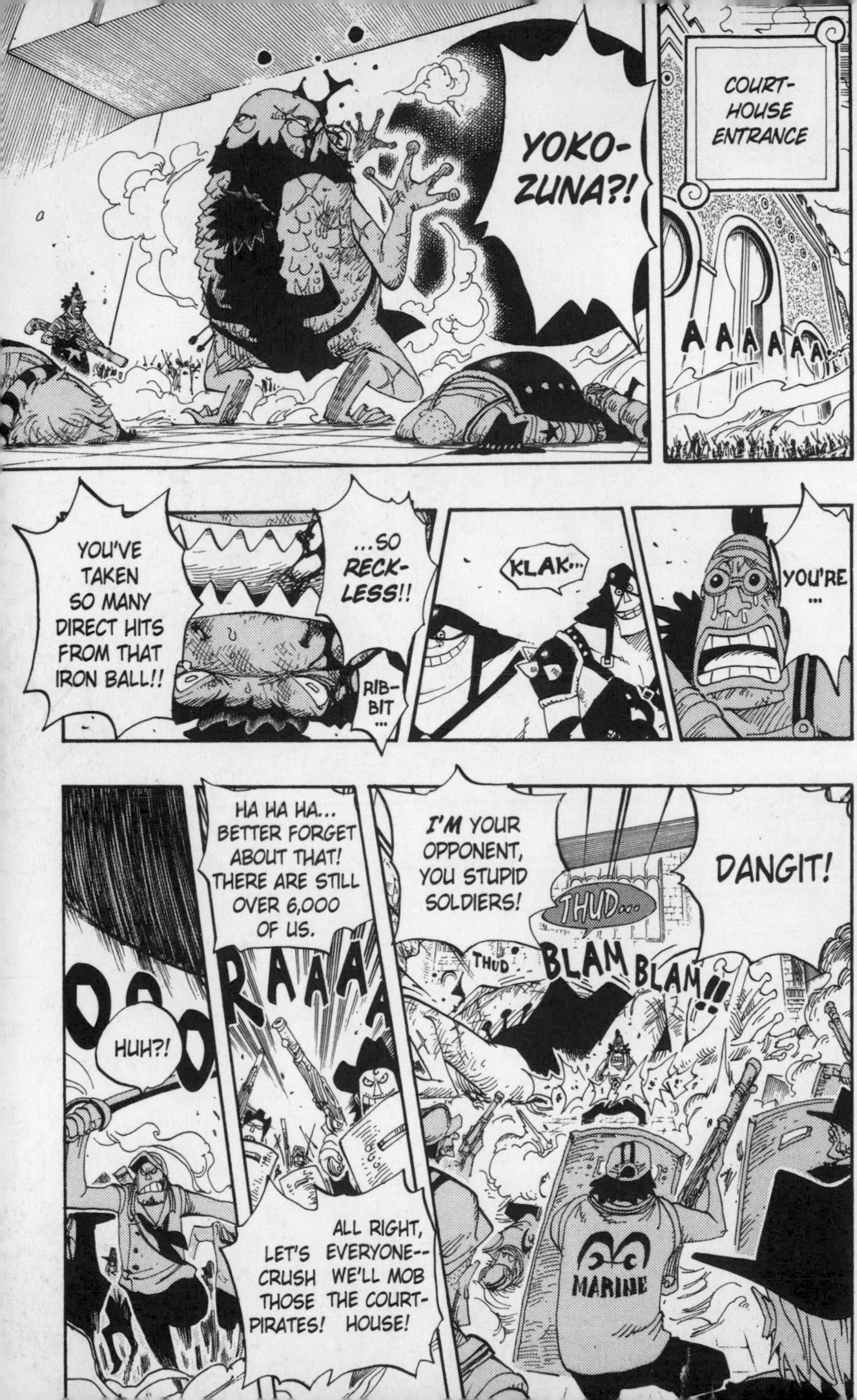
COURT-HOUSE ENTRANCE
AAAAAA
YOKO-ZUNA?!
YOU'RE ...
KLAK...
...SO RECK-LESS!!
RIB-BIT ...
YOU'VE TAKEN SO MANY DIRECT HITS FROM THAT IRON BALL!!
DANGIT!
I'M YOUR OPPONENT, YOU STUPID SOLDIERS!
THUD...
THUD
BLAM BLAM!!
ALL RIGHT, EVERYONE-- WE'LL MOB THE COURT-HOUSE!
HA HA HA... BETTER FORGET ABOUT THAT! THERE ARE STILL OVER 6,000 OF US.
RAAAA
LET'S CRUSH THOSE PIRATES!
OOO
HUH?!
MARINE

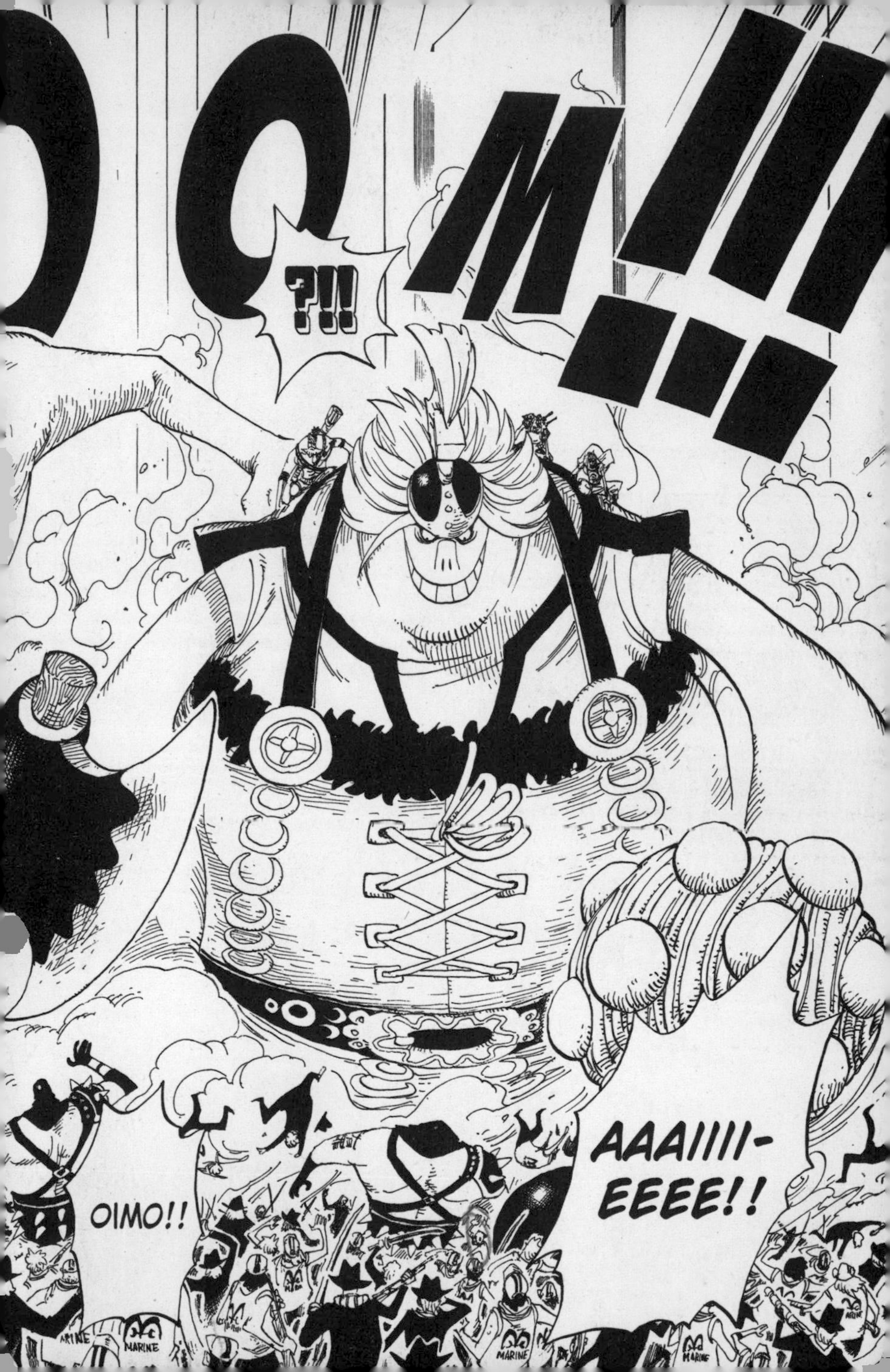
OOM!!!
?!!
AAAIIII-EEEE!!
OIMO!!

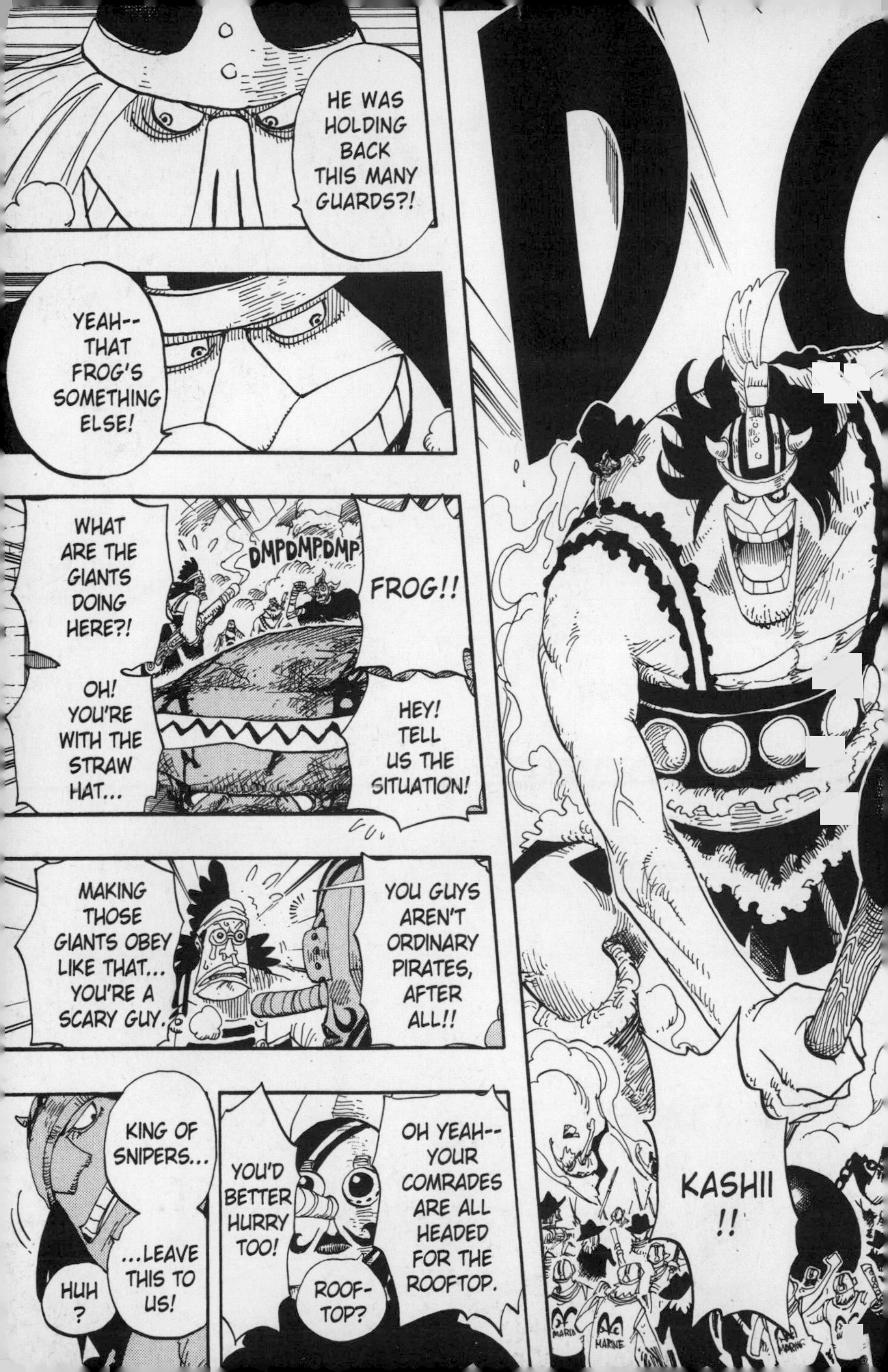
DO
KASHII !!
HE WAS HOLDING BACK THIS MANY GUARDS?!
YEAH-- THAT FROG'S SOMETHING ELSE!
FROG!!
DMPDMPDMP
WHAT ARE THE GIANTS DOING HERE?!
HEY! TELL US THE SITUATION!
OH! YOU'RE WITH THE STRAW HAT...
YOU GUYS AREN'T ORDINARY PIRATES, AFTER ALL!!
MAKING THOSE GIANTS OBEY LIKE THAT... YOU'RE A SCARY GUY.
OH YEAH-- YOUR COMRADES ARE ALL HEADED FOR THE ROOFTOP.
YOU'D BETTER HURRY TOO!
ROOF-TOP?
KING OF SNIPERS...
...LEAVE THIS TO US!
HUH ?

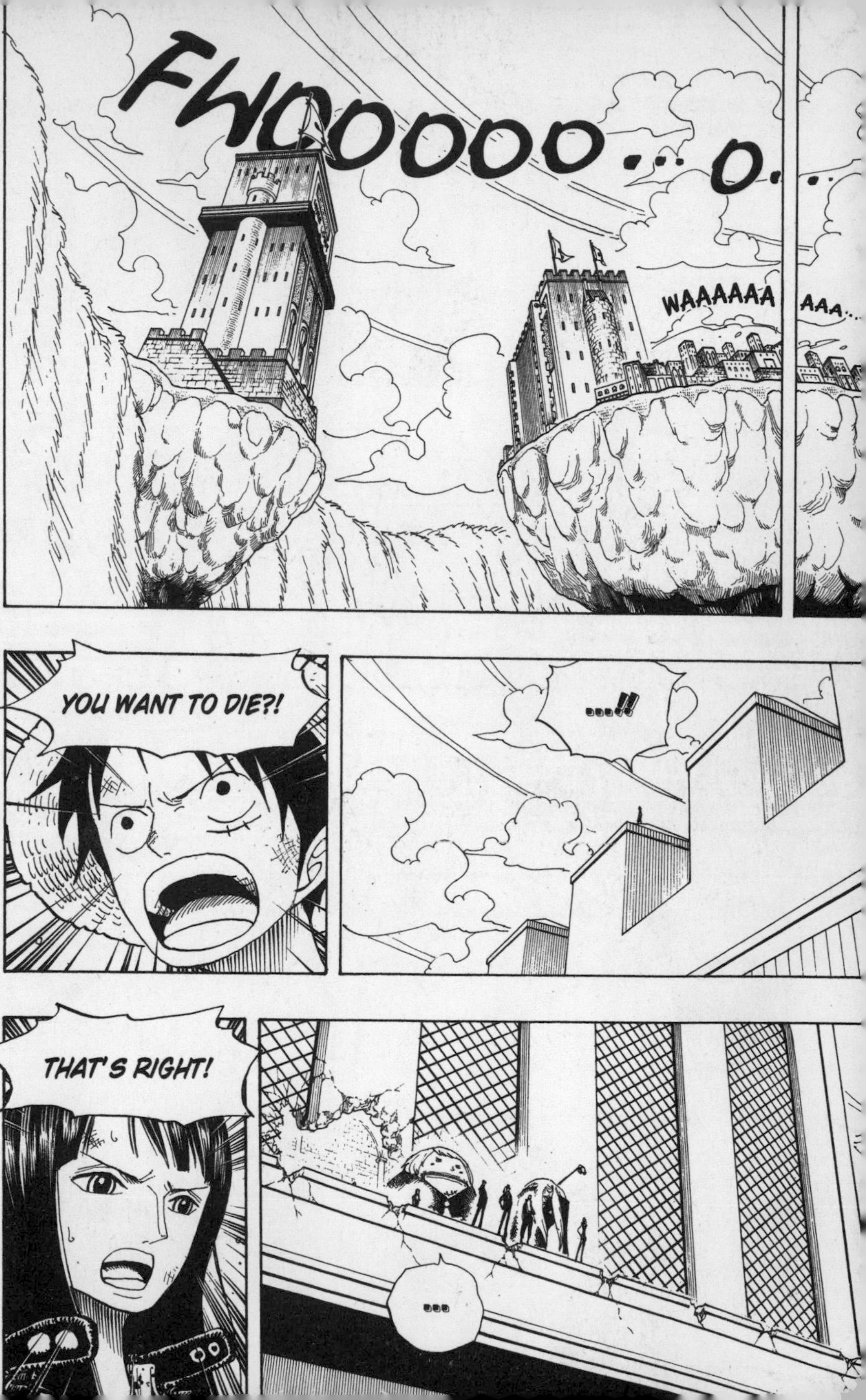
FWOOOOO... O...
WAAAAAA AAA...
...!!
YOU WANT TO DIE?!
...
THAT'S RIGHT!

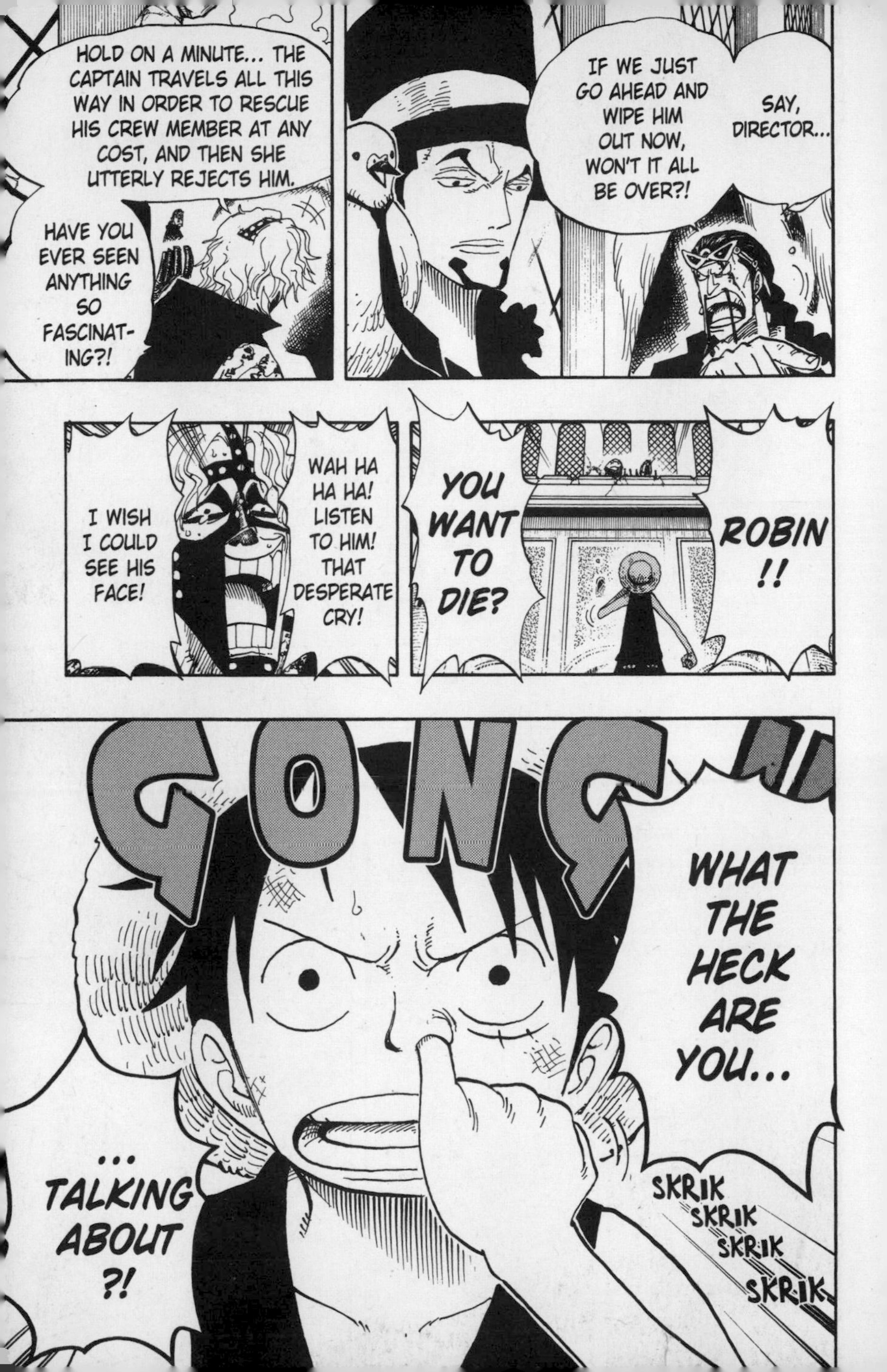
SAY, DIRECTOR...
IF WE JUST GO AHEAD AND WIPE HIM OUT NOW, WON'T IT ALL BE OVER?!
HOLD ON A MINUTE... THE CAPTAIN TRAVELS ALL THIS WAY IN ORDER TO RESCUE HIS CREW MEMBER AT ANY COST, AND THEN SHE UTTERLY REJECTS HIM.
HAVE YOU EVER SEEN ANYTHING SO FASCINAT-ING?!
ROBIN!!
YOU WANT TO DIE?
WAH HA HA HA! LISTEN TO HIM! THAT DESPERATE CRY!
I WISH I COULD SEE HIS FACE!
GONG
WHAT THE HECK ARE YOU...
SKRIK SKRIK SKRIK SKRIK
...TALKING ABOUT?!

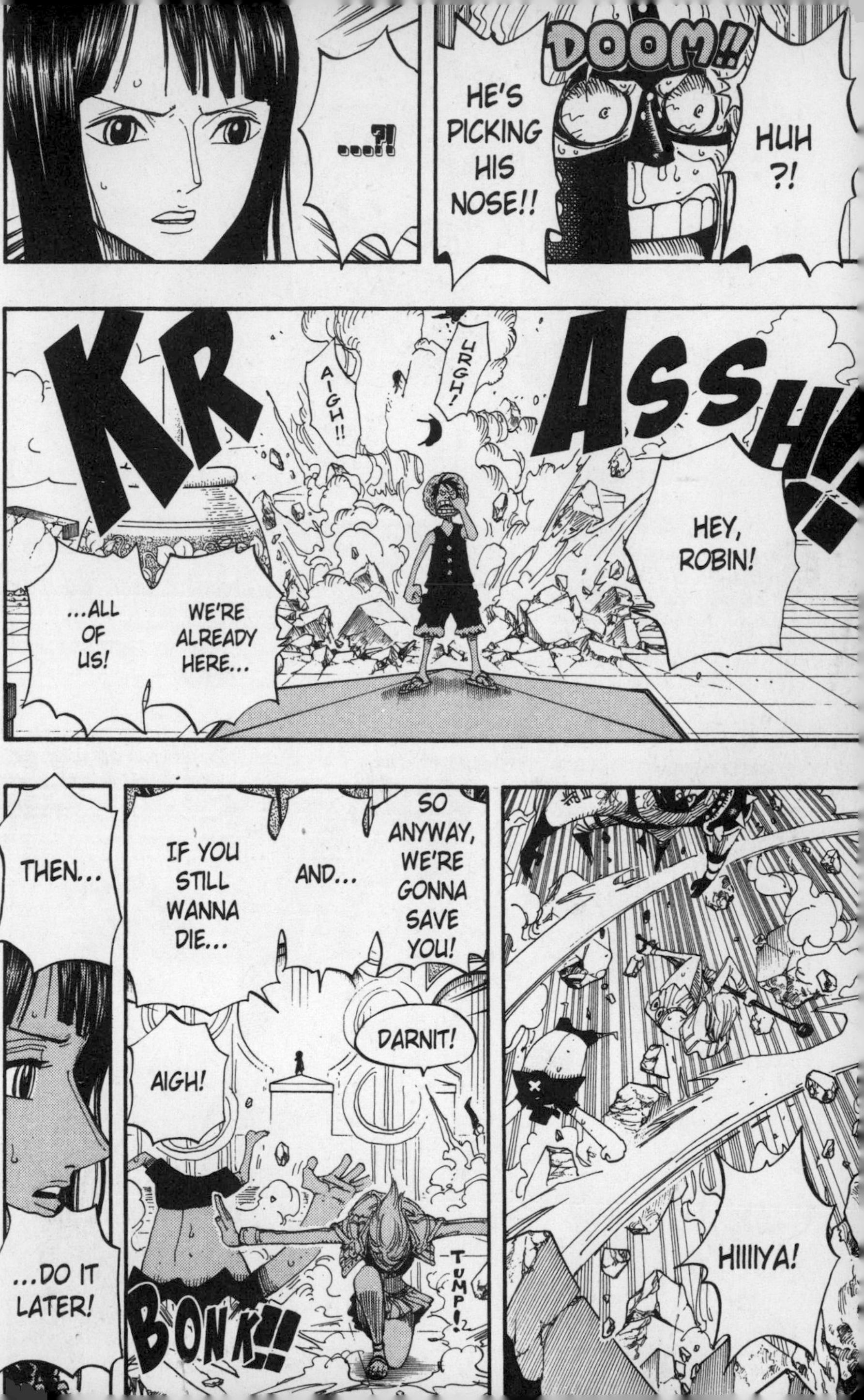
DOOM!!
HUH ?!
HE'S PICKING HIS NOSE!!
...?!
KRASSH!!
URGH!
AIGH!!
HEY, ROBIN!
WE'RE ALREADY HERE...
...ALL OF US!
HIIIIYA!
SO ANYWAY, WE'RE GONNA SAVE YOU!
AND...
IF YOU STILL WANNA DIE...
DARNIT!
AIGH!
TUMP!
BONK!!
THEN...
...DO IT LATER!

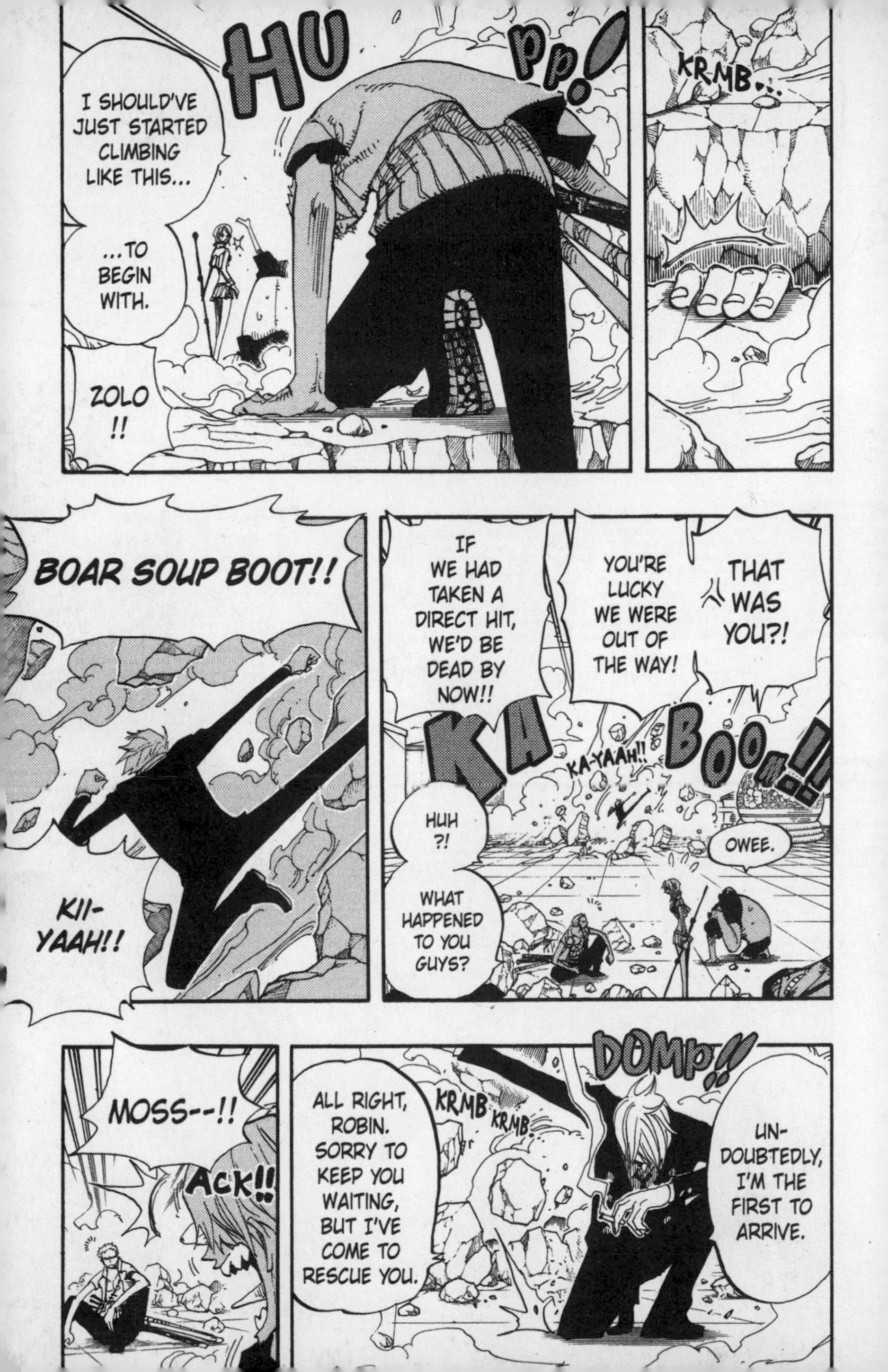
KRMB...
HUPP!
I SHOULD'VE JUST STARTED CLIMBING LIKE THIS...
...TO BEGIN WITH.
ZOLO!!
THAT WAS YOU?!
YOU'RE LUCKY WE WERE OUT OF THE WAY!
IF WE HAD TAKEN A DIRECT HIT, WE'D BE DEAD BY NOW!!
KA BOOM!!
KA-YAAH!!
OWEE.
HUH?!
WHAT HAPPENED TO YOU GUYS?
BOAR SOUP BOOT!!
KII-YAAH!!
DOMP!!
UN-DOUBTEDLY, I'M THE FIRST TO ARRIVE.
KRMB
KRMB
ALL RIGHT, ROBIN. SORRY TO KEEP YOU WAITING, BUT I'VE COME TO RESCUE YOU.
MOSS--!!
ACK!!

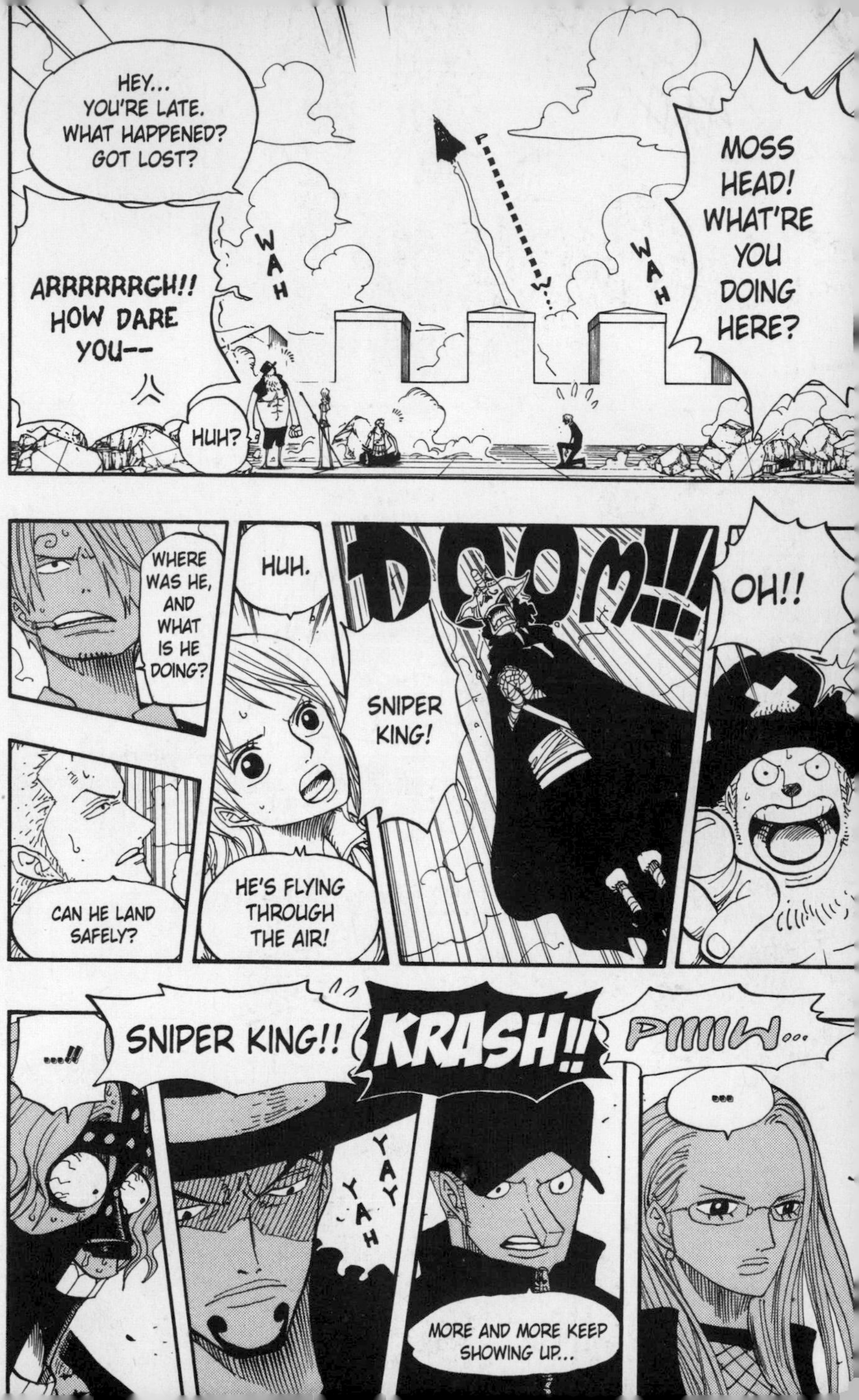
MOSS HEAD! WHAT'RE YOU DOING HERE?
WAH
WAH
HEY... YOU'RE LATE. WHAT HAPPENED? GOT LOST?
ARRRRRRGH!! HOW DARE YOU--
HUH?
OH!!
DOOM!!!
SNIPER KING!
HUH.
HE'S FLYING THROUGH THE AIR!
WHERE WAS HE, AND WHAT IS HE DOING?
CAN HE LAND SAFELY?
PIIIW...
...
KRASH!!
YAY
YAH
MORE AND MORE KEEP SHOWING UP...
SNIPER KING!!
...!!

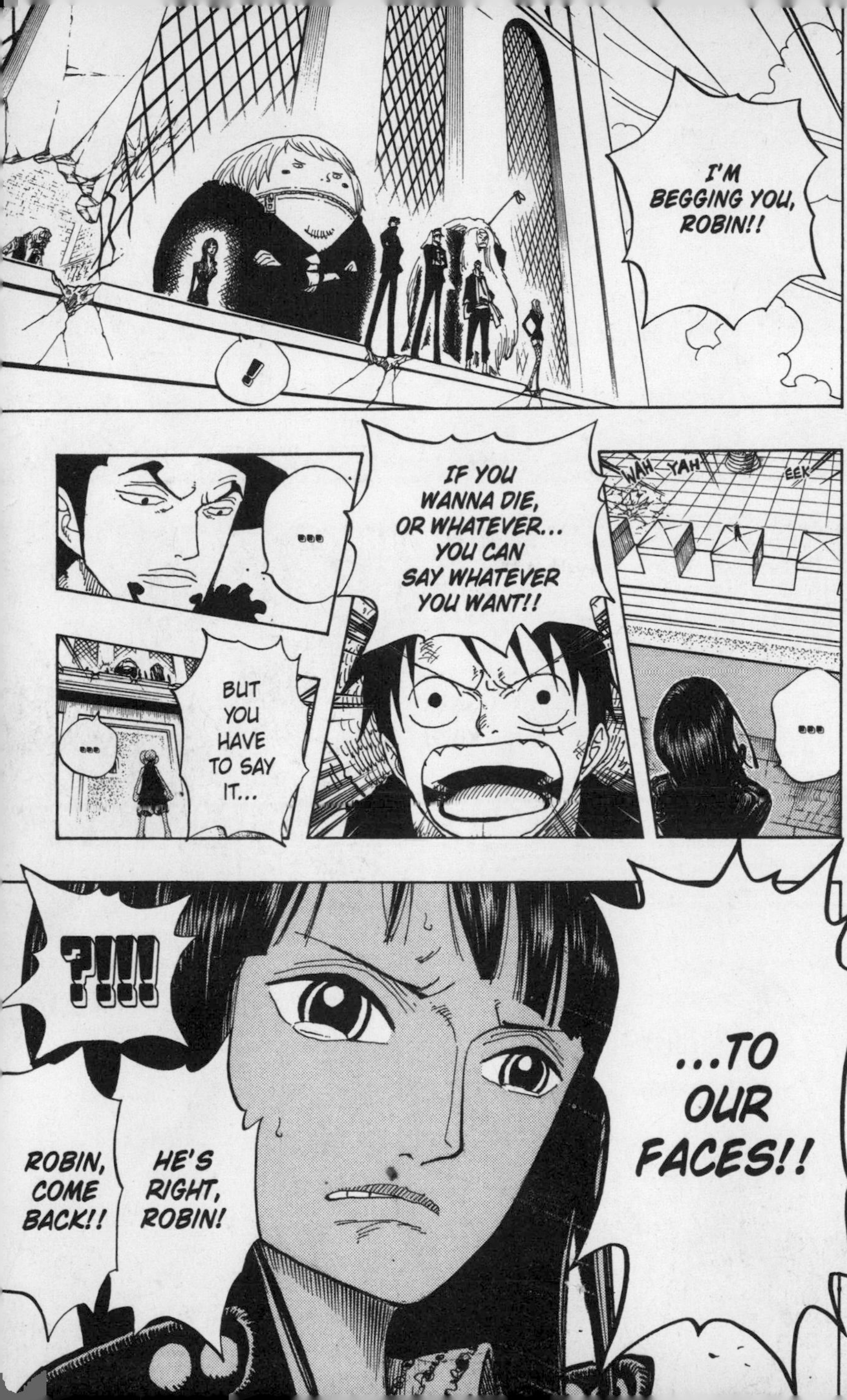

I'M BEGGING YOU, ROBIN!!
!
EEK
YAH
WAH
...
IF YOU WANNA DIE, OR WHATEVER... YOU CAN SAY WHATEVER YOU WANT!!
...
BUT YOU HAVE TO SAY IT...
...
...TO OUR FACES!!
?!!!
HE'S RIGHT, ROBIN!
ROBIN, COME BACK!!

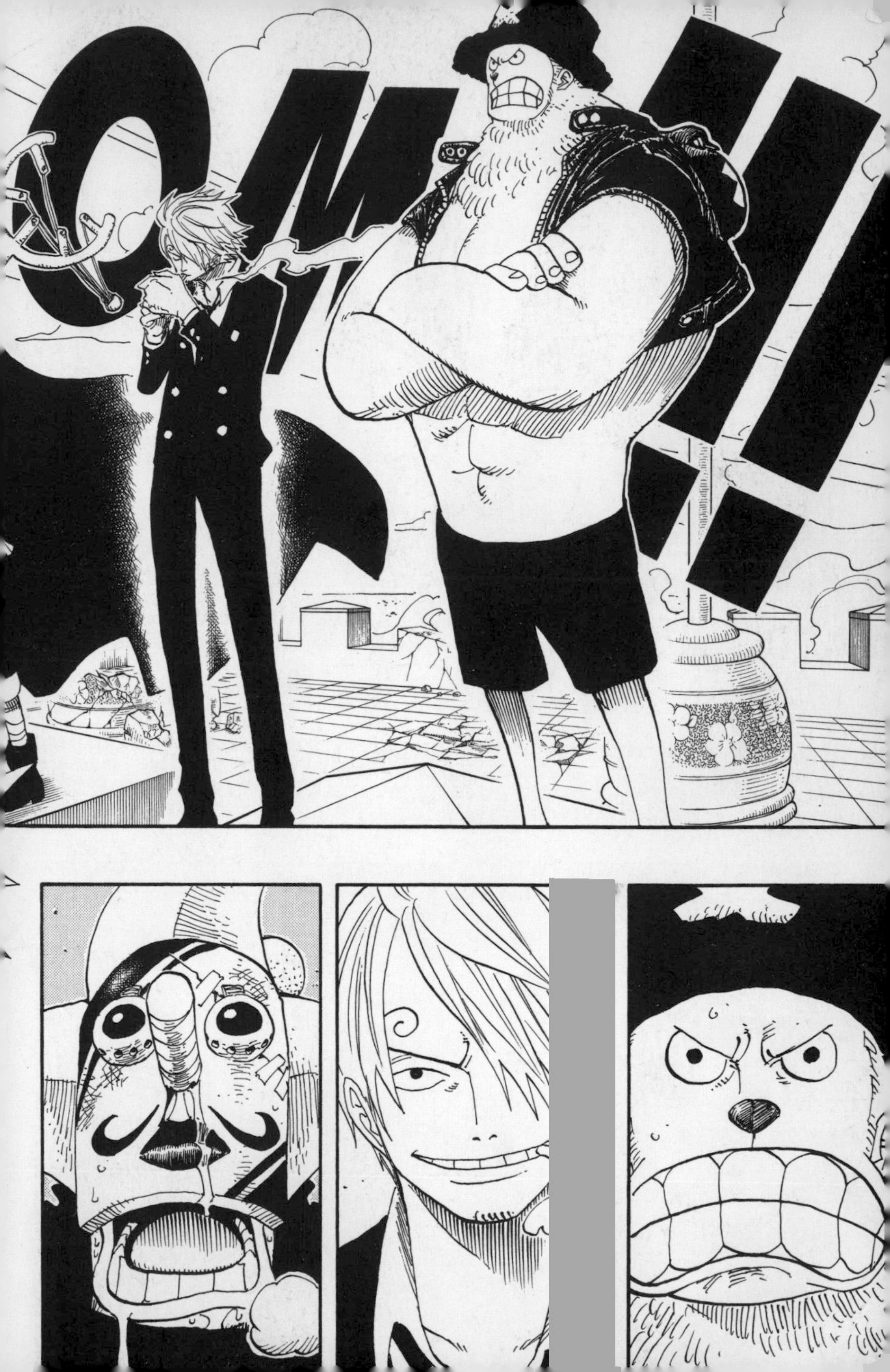
OM!!

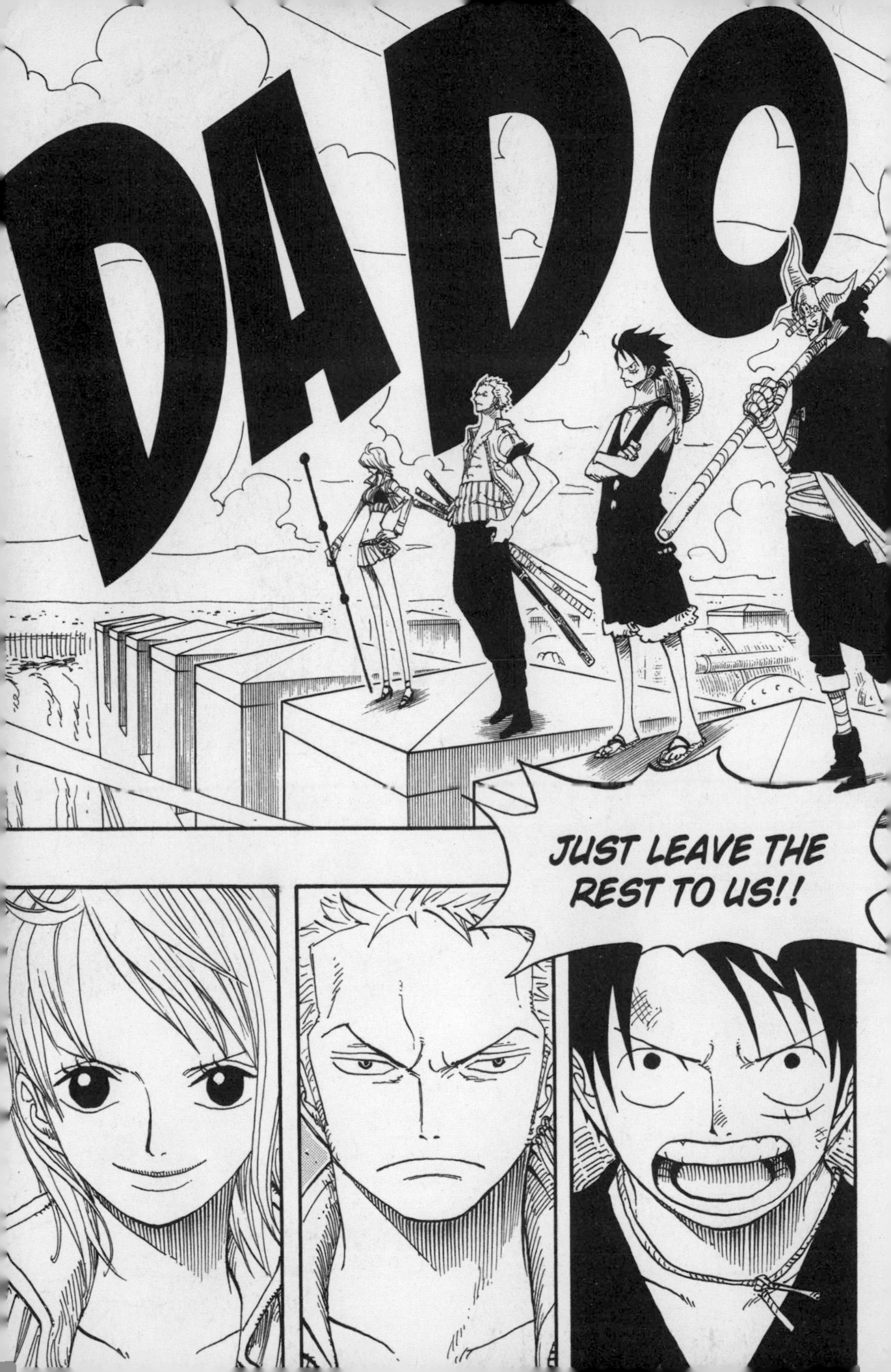
DADO
JUST LEAVE THE REST TO US!!

THEY CALLED A DEMON

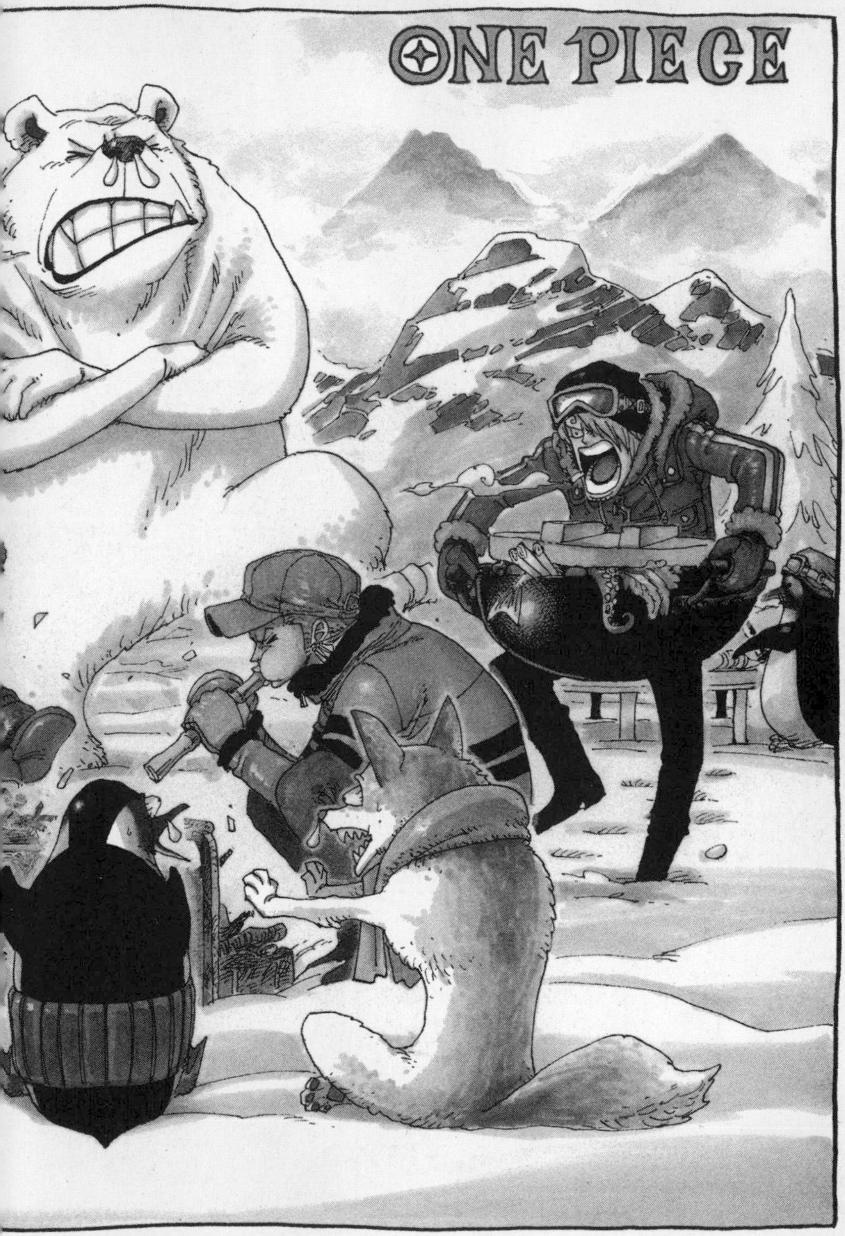
ONE PIECE

Chapter 391: THE GIRL

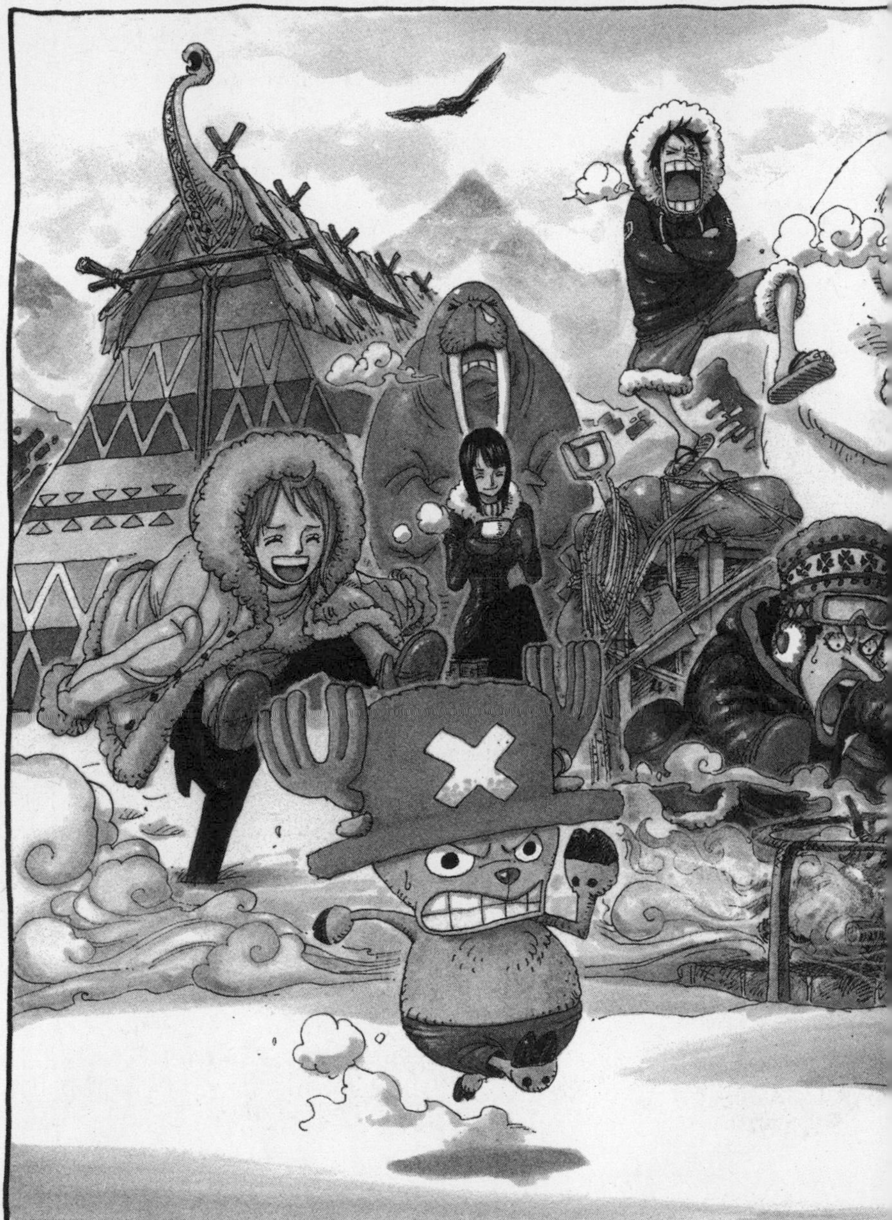

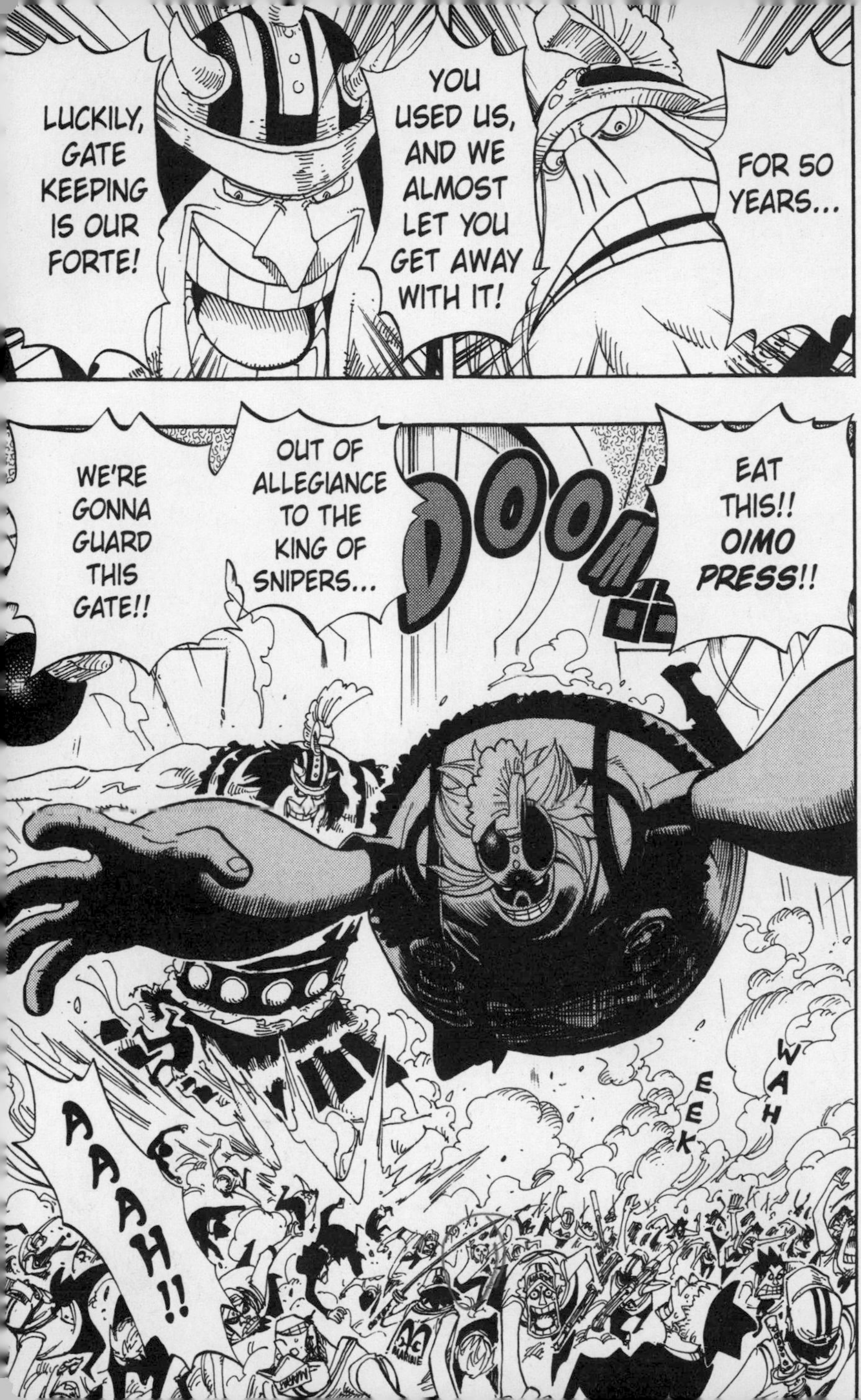
FOR 50 YEARS...
YOU USED US, AND WE ALMOST LET YOU GET AWAY WITH IT!
LUCKILY, GATE KEEPING IS OUR FORTE!
EAT THIS!! OIMO PRESS!!
DOOM
OUT OF ALLEGIANCE TO THE KING OF SNIPERS...
WE'RE GONNA GUARD THIS GATE!!
WAH
EEK
AAAAH!!

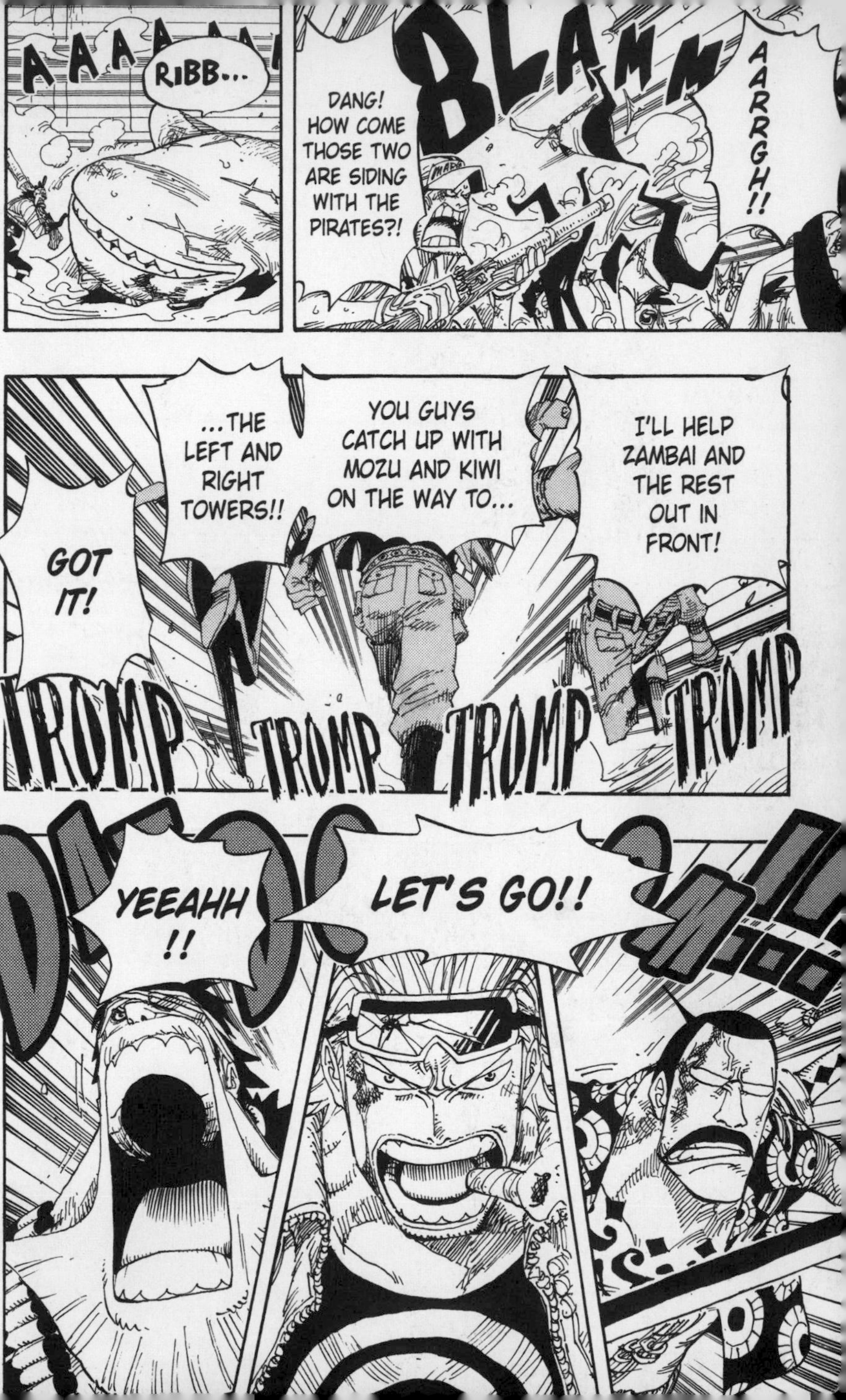
AARRGH!!
BLAMM
DANG! HOW COME THOSE TWO ARE SIDING WITH THE PIRATES?!
RIBB...
I'LL HELP ZAMBAI AND THE REST OUT IN FRONT!
YOU GUYS CATCH UP WITH MOZU AND KIWI ON THE WAY TO...
...THE LEFT AND RIGHT TOWERS!!
GOT IT!
TROMP
TROMP
TROMP
TROMP
LET'S GO!!
YEEAHH!!

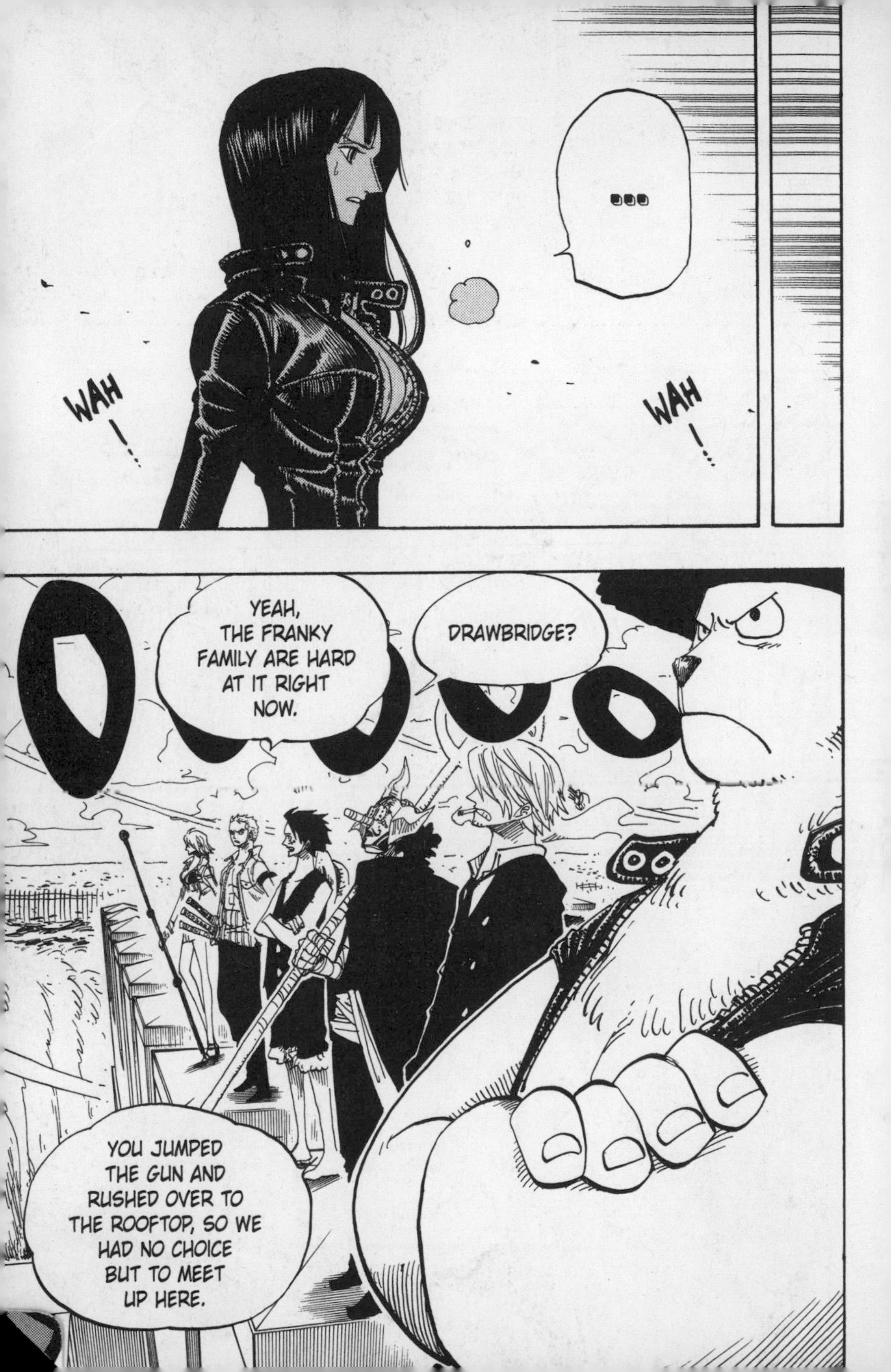
...
WAH!...
WAH!...
DRAWBRIDGE?
YEAH, THE FRANKY FAMILY ARE HARD AT IT RIGHT NOW.
YOU JUMPED THE GUN AND RUSHED OVER TO THE ROOFTOP, SO WE HAD NO CHOICE BUT TO MEET UP HERE.

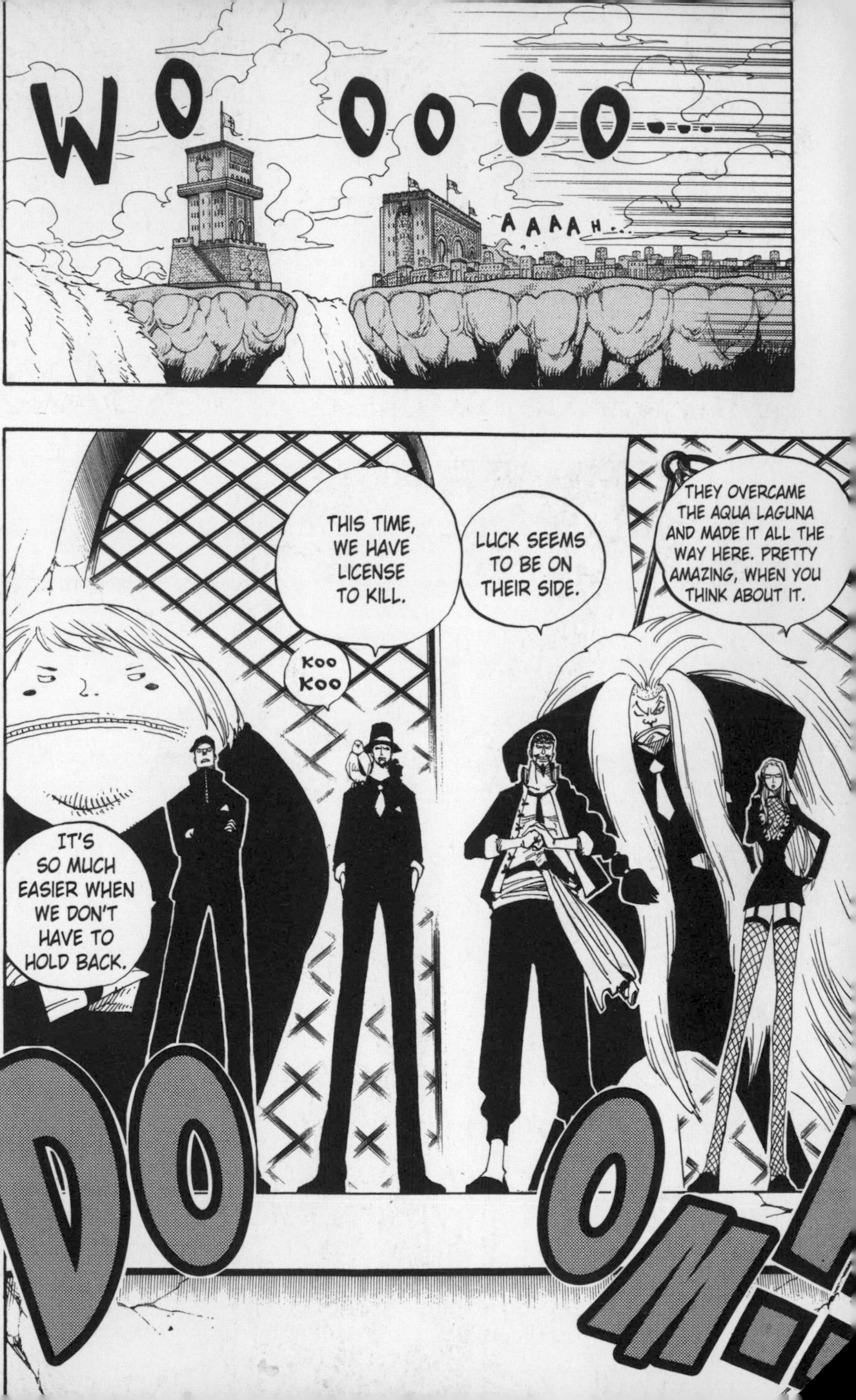
WOOOOO...
AAAAH...
THEY OVERCAME THE AQUA LAGUNA AND MADE IT ALL THE WAY HERE. PRETTY AMAZING, WHEN YOU THINK ABOUT IT.
LUCK SEEMS TO BE ON THEIR SIDE.
THIS TIME, WE HAVE LICENSE TO KILL.
KOO KOO
IT'S SO MUCH EASIER WHEN WE DON'T HAVE TO HOLD BACK.
DOOM...

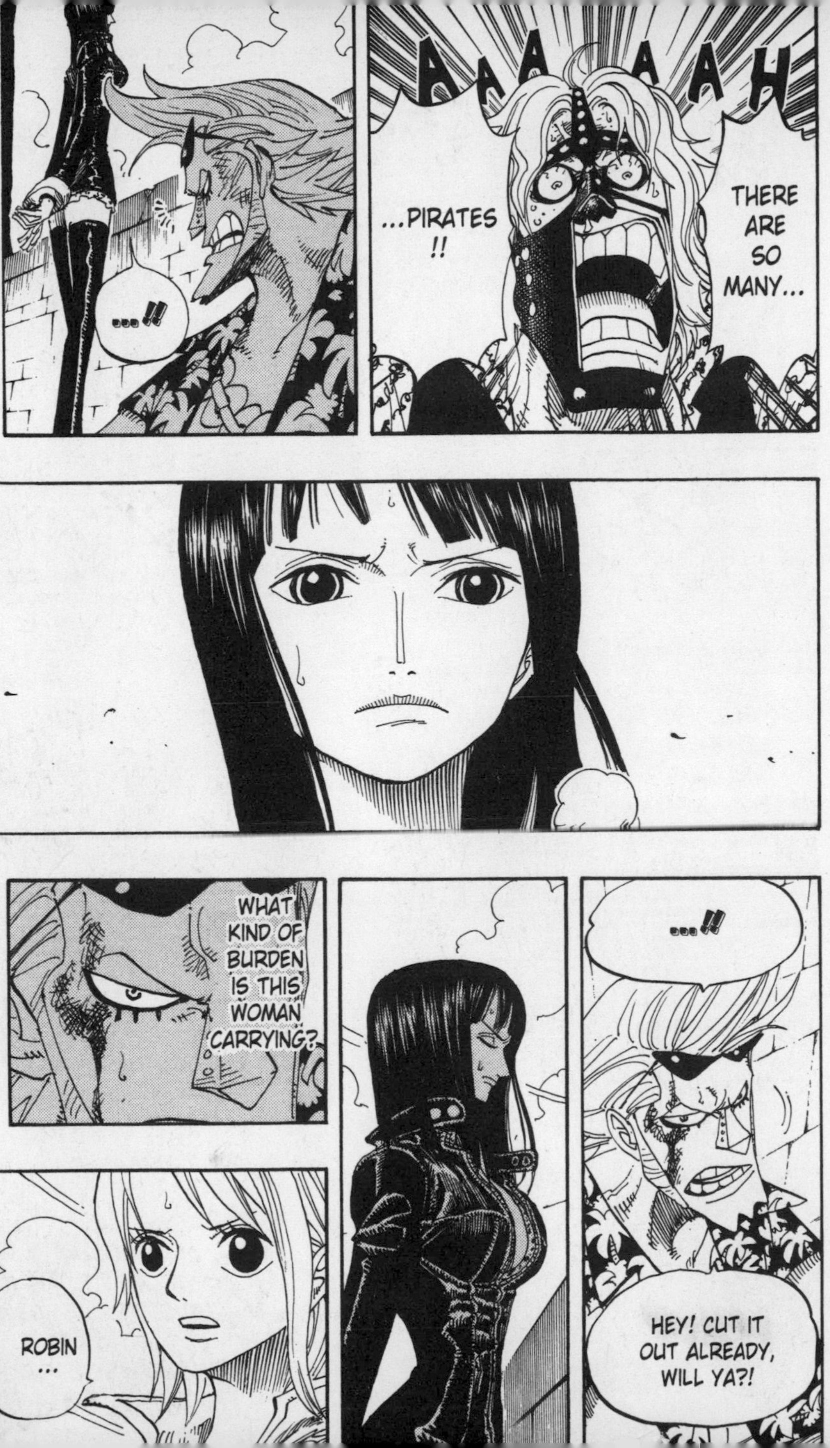
AAAAAH
THERE ARE SO MANY...
...PIRATES !!
...!!
...!!
HEY! CUT IT OUT ALREADY, WILL YA?!
WHAT KIND OF BURDEN IS THIS WOMAN CARRYING?
ROBIN ...

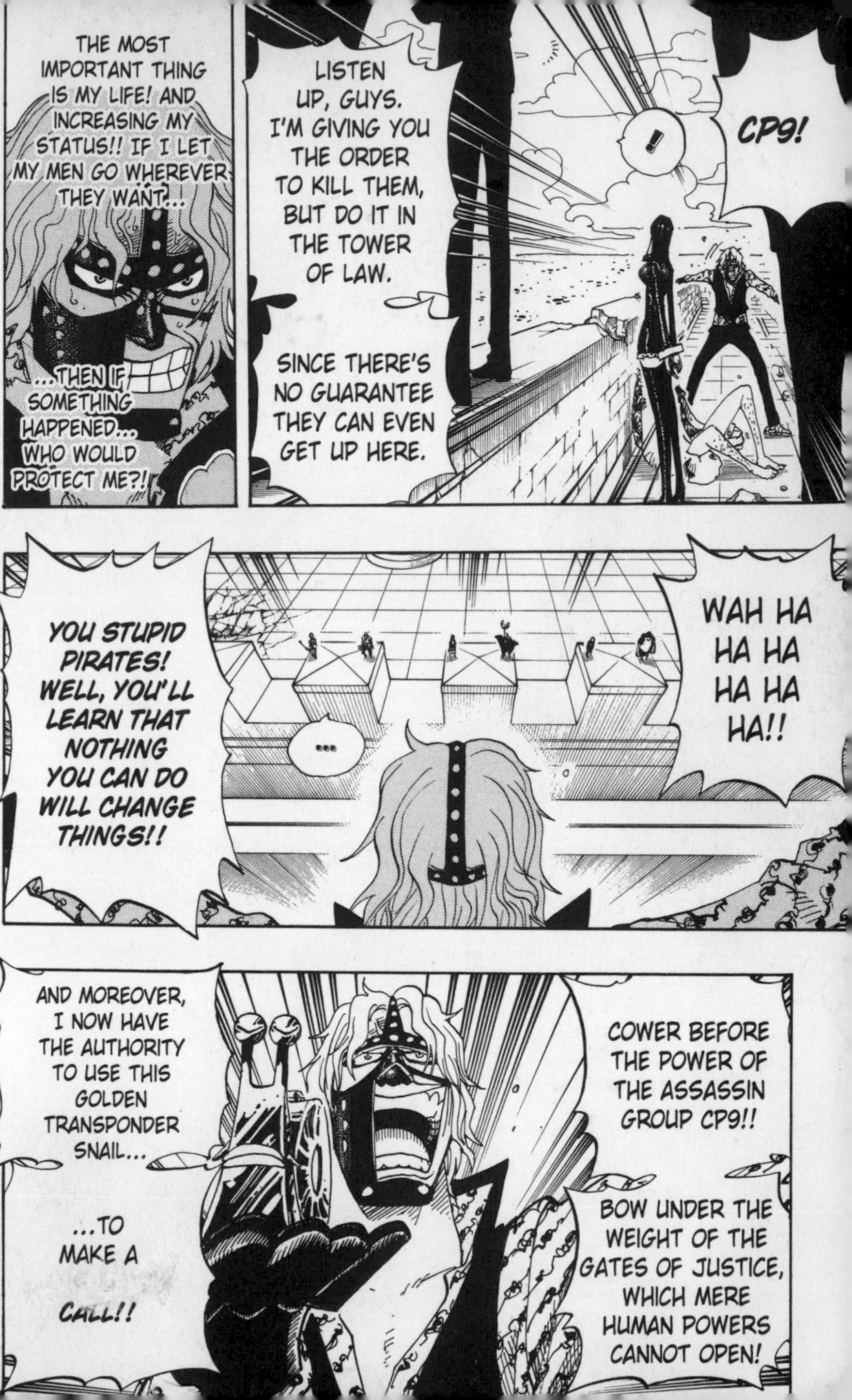
CP9!
!
LISTEN UP, GUYS. I'M GIVING YOU THE ORDER TO KILL THEM, BUT DO IT IN THE TOWER OF LAW.
SINCE THERE'S NO GUARANTEE THEY CAN EVEN GET UP HERE.
THE MOST IMPORTANT THING IS MY LIFE! AND INCREASING MY STATUS!! IF I LET MY MEN GO WHEREVER THEY WANT...
...THEN IF SOMETHING HAPPENED... WHO WOULD PROTECT ME?!
WAH HA HA HA HA HA HA!!
...
YOU STUPID PIRATES! WELL, YOU'LL LEARN THAT NOTHING YOU CAN DO WILL CHANGE THINGS!!
COWER BEFORE THE POWER OF THE ASSASSIN GROUP CP9!!
BOW UNDER THE WEIGHT OF THE GATES OF JUSTICE, WHICH MERE HUMAN POWERS CANNOT OPEN!
AND MOREOVER, I NOW HAVE THE AUTHORITY TO USE THIS GOLDEN TRANSPONDER SNAIL...
...TO MAKE A
CALL!!

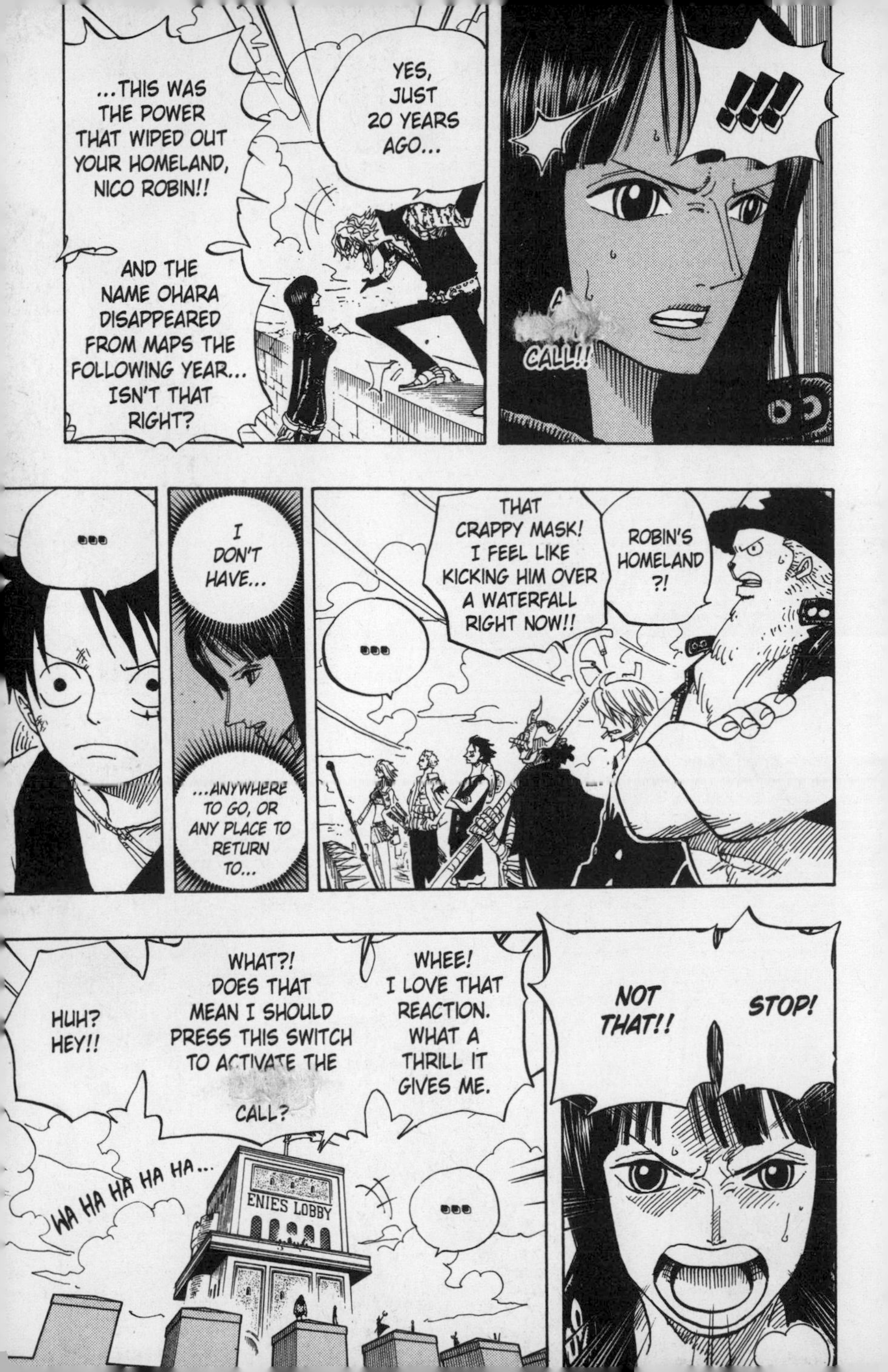
!!!
A
CALL!!
YES, JUST 20 YEARS AGO...
...THIS WAS THE POWER THAT WIPED OUT YOUR HOMELAND, NICO ROBIN!!
AND THE NAME OHARA DISAPPEARED FROM MAPS THE FOLLOWING YEAR... ISN'T THAT RIGHT?
ROBIN'S HOMELAND?!
THAT CRAPPY MASK! I FEEL LIKE KICKING HIM OVER A WATERFALL RIGHT NOW!!
...
I DON'T HAVE...
...ANYWHERE TO GO, OR ANY PLACE TO RETURN TO...
...
STOP!
NOT THAT!!
WHEE! I LOVE THAT REACTION. WHAT A THRILL IT GIVES ME.
WHAT?! DOES THAT MEAN I SHOULD PRESS THIS SWITCH TO ACTIVATE THE
CALL?
HUH? HEY!!
WA HA HA HA HA...
ENIES LOBBY
...

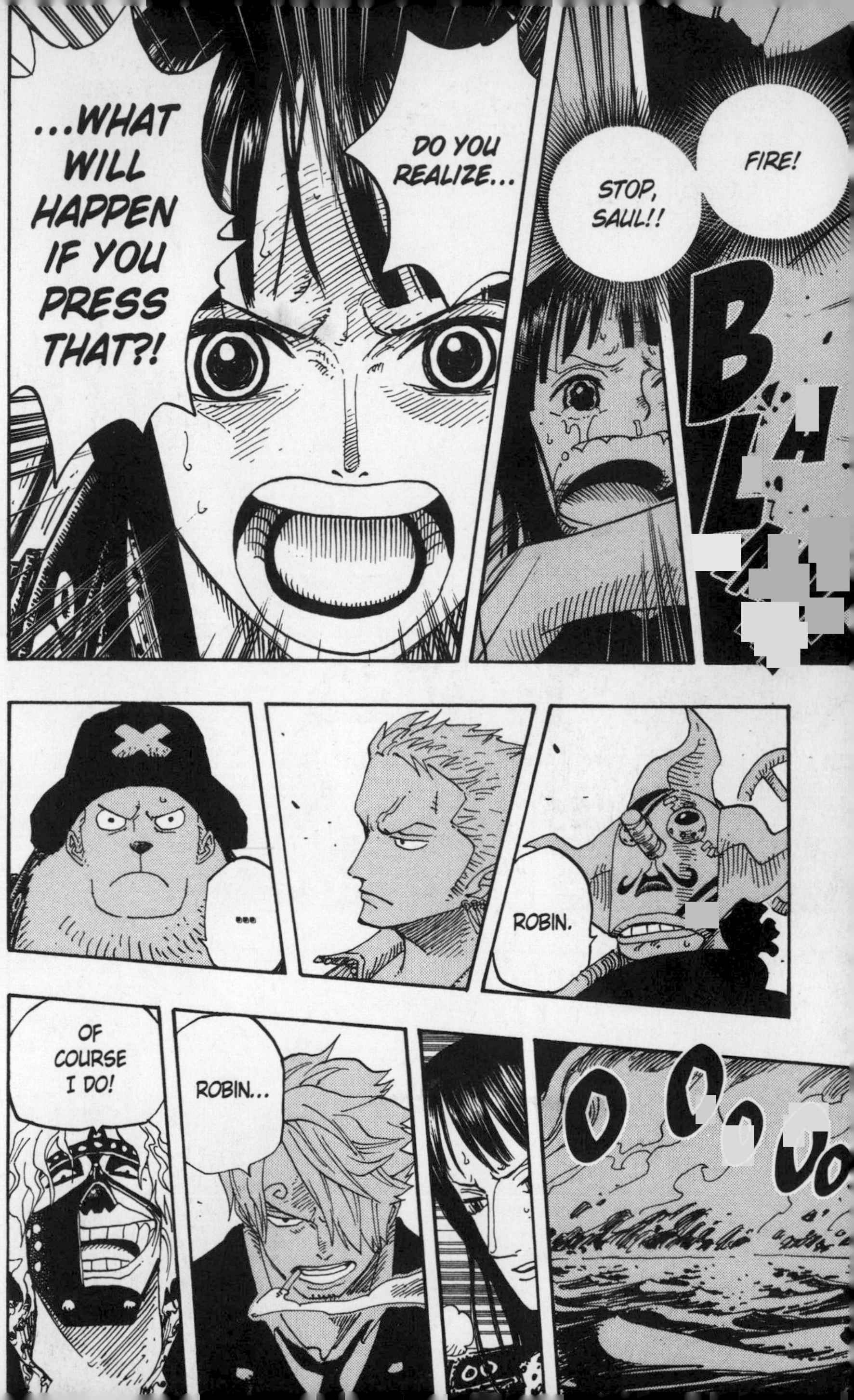
FIRE!
STOP, SAUL!!
DO YOU REALIZE...
...WHAT WILL HAPPEN IF YOU PRESS THAT?!
ROBIN.
...
ROBIN...
OF COURSE I DO!

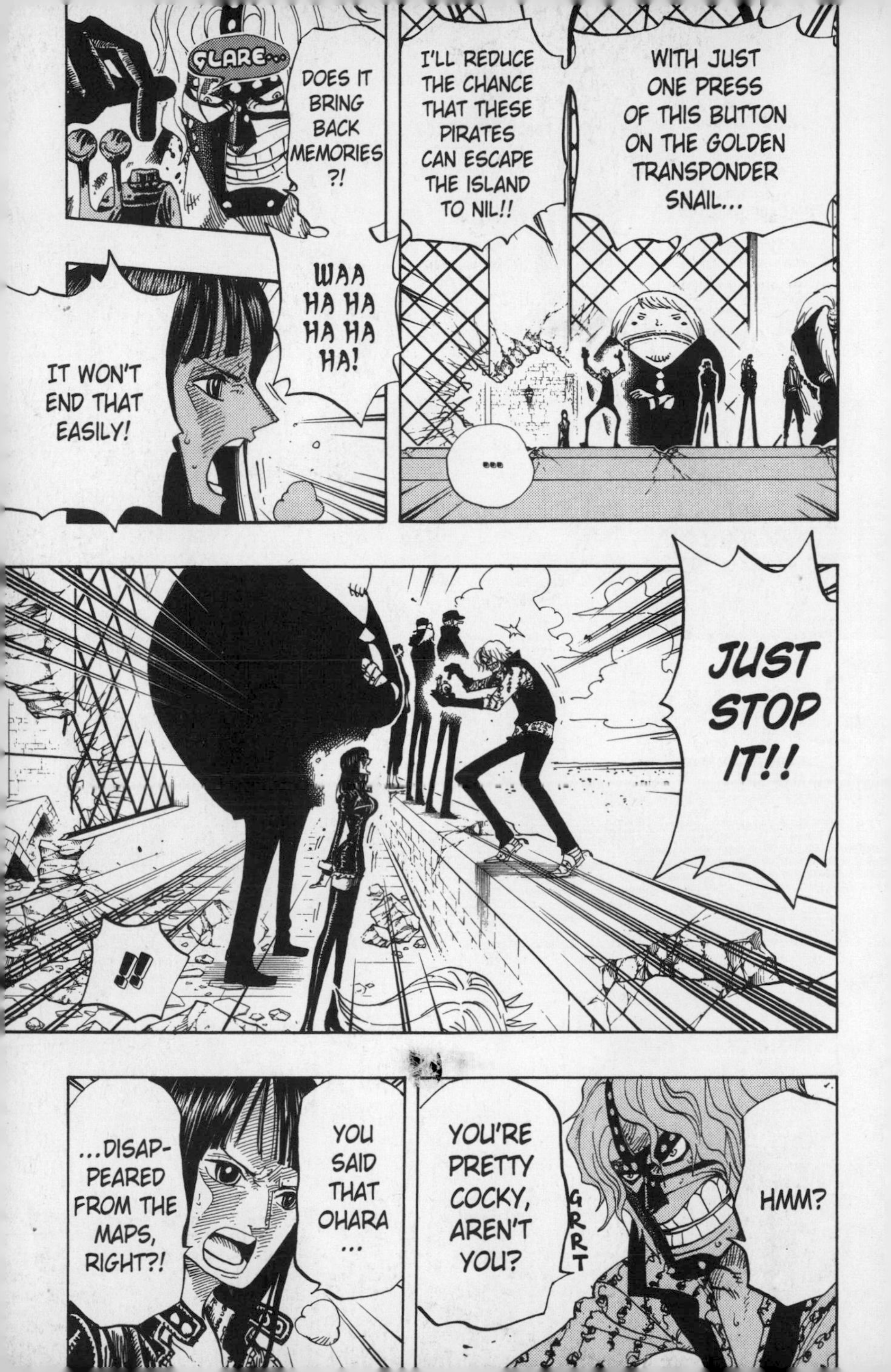
WITH JUST ONE PRESS OF THIS BUTTON ON THE GOLDEN TRANSPONDER SNAIL...
I'LL REDUCE THE CHANCE THAT THESE PIRATES CAN ESCAPE THE ISLAND TO NIL!!
...
GLARE...
DOES IT BRING BACK MEMORIES?!
WAA HA HA HA HA HA!
IT WON'T END THAT EASILY!
JUST STOP IT!!
!!
HMM?
GRRRT
YOU'RE PRETTY COCKY, AREN'T YOU?
YOU SAID THAT OHARA...
...DISAPPEARED FROM THE MAPS, RIGHT?!

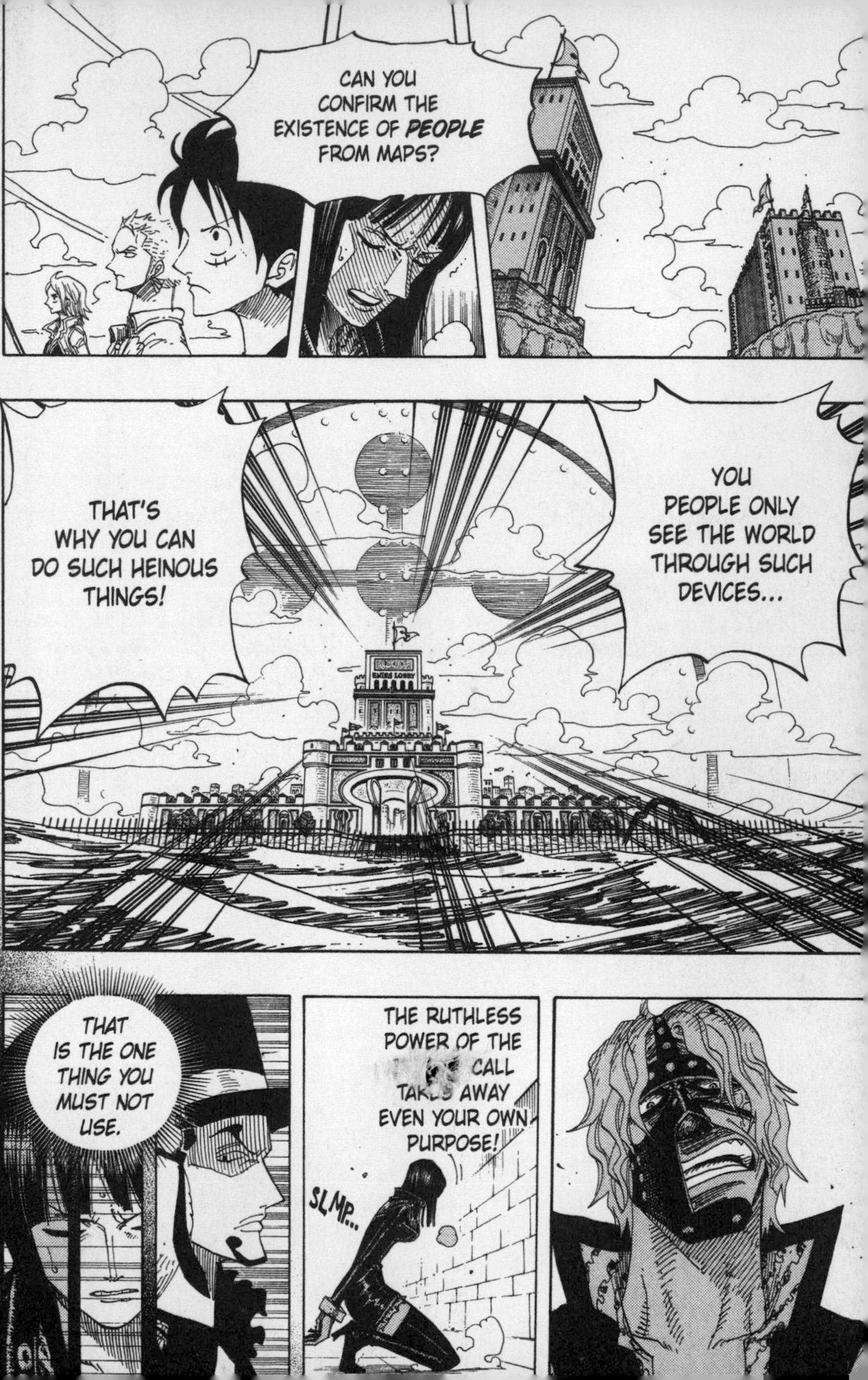
CAN YOU CONFIRM THE EXISTENCE OF *PEOPLE* FROM MAPS?
YOU PEOPLE ONLY SEE THE WORLD THROUGH SUCH DEVICES...
THAT'S WHY YOU CAN DO SUCH HEINOUS THINGS!
THE RUTHLESS POWER OF THE CALL TAKES AWAY EVEN YOUR OWN PURPOSE!
SLMP...
THAT IS THE ONE THING YOU MUST NOT USE.

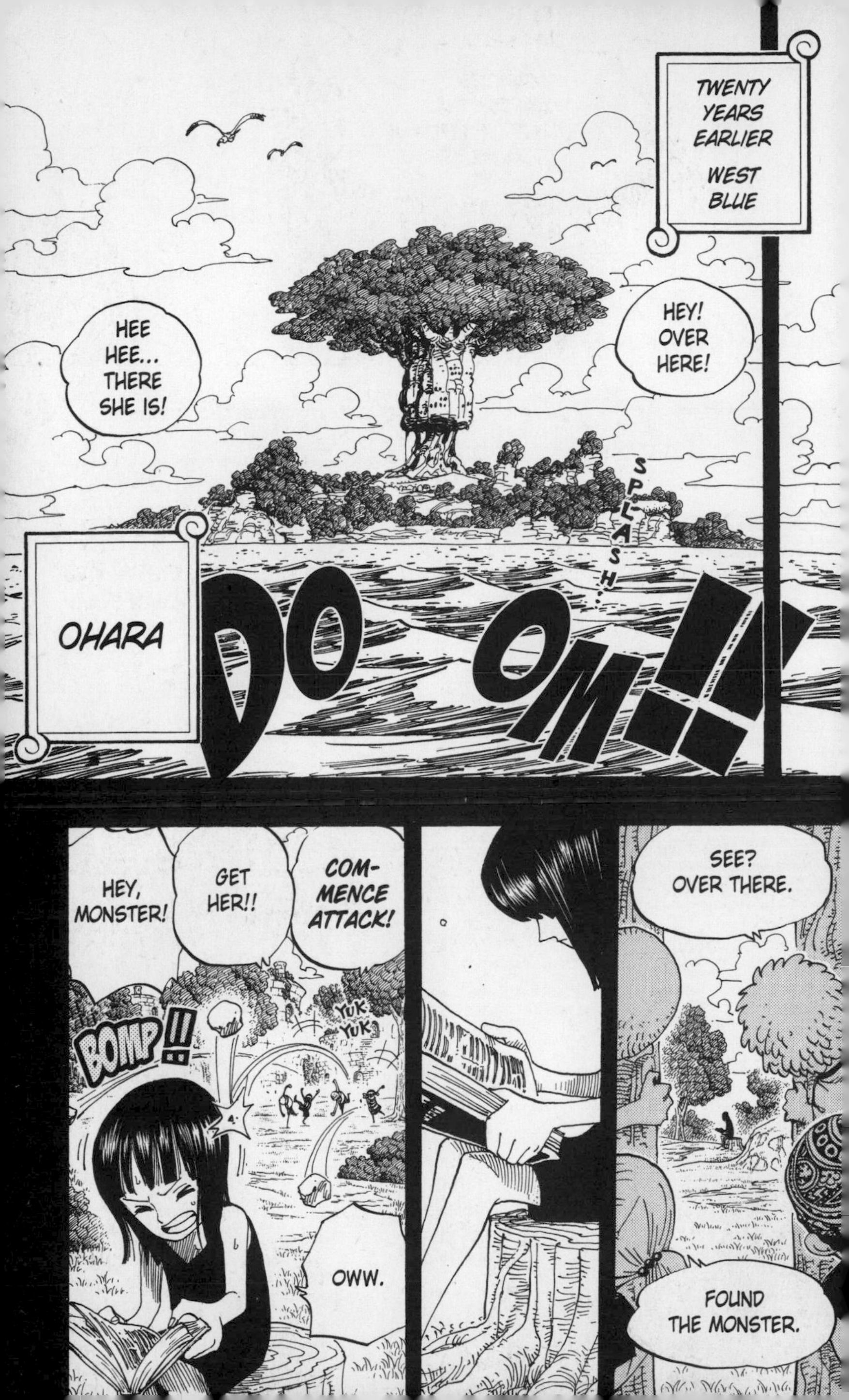
TWENTY YEARS EARLIER
WEST BLUE
HEY! OVER HERE!
HEE HEE... THERE SHE IS!
SPLASH...
OHARA
DO-OM!!
SEE? OVER THERE.
FOUND THE MONSTER.
COM-MENCE ATTACK!
GET HER!!
HEY, MONSTER!
YUK YUK
BOMP!!
OWW.

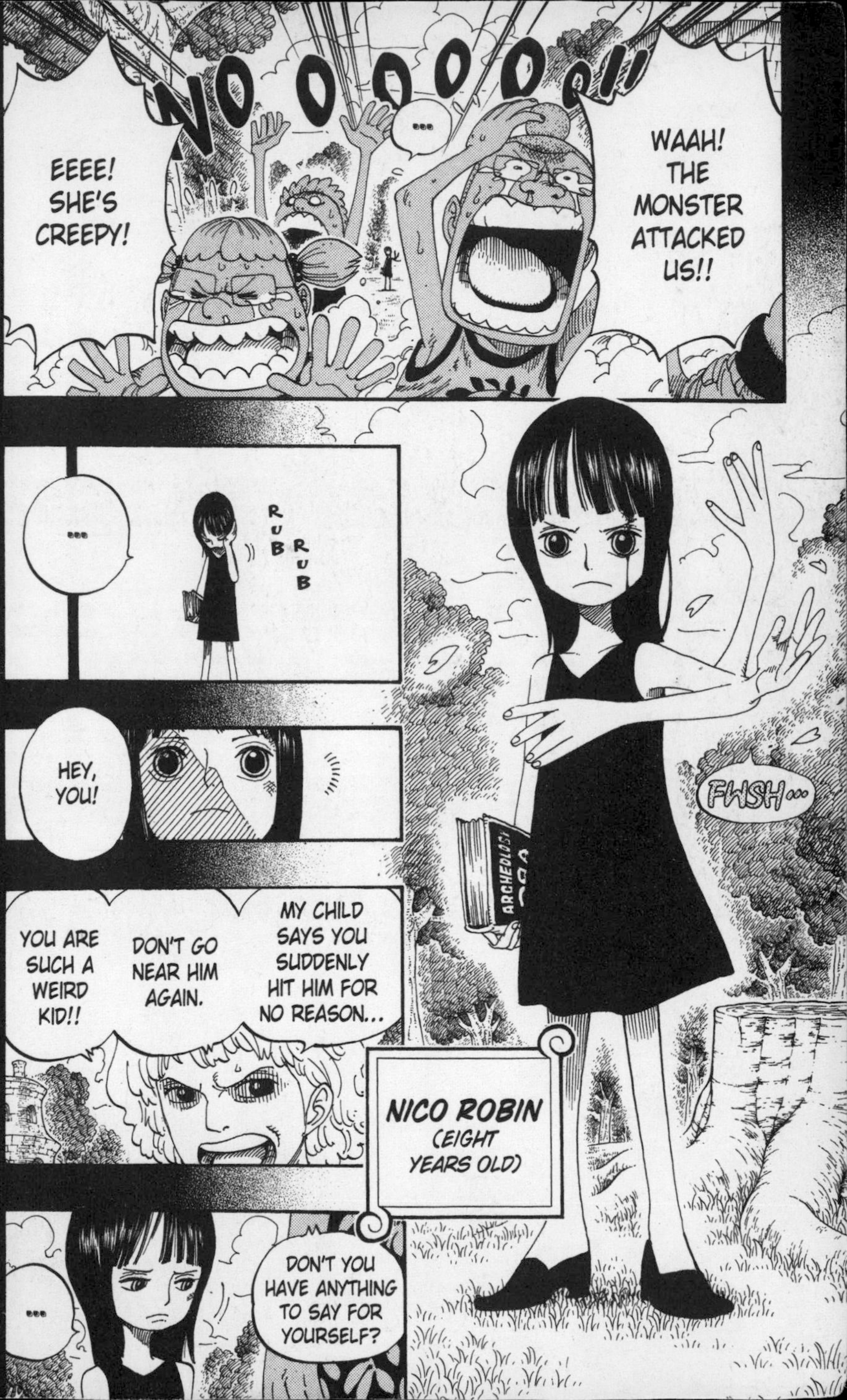
NOOOOO!!
WAAH! THE MONSTER ATTACKED US!!
...
EEEE! SHE'S CREEPY!
FWSH...
ARCHEOLOGY
NICO ROBIN (EIGHT YEARS OLD)
RUB RUB
...
HEY, YOU!
MY CHILD SAYS YOU SUDDENLY HIT HIM FOR NO REASON...
DON'T GO NEAR HIM AGAIN.
YOU ARE SUCH A WEIRD KID!!
DON'T YOU HAVE ANYTHING TO SAY FOR YOURSELF?
...

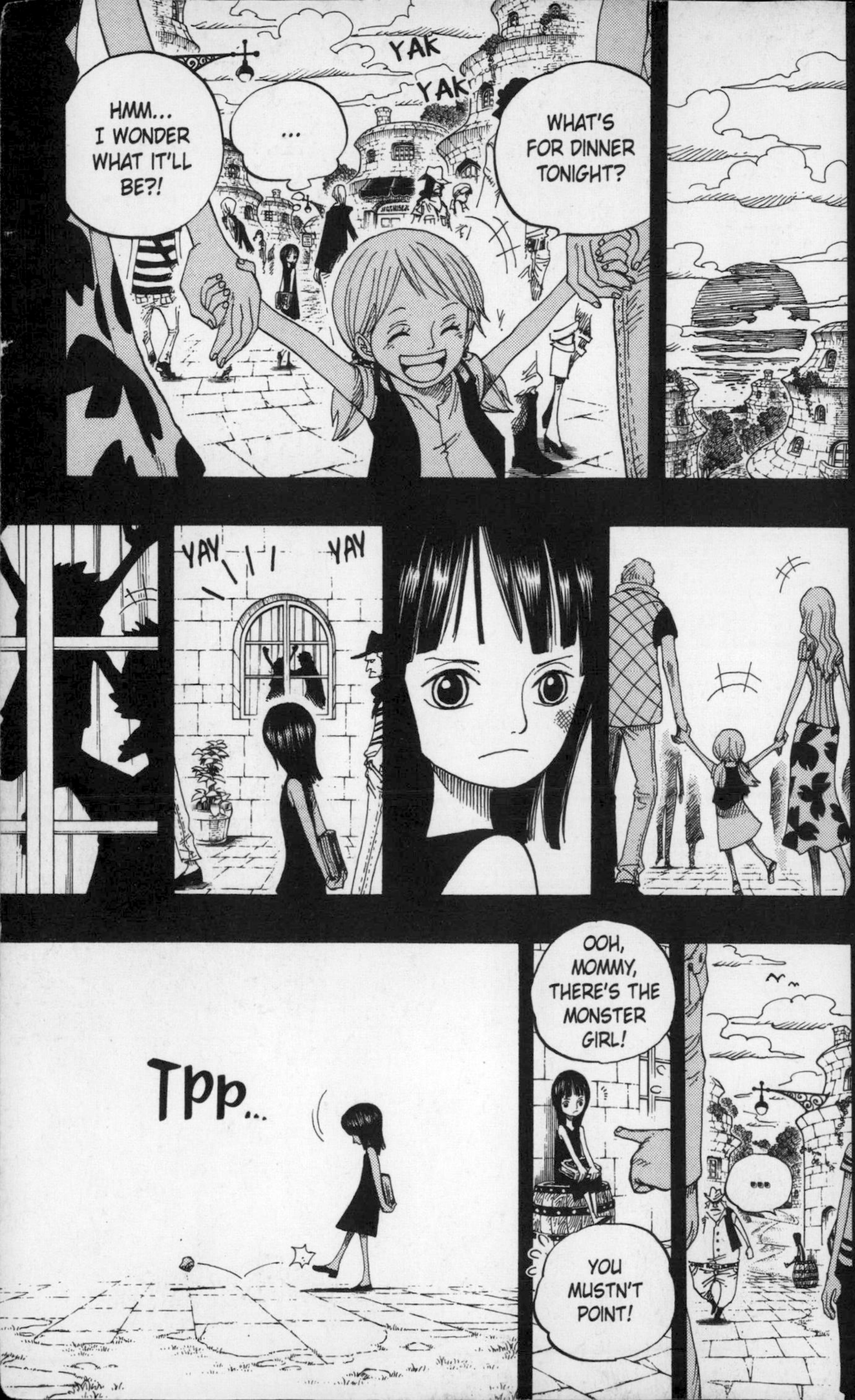
YAK
YAK
WHAT'S FOR DINNER TONIGHT?
...
HMM... I WONDER WHAT IT'LL BE?!
YAY
YAY
...
OOH, MOMMY, THERE'S THE MONSTER GIRL!
YOU MUSTN'T POINT!
Tpp...

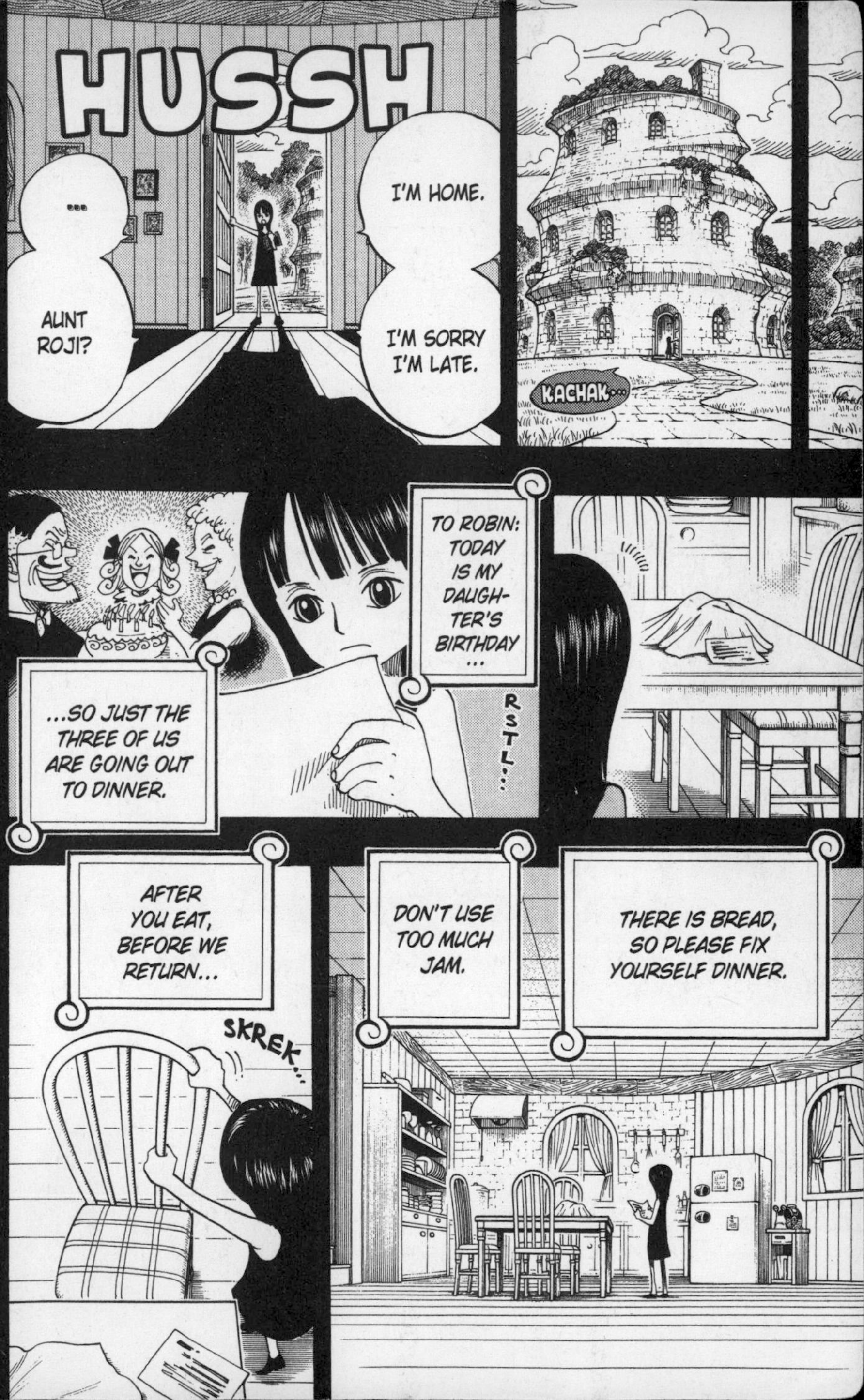
KACHAK...
HUSSH
I'M HOME.
I'M SORRY I'M LATE.
...
AUNT ROJI?
TO ROBIN: TODAY IS MY DAUGHTER'S BIRTHDAY...
RSTL...
...SO JUST THE THREE OF US ARE GOING OUT TO DINNER.
THERE IS BREAD, SO PLEASE FIX YOURSELF DINNER.
DON'T USE TOO MUCH JAM.
AFTER YOU EAT, BEFORE WE RETURN...
SKREK...

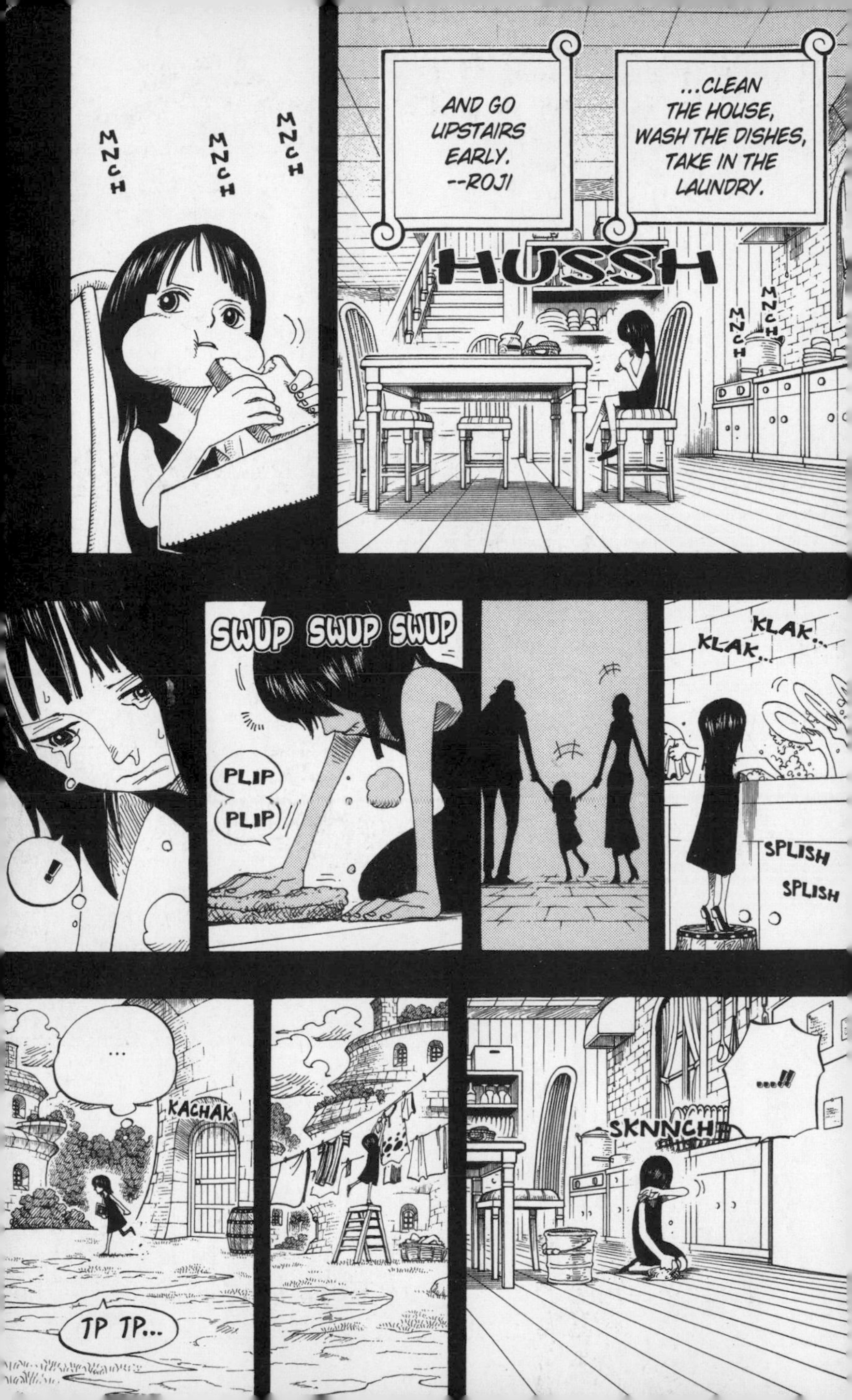
...CLEAN THE HOUSE, WASH THE DISHES, TAKE IN THE LAUNDRY.
AND GO UPSTAIRS EARLY. --ROJI
HUSSH
MNCH MNCH
MNCH MNCH MNCH
KLAK... KLAK...
SPLISH SPLISH
SWUP SWUP SWUP
PLIP PLIP
!
SKNNCH
...!!
...
KACHAK
TP TP...

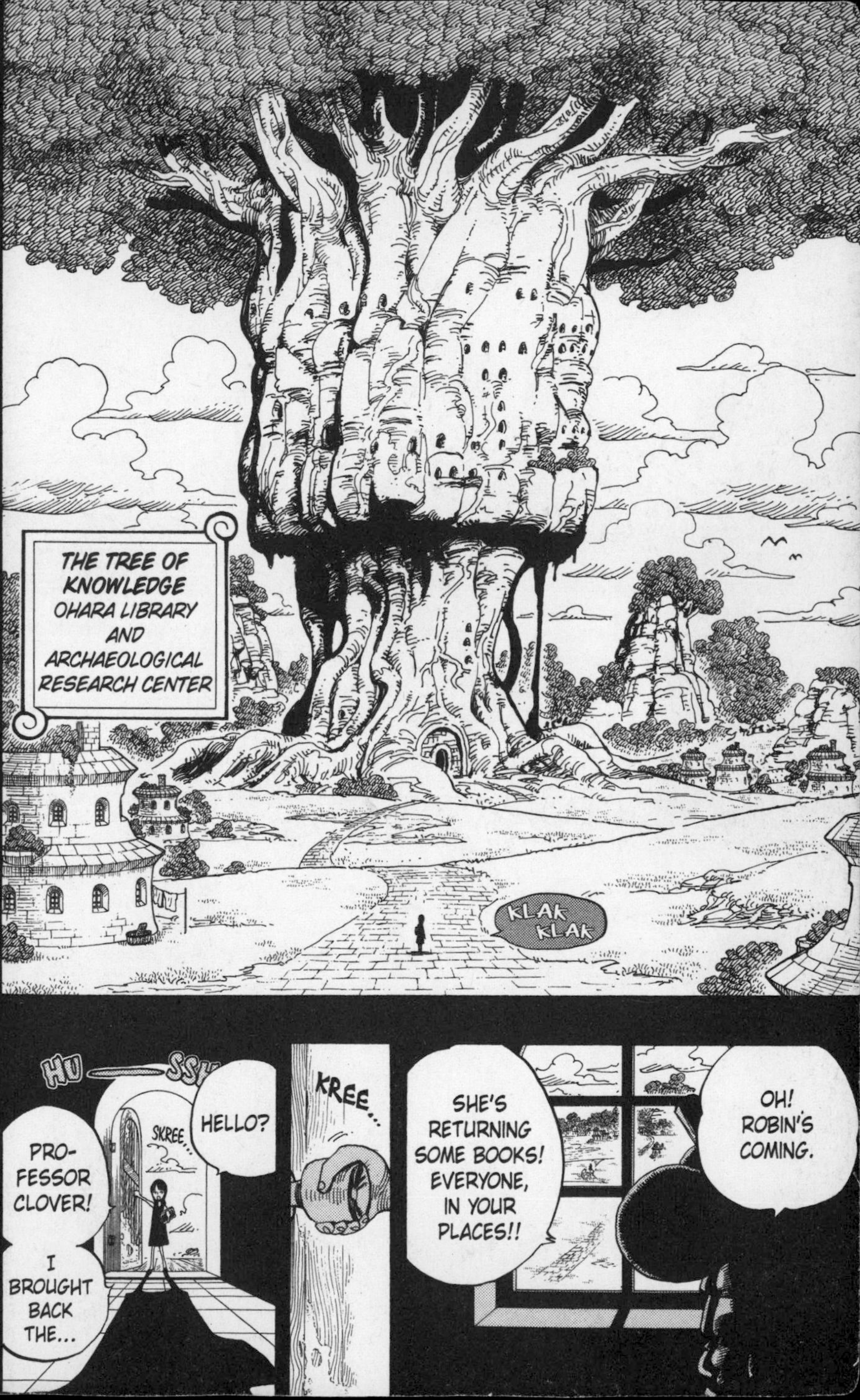
THE TREE OF KNOWLEDGE
OHARA LIBRARY AND ARCHAEOLOGICAL RESEARCH CENTER
KLAK KLAK
OH! ROBIN'S COMING.
SHE'S RETURNING SOME BOOKS! EVERYONE, IN YOUR PLACES!!
KREE...
HU——SSH
HELLO?
SKREE...
PRO-FESSOR CLOVER!
I BROUGHT BACK THE...

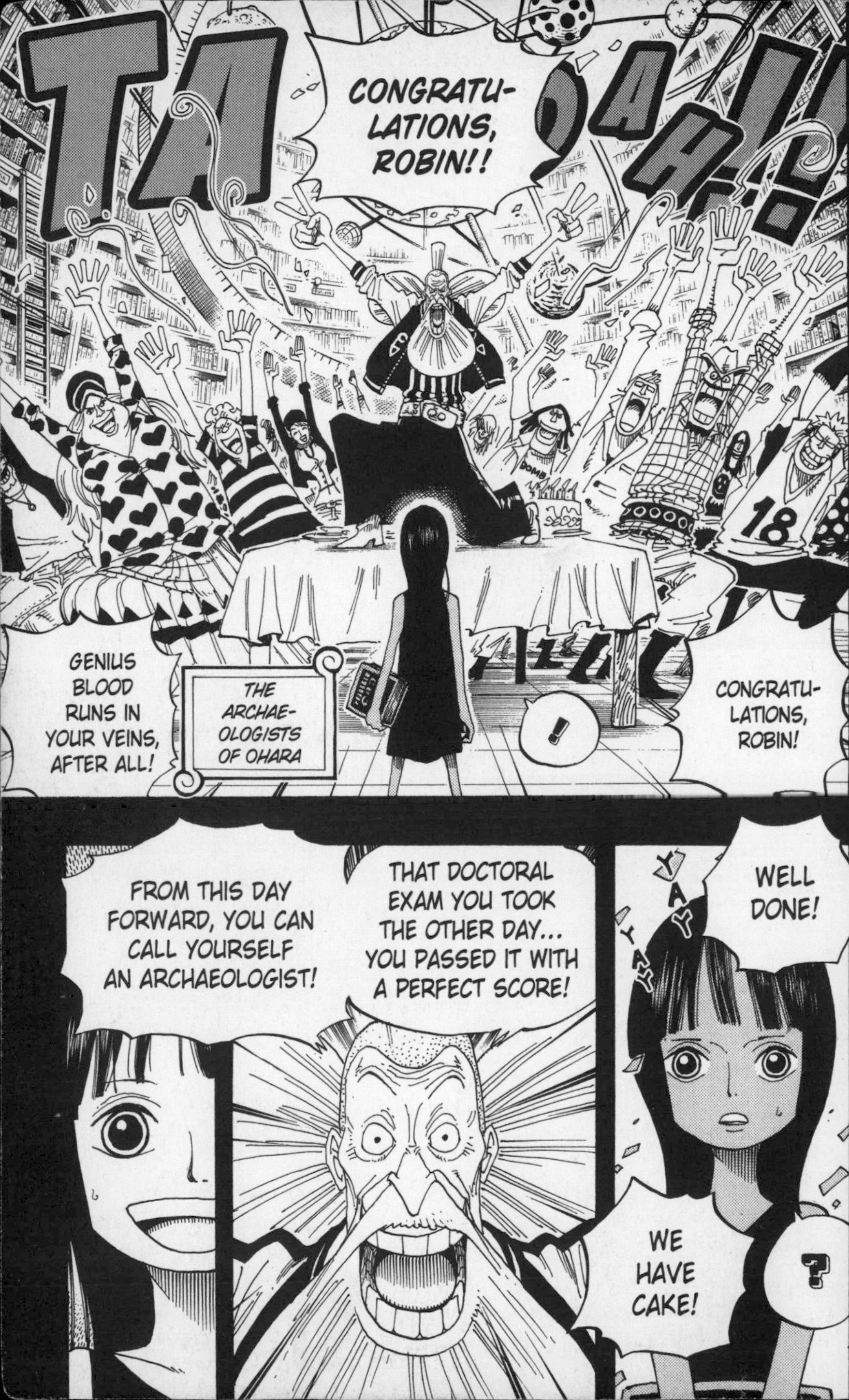
T.A DAAH!!
CONGRATULATIONS, ROBIN!!
CONGRATULATIONS, ROBIN!
!
THE ARCHAEOLOGISTS OF OHARA
GENIUS BLOOD RUNS IN YOUR VEINS, AFTER ALL!
WELL DONE!
YAY YAY
WE HAVE CAKE!
?
THAT DOCTORAL EXAM YOU TOOK THE OTHER DAY... YOU PASSED IT WITH A PERFECT SCORE!
FROM THIS DAY FORWARD, YOU CAN CALL YOURSELF AN ARCHAEOLOGIST!

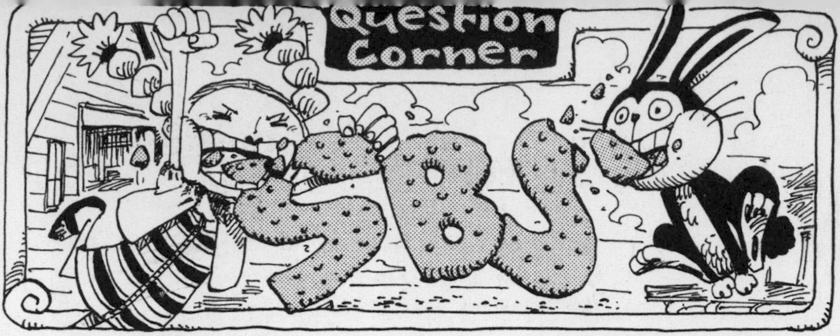
Question Corner
SBS

Q: In chapter 367, Sanji breaks a Transponder Snail. That's terrible!! The Transponder Snail didn't do a thing to him! Do you want the Transponder Snail to cry? It'll scream out in pain, y'know? Maybe its body won't hurt, but it'll cry because of emotional hurt. So let's apologize.

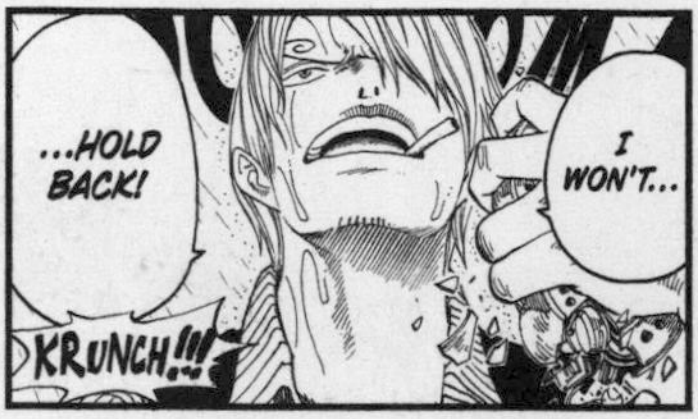
I WON'T...
...HOLD BACK!
KRUNCH!!!

--Naoko

A: Well, err... I thought that's the impression you'd get, but there's no need to worry. The illustration on the right is a Transponder Snail in the wild. It is able to communicate with its cohorts through the use of electrical waves (thought waves).

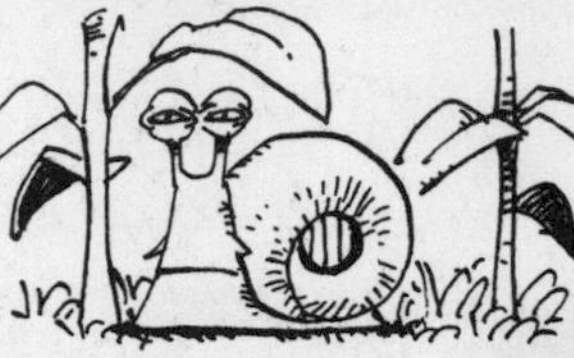

And humans attach a button receiver to contact a specific Transponder Snail. Hence, even if the receiver is crushed, it doesn't hurt the transponder Snail itself.

Q: Mr. Oda, you are guilty of sexual harassment.

--Representative of all girls

A: What?! I didn't say anything that can be called harassment!! I have no idea what you're talking about.

Q: Nami's bust measurement of 95 equals what cup size?

--Nami-loving Man

A: So you're the culprit! Questions like yours are why the girls are protesting up above!! Although I'm curious too! ♥ But cup size is hard to determine. They use terms like "band size" and "cup size" that I don't understand. I wish our female readers would enlighten us. What are Nami and Robin's cup sizes? (←sexual harassment)

Chapter 392: DERESHI

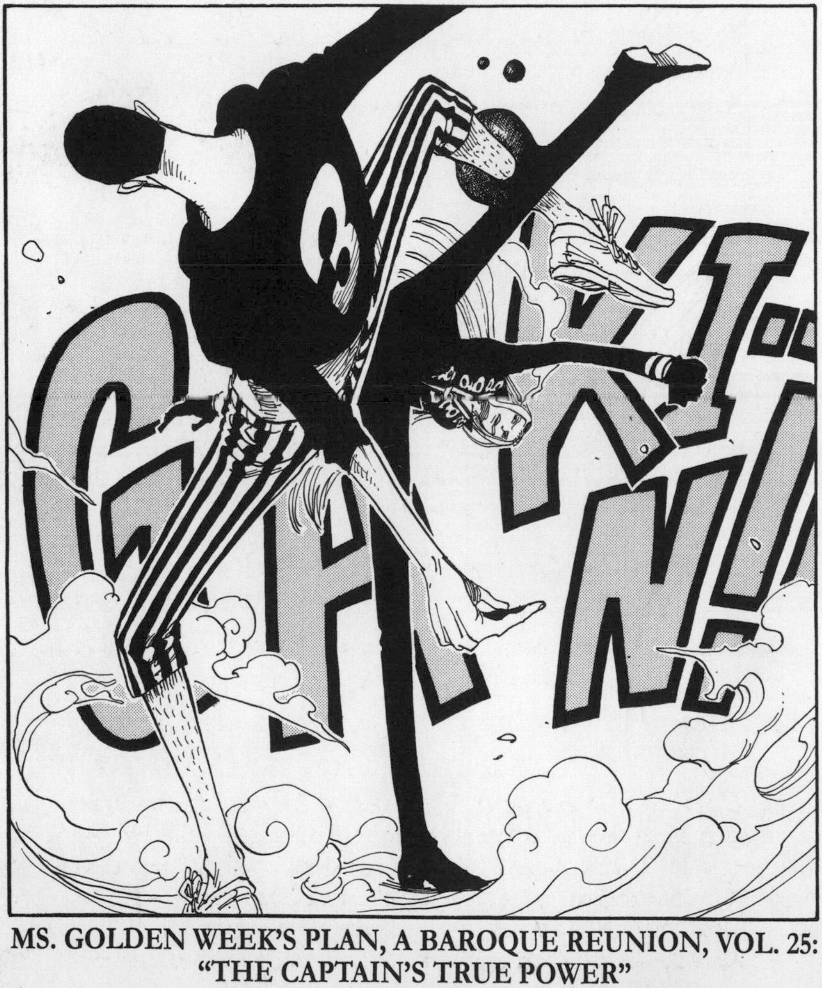

MS. GOLDEN WEEK'S PLAN, A BAROQUE REUNION, VOL. 25:
"THE CAPTAIN'S TRUE POWER"

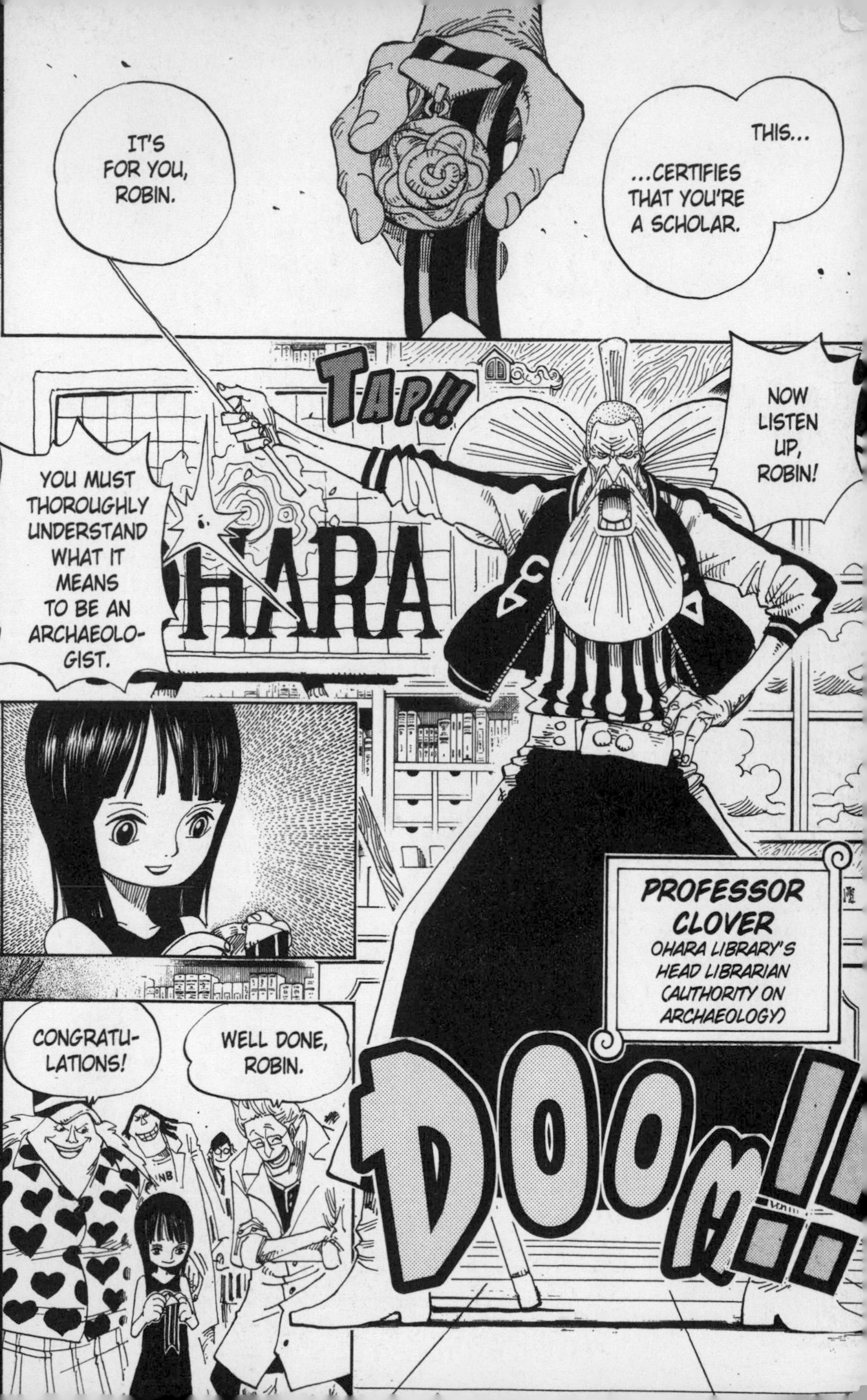
THIS...
...CERTIFIES THAT YOU'RE A SCHOLAR.
IT'S FOR YOU, ROBIN.
TAP!!
NOW LISTEN UP, ROBIN!
YOU MUST THOROUGHLY UNDERSTAND WHAT IT MEANS TO BE AN ARCHAEOLO-GIST.
HARA
PROFESSOR CLOVER
OHARA LIBRARY'S HEAD LIBRARIAN (AUTHORITY ON ARCHAEOLOGY)
DOOM!!
WELL DONE, ROBIN.
CONGRATU-LATIONS!

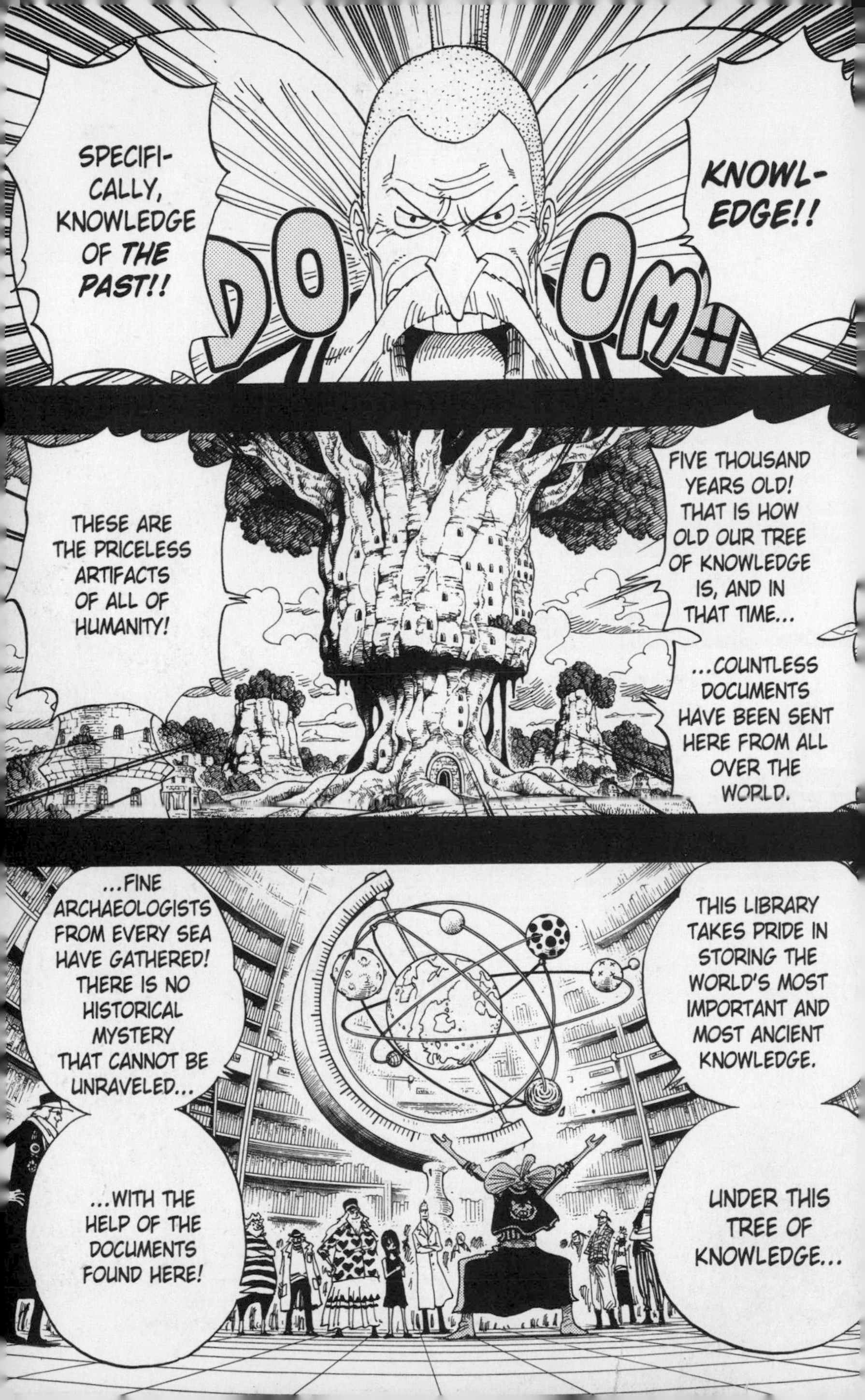
KNOWL-EDGE!!
SPECIFICALLY, KNOWLEDGE OF THE PAST!!
DOOM
FIVE THOUSAND YEARS OLD! THAT IS HOW OLD OUR TREE OF KNOWLEDGE IS, AND IN THAT TIME...
...COUNTLESS DOCUMENTS HAVE BEEN SENT HERE FROM ALL OVER THE WORLD.
THESE ARE THE PRICELESS ARTIFACTS OF ALL OF HUMANITY!
THIS LIBRARY TAKES PRIDE IN STORING THE WORLD'S MOST IMPORTANT AND MOST ANCIENT KNOWLEDGE.
UNDER THIS TREE OF KNOWLEDGE...
...FINE ARCHAEOLOGISTS FROM EVERY SEA HAVE GATHERED! THERE IS NO HISTORICAL MYSTERY THAT CANNOT BE UNRAVELED...
...WITH THE HELP OF THE DOCUMENTS FOUND HERE!

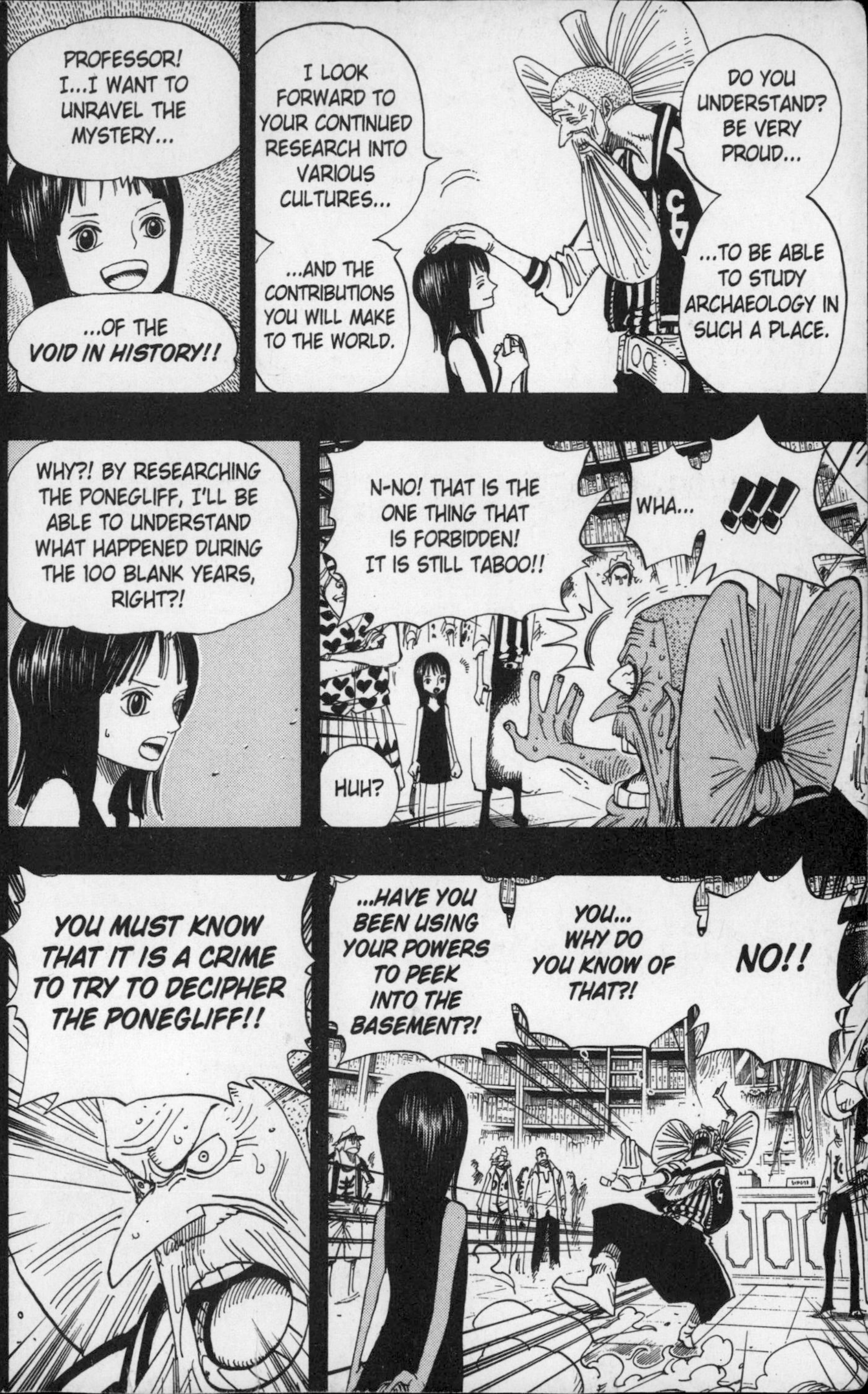
DO YOU UNDERSTAND? BE VERY PROUD...
...TO BE ABLE TO STUDY ARCHAEOLOGY IN SUCH A PLACE.
I LOOK FORWARD TO YOUR CONTINUED RESEARCH INTO VARIOUS CULTURES...
...AND THE CONTRIBUTIONS YOU WILL MAKE TO THE WORLD.
PROFESSOR! I...I WANT TO UNRAVEL THE MYSTERY...
...OF THE VOID IN HISTORY!!
WHA... !!!
N-NO! THAT IS THE ONE THING THAT IS FORBIDDEN! IT IS STILL TABOO!!
HUH?
WHY?! BY RESEARCHING THE PONEGLIFF, I'LL BE ABLE TO UNDERSTAND WHAT HAPPENED DURING THE 100 BLANK YEARS, RIGHT?!
NO!!
YOU... WHY DO YOU KNOW OF THAT?!
...HAVE YOU BEEN USING YOUR POWERS TO PEEK INTO THE BASEMENT?!
YOU MUST KNOW THAT IT IS A CRIME TO TRY TO DECIPHER THE PONEGLIFF!!

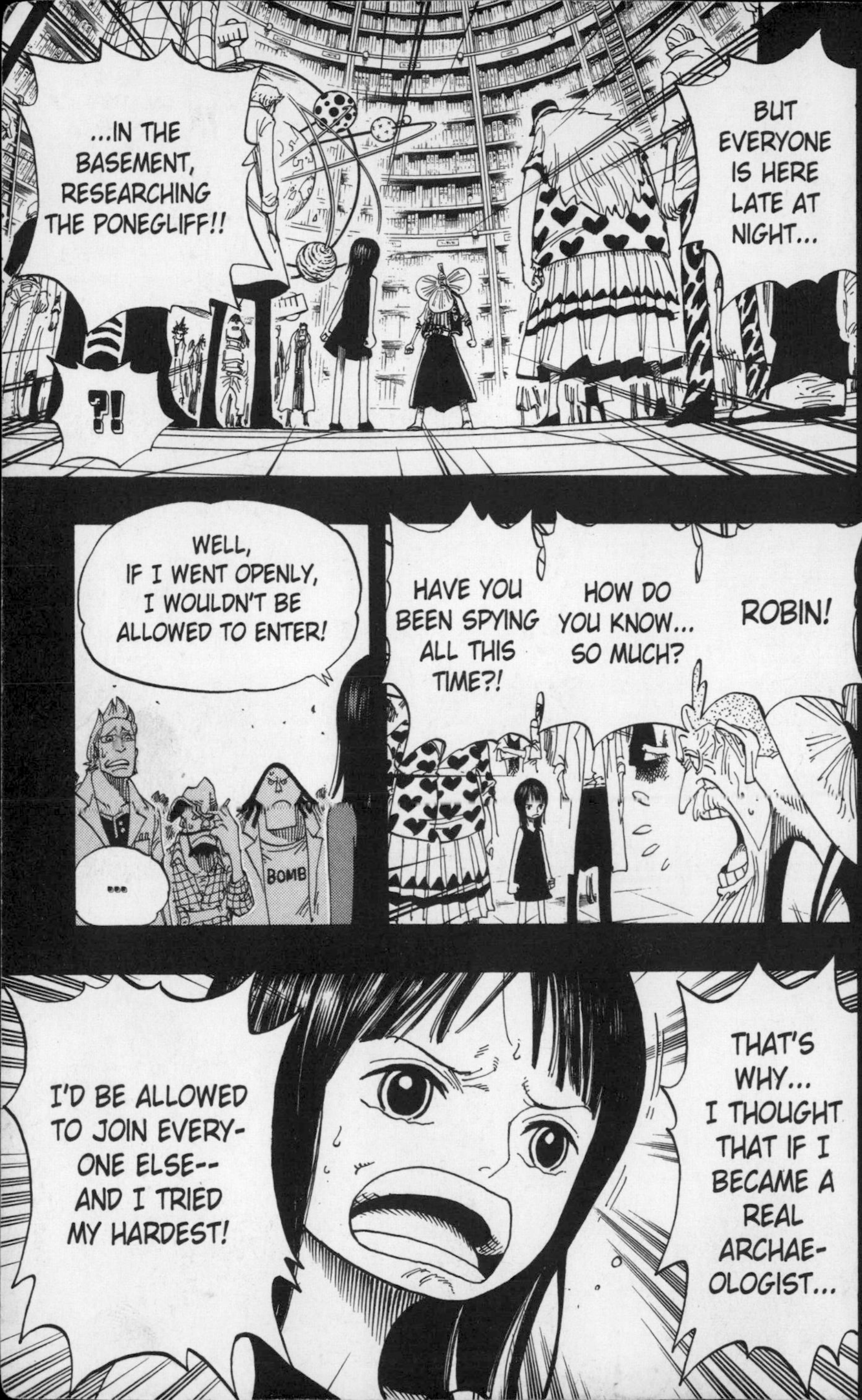
BUT EVERYONE IS HERE LATE AT NIGHT...
...IN THE BASEMENT, RESEARCHING THE PONEGLIFF!!
?!
ROBIN!
HOW DO YOU KNOW... SO MUCH?
HAVE YOU BEEN SPYING ALL THIS TIME?!
WELL, IF I WENT OPENLY, I WOULDN'T BE ALLOWED TO ENTER!
...
BOMB
THAT'S WHY... I THOUGHT THAT IF I BECAME A REAL ARCHAEOLOGIST...
I'D BE ALLOWED TO JOIN EVERY-ONE ELSE-- AND I TRIED MY HARDEST!

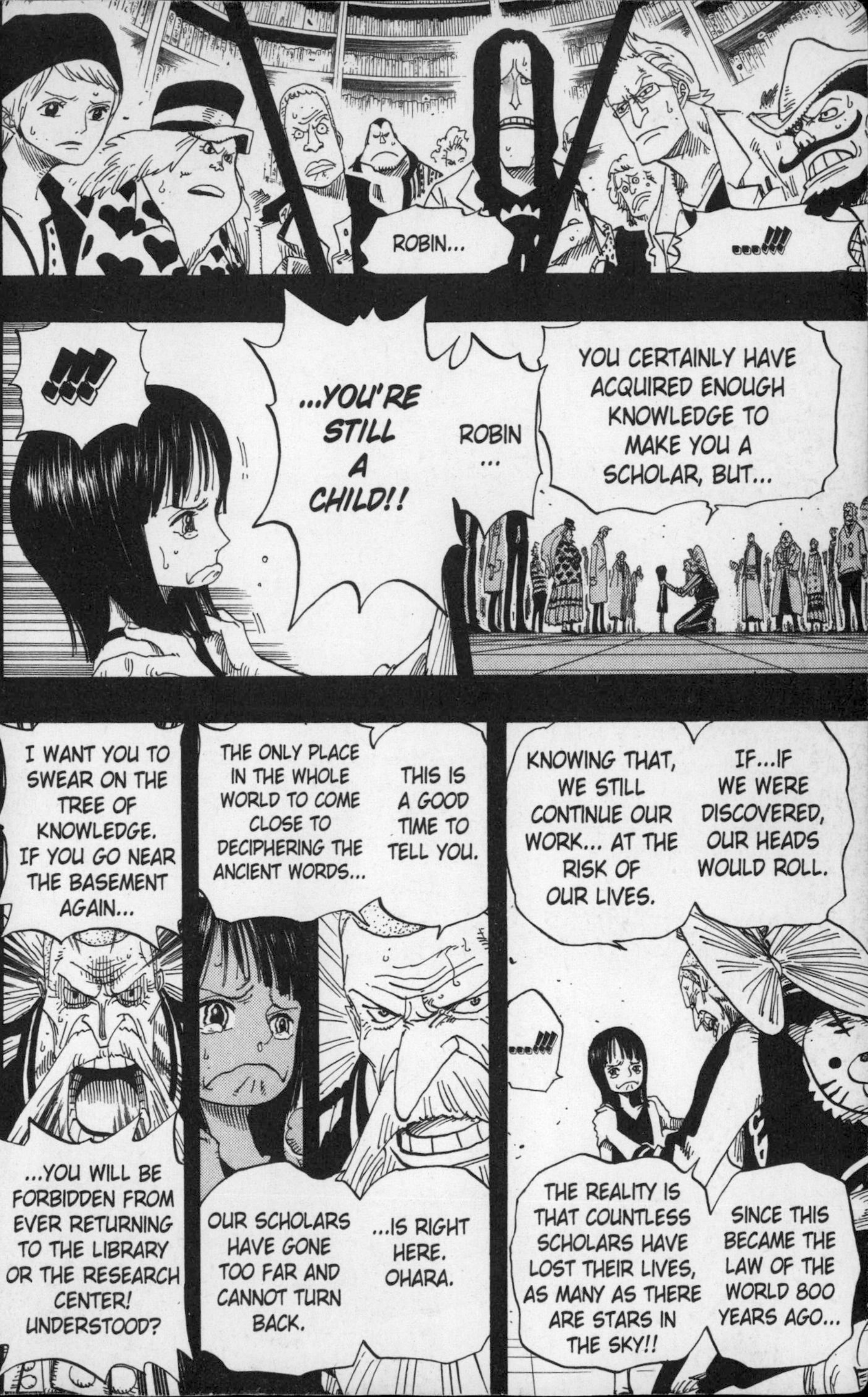

...!!!
ROBIN...
YOU CERTAINLY HAVE ACQUIRED ENOUGH KNOWLEDGE TO MAKE YOU A SCHOLAR, BUT...
ROBIN ...
...YOU'RE STILL A CHILD!!
!!!
IF...IF WE WERE DISCOVERED, OUR HEADS WOULD ROLL.
KNOWING THAT, WE STILL CONTINUE OUR WORK... AT THE RISK OF OUR LIVES.
...!!!
SINCE THIS BECAME THE LAW OF THE WORLD 800 YEARS AGO...
THE REALITY IS THAT COUNTLESS SCHOLARS HAVE LOST THEIR LIVES, AS MANY AS THERE ARE STARS IN THE SKY!!
THIS IS A GOOD TIME TO TELL YOU.
THE ONLY PLACE IN THE WHOLE WORLD TO COME CLOSE TO DECIPHERING THE ANCIENT WORDS...
...IS RIGHT HERE. OHARA.
OUR SCHOLARS HAVE GONE TOO FAR AND CANNOT TURN BACK.
I WANT YOU TO SWEAR ON THE TREE OF KNOWLEDGE. IF YOU GO NEAR THE BASEMENT AGAIN...
...YOU WILL BE FORBIDDEN FROM EVER RETURNING TO THE LIBRARY OR THE RESEARCH CENTER! UNDERSTOOD?

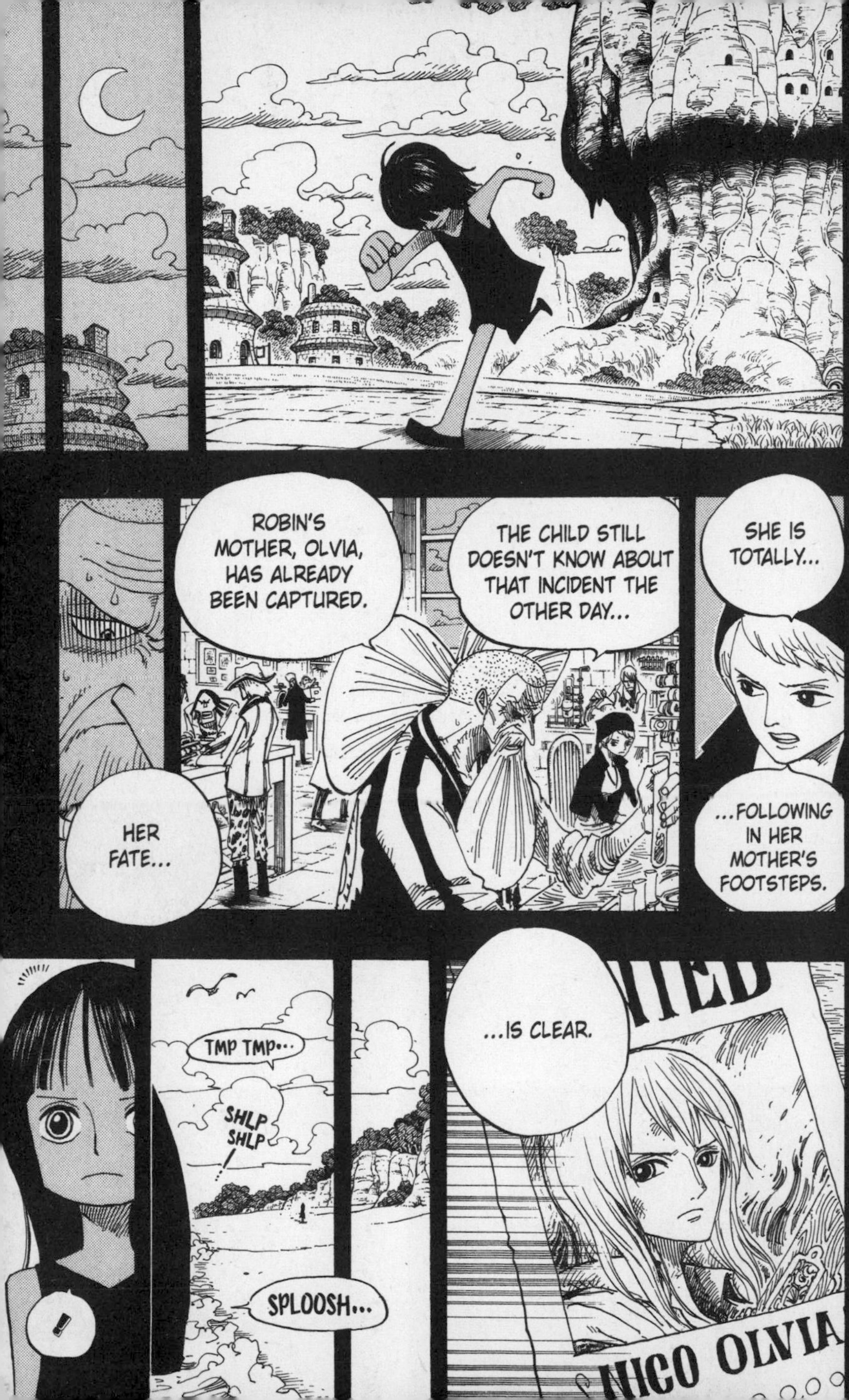

SHE IS TOTALLY...
...FOLLOWING IN HER MOTHER'S FOOTSTEPS.
THE CHILD STILL DOESN'T KNOW ABOUT THAT INCIDENT THE OTHER DAY...
ROBIN'S MOTHER, OLVIA, HAS ALREADY BEEN CAPTURED.
HER FATE...
...IS CLEAR.
NICO OLVIA
TMP TMP...
SHLP SHLP
SPLOOSH...
!

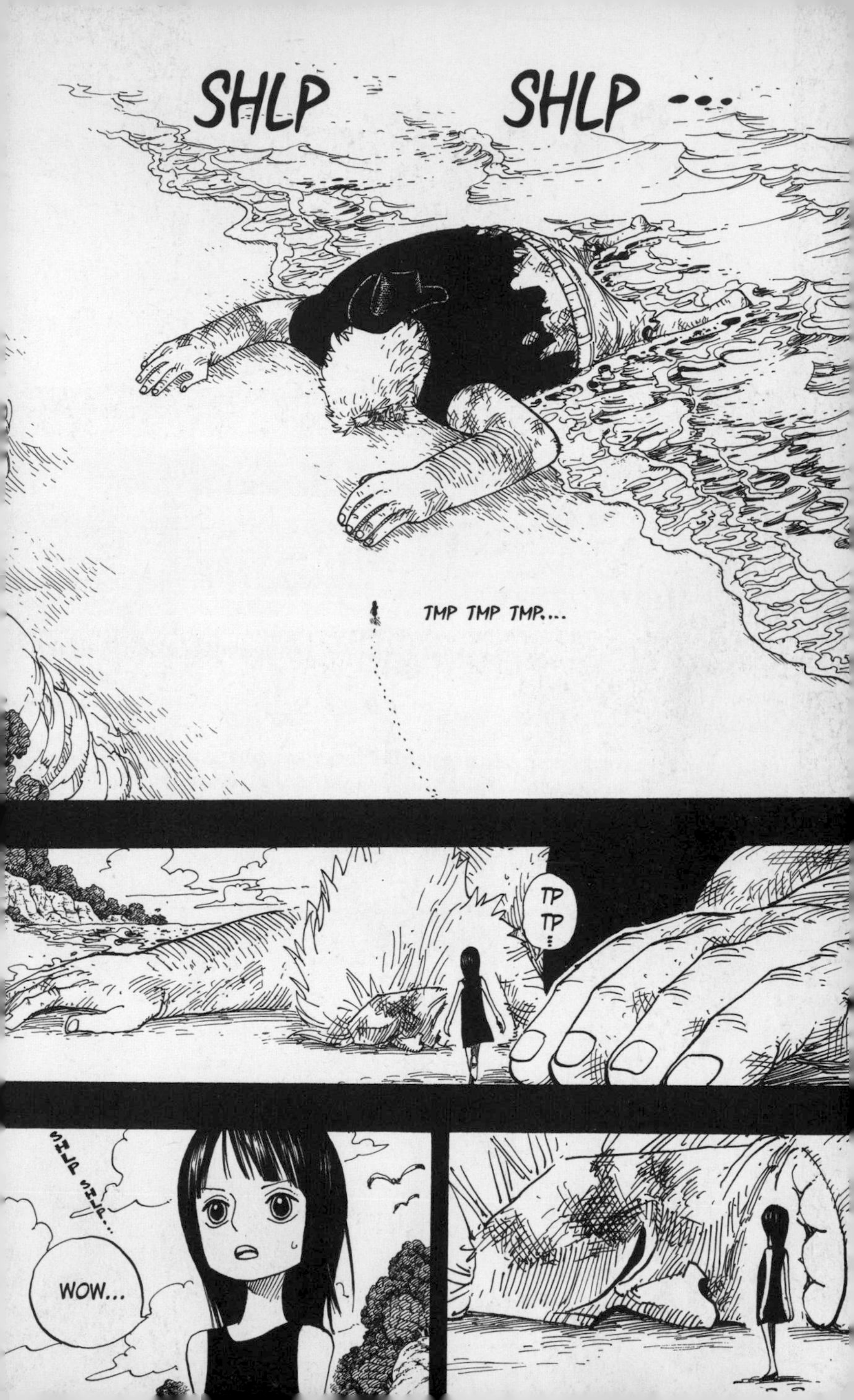
SHLP SHLP ...
TMP TMP TMP....
TP TP...
SHLP SHLP...
WOW...

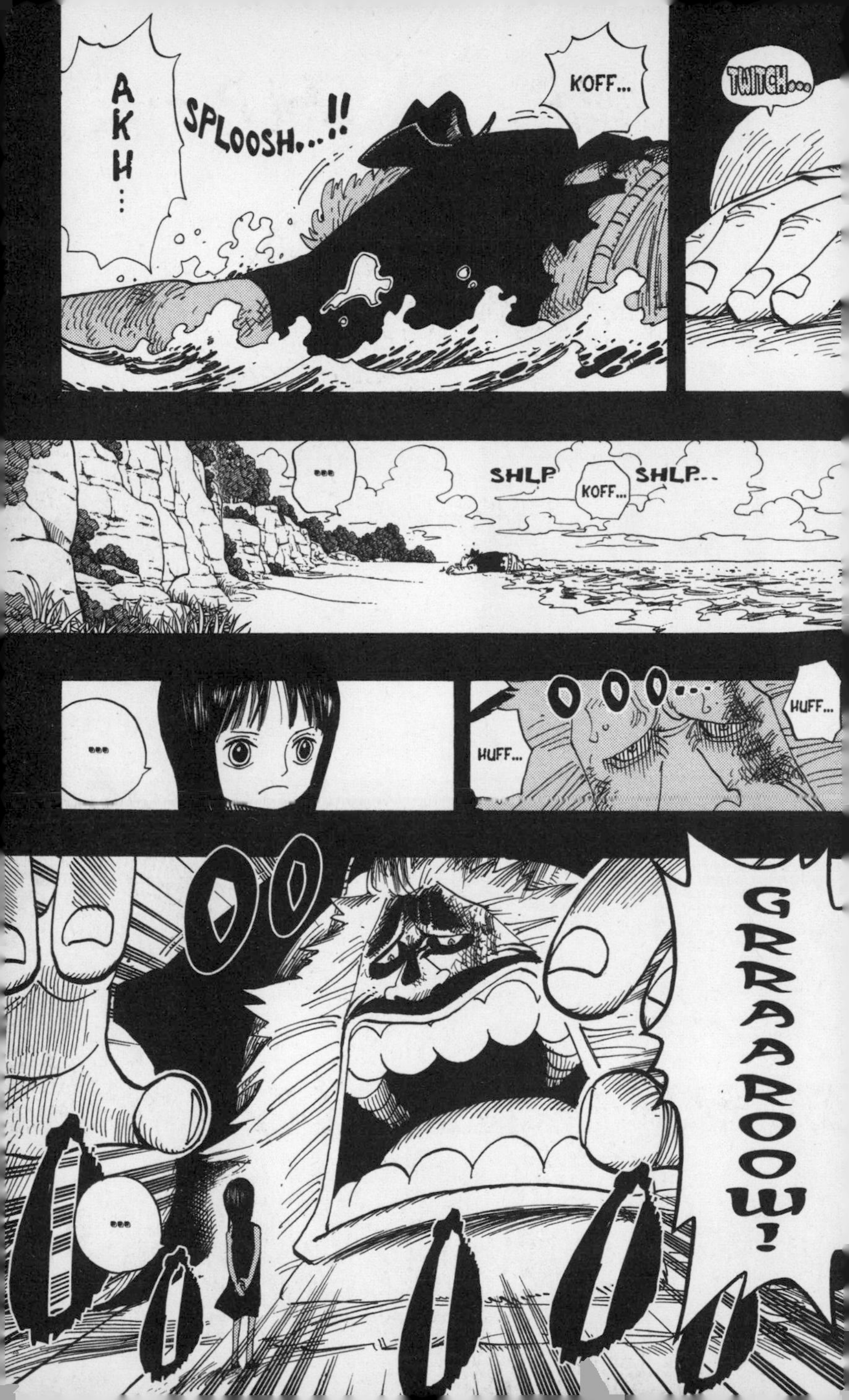

TWITCH...
KOFF...
SPLOOSH...!!
AKH...
SHLP...
KOFF...
SHLP
...
HUFF...
HUFF...
...
GRRAAROOOW!
...

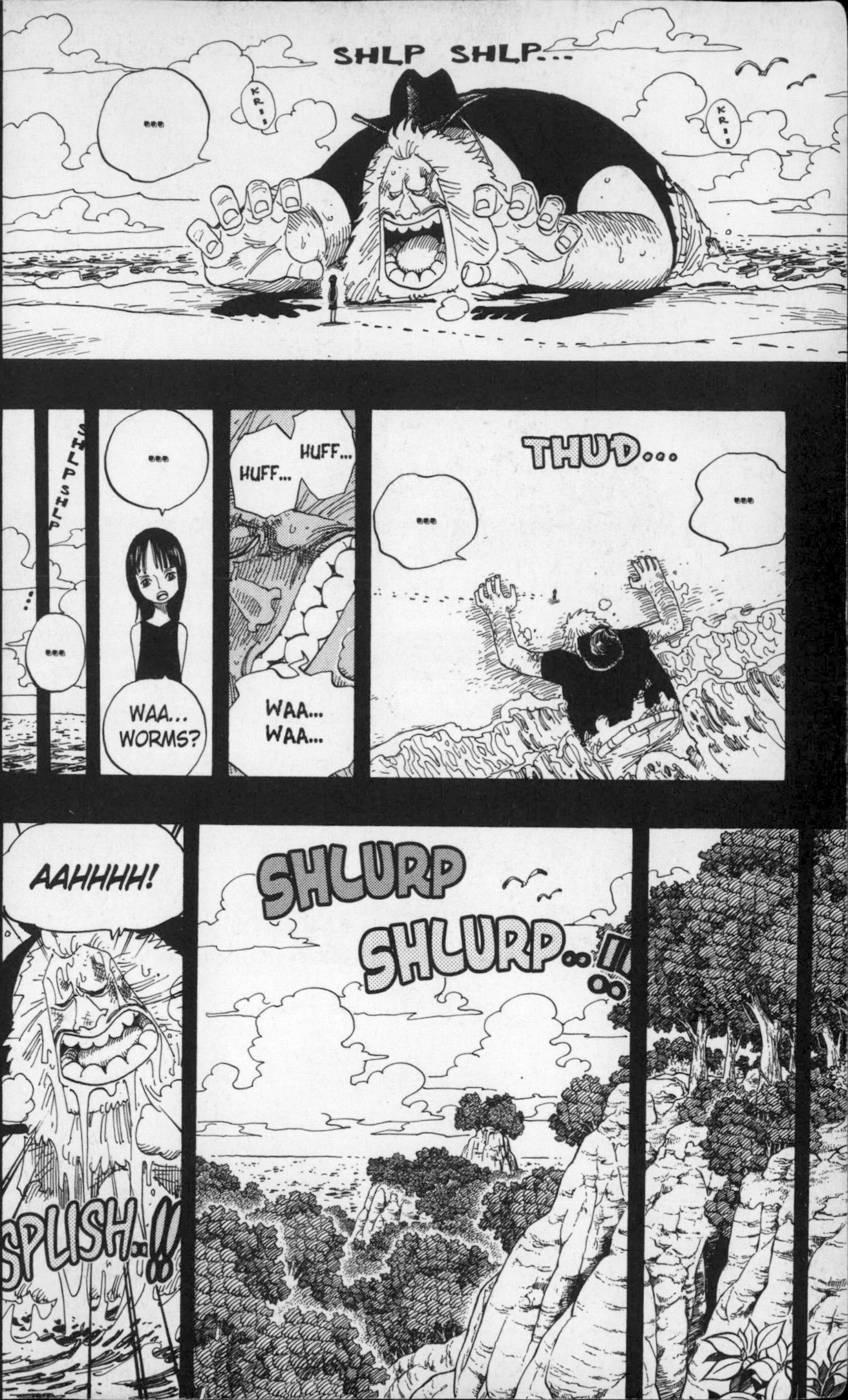
SHLP SHLP...
KRI!
...
KRI!
THUD...
...
...
HUFF...
HUFF...
WAA...
WAA...
...
WAA...
WORMS?
SHLP SHLP
...
...
SHLURP
SHLURP..!!
AAHHHH!
SPLISH..!!

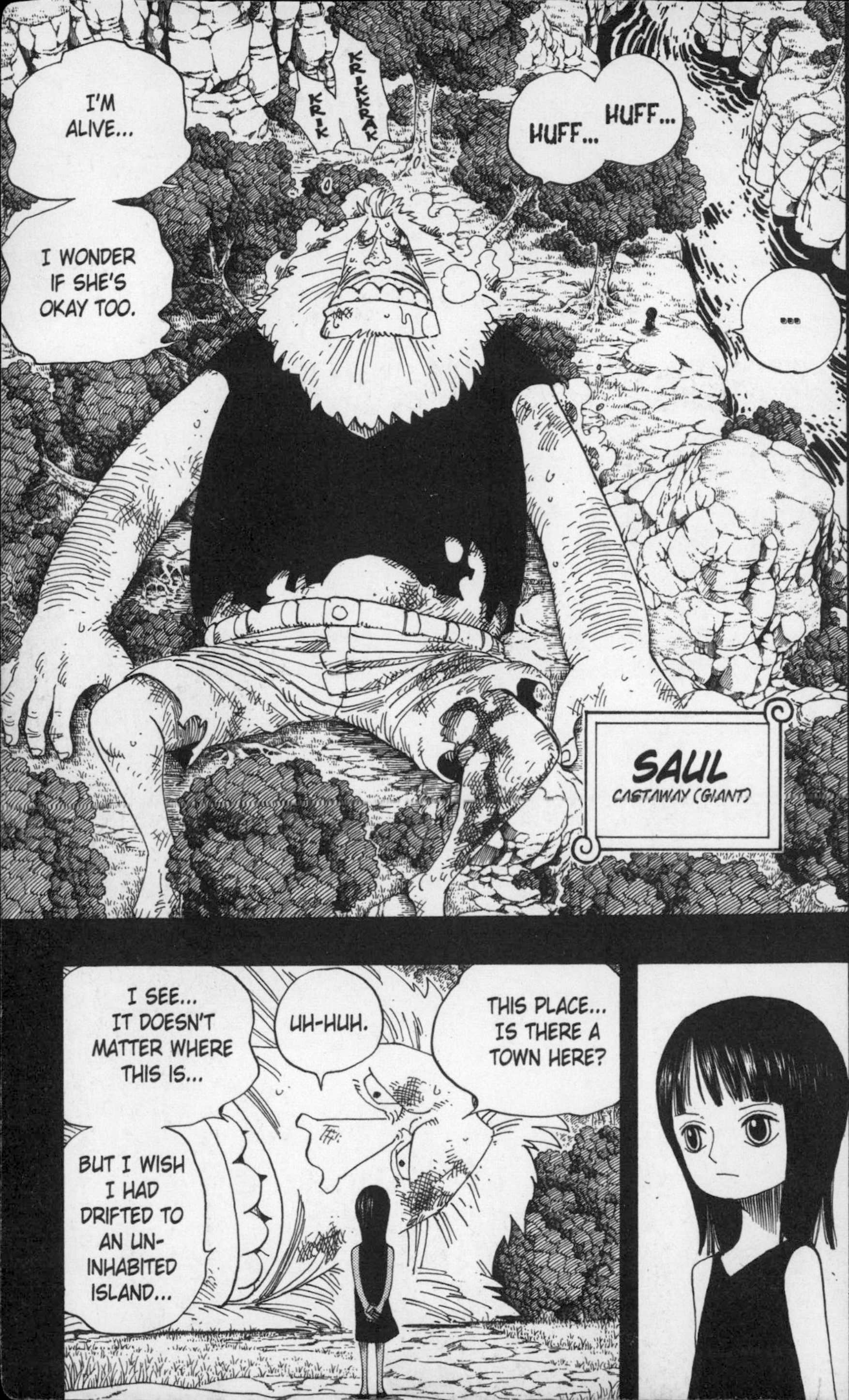
HUFF... HUFF...
KRIKKRAK
KRIK
I'M ALIVE...
...
I WONDER IF SHE'S OKAY TOO.
SAUL
CASTAWAY (GIANT)
THIS PLACE... IS THERE A TOWN HERE?
UH-HUH.
I SEE... IT DOESN'T MATTER WHERE THIS IS...
BUT I WISH I HAD DRIFTED TO AN UN-INHABITED ISLAND...

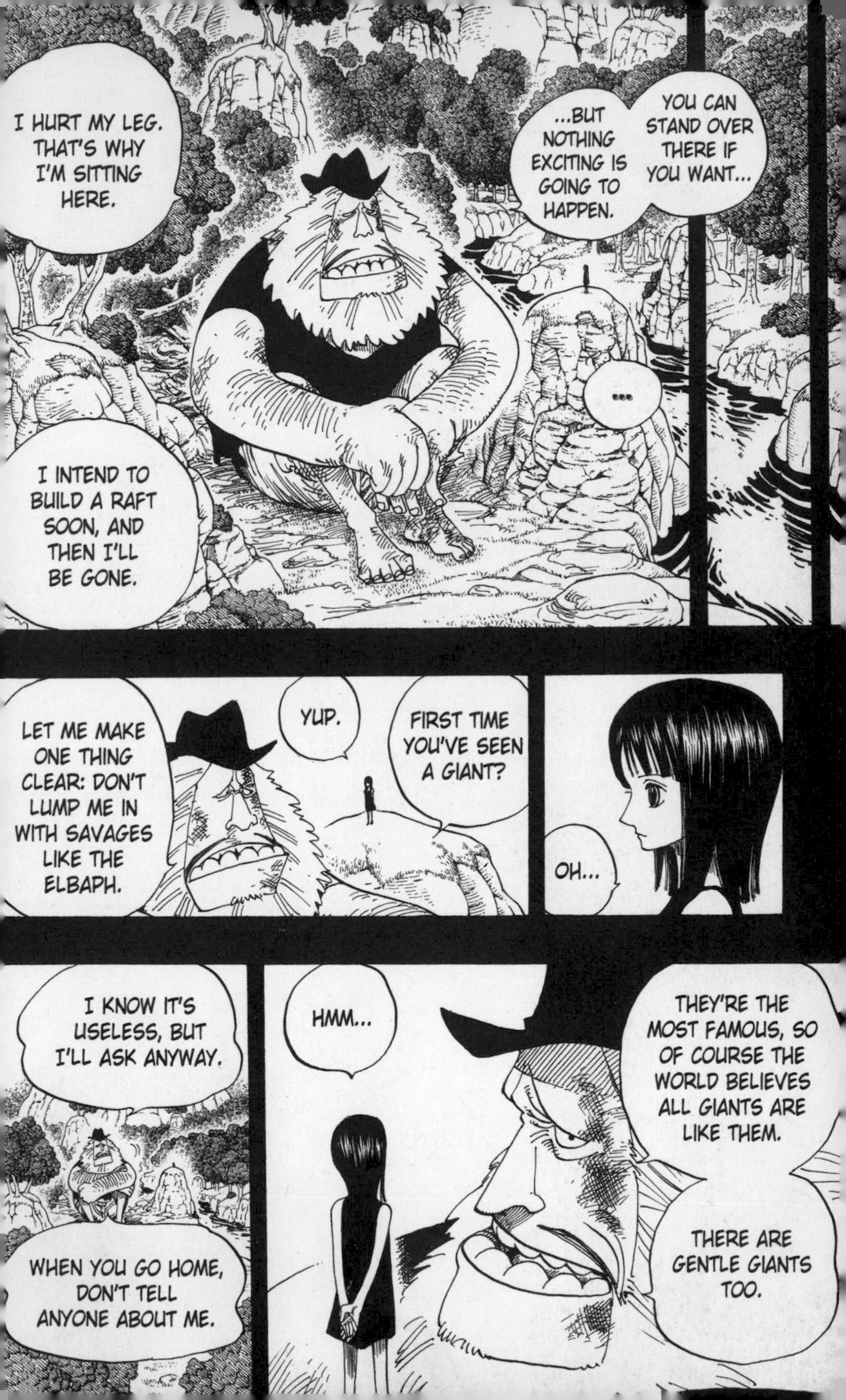
YOU CAN STAND OVER THERE IF YOU WANT...
...BUT NOTHING EXCITING IS GOING TO HAPPEN.
...
I HURT MY LEG. THAT'S WHY I'M SITTING HERE.
I INTEND TO BUILD A RAFT SOON, AND THEN I'LL BE GONE.
OH...
FIRST TIME YOU'VE SEEN A GIANT?
YUP.
LET ME MAKE ONE THING CLEAR: DON'T LUMP ME IN WITH SAVAGES LIKE THE ELBAPH.
THEY'RE THE MOST FAMOUS, SO OF COURSE THE WORLD BELIEVES ALL GIANTS ARE LIKE THEM.
THERE ARE GENTLE GIANTS TOO.
HMM...
I KNOW IT'S USELESS, BUT I'LL ASK ANYWAY.
WHEN YOU GO HOME, DON'T TELL ANYONE ABOUT ME.

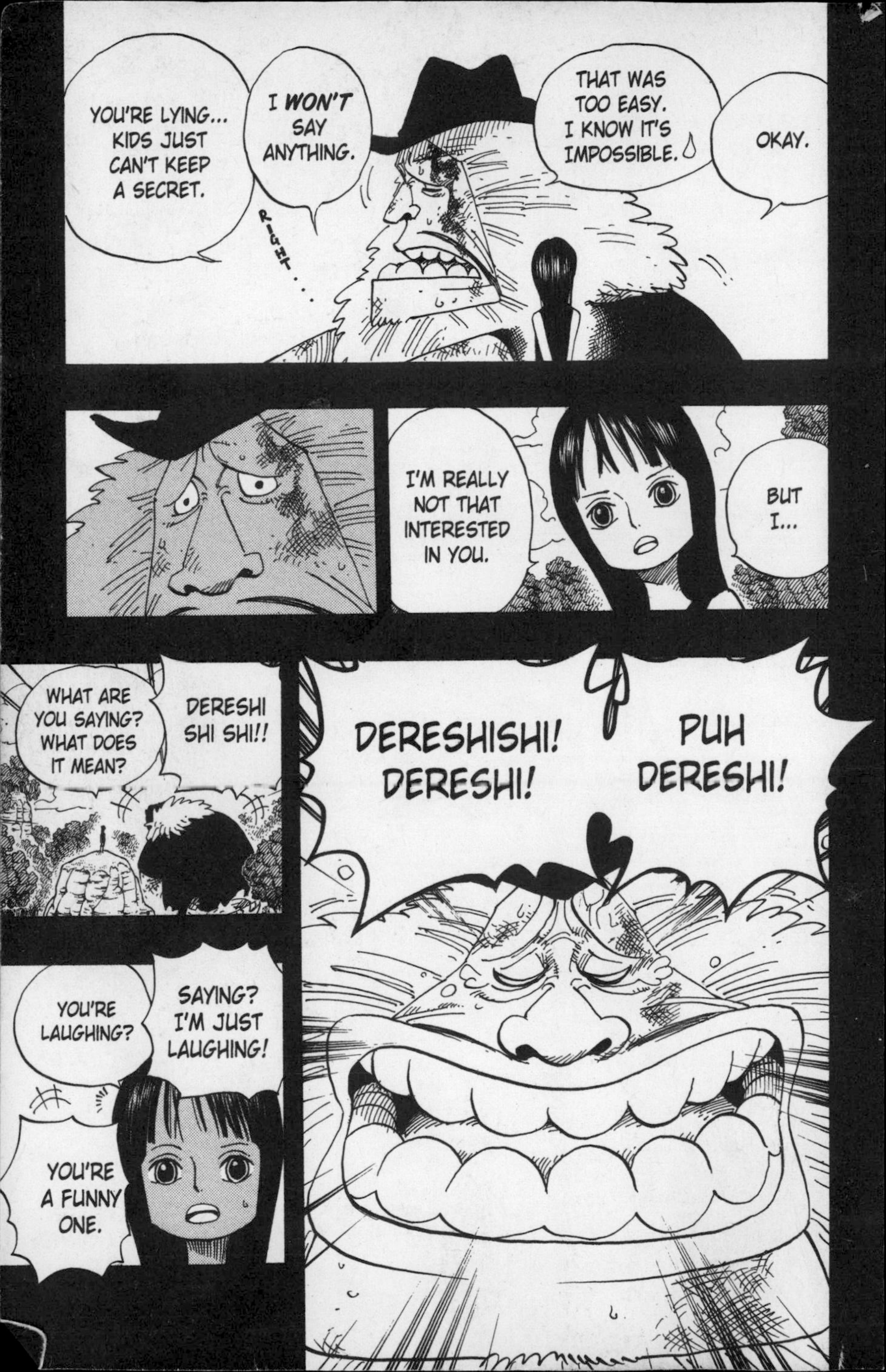
OKAY.
THAT WAS TOO EASY. I KNOW IT'S IMPOSSIBLE.
I WON'T SAY ANYTHING.
RIGHT...
YOU'RE LYING... KIDS JUST CAN'T KEEP A SECRET.
BUT I...
I'M REALLY NOT THAT INTERESTED IN YOU.
PUH DERESHI!
DERESHISHI! DERESHI!
DERESHI SHI SHI!!
WHAT ARE YOU SAYING? WHAT DOES IT MEAN?
SAYING? I'M JUST LAUGHING!
YOU'RE LAUGHING?
YOU'RE A FUNNY ONE.

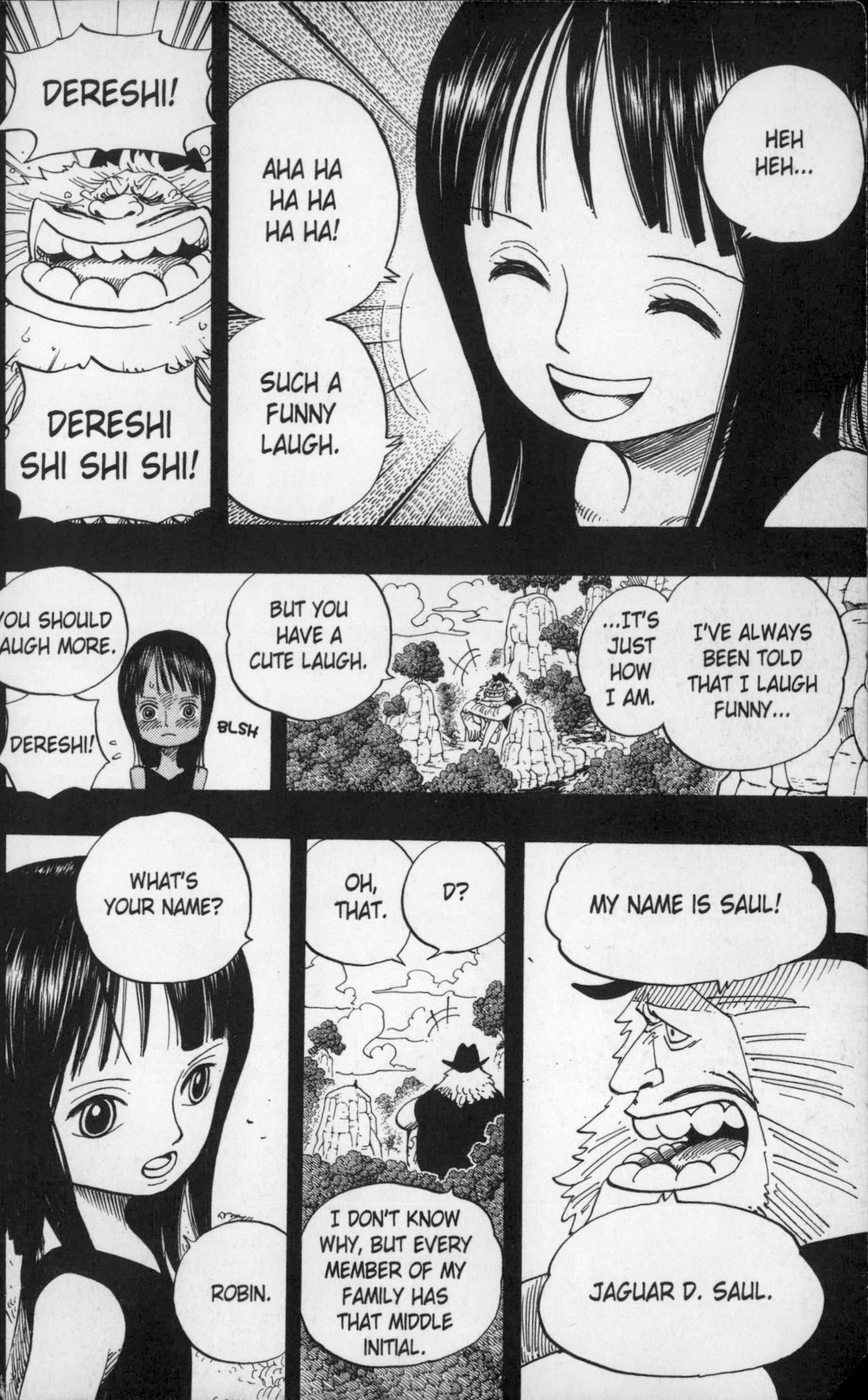
HEH HEH...
AHA HA HA HA HA HA!
SUCH A FUNNY LAUGH.
DERESHI!
DERESHI SHI SHI SHI!
I'VE ALWAYS BEEN TOLD THAT I LAUGH FUNNY...
...IT'S JUST HOW I AM.
BUT YOU HAVE A CUTE LAUGH.
YOU SHOULD LAUGH MORE.
BLSH
DERESHI!
MY NAME IS SAUL!
JAGUAR D. SAUL.
D?
OH, THAT.
I DON'T KNOW WHY, BUT EVERY MEMBER OF MY FAMILY HAS THAT MIDDLE INITIAL.
WHAT'S YOUR NAME?
ROBIN.

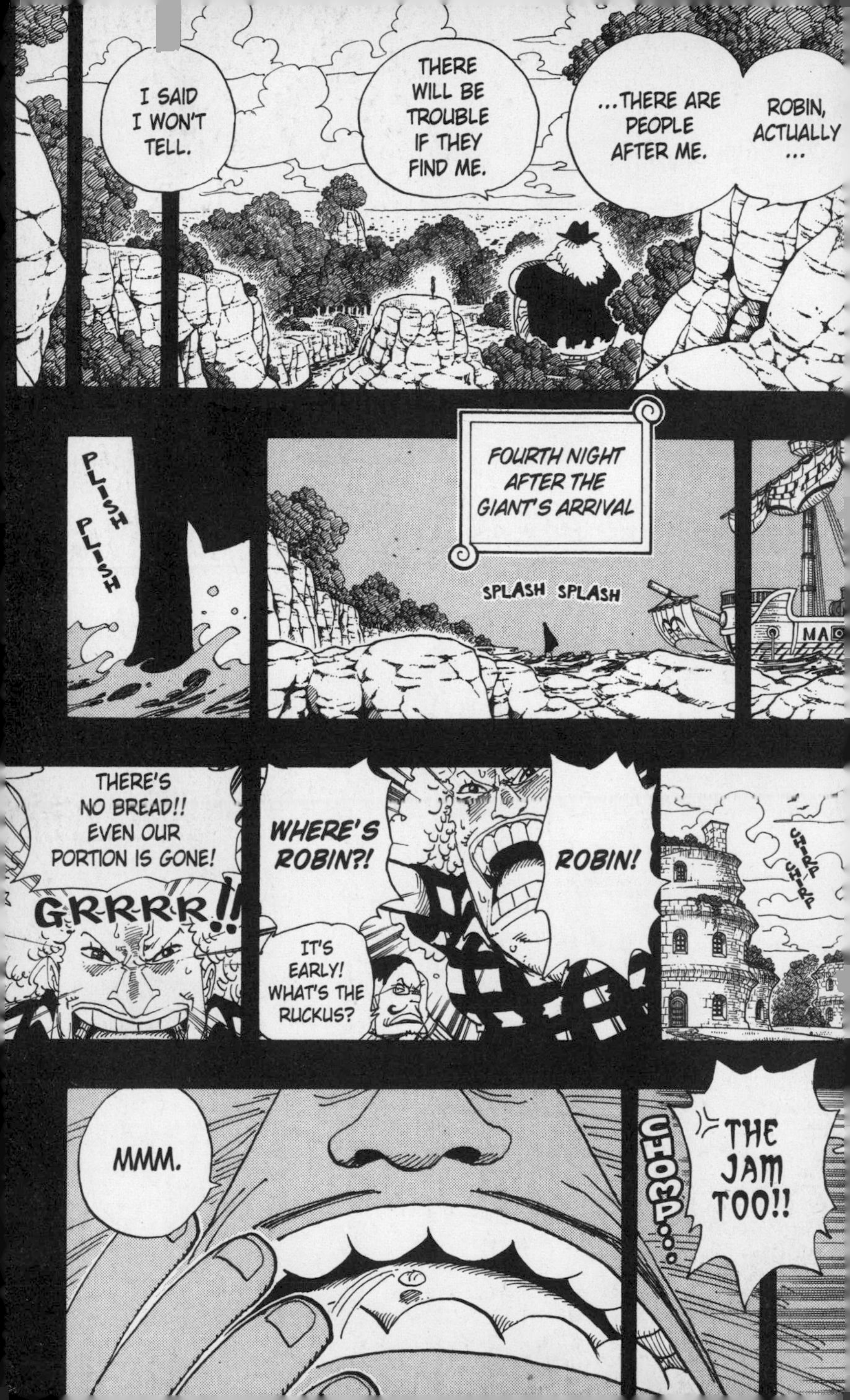

ROBIN, ACTUALLY...
...THERE ARE PEOPLE AFTER ME.
THERE WILL BE TROUBLE IF THEY FIND ME.
I SAID I WON'T TELL.
FOURTH NIGHT AFTER THE GIANT'S ARRIVAL
SPLASH SPLASH
PLISH PLISH
CHIRP CHIRP
ROBIN!
WHERE'S ROBIN?!
IT'S EARLY! WHAT'S THE RUCKUS?
THERE'S NO BREAD!! EVEN OUR PORTION IS GONE!
GRRRR!!
THE JAM TOO!!
CHOMP...
MMM.

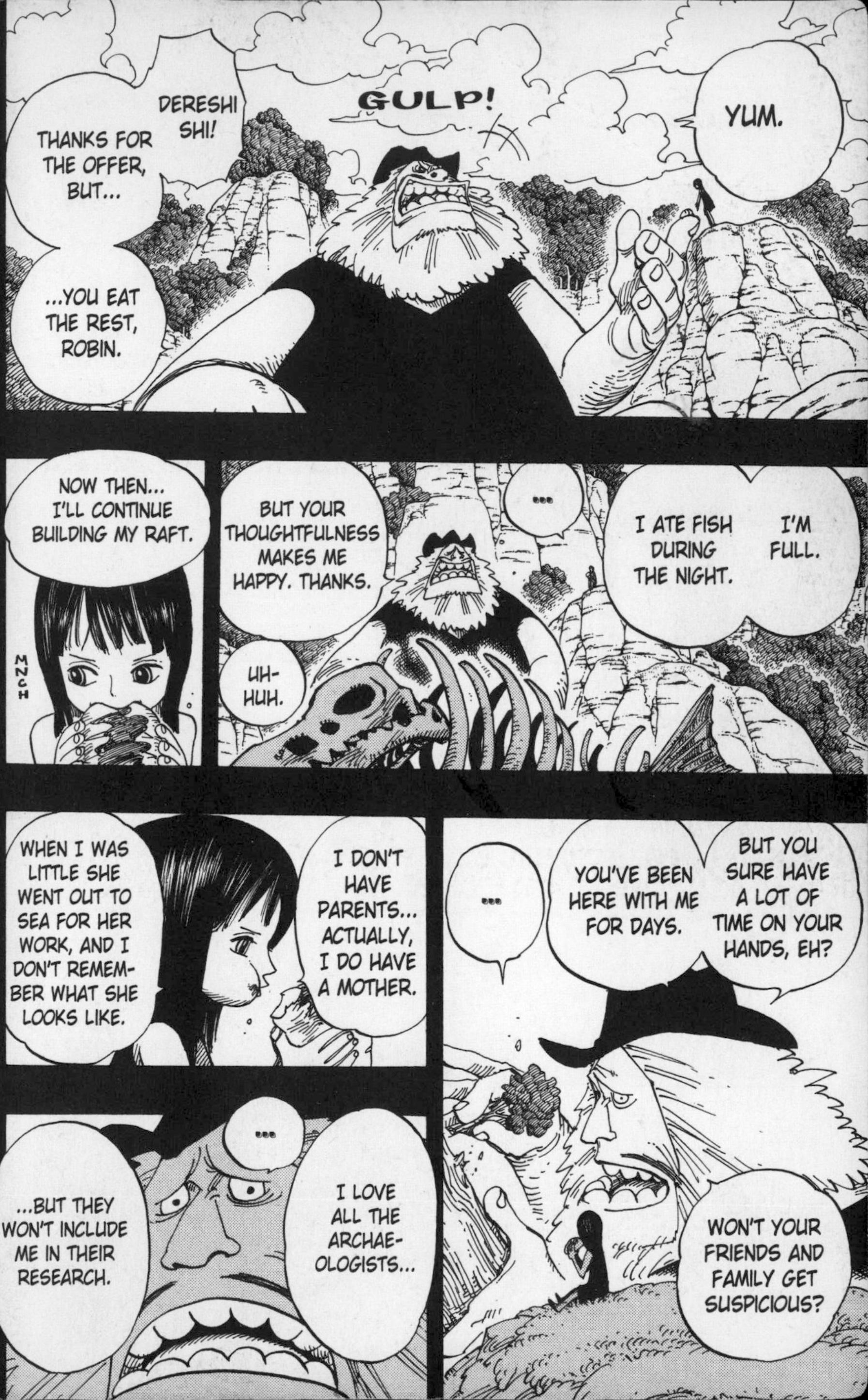
YUM.
GULP!
DERESHI SHI!
THANKS FOR THE OFFER, BUT...
...YOU EAT THE REST, ROBIN.
I'M FULL.
I ATE FISH DURING THE NIGHT.
...
BUT YOUR THOUGHTFULNESS MAKES ME HAPPY. THANKS.
UH-HUH.
NOW THEN... I'LL CONTINUE BUILDING MY RAFT.
MNCH
BUT YOU SURE HAVE A LOT OF TIME ON YOUR HANDS, EH?
YOU'VE BEEN HERE WITH ME FOR DAYS.
...
WON'T YOUR FRIENDS AND FAMILY GET SUSPICIOUS?
I DON'T HAVE PARENTS... ACTUALLY, I DO HAVE A MOTHER.
WHEN I WAS LITTLE SHE WENT OUT TO SEA FOR HER WORK, AND I DON'T REMEMBER WHAT SHE LOOKS LIKE.
...
I LOVE ALL THE ARCHAEOLOGISTS...
...BUT THEY WON'T INCLUDE ME IN THEIR RESEARCH.

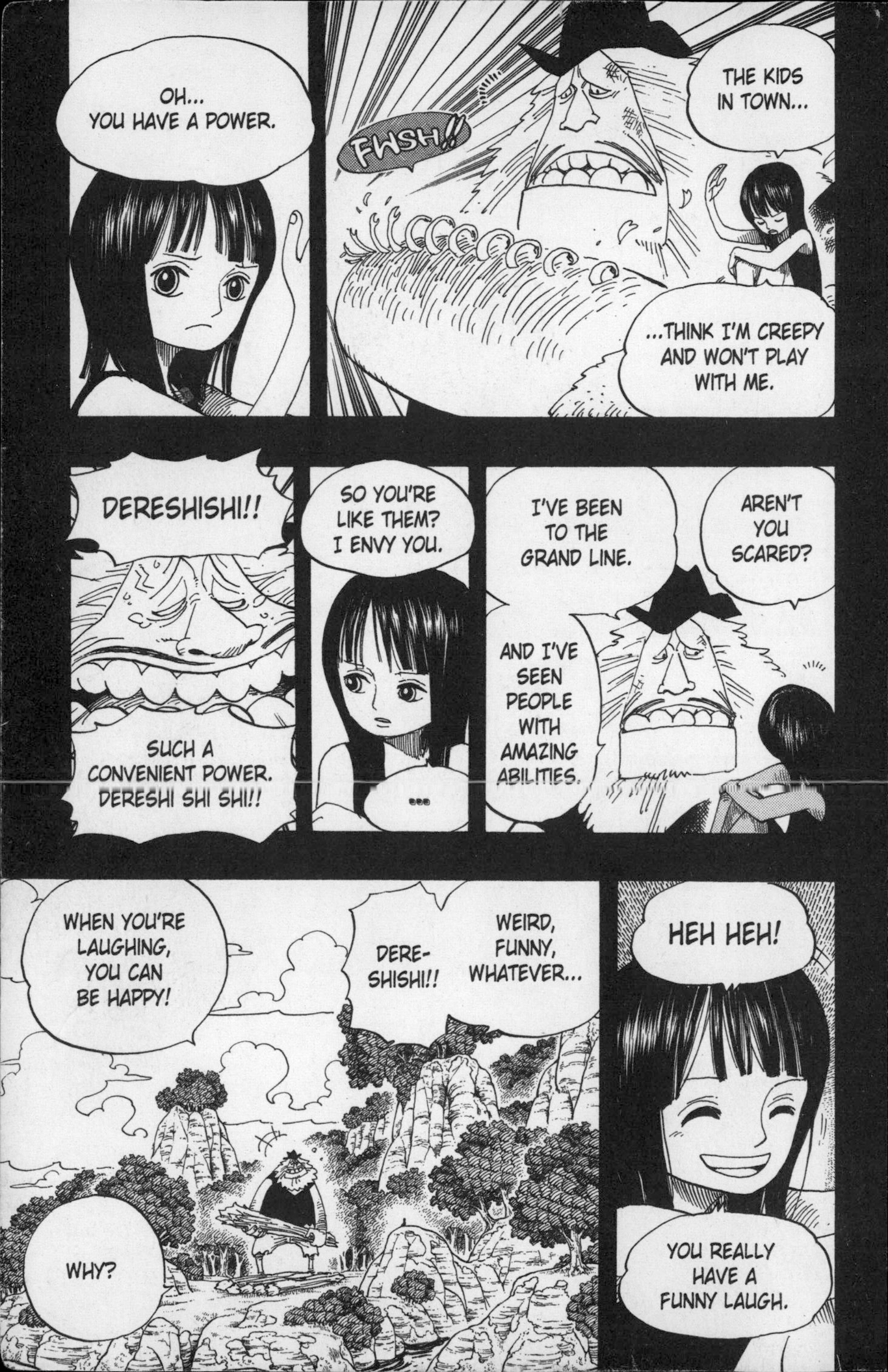
THE KIDS IN TOWN...
FWSH!!
...THINK I'M CREEPY AND WON'T PLAY WITH ME.
OH... YOU HAVE A POWER.
AREN'T YOU SCARED?
I'VE BEEN TO THE GRAND LINE.
AND I'VE SEEN PEOPLE WITH AMAZING ABILITIES.
SO YOU'RE LIKE THEM? I ENVY YOU.
...
DERESHISHI!!
SUCH A CONVENIENT POWER. DERESHI SHI SHI!!
HEH HEH!
YOU REALLY HAVE A FUNNY LAUGH.
WEIRD, FUNNY, WHATEVER...
DERE-SHISHI!!
WHEN YOU'RE LAUGHING, YOU CAN BE HAPPY!
WHY?

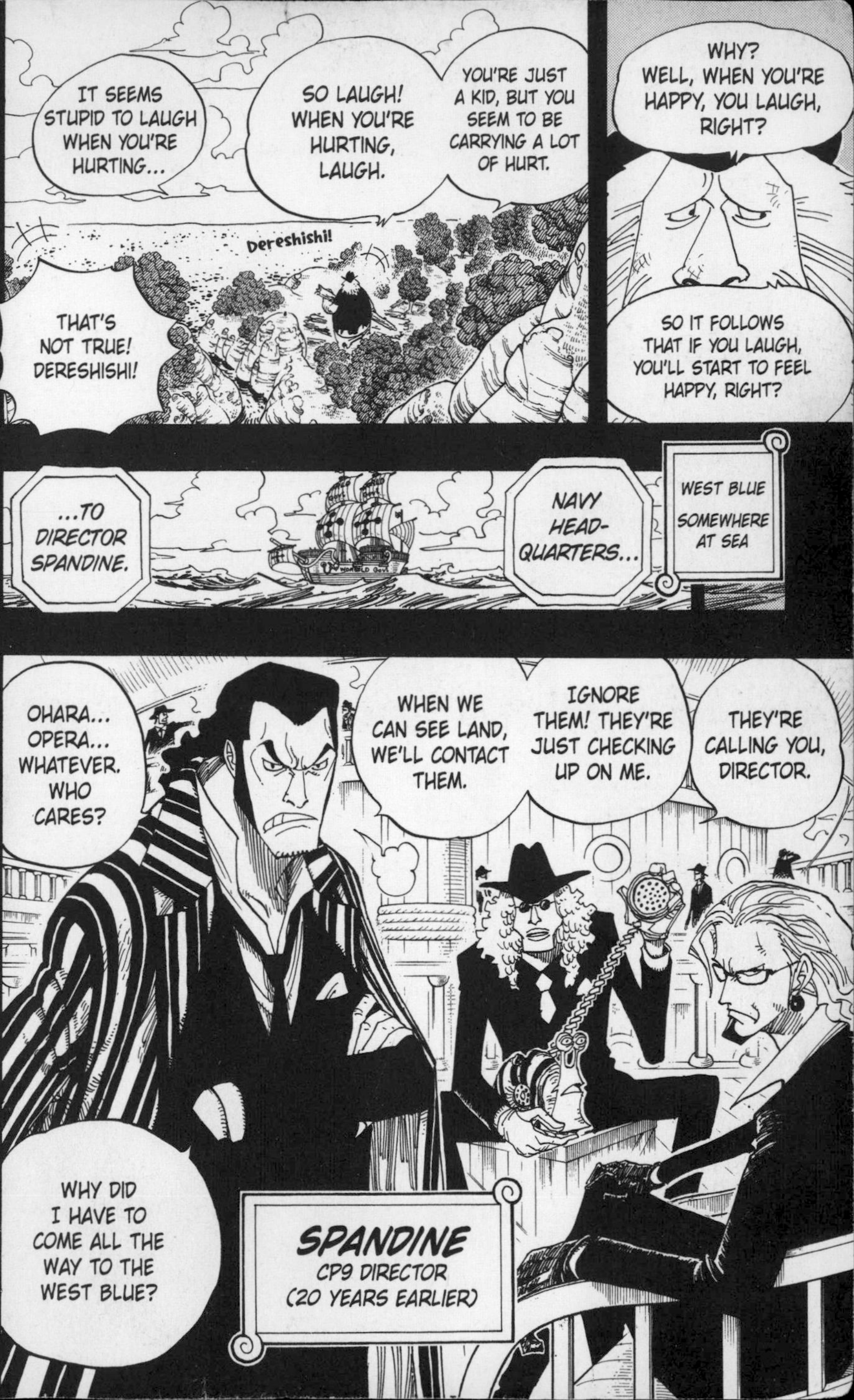
WHY? WELL, WHEN YOU'RE HAPPY, YOU LAUGH, RIGHT?
SO IT FOLLOWS THAT IF YOU LAUGH, YOU'LL START TO FEEL HAPPY, RIGHT?
YOU'RE JUST A KID, BUT YOU SEEM TO BE CARRYING A LOT OF HURT.
SO LAUGH! WHEN YOU'RE HURTING, LAUGH.
IT SEEMS STUPID TO LAUGH WHEN YOU'RE HURTING...
Dereshishi!
THAT'S NOT TRUE! DERESHISHI!
WEST BLUE SOMEWHERE AT SEA
NAVY HEAD-QUARTERS...
...TO DIRECTOR SPANDINE.
THEY'RE CALLING YOU, DIRECTOR.
IGNORE THEM! THEY'RE JUST CHECKING UP ON ME.
WHEN WE CAN SEE LAND, WE'LL CONTACT THEM.
OHARA... OPERA... WHATEVER. WHO CARES?
SPANDINE
CP9 DIRECTOR
(20 YEARS EARLIER)
WHY DID I HAVE TO COME ALL THE WAY TO THE WEST BLUE?

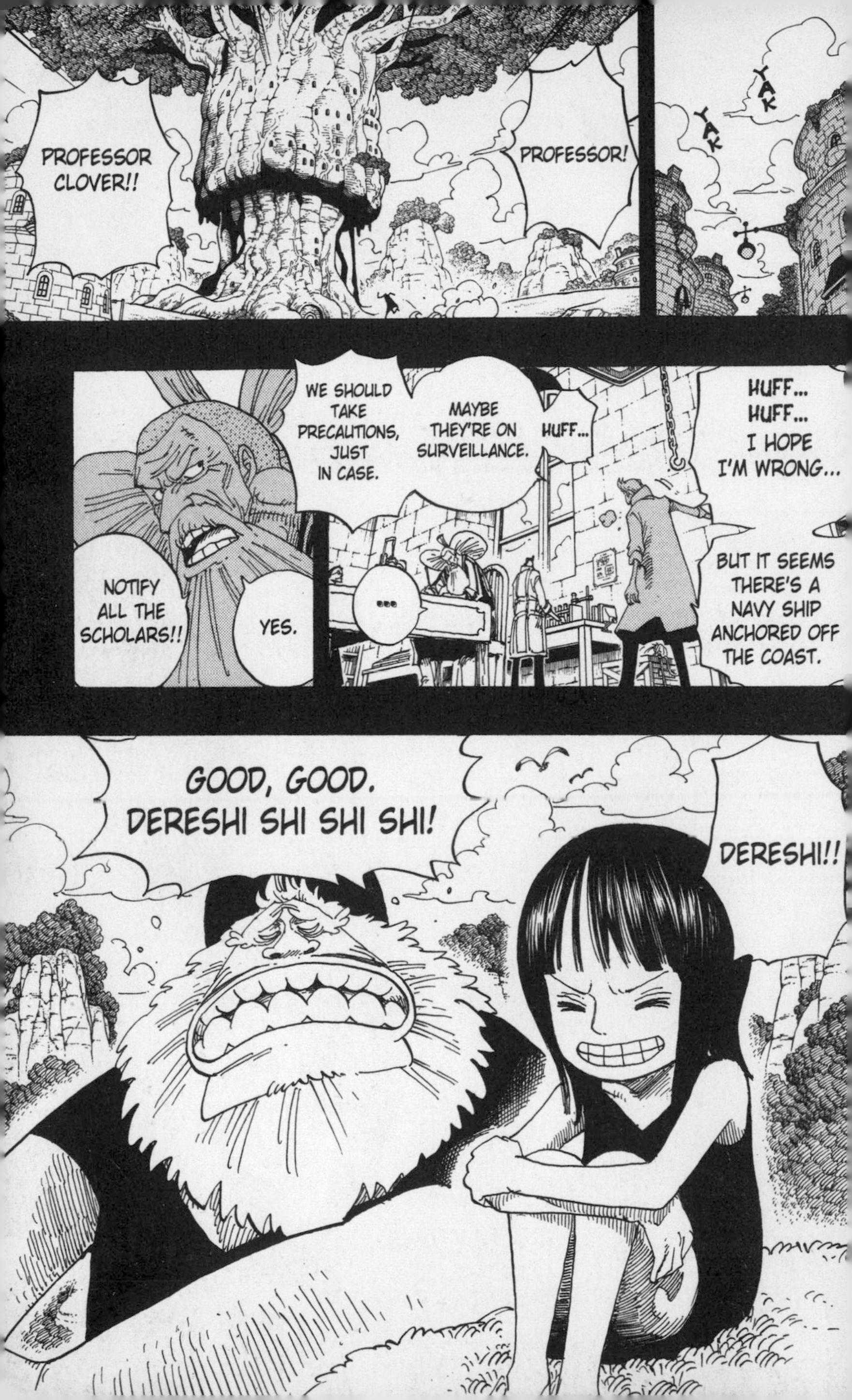
YAK
YAK
PROFESSOR!
PROFESSOR CLOVER!!
HUFF... HUFF... I HOPE I'M WRONG...
BUT IT SEEMS THERE'S A NAVY SHIP ANCHORED OFF THE COAST.
HUFF...
MAYBE THEY'RE ON SURVEILLANCE.
WE SHOULD TAKE PRECAUTIONS, JUST IN CASE.
...
NOTIFY ALL THE SCHOLARS!!
YES.
GOOD, GOOD. DERESHI SHI SHI SHI!
DERESHI!!

Chapter 393:
Olvia

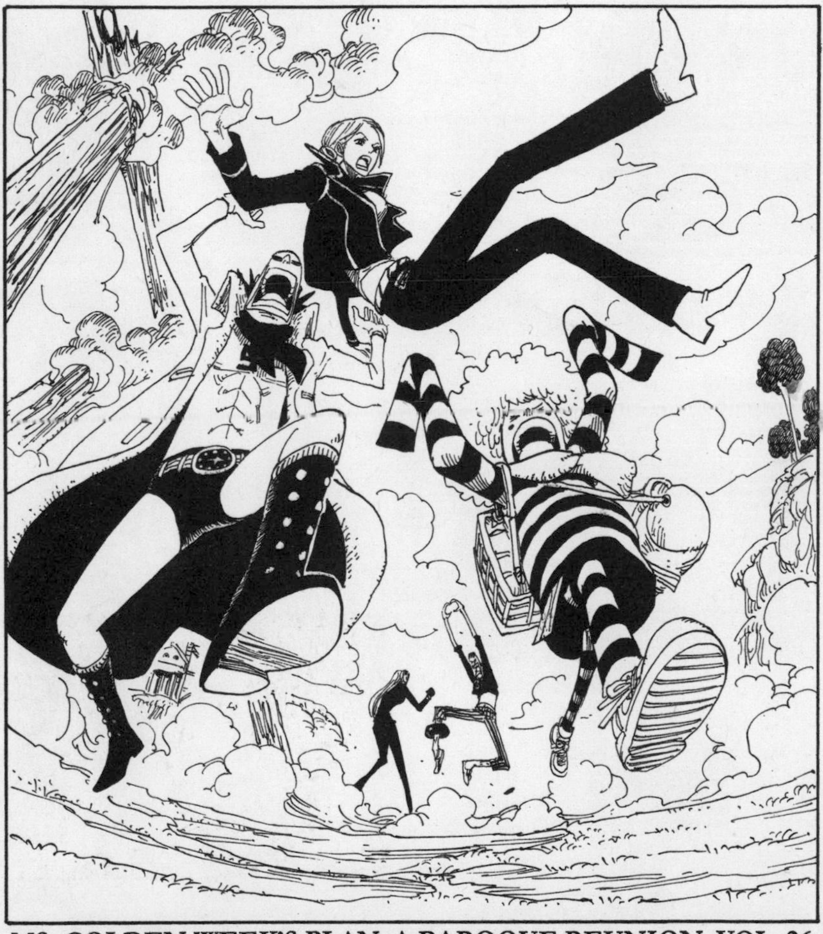

MS. GOLDEN WEEK'S PLAN, A BAROQUE REUNION, VOL. 26:
"WAIT FOR AN OPENING AND RESCUE"

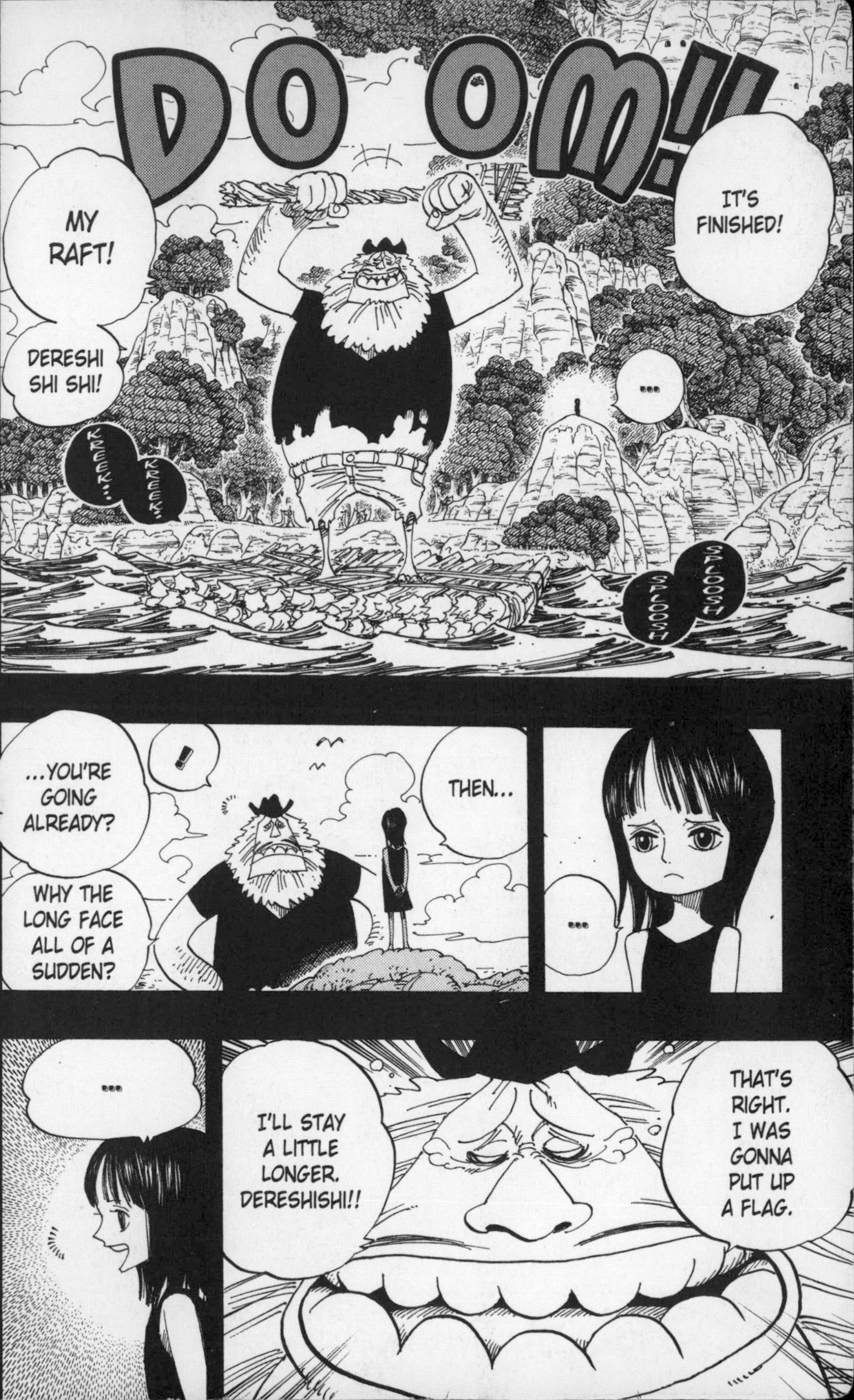
DO OM!!
IT'S FINISHED!
MY RAFT!
DERESHI SHI SHI!
...
SPLOOSH
SPLOOSH
KREEK
KREEK
...
THEN...
!
...YOU'RE GOING ALREADY?
WHY THE LONG FACE ALL OF A SUDDEN?
THAT'S RIGHT. I WAS GONNA PUT UP A FLAG.
I'LL STAY A LITTLE LONGER. DERESHISHI!!
...

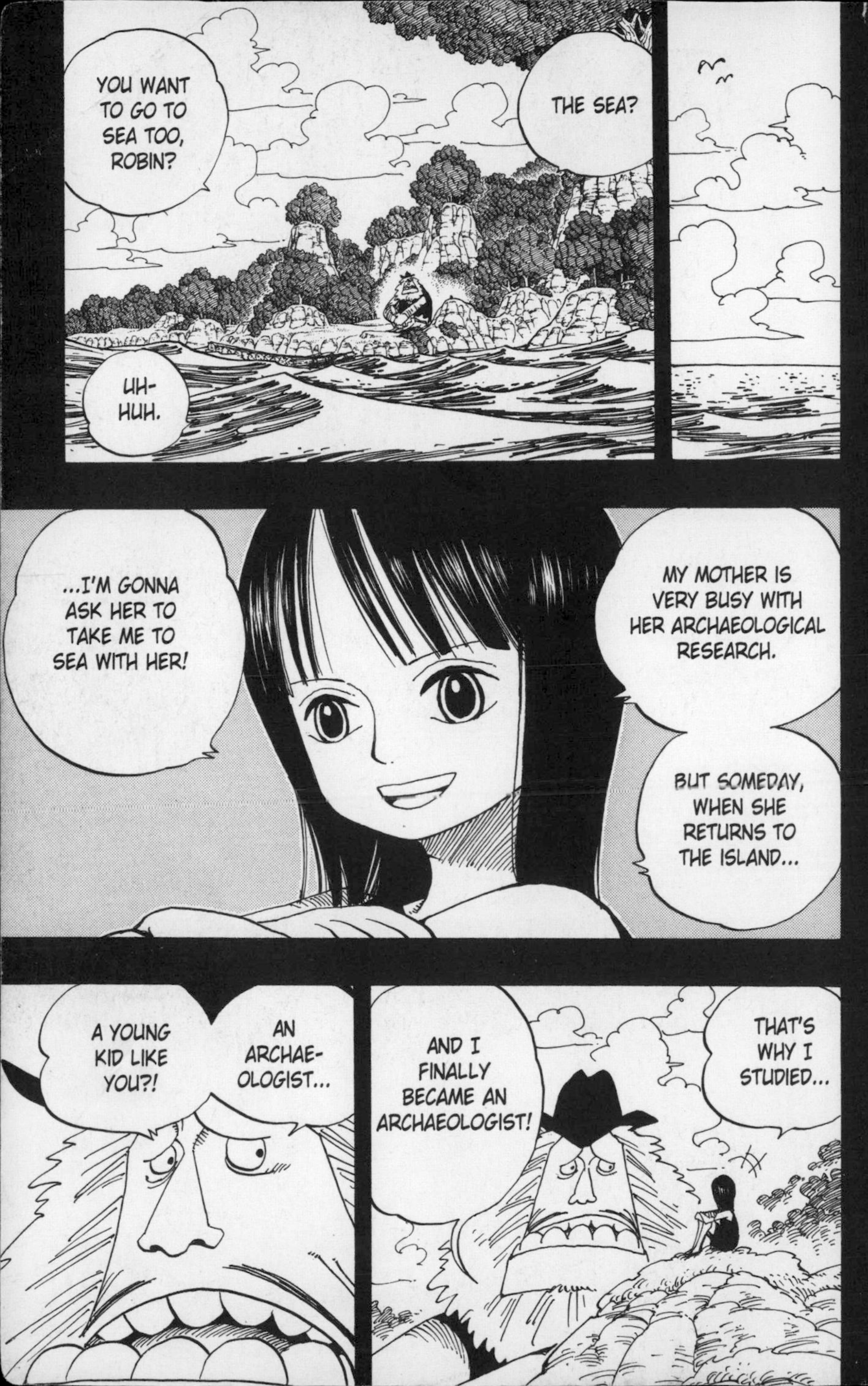
THE SEA?
YOU WANT TO GO TO SEA TOO, ROBIN?
UH-HUH.
MY MOTHER IS VERY BUSY WITH HER ARCHAEOLOGICAL RESEARCH.
BUT SOMEDAY, WHEN SHE RETURNS TO THE ISLAND...
...I'M GONNA ASK HER TO TAKE ME TO SEA WITH HER!
THAT'S WHY I STUDIED...
AND I FINALLY BECAME AN ARCHAEOLOGIST!
AN ARCHAE-OLOGIST...
A YOUNG KID LIKE YOU?!

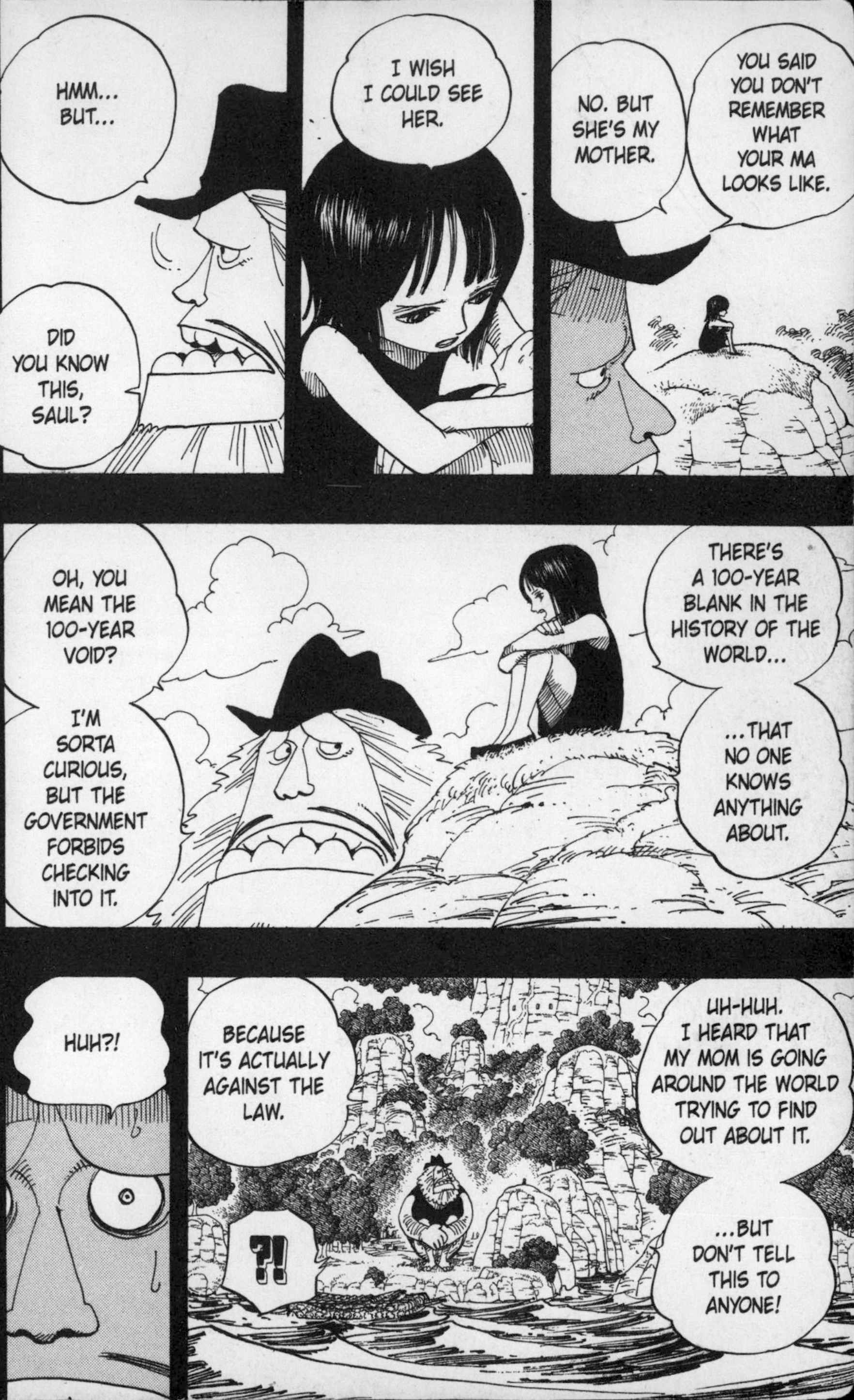
YOU SAID YOU DON'T REMEMBER WHAT YOUR MA LOOKS LIKE.
NO. BUT SHE'S MY MOTHER.
I WISH I COULD SEE HER.
HMM... BUT...
DID YOU KNOW THIS, SAUL?
THERE'S A 100-YEAR BLANK IN THE HISTORY OF THE WORLD...
...THAT NO ONE KNOWS ANYTHING ABOUT.
OH, YOU MEAN THE 100-YEAR VOID?
I'M SORTA CURIOUS, BUT THE GOVERNMENT FORBIDS CHECKING INTO IT.
UH-HUH. I HEARD THAT MY MOM IS GOING AROUND THE WORLD TRYING TO FIND OUT ABOUT IT.
...BUT DON'T TELL THIS TO ANYONE!
BECAUSE IT'S ACTUALLY AGAINST THE LAW.
?!
HUH?!

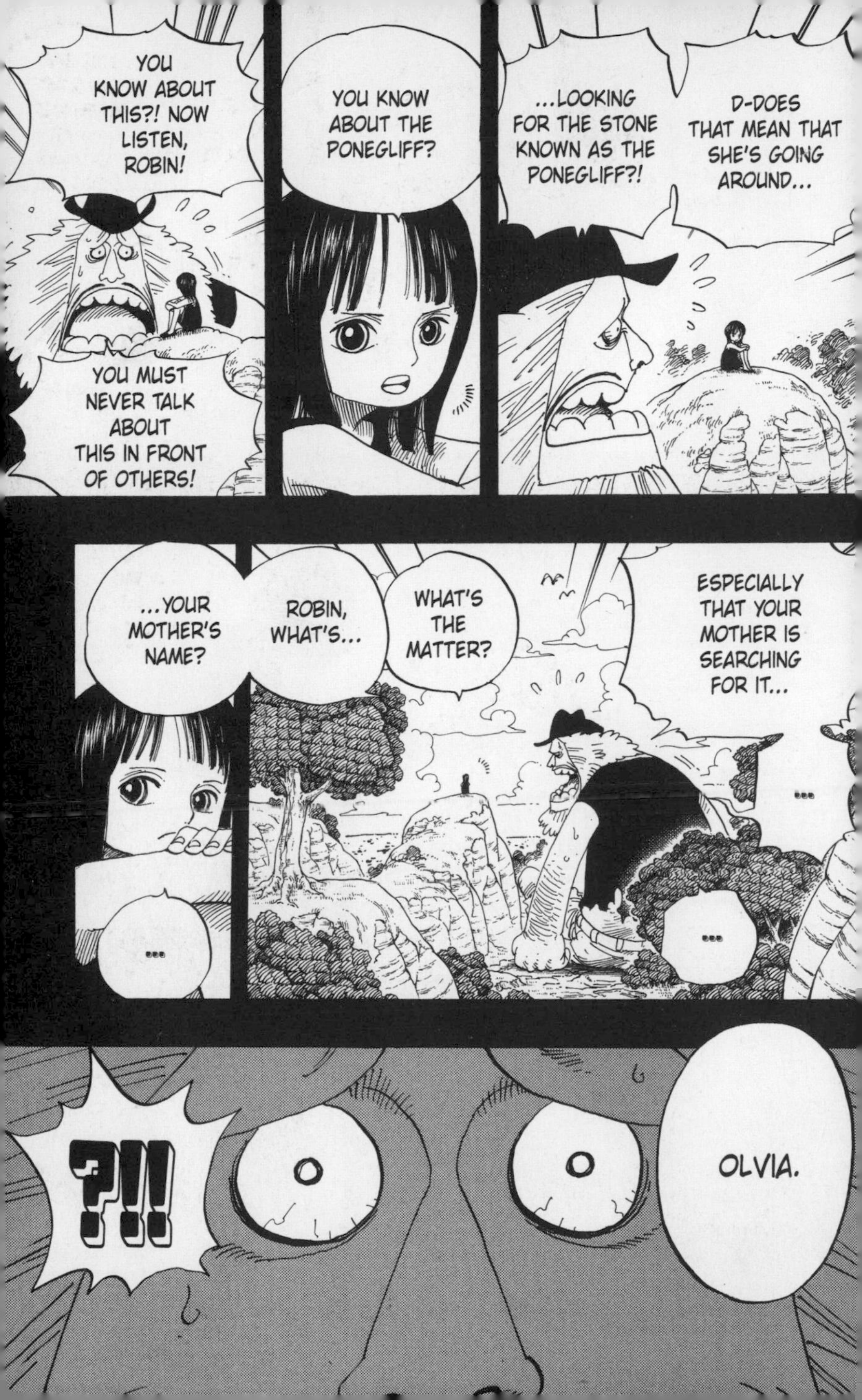
D-DOES THAT MEAN THAT SHE'S GOING AROUND...
...LOOKING FOR THE STONE KNOWN AS THE PONEGLIFF?!
YOU KNOW ABOUT THE PONEGLIFF?
YOU KNOW ABOUT THIS?! NOW LISTEN, ROBIN!
YOU MUST NEVER TALK ABOUT THIS IN FRONT OF OTHERS!
ESPECIALLY THAT YOUR MOTHER IS SEARCHING FOR IT...
...
WHAT'S THE MATTER?
ROBIN, WHAT'S...
...
...YOUR MOTHER'S NAME?
...
OLVIA.
?!!

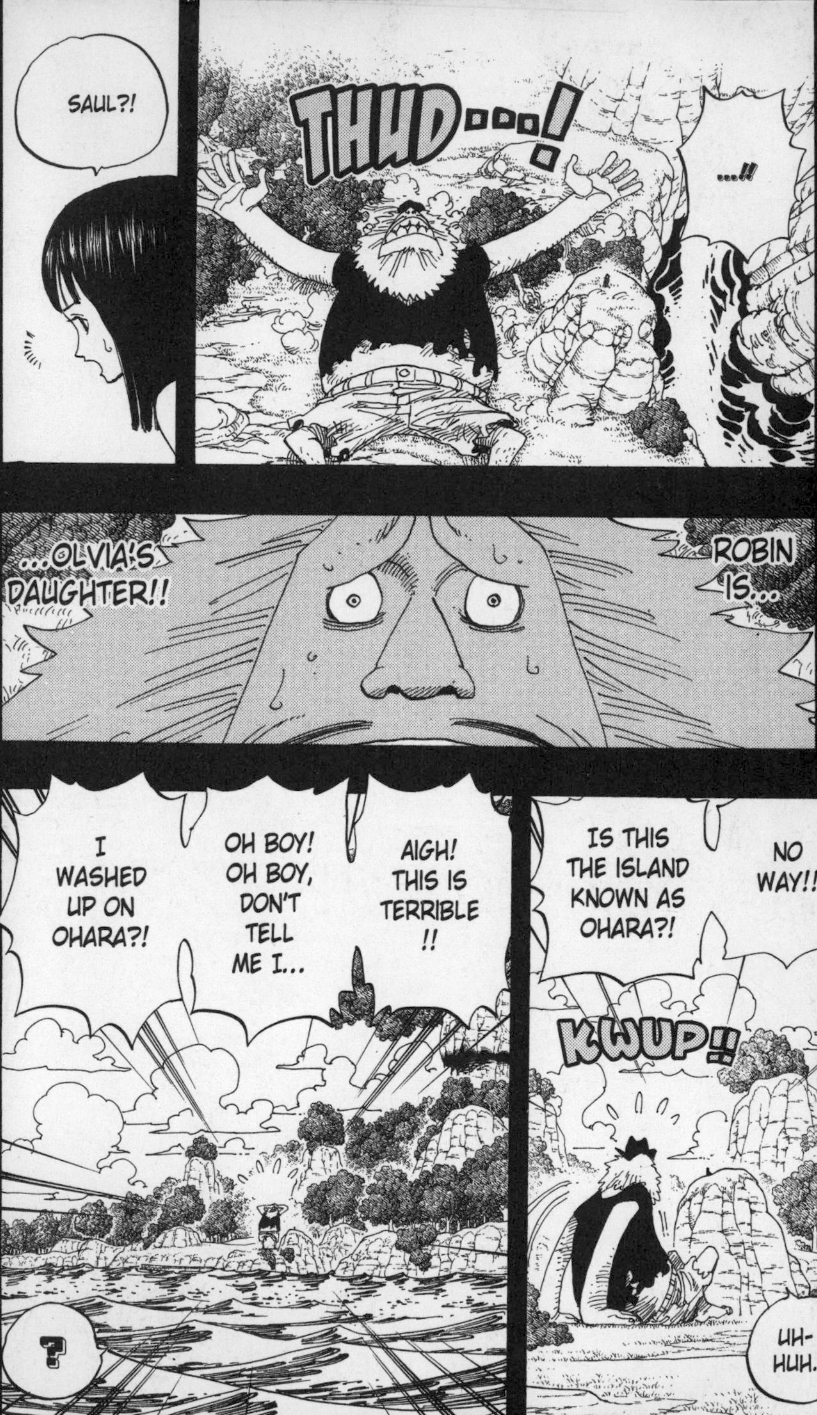
THUD...!
...!!
SAUL?!
ROBIN IS...
...OLVIA'S DAUGHTER!!
NO WAY!!
IS THIS THE ISLAND KNOWN AS OHARA?!
KWUP!!
UH-HUH.
AIGH! THIS IS TERRIBLE!!
OH BOY! OH BOY, DON'T TELL ME I...
I WASHED UP ON OHARA?!
?

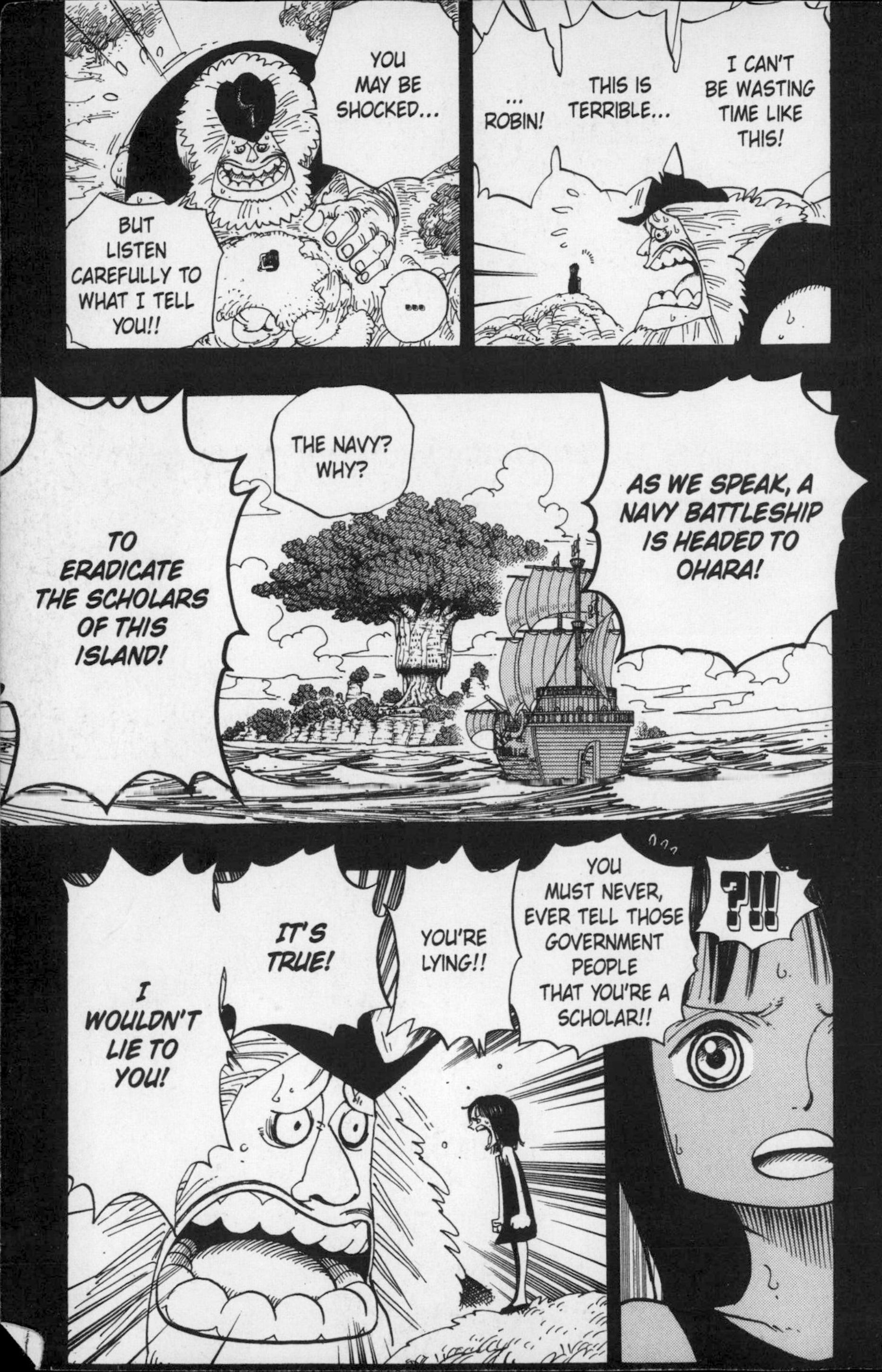
I CAN'T BE WASTING TIME LIKE THIS!
THIS IS TERRIBLE...
... ROBIN!
YOU MAY BE SHOCKED...
BUT LISTEN CAREFULLY TO WHAT I TELL YOU!!
...
AS WE SPEAK, A NAVY BATTLESHIP IS HEADED TO OHARA!
THE NAVY? WHY?
TO ERADICATE THE SCHOLARS OF THIS ISLAND!
?!!
YOU MUST NEVER, EVER TELL THOSE GOVERNMENT PEOPLE THAT YOU'RE A SCHOLAR!!
YOU'RE LYING!!
IT'S TRUE!
I WOULDN'T LIE TO YOU!

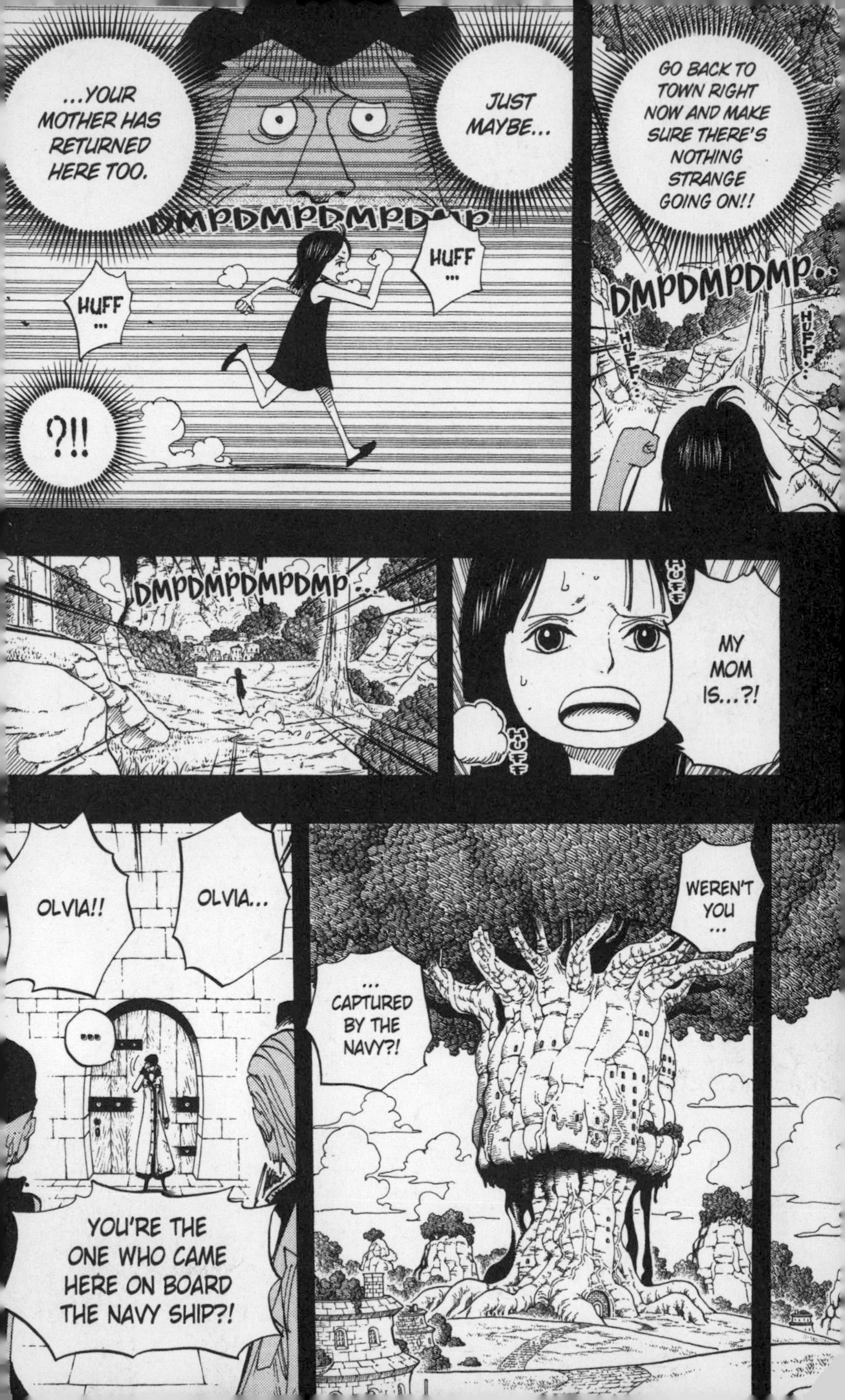
GO BACK TO TOWN RIGHT NOW AND MAKE SURE THERE'S NOTHING STRANGE GOING ON!!
DMPDMPDMP..
HUFF..
HUFF..
JUST MAYBE...
...YOUR MOTHER HAS RETURNED HERE TOO.
DMPDMPDMPDMP
HUFF...
HUFF...
?!!
HUFF
MY MOM IS...?!
HUFF
DMPDMPDMPDMP...
WEREN'T YOU...
...CAPTURED BY THE NAVY?!
OLVIA...
OLVIA!!
...
YOU'RE THE ONE WHO CAME HERE ON BOARD THE NAVY SHIP?!

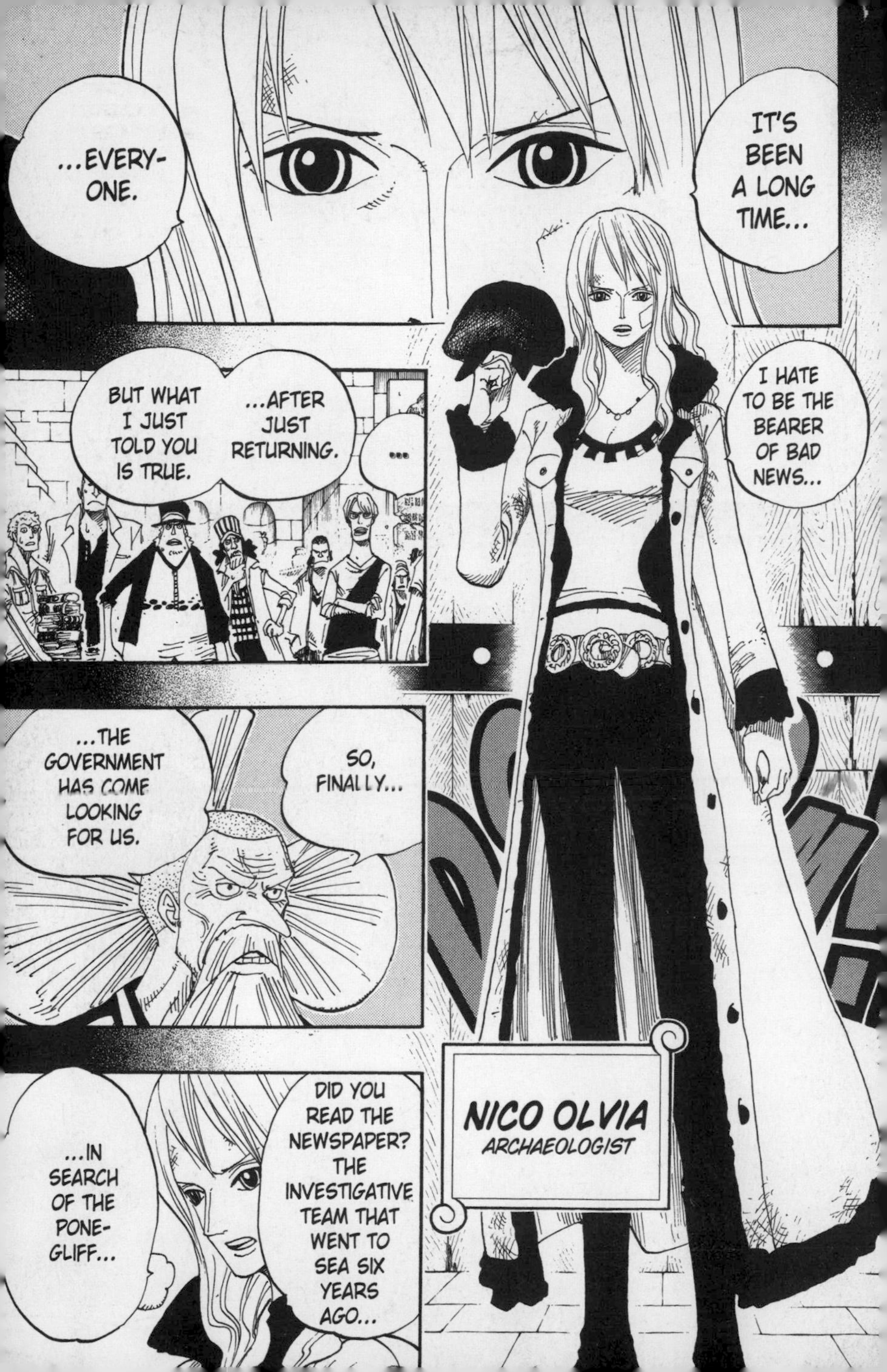
IT'S BEEN A LONG TIME...
...EVERY-ONE.
I HATE TO BE THE BEARER OF BAD NEWS...
NICO OLVIA
ARCHAEOLOGIST
...
...AFTER JUST RETURNING.
BUT WHAT I JUST TOLD YOU IS TRUE.
SO, FINALLY...
...THE GOVERNMENT HAS COME LOOKING FOR US.
DID YOU READ THE NEWSPAPER? THE INVESTIGATIVE TEAM THAT WENT TO SEA SIX YEARS AGO...
...IN SEARCH OF THE PONE-GLIFF...

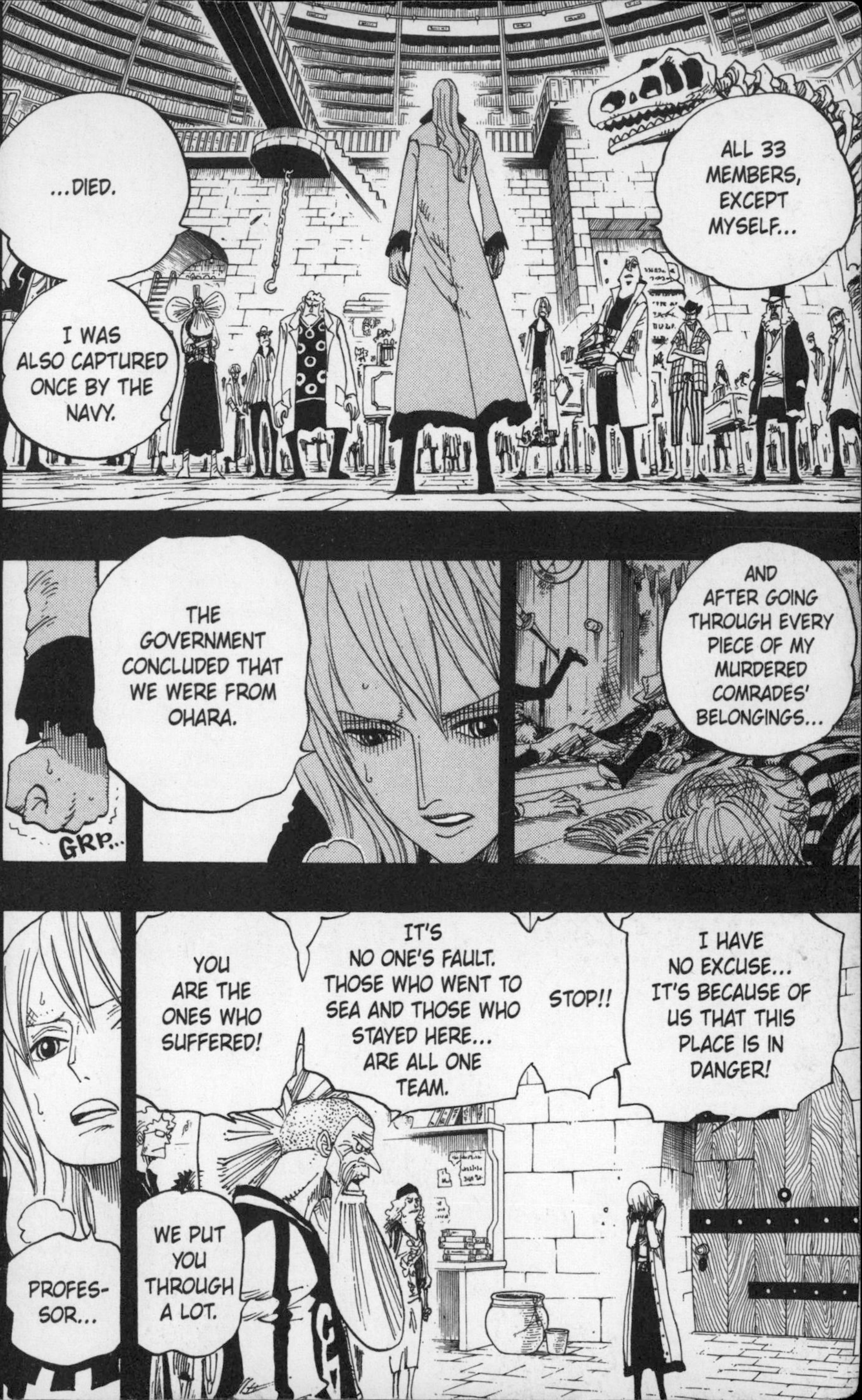
ALL 33 MEMBERS, EXCEPT MYSELF...
...DIED.
I WAS ALSO CAPTURED ONCE BY THE NAVY.
AND AFTER GOING THROUGH EVERY PIECE OF MY MURDERED COMRADES' BELONGINGS...
THE GOVERNMENT CONCLUDED THAT WE WERE FROM OHARA.
GRP...
I HAVE NO EXCUSE... IT'S BECAUSE OF US THAT THIS PLACE IS IN DANGER!
STOP!!
IT'S NO ONE'S FAULT. THOSE WHO WENT TO SEA AND THOSE WHO STAYED HERE... ARE ALL ONE TEAM.
YOU ARE THE ONES WHO SUFFERED!
WE PUT YOU THROUGH A LOT.
PROFES-SOR...

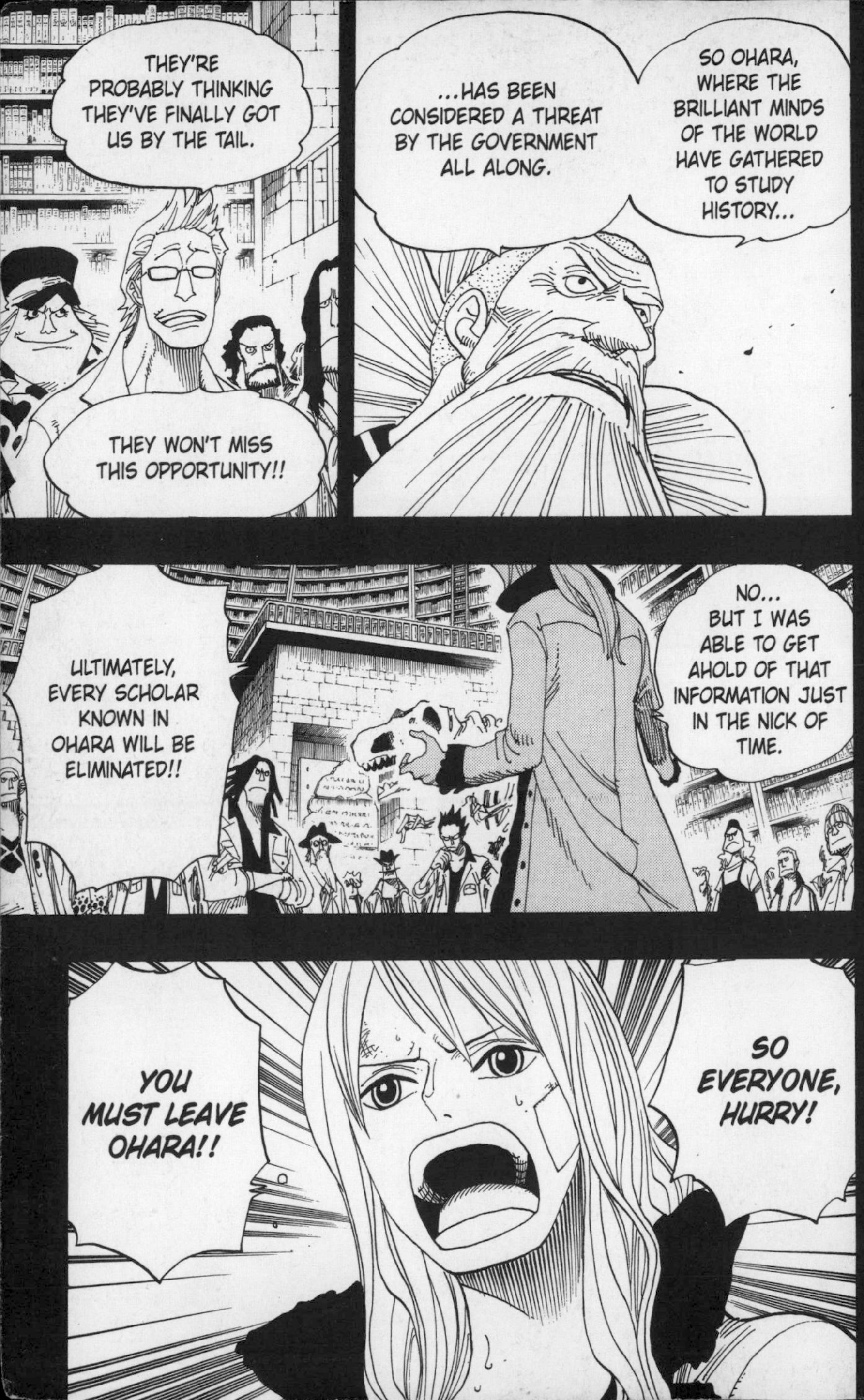
SO OHARA, WHERE THE BRILLIANT MINDS OF THE WORLD HAVE GATHERED TO STUDY HISTORY...
...HAS BEEN CONSIDERED A THREAT BY THE GOVERNMENT ALL ALONG.
THEY'RE PROBABLY THINKING THEY'VE FINALLY GOT US BY THE TAIL.
THEY WON'T MISS THIS OPPORTUNITY!!
NO... BUT I WAS ABLE TO GET AHOLD OF THAT INFORMATION JUST IN THE NICK OF TIME.
ULTIMATELY, EVERY SCHOLAR KNOWN IN OHARA WILL BE ELIMINATED!!
SO EVERYONE, HURRY!
YOU MUST LEAVE OHARA!!

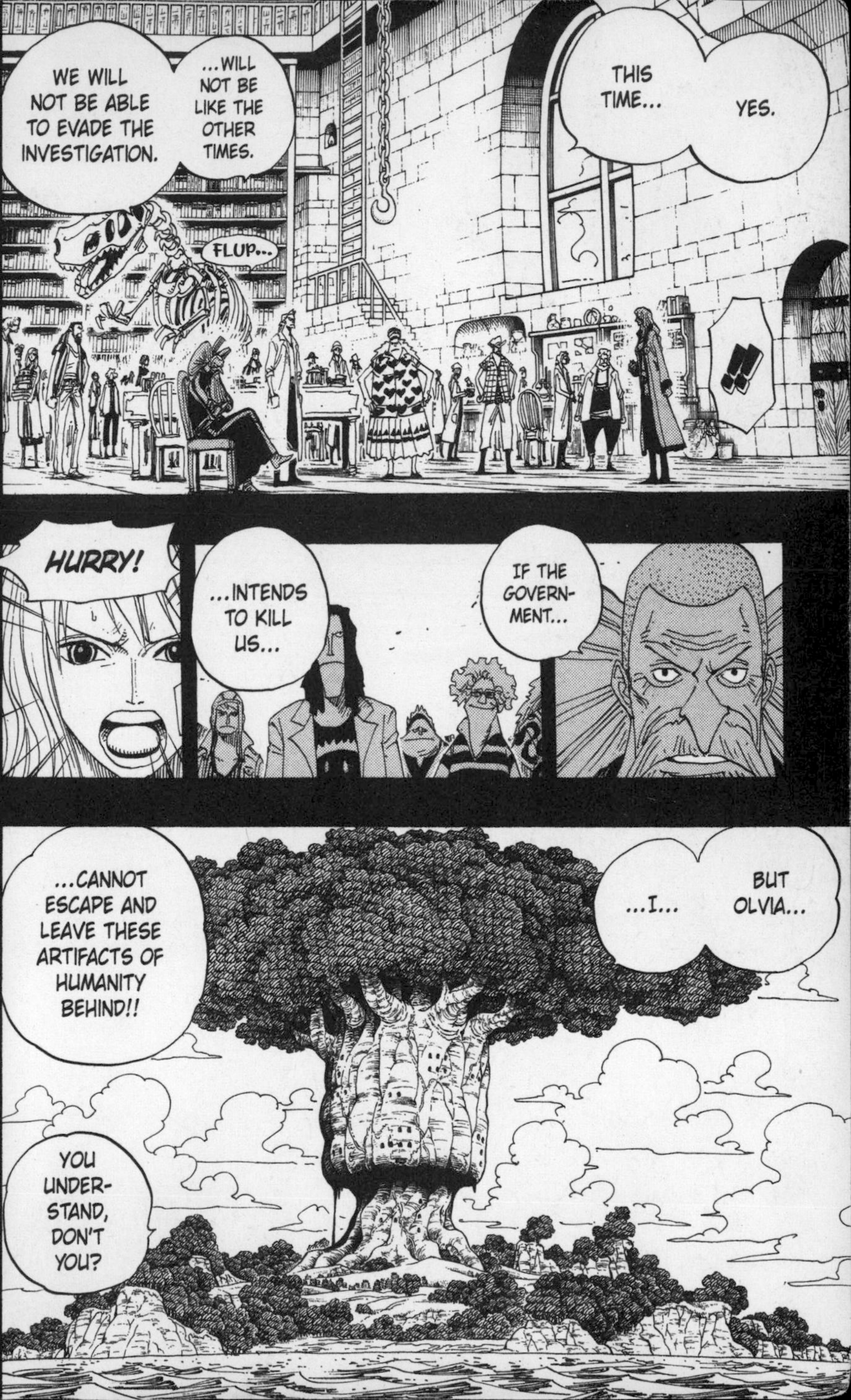
YES.
THIS TIME...
...WILL NOT BE LIKE THE OTHER TIMES.
WE WILL NOT BE ABLE TO EVADE THE INVESTIGATION.
FLUP...
!!
IF THE GOVERN-MENT...
...INTENDS TO KILL US...
HURRY!
BUT OLVIA...
...I...
...CANNOT ESCAPE AND LEAVE THESE ARTIFACTS OF HUMANITY BEHIND!!
YOU UNDER-STAND, DON'T YOU?

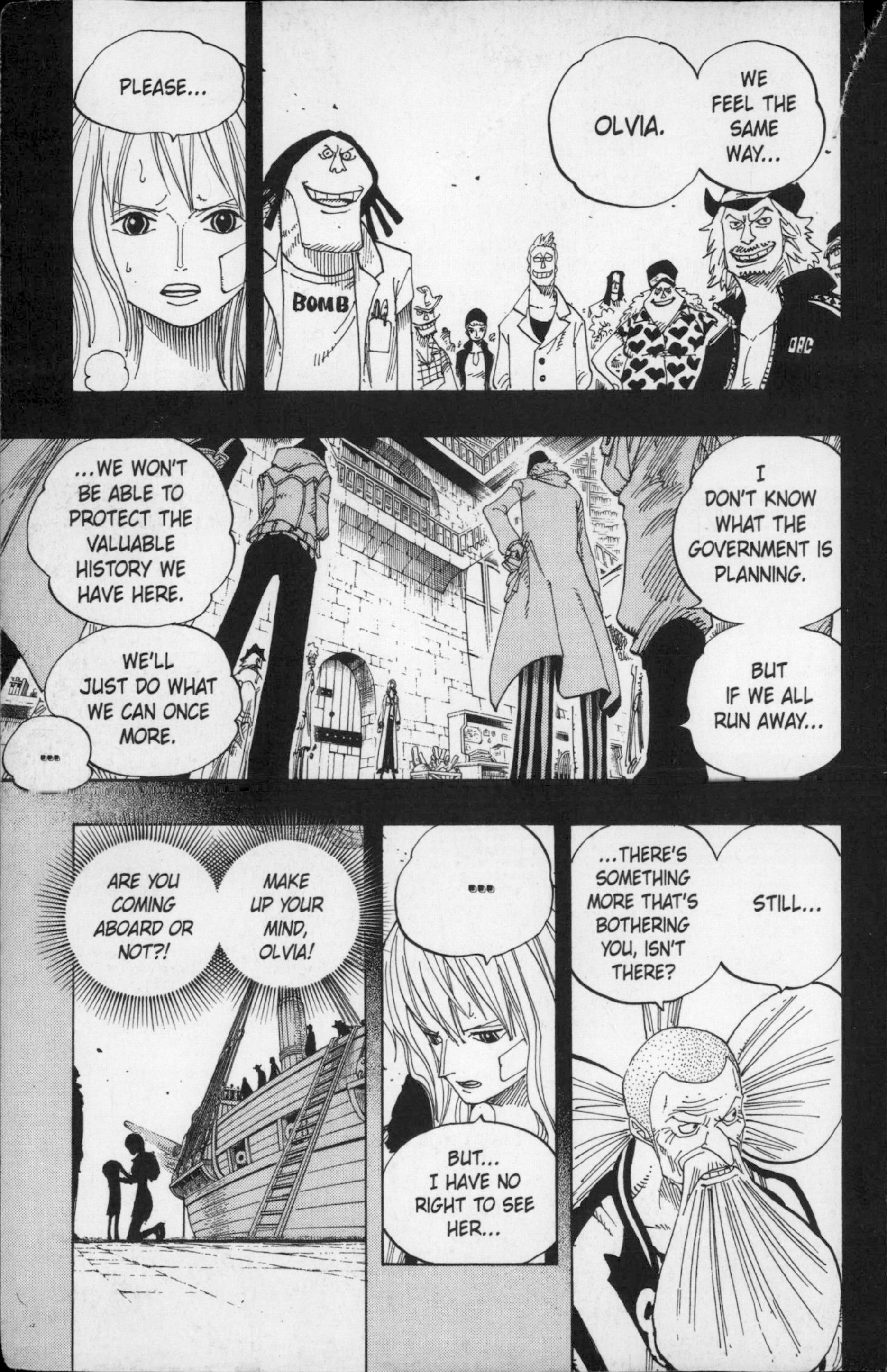
WE FEEL THE SAME WAY...
OLVIA.
PLEASE...
I DON'T KNOW WHAT THE GOVERNMENT IS PLANNING.
BUT IF WE ALL RUN AWAY...
...WE WON'T BE ABLE TO PROTECT THE VALUABLE HISTORY WE HAVE HERE.
WE'LL JUST DO WHAT WE CAN ONCE MORE.
...
STILL...
...THERE'S SOMETHING MORE THAT'S BOTHERING YOU, ISN'T THERE?
...
BUT... I HAVE NO RIGHT TO SEE HER...
MAKE UP YOUR MIND, OLVIA!
ARE YOU COMING ABOARD OR NOT?!
BOMB

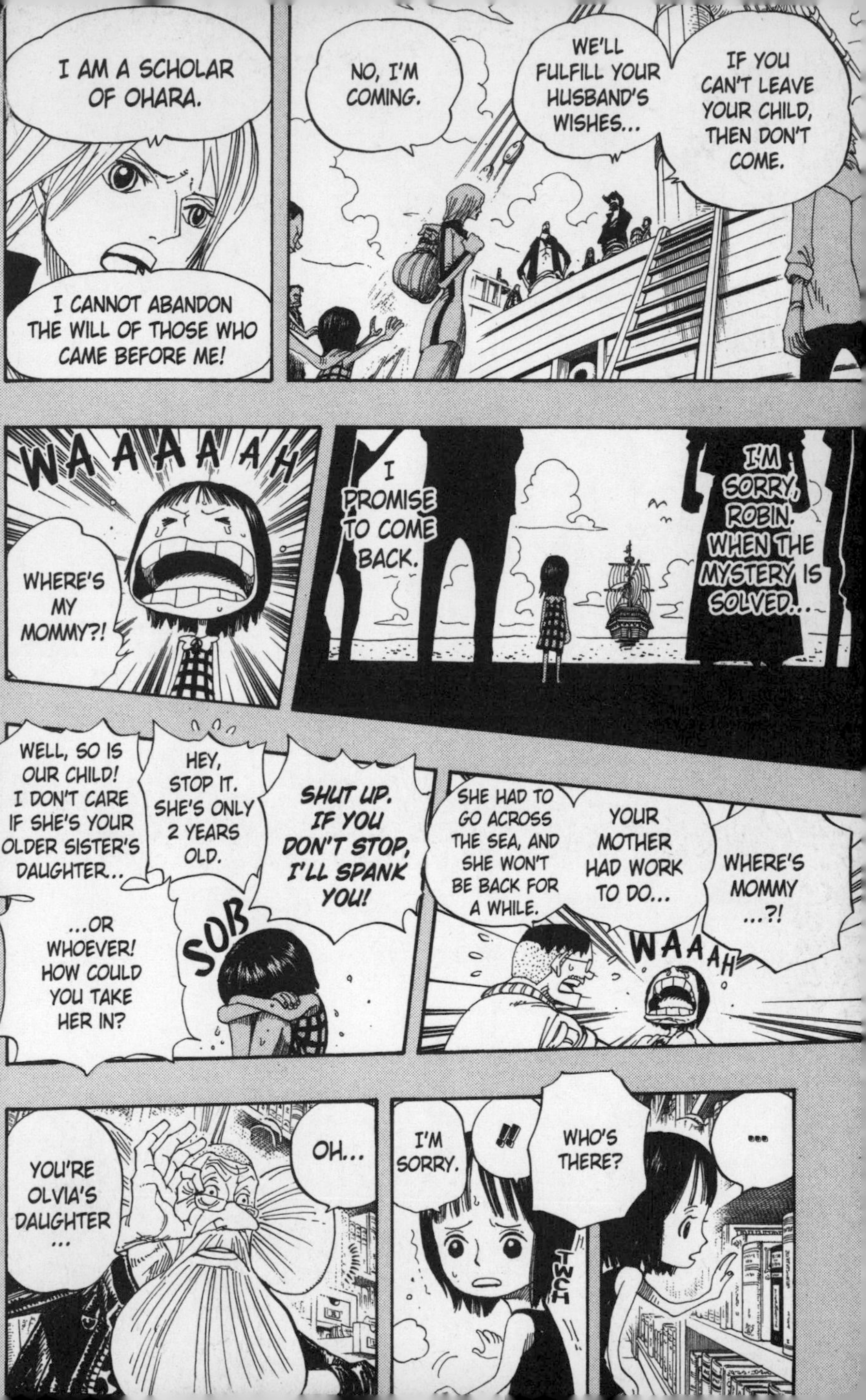
IF YOU CAN'T LEAVE YOUR CHILD, THEN DON'T COME.
WE'LL FULFILL YOUR HUSBAND'S WISHES...
NO, I'M COMING.
I AM A SCHOLAR OF OHARA.
I CANNOT ABANDON THE WILL OF THOSE WHO CAME BEFORE ME!
I'M SORRY, ROBIN. WHEN THE MYSTERY IS SOLVED...
I PROMISE TO COME BACK.
WAAAAAH
WHERE'S MY MOMMY?!
WHERE'S MOMMY ...?!
YOUR MOTHER HAD WORK TO DO...
SHE HAD TO GO ACROSS THE SEA, AND SHE WON'T BE BACK FOR A WHILE.
WAAAH
SHUT UP. IF YOU DON'T STOP, I'LL SPANK YOU!
HEY, STOP IT. SHE'S ONLY 2 YEARS OLD.
WELL, SO IS OUR CHILD! I DON'T CARE IF SHE'S YOUR OLDER SISTER'S DAUGHTER...
...OR WHOEVER! HOW COULD YOU TAKE HER IN?
SOB
...
WHO'S THERE?
!!
TWCH
I'M SORRY.
OH...
YOU'RE OLVIA'S DAUGHTER ...

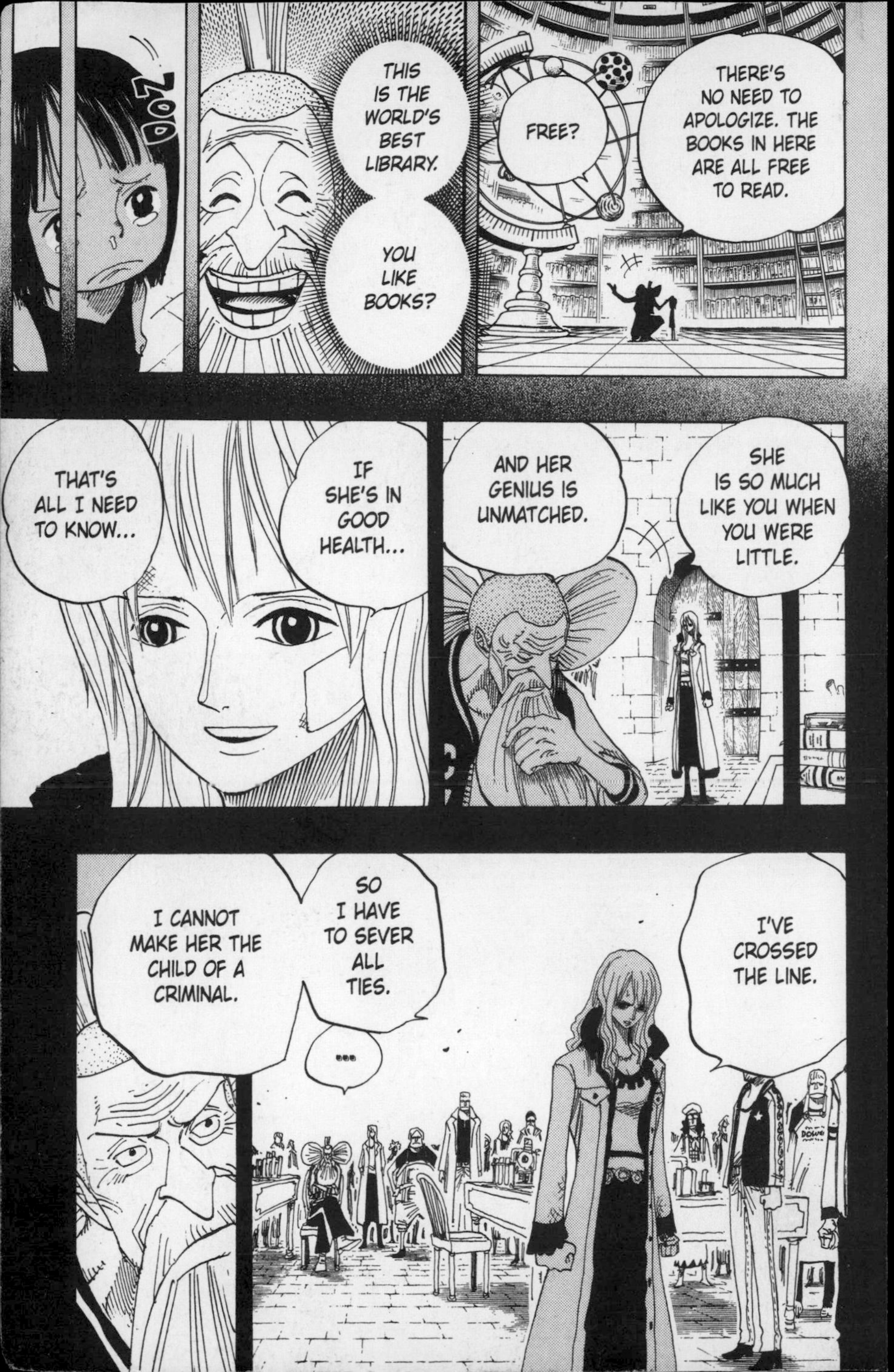
THERE'S NO NEED TO APOLOGIZE. THE BOOKS IN HERE ARE ALL FREE TO READ.
FREE?
THIS IS THE WORLD'S BEST LIBRARY.
YOU LIKE BOOKS?
SHE IS SO MUCH LIKE YOU WHEN YOU WERE LITTLE.
AND HER GENIUS IS UNMATCHED.
IF SHE'S IN GOOD HEALTH...
THAT'S ALL I NEED TO KNOW...
I'VE CROSSED THE LINE.
SO I HAVE TO SEVER ALL TIES.
I CANNOT MAKE HER THE CHILD OF A CRIMINAL.
...

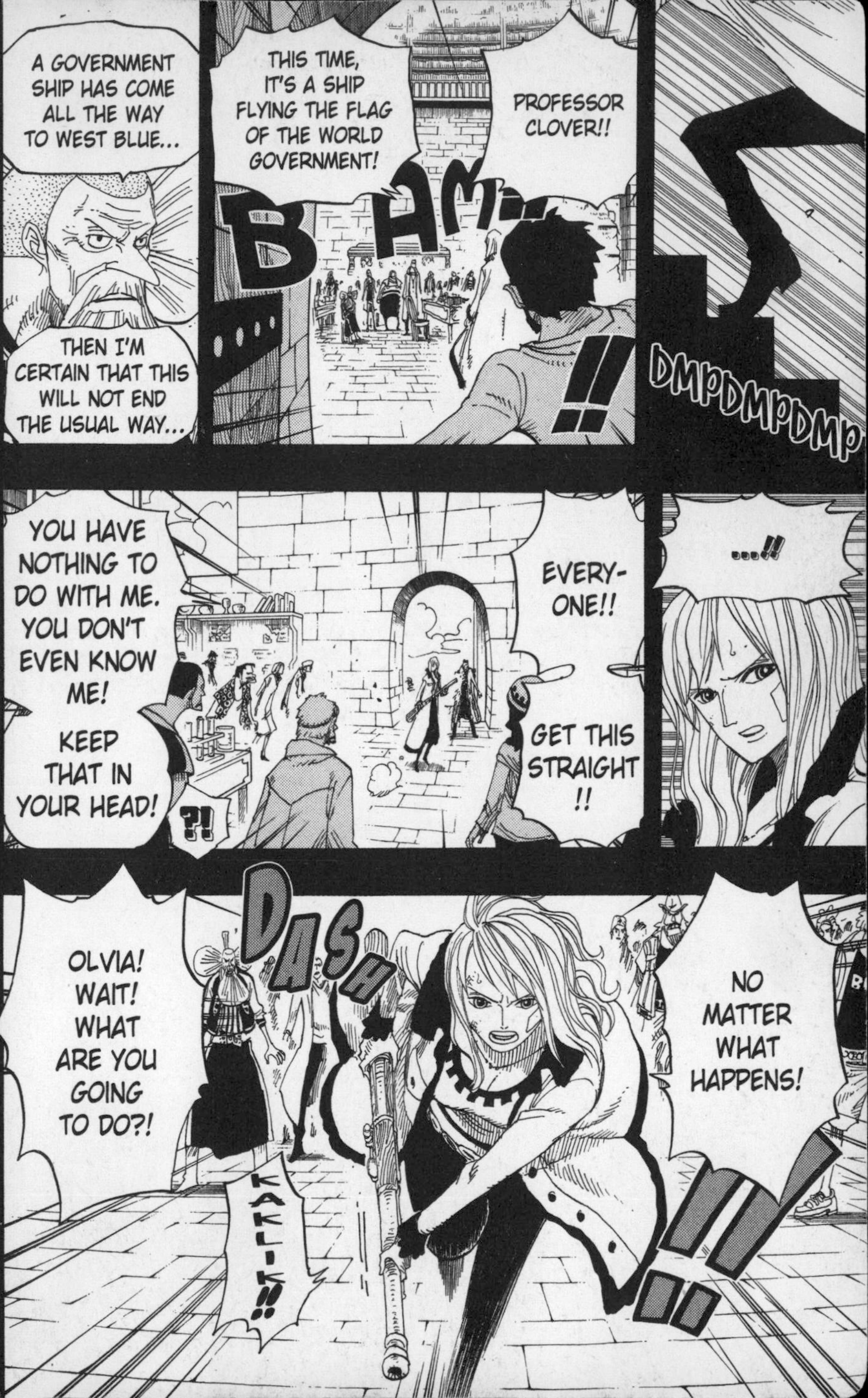
DMPDMPDMP
PROFESSOR CLOVER!!
THIS TIME, IT'S A SHIP FLYING THE FLAG OF THE WORLD GOVERNMENT!
BAM
!!
A GOVERNMENT SHIP HAS COME ALL THE WAY TO WEST BLUE...
THEN I'M CERTAIN THAT THIS WILL NOT END THE USUAL WAY...
...!!
EVERY-ONE!!
YOU HAVE NOTHING TO DO WITH ME. YOU DON'T EVEN KNOW ME!
GET THIS STRAIGHT!!
KEEP THAT IN YOUR HEAD!
?!
NO MATTER WHAT HAPPENS!
!!
DASH
OLVIA! WAIT! WHAT ARE YOU GOING TO DO?!
KAKLIK!!

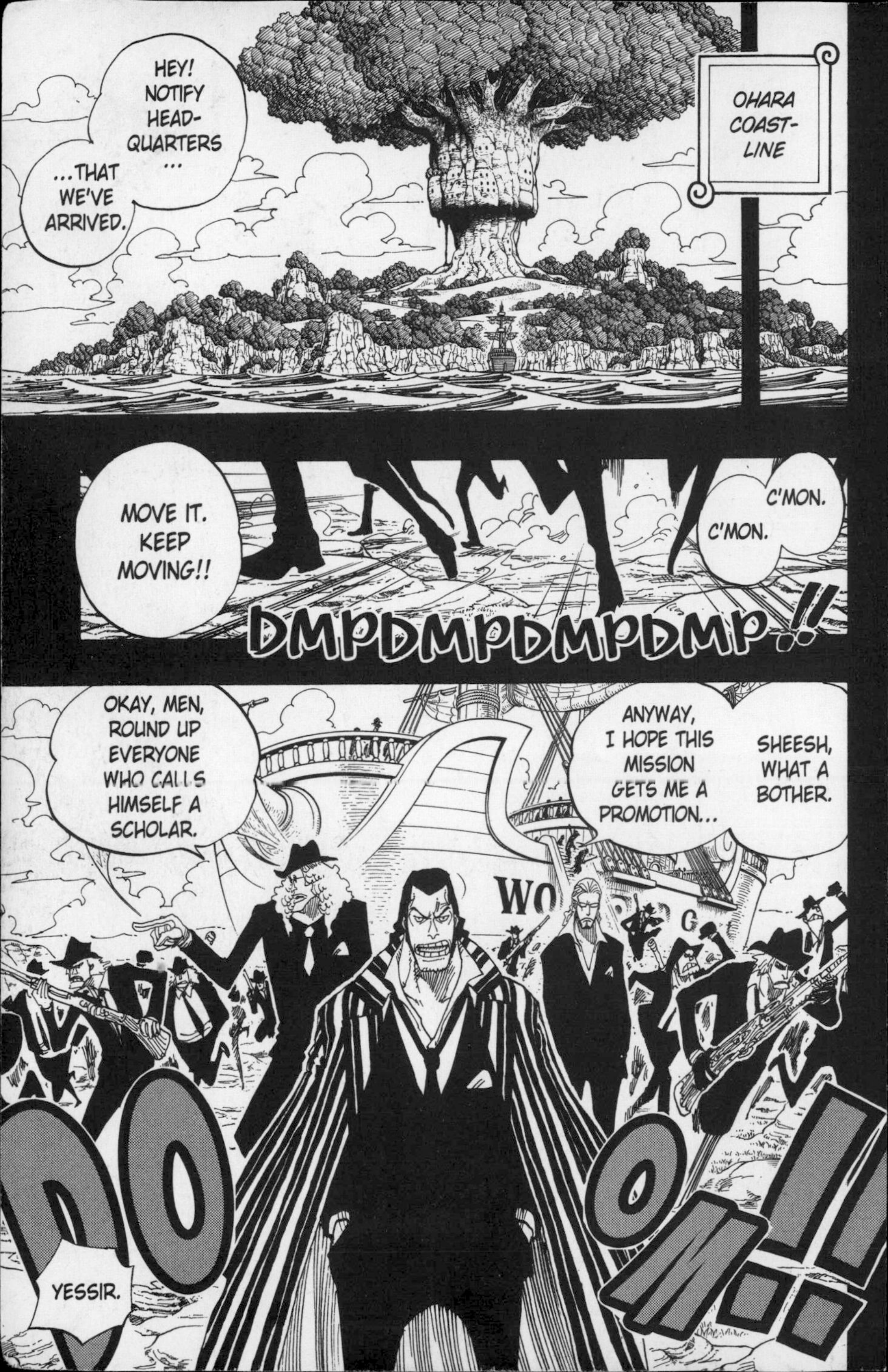
OHARA COAST-LINE
HEY! NOTIFY HEAD-QUARTERS...
...THAT WE'VE ARRIVED.
C'MON.
C'MON.
MOVE IT. KEEP MOVING!!
DMPDMPDMPDMP!!
SHEESH, WHAT A BOTHER.
ANYWAY, I HOPE THIS MISSION GETS ME A PROMOTION...
OKAY, MEN, ROUND UP EVERYONE WHO CALLS HIMSELF A SCHOLAR.
DOOON!!
YESSIR.

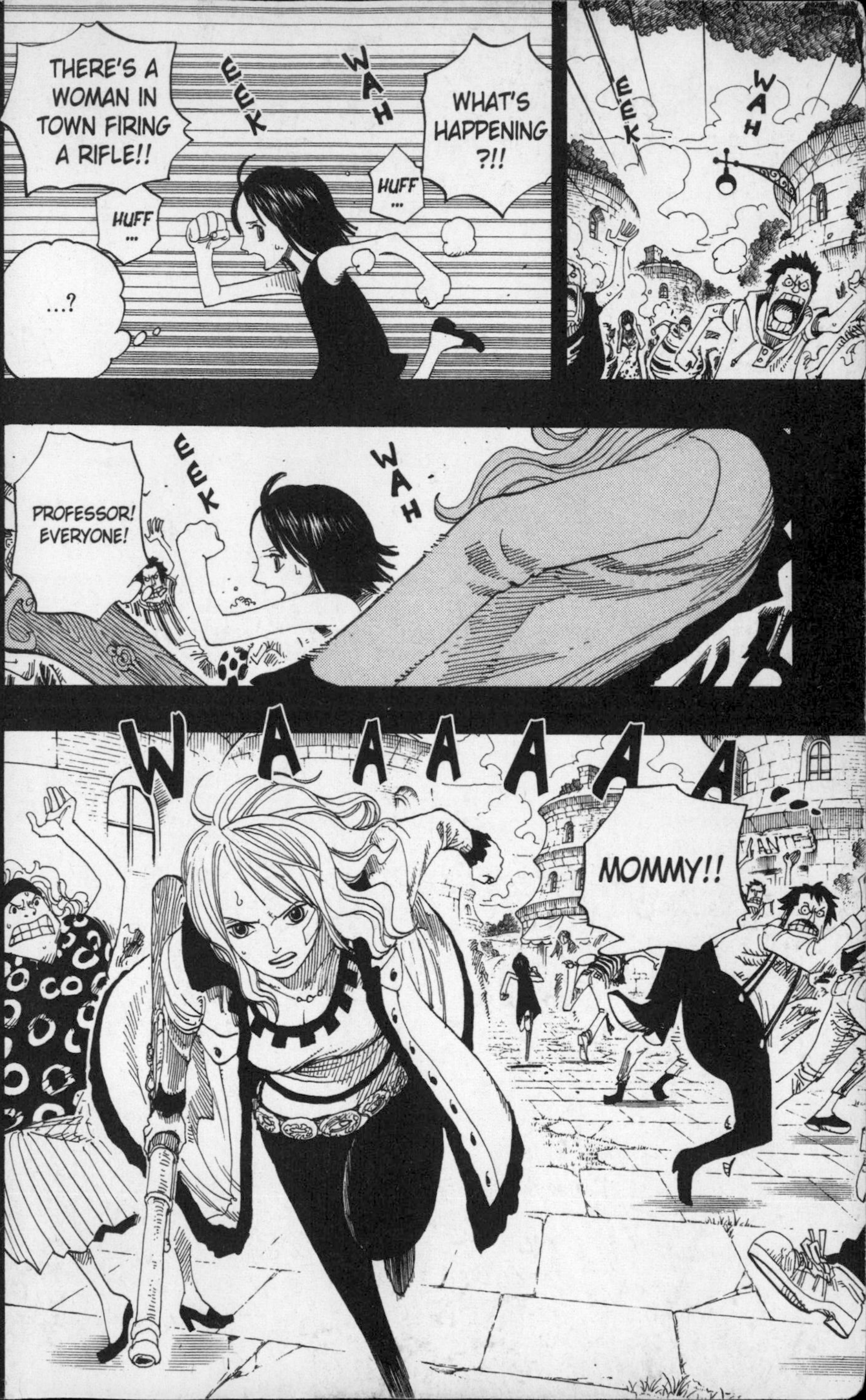
WAH
EEK
WHAT'S HAPPENING ?!!
WAH
EEK
HUFF ...
THERE'S A WOMAN IN TOWN FIRING A RIFLE!!
HUFF ...
...?
WAH
EEK
PROFESSOR! EVERYONE!
WAAAAAA
MOMMY!!

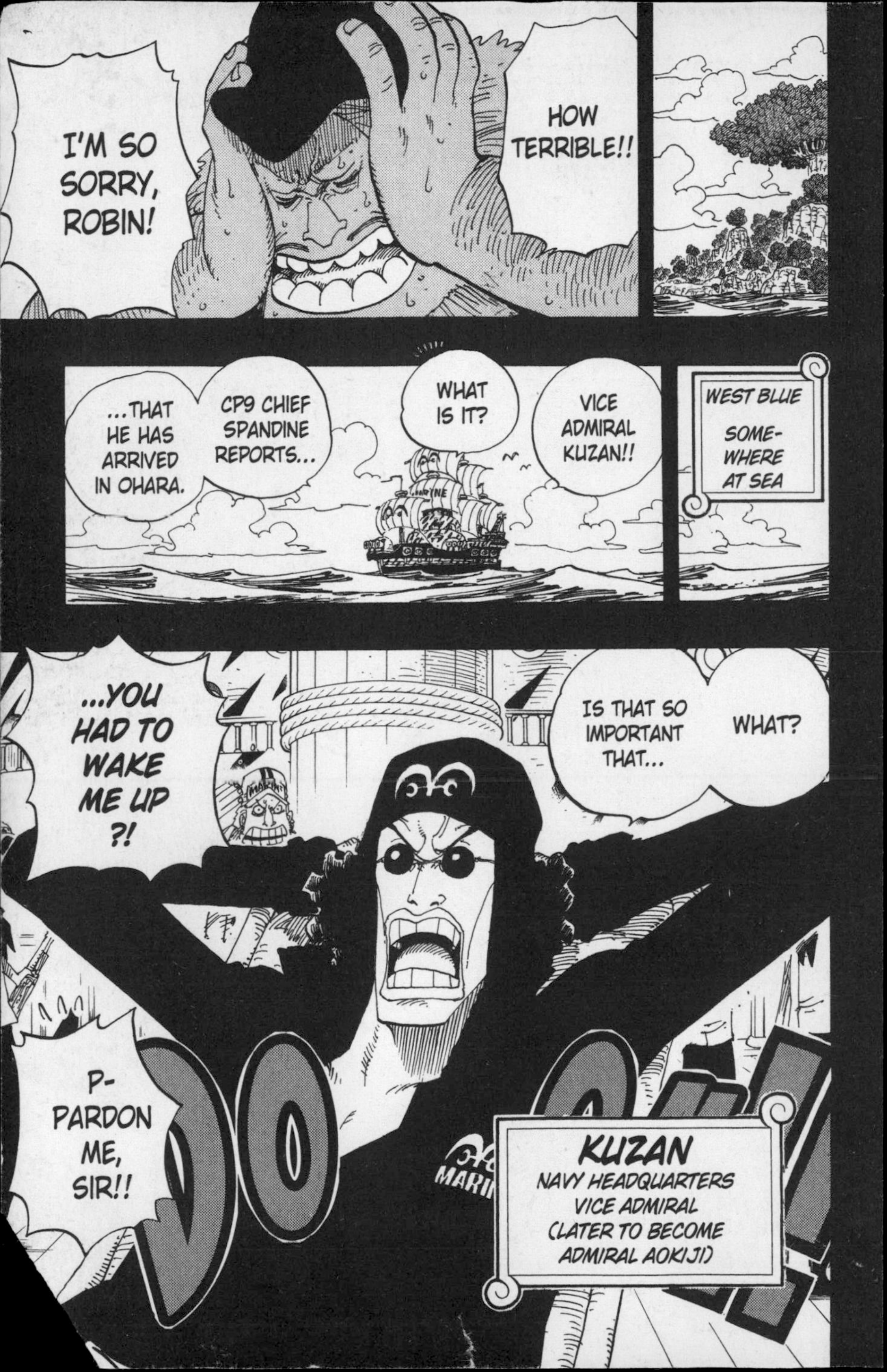
HOW TERRIBLE!!
I'M SO SORRY, ROBIN!
WEST BLUE
SOME-WHERE AT SEA
VICE ADMIRAL KUZAN!!
WHAT IS IT?
CP9 CHIEF SPANDINE REPORTS...
...THAT HE HAS ARRIVED IN OHARA.
WHAT?
IS THAT SO IMPORTANT THAT...
...YOU HAD TO WAKE ME UP ?!
KUZAN
NAVY HEADQUARTERS VICE ADMIRAL (LATER TO BECOME ADMIRAL AOKIJI)
P-PARDON ME, SIR!!

THE DEMONS OF OHARA

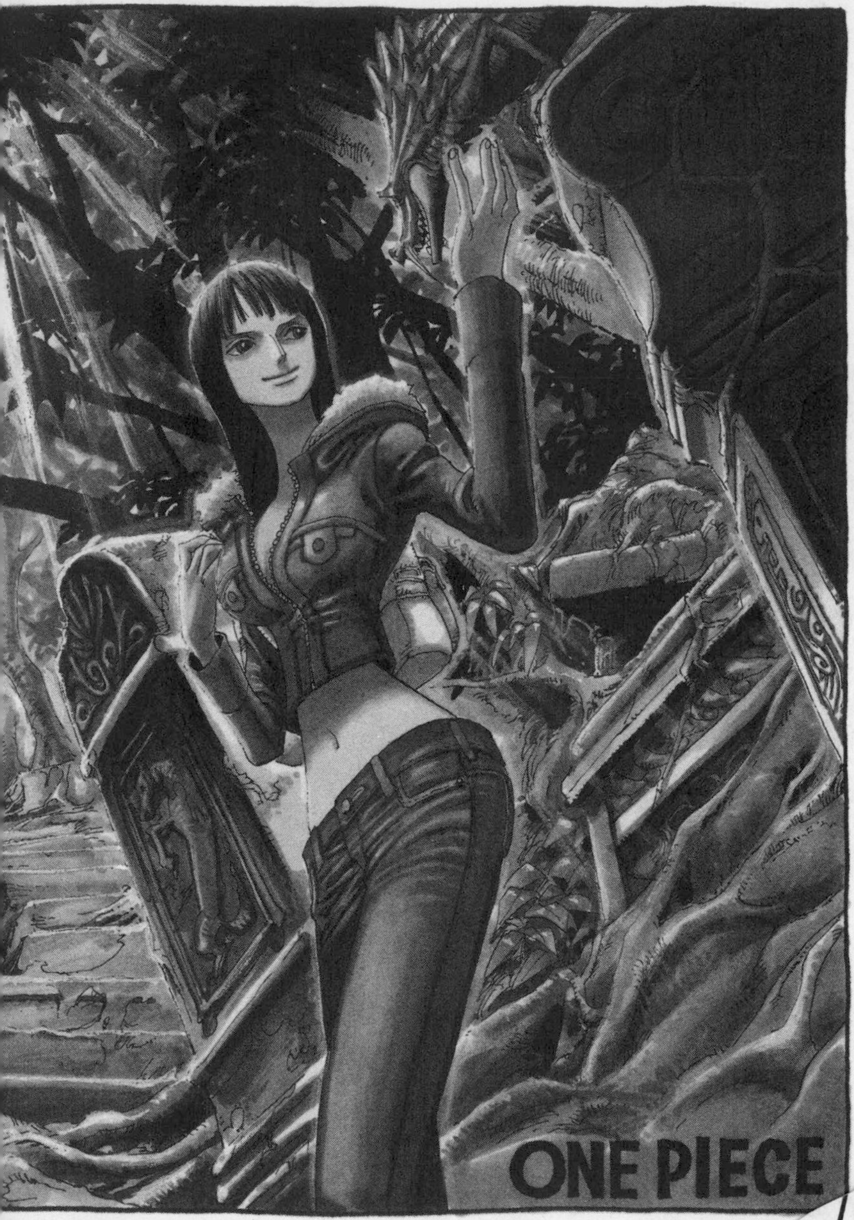
ONE PIECE

Chapter 394:

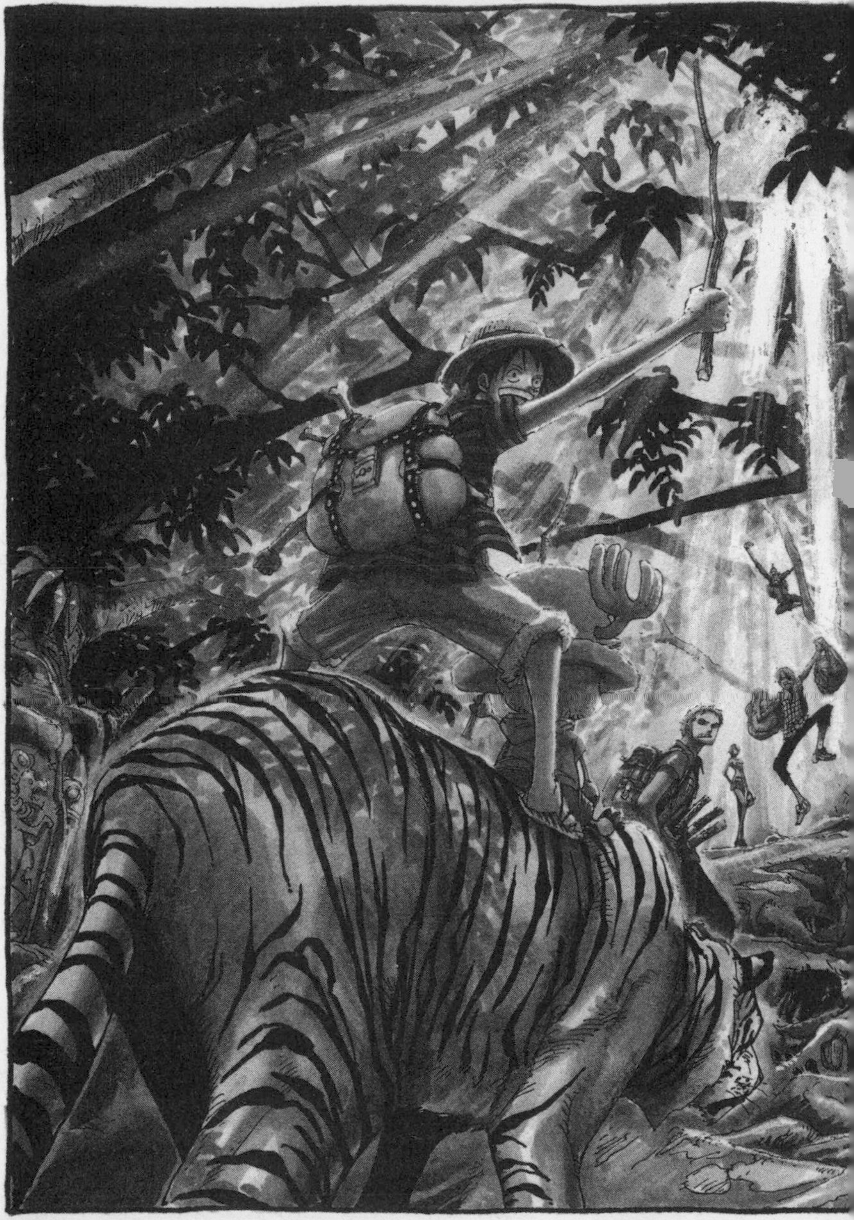

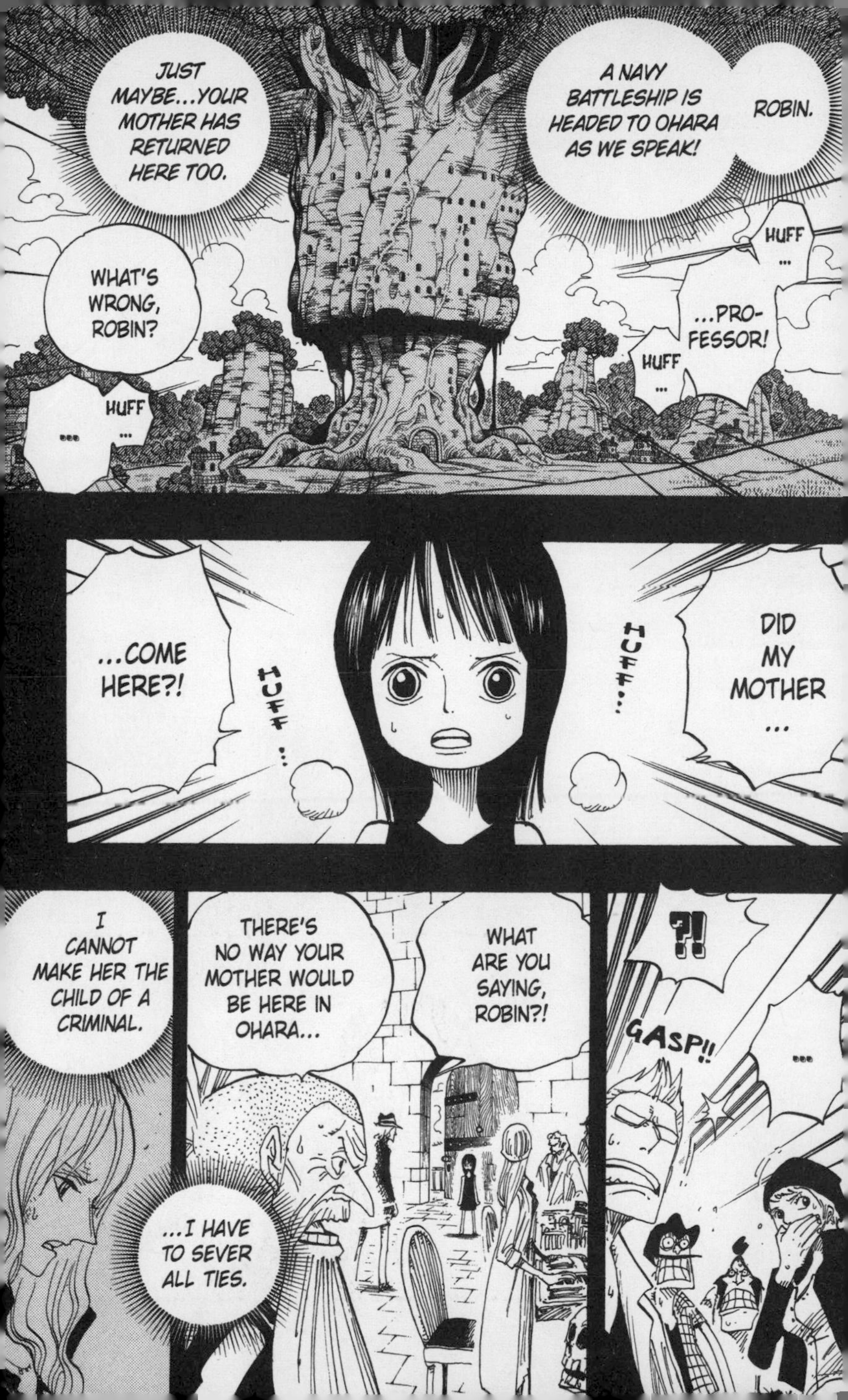
ROBIN.
A NAVY BATTLESHIP IS HEADED TO OHARA AS WE SPEAK!
JUST MAYBE...YOUR MOTHER HAS RETURNED HERE TOO.
HUFF...
...PRO-FESSOR!
HUFF...
WHAT'S WRONG, ROBIN?
HUFF...
...
DID MY MOTHER...
HUFF...
HUFF...
...COME HERE?!
?!
...
GASP!!
WHAT ARE YOU SAYING, ROBIN?!
THERE'S NO WAY YOUR MOTHER WOULD BE HERE IN OHARA...
...I HAVE TO SEVER ALL TIES.
I CANNOT MAKE HER THE CHILD OF A CRIMINAL.

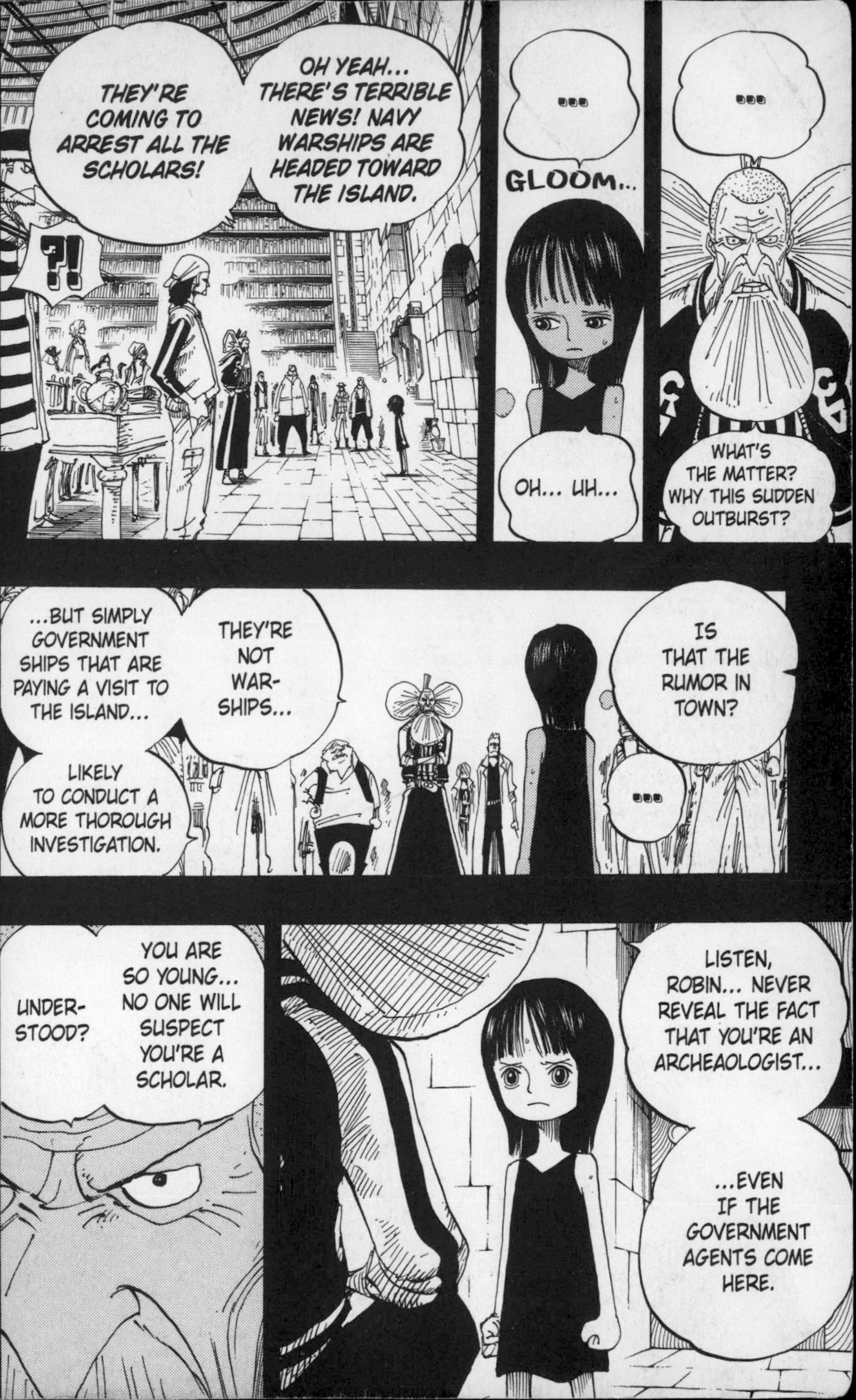
...
WHAT'S THE MATTER? WHY THIS SUDDEN OUTBURST?
...
GLOOM...
OH... UH...
OH YEAH... THERE'S TERRIBLE NEWS! NAVY WARSHIPS ARE HEADED TOWARD THE ISLAND.
THEY'RE COMING TO ARREST ALL THE SCHOLARS!
?!
IS THAT THE RUMOR IN TOWN?
...
THEY'RE NOT WAR-SHIPS...
...BUT SIMPLY GOVERNMENT SHIPS THAT ARE PAYING A VISIT TO THE ISLAND...
LIKELY TO CONDUCT A MORE THOROUGH INVESTIGATION.
LISTEN, ROBIN... NEVER REVEAL THE FACT THAT YOU'RE AN ARCHEAOLOGIST...
...EVEN IF THE GOVERNMENT AGENTS COME HERE.
YOU ARE SO YOUNG... NO ONE WILL SUSPECT YOU'RE A SCHOLAR.
UNDER-STOOD?

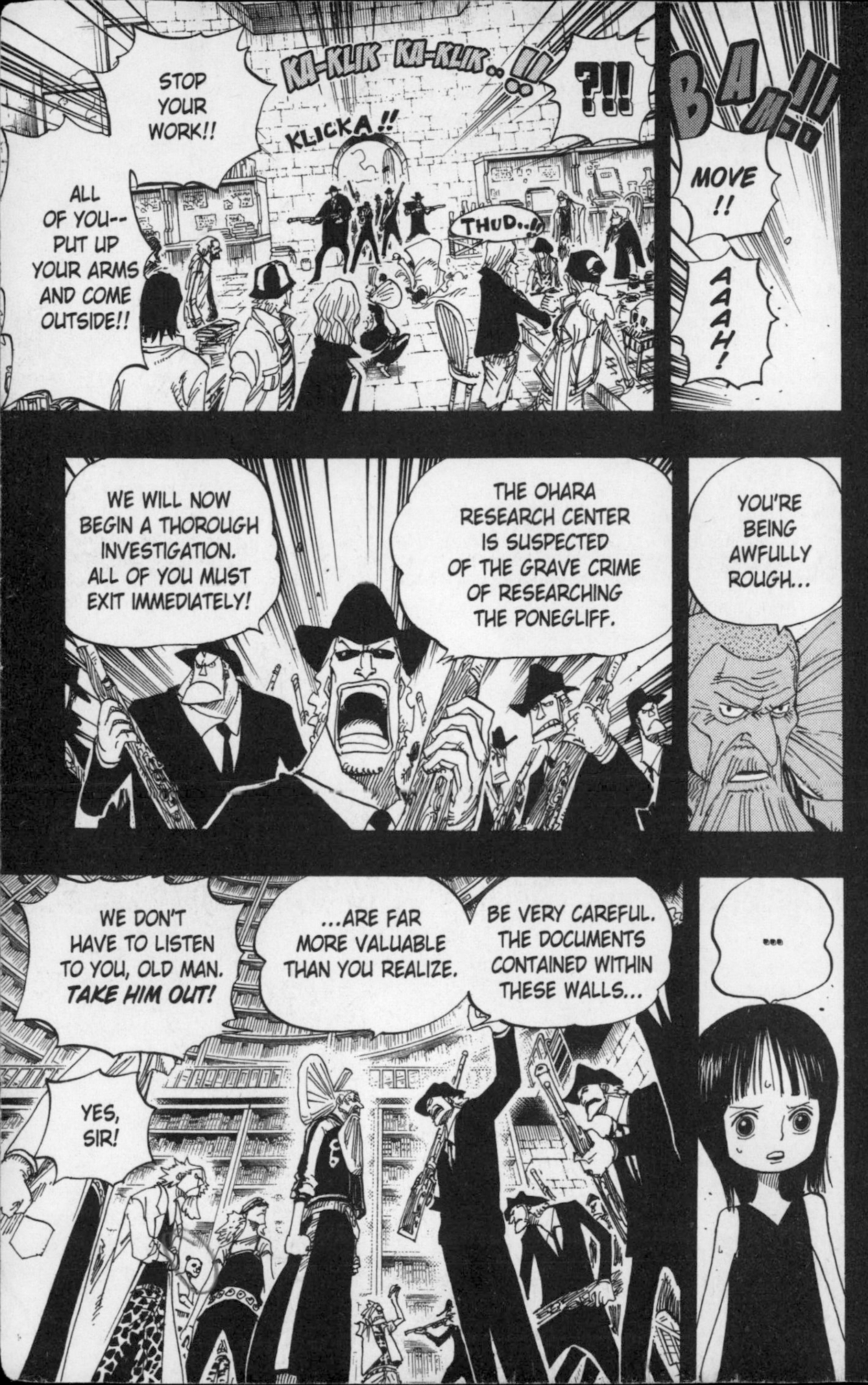
BAM!!
MOVE!!
AAAH!
?!!
KA-KLIK KA-KLIK..!!
STOP YOUR WORK!!
KLICKA!!
THUD..!!
ALL OF YOU-- PUT UP YOUR ARMS AND COME OUTSIDE!!
YOU'RE BEING AWFULLY ROUGH...
THE OHARA RESEARCH CENTER IS SUSPECTED OF THE GRAVE CRIME OF RESEARCHING THE PONEGLIFF.
WE WILL NOW BEGIN A THOROUGH INVESTIGATION. ALL OF YOU MUST EXIT IMMEDIATELY!
...
BE VERY CAREFUL. THE DOCUMENTS CONTAINED WITHIN THESE WALLS...
...ARE FAR MORE VALUABLE THAN YOU REALIZE.
WE DON'T HAVE TO LISTEN TO YOU, OLD MAN. TAKE HIM OUT!
YES, SIR!

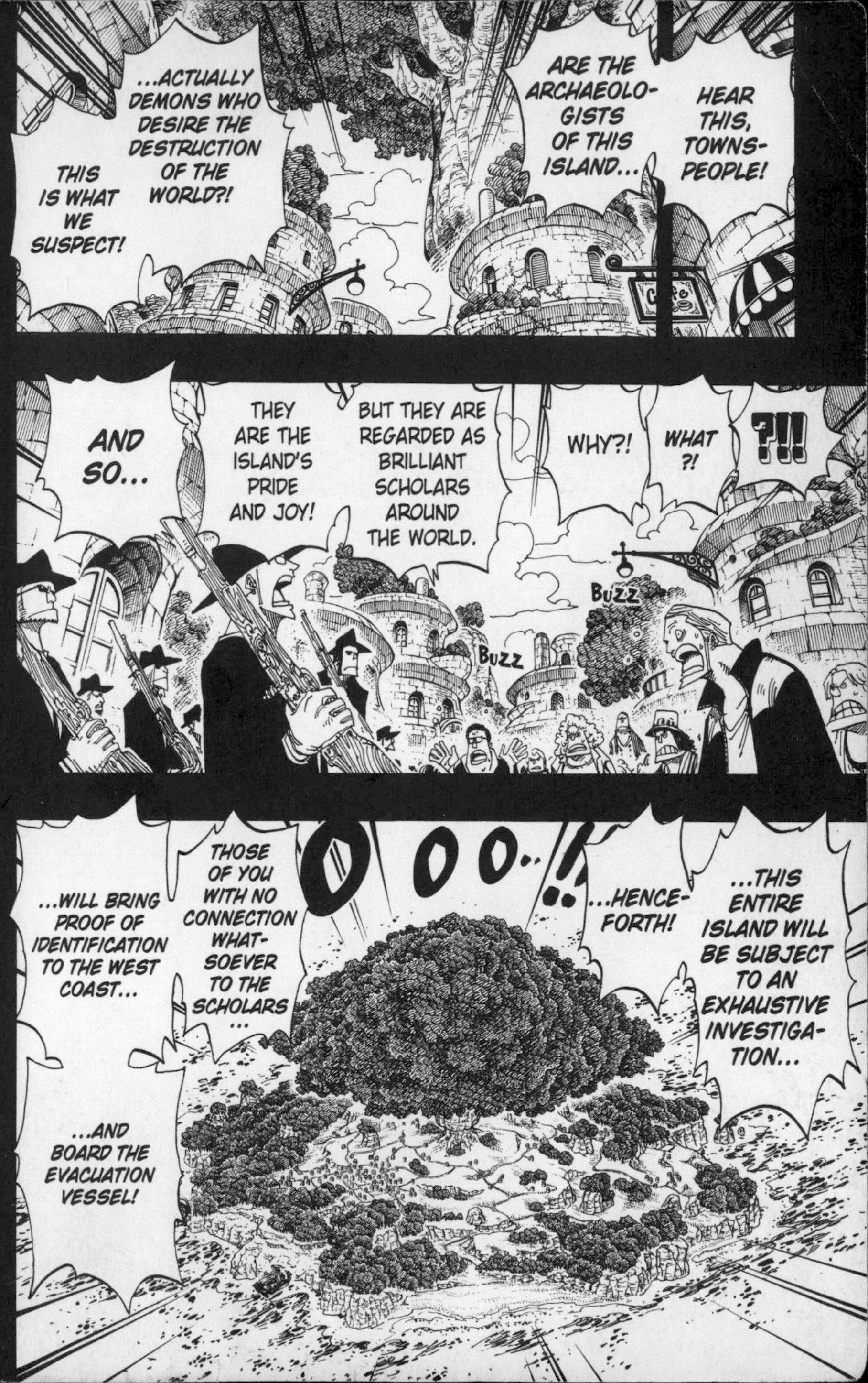
HEAR THIS, TOWNSPEOPLE!
ARE THE ARCHAEOLOGISTS OF THIS ISLAND...
...ACTUALLY DEMONS WHO DESIRE THE DESTRUCTION OF THE WORLD?!
THIS IS WHAT WE SUSPECT!
?!!
WHAT?!
WHY?!
BUT THEY ARE REGARDED AS BRILLIANT SCHOLARS AROUND THE WORLD.
THEY ARE THE ISLAND'S PRIDE AND JOY!
AND SO...
BUZZ
BUZZ
...THIS ENTIRE ISLAND WILL BE SUBJECT TO AN EXHAUSTIVE INVESTIGATION...
...HENCEFORTH!
OOO..!!
THOSE OF YOU WITH NO CONNECTION WHATSOEVER TO THE SCHOLARS...
...WILL BRING PROOF OF IDENTIFICATION TO THE WEST COAST...
...AND BOARD THE EVACUATION VESSEL!

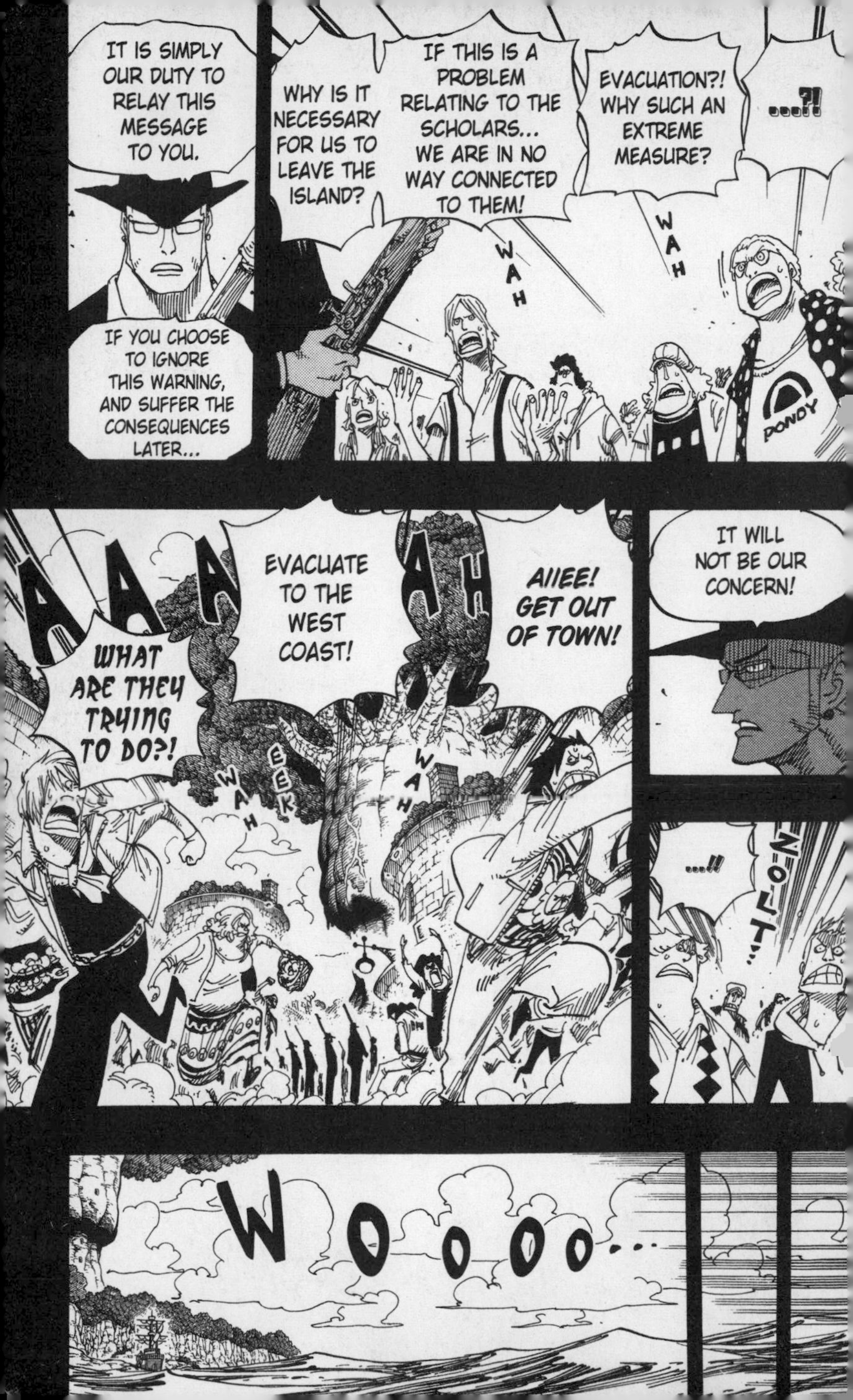
...?!
EVACUATION?! WHY SUCH AN EXTREME MEASURE?
WAH
IF THIS IS A PROBLEM RELATING TO THE SCHOLARS... WE ARE IN NO WAY CONNECTED TO THEM!
WAH
WHY IS IT NECESSARY FOR US TO LEAVE THE ISLAND?
IT IS SIMPLY OUR DUTY TO RELAY THIS MESSAGE TO YOU.
IF YOU CHOOSE TO IGNORE THIS WARNING, AND SUFFER THE CONSEQUENCES LATER...
IT WILL NOT BE OUR CONCERN!
...!!
JOLT
AIIEE! GET OUT OF TOWN!
AAAAH
EVACUATE TO THE WEST COAST!
WHAT ARE THEY TRYING TO DO?!
WAH
EEK
WAH
WOOOO...

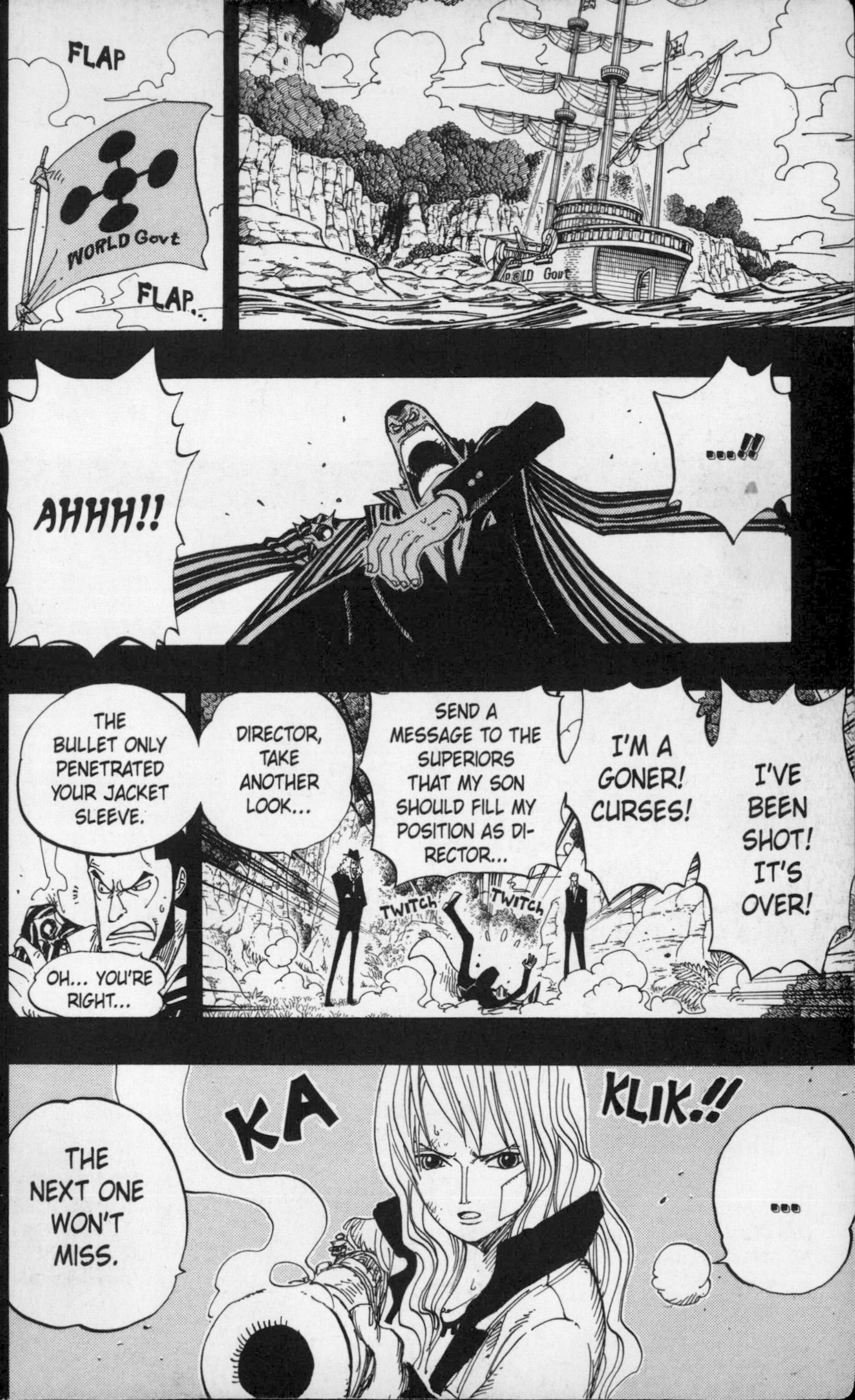
WORLD Govt
FLAP
WORLD Govt
FLAP...
...!!
AHHH!!
I'VE BEEN SHOT! IT'S OVER!
I'M A GONER! CURSES!
SEND A MESSAGE TO THE SUPERIORS THAT MY SON SHOULD FILL MY POSITION AS DI-RECTOR...
DIRECTOR, TAKE ANOTHER LOOK...
TWITCH
TWITCH
THE BULLET ONLY PENETRATED YOUR JACKET SLEEVE.
OH... YOU'RE RIGHT...
KA KLIK!!
...
THE NEXT ONE WON'T MISS.

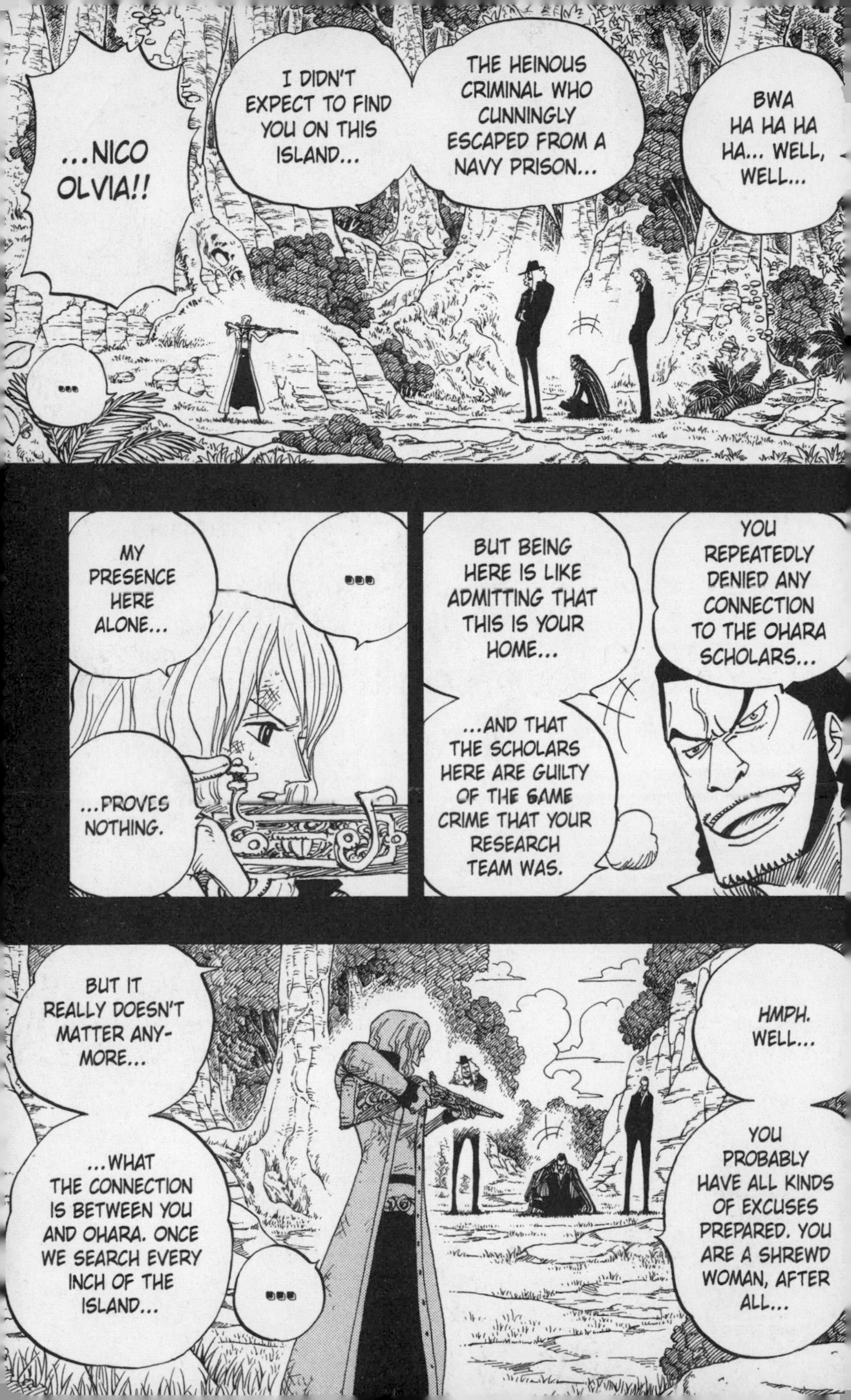
BWA HA HA HA... WELL, WELL...
THE HEINOUS CRIMINAL WHO CUNNINGLY ESCAPED FROM A NAVY PRISON...
I DIDN'T EXPECT TO FIND YOU ON THIS ISLAND...
...NICO OLVIA!!
...
YOU REPEATEDLY DENIED ANY CONNECTION TO THE OHARA SCHOLARS...
BUT BEING HERE IS LIKE ADMITTING THAT THIS IS YOUR HOME...
...AND THAT THE SCHOLARS HERE ARE GUILTY OF THE SAME CRIME THAT YOUR RESEARCH TEAM WAS.
...
MY PRESENCE HERE ALONE...
...PROVES NOTHING.
HMPH. WELL...
YOU PROBABLY HAVE ALL KINDS OF EXCUSES PREPARED. YOU ARE A SHREWD WOMAN, AFTER ALL...
BUT IT REALLY DOESN'T MATTER ANYMORE...
...WHAT THE CONNECTION IS BETWEEN YOU AND OHARA. ONCE WE SEARCH EVERY INCH OF THE ISLAND...
...

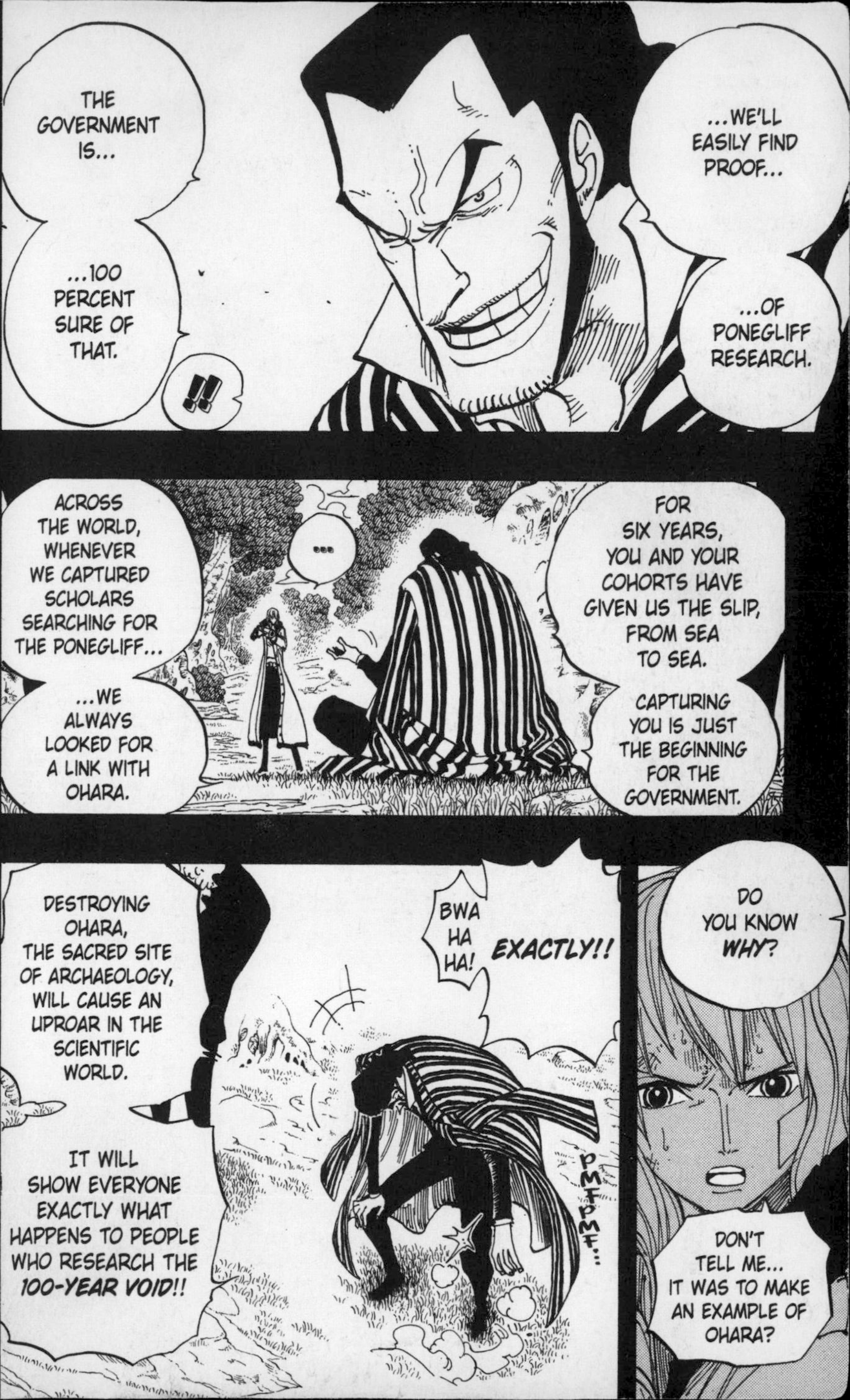
...WE'LL EASILY FIND PROOF...
...OF PONEGLIFF RESEARCH.
THE GOVERNMENT IS...
...100 PERCENT SURE OF THAT.
!!
FOR SIX YEARS, YOU AND YOUR COHORTS HAVE GIVEN US THE SLIP, FROM SEA TO SEA.
CAPTURING YOU IS JUST THE BEGINNING FOR THE GOVERNMENT.
...
ACROSS THE WORLD, WHENEVER WE CAPTURED SCHOLARS SEARCHING FOR THE PONEGLIFF...
...WE ALWAYS LOOKED FOR A LINK WITH OHARA.
DO YOU KNOW *WHY?*
DON'T TELL ME... IT WAS TO MAKE AN EXAMPLE OF OHARA?
BWA HA HA!
EXACTLY!!
DESTROYING OHARA, THE SACRED SITE OF ARCHAEOLOGY, WILL CAUSE AN UPROAR IN THE SCIENTIFIC WORLD.
PMF PMF...
IT WILL SHOW EVERYONE EXACTLY WHAT HAPPENS TO PEOPLE WHO RESEARCH THE ***100-YEAR VOID!!***

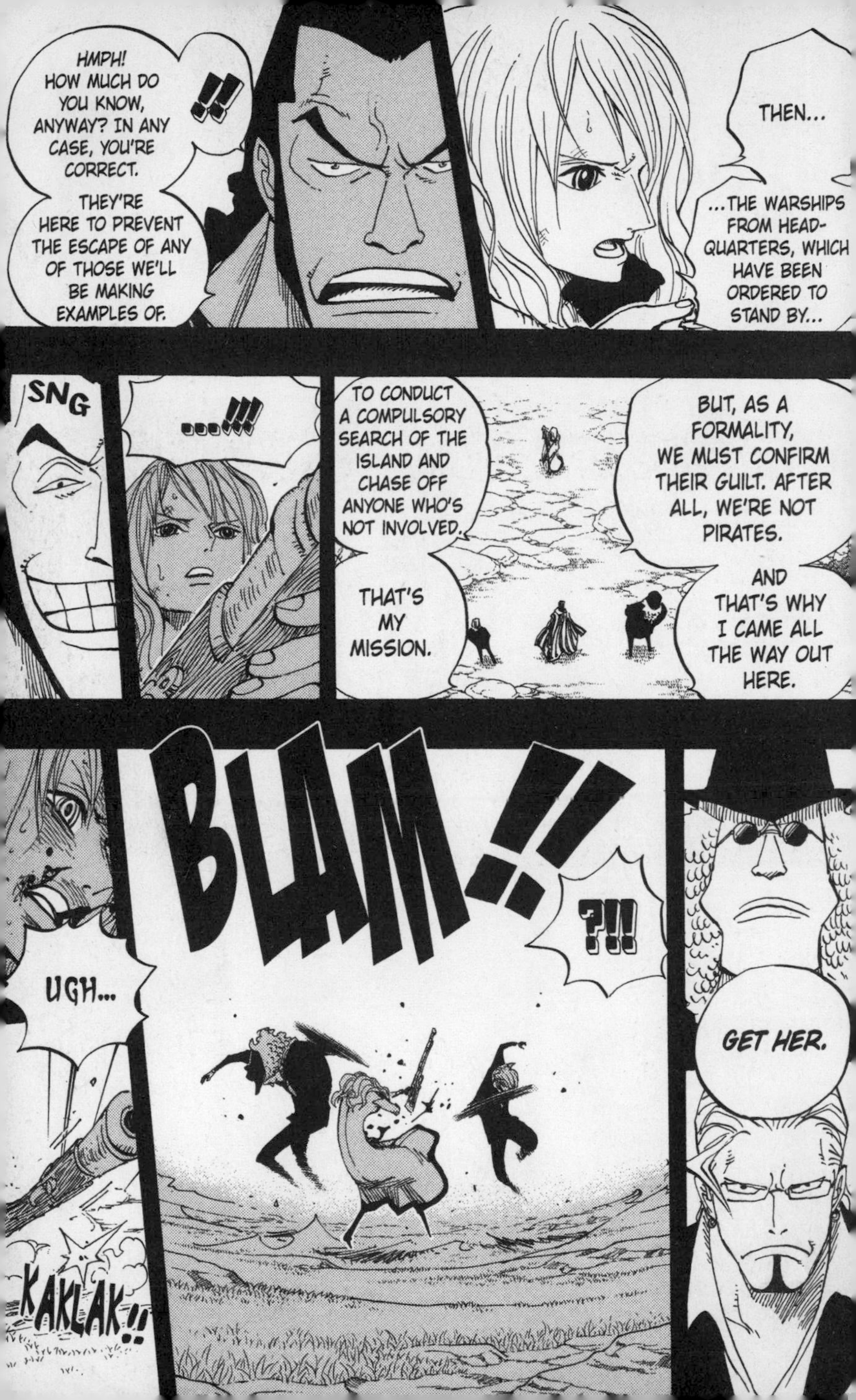
THEN...
...THE WARSHIPS FROM HEAD-QUARTERS, WHICH HAVE BEEN ORDERED TO STAND BY...
!!
HMPH! HOW MUCH DO YOU KNOW, ANYWAY? IN ANY CASE, YOU'RE CORRECT.
THEY'RE HERE TO PREVENT THE ESCAPE OF ANY OF THOSE WE'LL BE MAKING EXAMPLES OF.
BUT, AS A FORMALITY, WE MUST CONFIRM THEIR GUILT. AFTER ALL, WE'RE NOT PIRATES.
AND THAT'S WHY I CAME ALL THE WAY OUT HERE.
TO CONDUCT A COMPULSORY SEARCH OF THE ISLAND AND CHASE OFF ANYONE WHO'S NOT INVOLVED.
THAT'S MY MISSION.
...!!!
SNG
GET HER.
BLAM!!
?!!
UGH...
KAKLAK!!

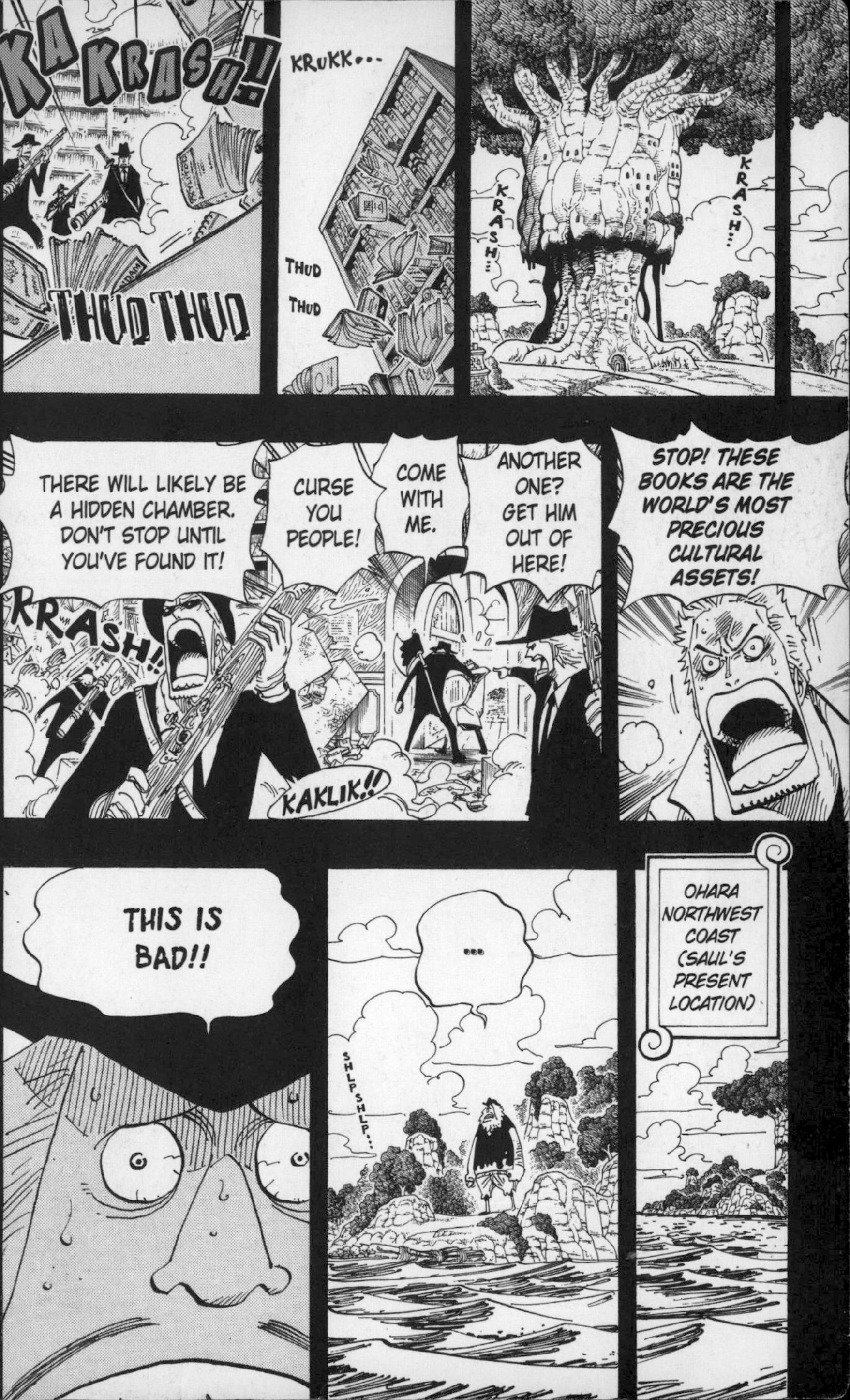
KRASH...
KRASH...
KRUKK...
THUD
THUD
KAKRASH!!
THUD THUD
STOP! THESE BOOKS ARE THE WORLD'S MOST PRECIOUS CULTURAL ASSETS!
ANOTHER ONE? GET HIM OUT OF HERE!
COME WITH ME.
KAKLIK!!
CURSE YOU PEOPLE!
THERE WILL LIKELY BE A HIDDEN CHAMBER. DON'T STOP UNTIL YOU'VE FOUND IT!
KRASH!!
OHARA NORTHWEST COAST (SAUL'S PRESENT LOCATION)
...
SHLP SHLP...
THIS IS BAD!!

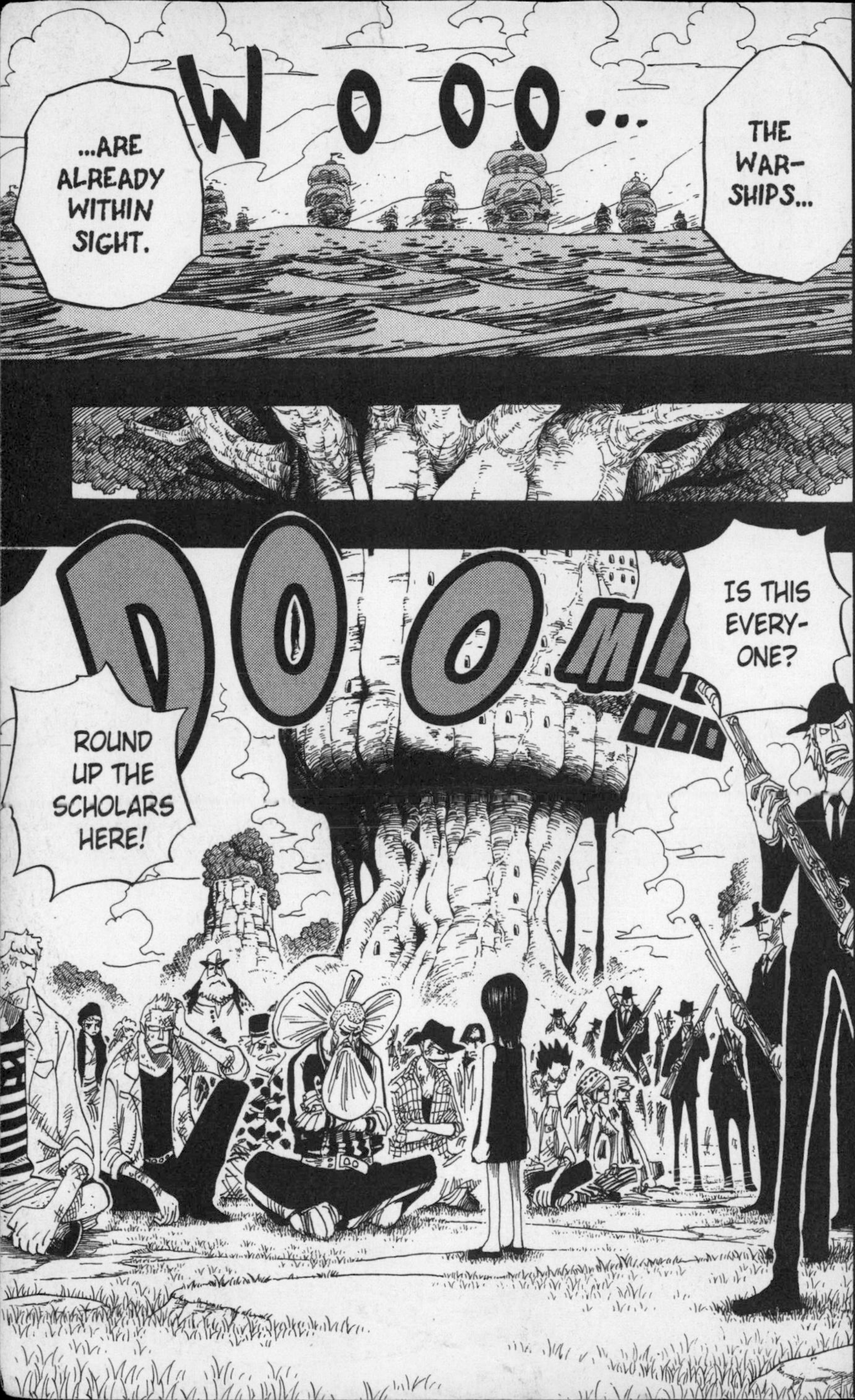
THE WAR-SHIPS...
WOOO...
...ARE ALREADY WITHIN SIGHT.
DOOM...
IS THIS EVERY-ONE?
ROUND UP THE SCHOLARS HERE!

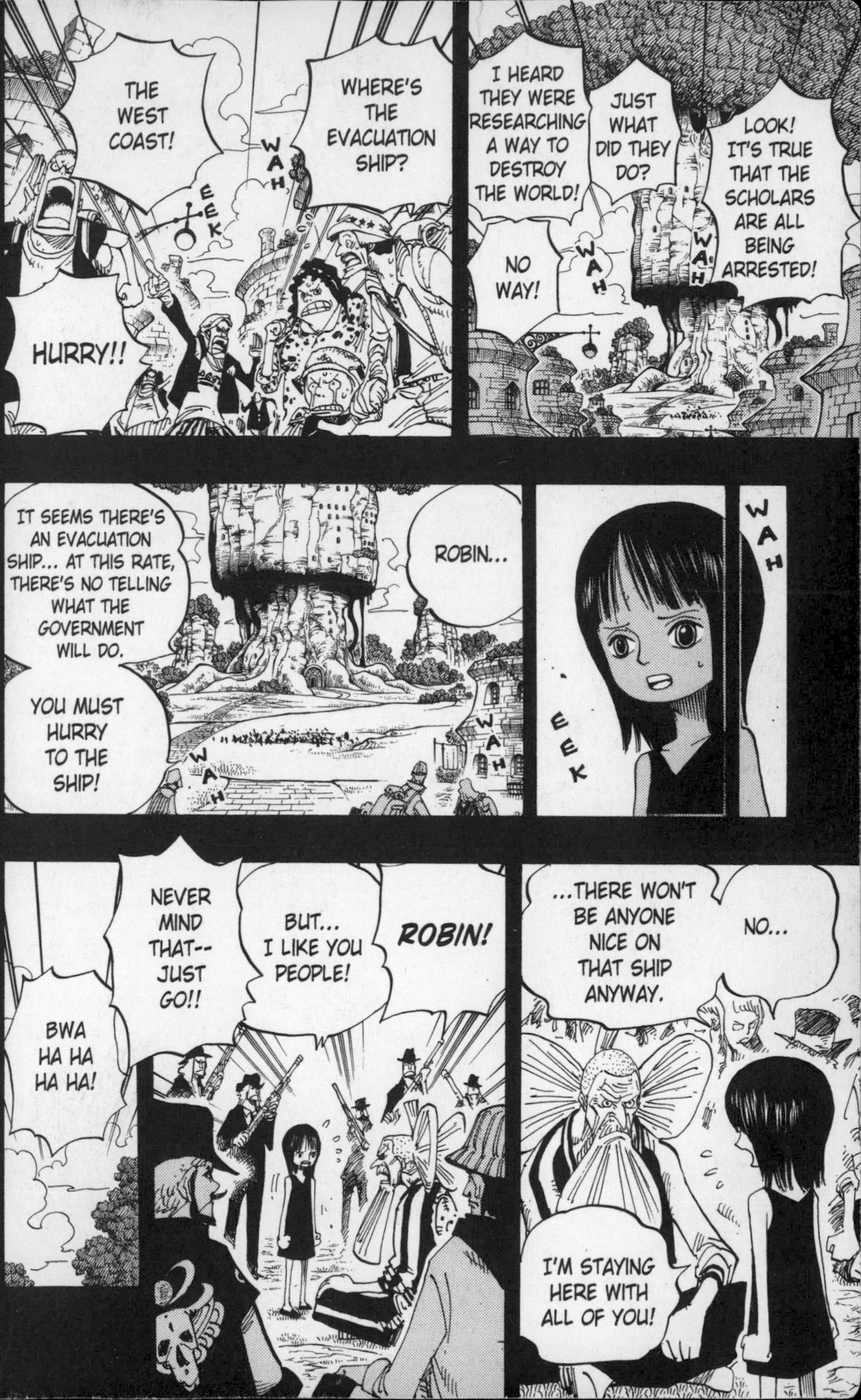
LOOK! IT'S TRUE THAT THE SCHOLARS ARE ALL BEING ARRESTED!
WAH
JUST WHAT DID THEY DO?
I HEARD THEY WERE RESEARCHING A WAY TO DESTROY THE WORLD!
WAH
NO WAY!
WHERE'S THE EVACUATION SHIP?
WAH
THE WEST COAST!
EEK
HURRY!!
WAH
EEK
ROBIN...
IT SEEMS THERE'S AN EVACUATION SHIP... AT THIS RATE, THERE'S NO TELLING WHAT THE GOVERNMENT WILL DO.
WAH
YOU MUST HURRY TO THE SHIP!
WAH
NO...
...THERE WON'T BE ANYONE NICE ON THAT SHIP ANYWAY.
I'M STAYING HERE WITH ALL OF YOU!
ROBIN!
BUT... I LIKE YOU PEOPLE!
NEVER MIND THAT-- JUST GO!!
BWA HA HA HA HA!

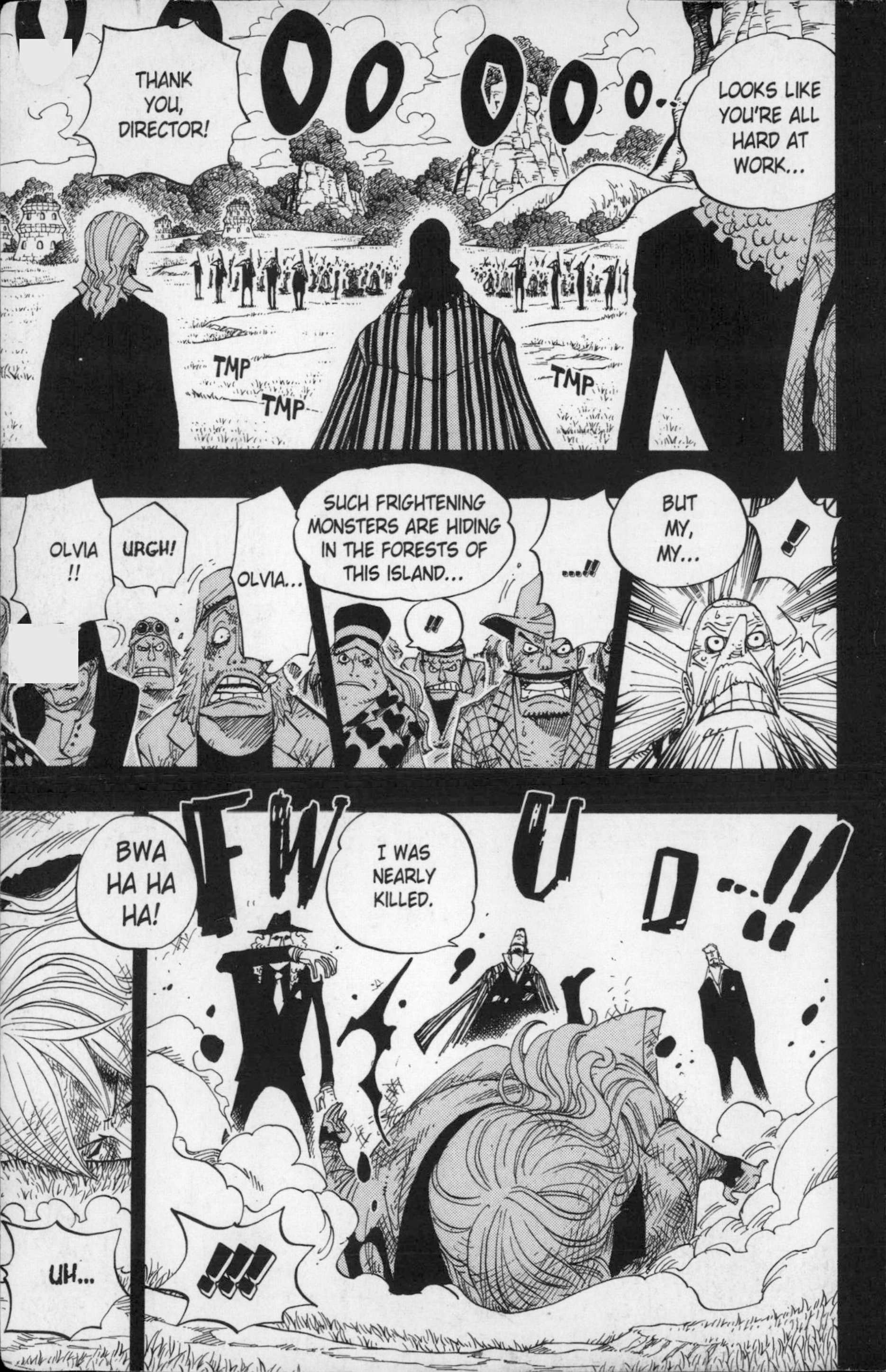
LOOKS LIKE YOU'RE ALL HARD AT WORK...
OOOOO...
THANK YOU, DIRECTOR!
TMP
TMP
TMP
!
BUT MY, MY...
...!!
SUCH FRIGHTENING MONSTERS ARE HIDING IN THE FORESTS OF THIS ISLAND...
!!
OLVIA...
URGH!
OLVIA !!
FWUD...!!
I WAS NEARLY KILLED.
BWA HA HA HA!
!!!
UH...

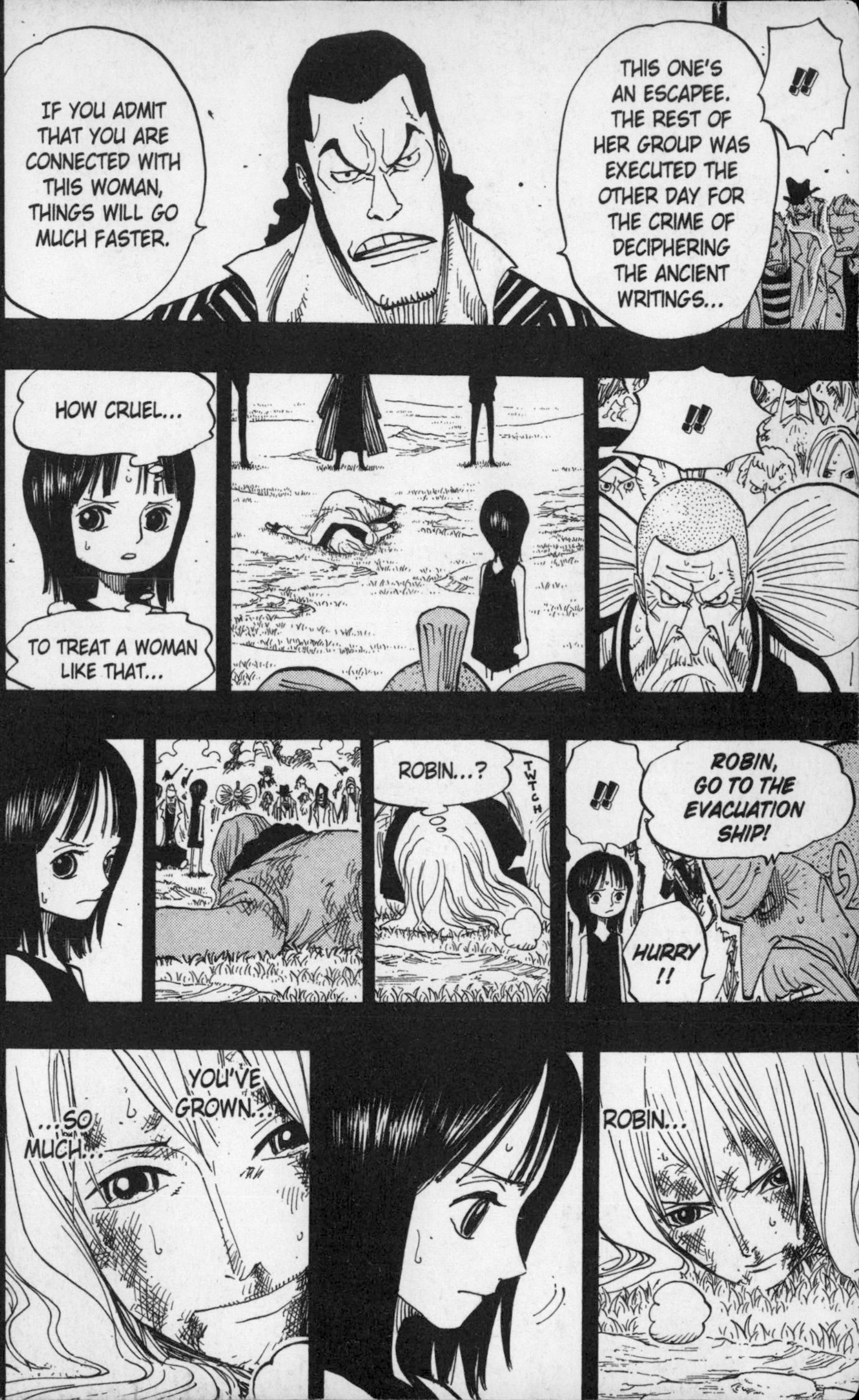
!!
THIS ONE'S AN ESCAPEE. THE REST OF HER GROUP WAS EXECUTED THE OTHER DAY FOR THE CRIME OF DECIPHERING THE ANCIENT WRITINGS...
IF YOU ADMIT THAT YOU ARE CONNECTED WITH THIS WOMAN, THINGS WILL GO MUCH FASTER.
!!
HOW CRUEL...
TO TREAT A WOMAN LIKE THAT...
ROBIN, GO TO THE EVACUATION SHIP!
!!
HURRY !!
TWTCH
ROBIN...?
ROBIN...
YOU'VE GROWN...
...SO MUCH...

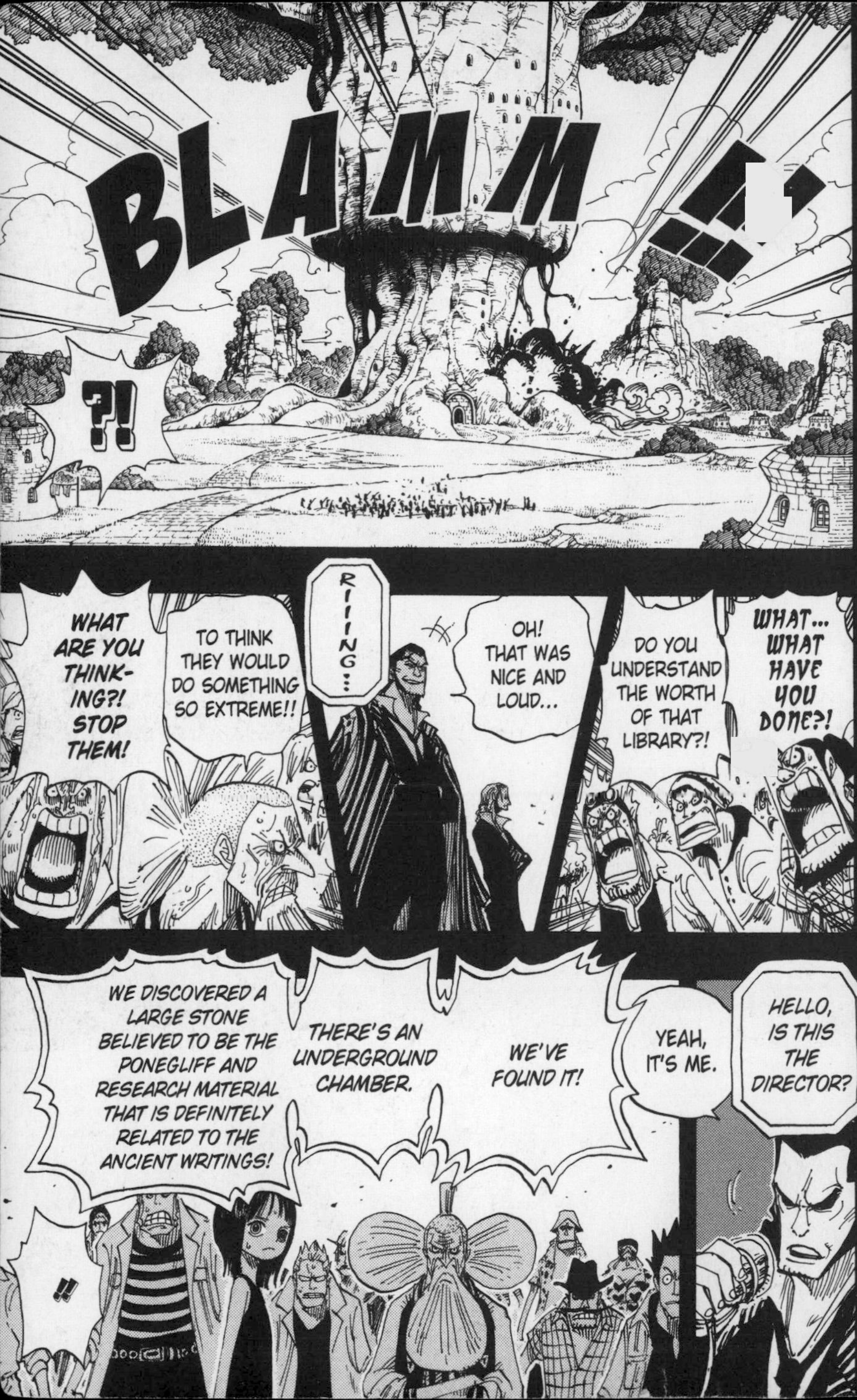
BLAMM!!
?!
WHAT... WHAT HAVE YOU DONE?!
DO YOU UNDERSTAND THE WORTH OF THAT LIBRARY?!
OH! THAT WAS NICE AND LOUD...
RIIING...
TO THINK THEY WOULD DO SOMETHING SO EXTREME!!
WHAT ARE YOU THINKING?! STOP THEM!
HELLO, IS THIS THE DIRECTOR?
YEAH, IT'S ME.
WE'VE FOUND IT!
THERE'S AN UNDERGROUND CHAMBER.
WE DISCOVERED A LARGE STONE BELIEVED TO BE THE PONEGLIFF AND RESEARCH MATERIAL THAT IS DEFINITELY RELATED TO THE ANCIENT WRITINGS!
!!

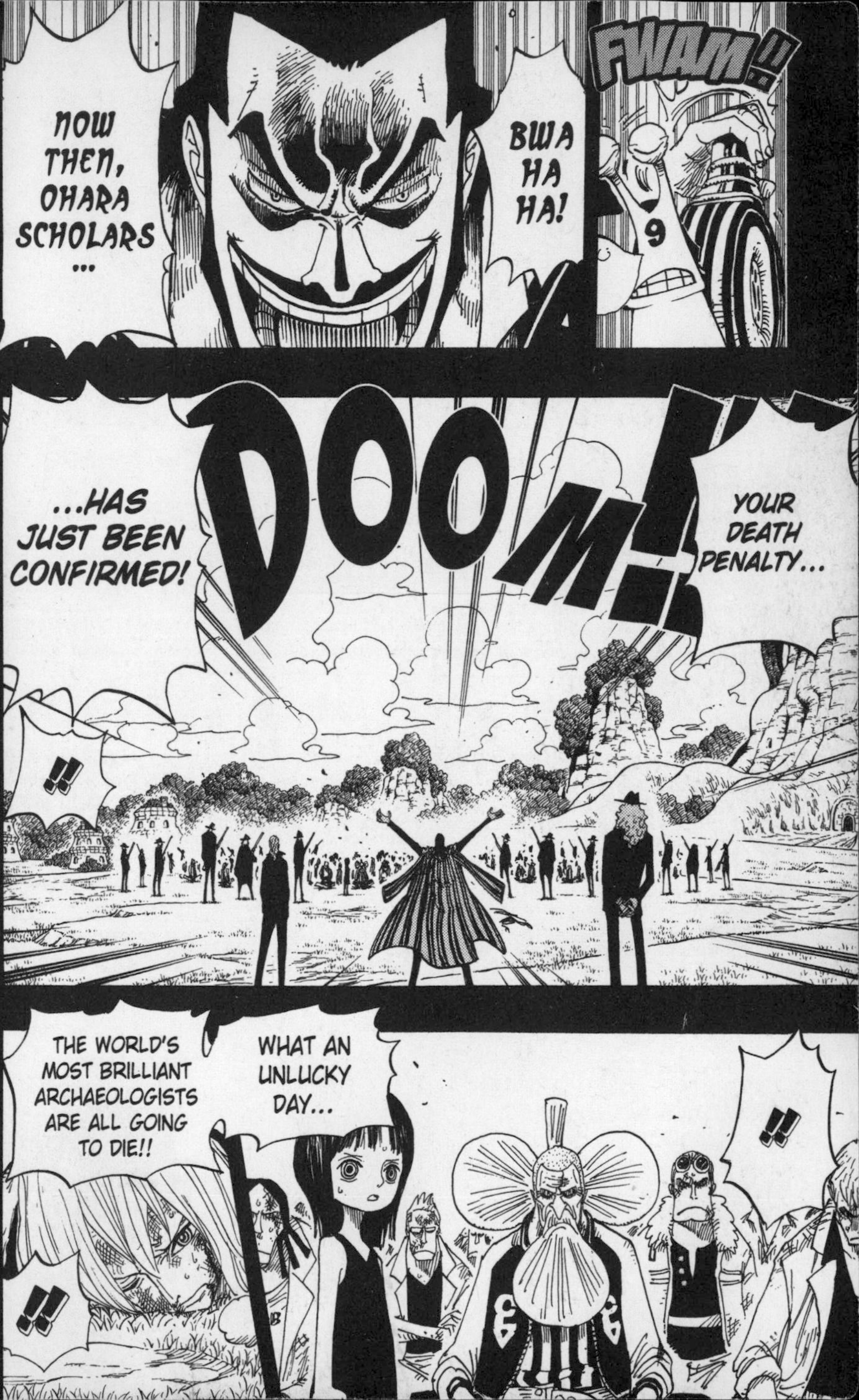
FWAM!!
BWA HA HA!
NOW THEN, OHARA SCHOLARS...
YOUR DEATH PENALTY...
DOOM!!
...HAS JUST BEEN CONFIRMED!
!!
!!
WHAT AN UNLUCKY DAY...
THE WORLD'S MOST BRILLIANT ARCHAEOLOGISTS ARE ALL GOING TO DIE!!
!!

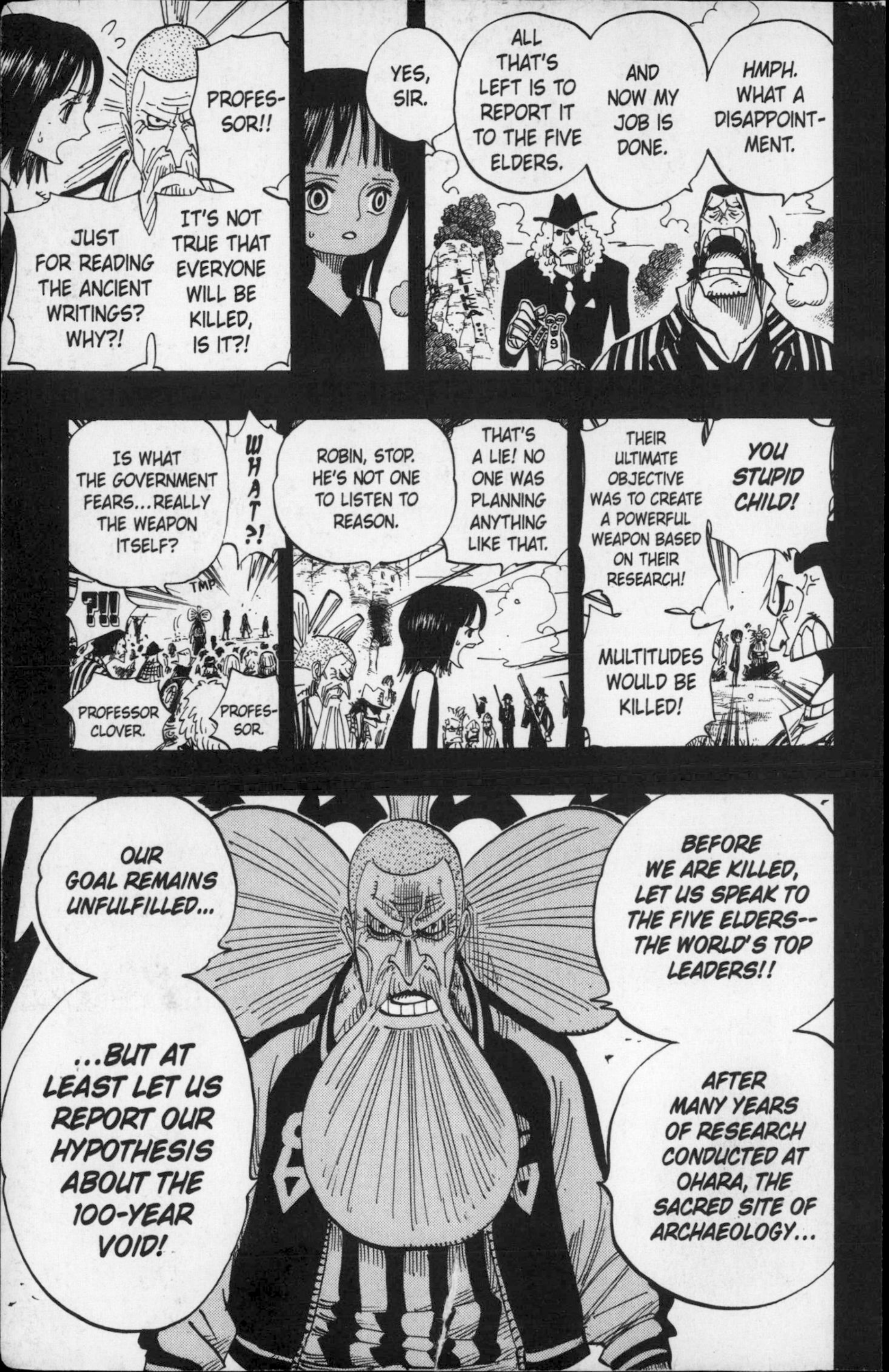
HMPH. WHAT A DISAPPOINTMENT.
AND NOW MY JOB IS DONE.
ALL THAT'S LEFT IS TO REPORT IT TO THE FIVE ELDERS.
YES, SIR.
PROFESSOR!!
IT'S NOT TRUE THAT EVERYONE WILL BE KILLED, IS IT?!
JUST FOR READING THE ANCIENT WRITINGS? WHY?!
YOU STUPID CHILD!
THEIR ULTIMATE OBJECTIVE WAS TO CREATE A POWERFUL WEAPON BASED ON THEIR RESEARCH!
MULTITUDES WOULD BE KILLED!
THAT'S A LIE! NO ONE WAS PLANNING ANYTHING LIKE THAT.
ROBIN, STOP. HE'S NOT ONE TO LISTEN TO REASON.
WHAT?!
IS WHAT THE GOVERNMENT FEARS...REALLY THE WEAPON ITSELF?
TMP
?!!
PROFESSOR.
PROFESSOR CLOVER.
BEFORE WE ARE KILLED, LET US SPEAK TO THE FIVE ELDERS-- THE WORLD'S TOP LEADERS!!
AFTER MANY YEARS OF RESEARCH CONDUCTED AT OHARA, THE SACRED SITE OF ARCHAEOLOGY...
OUR GOAL REMAINS UNFULFILLED...
...BUT AT LEAST LET US REPORT OUR HYPOTHESIS ABOUT THE 100-YEAR VOID!

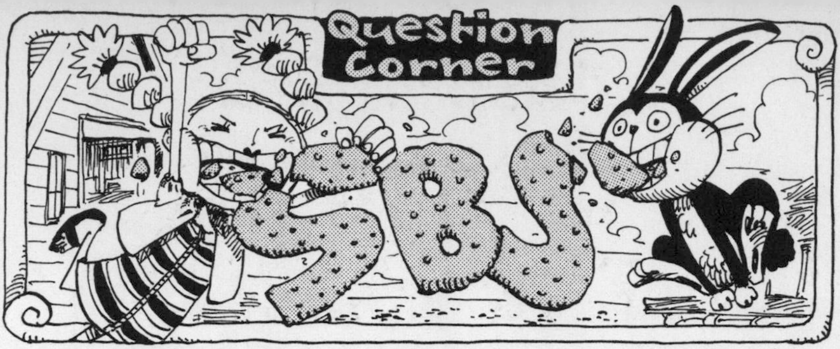
Question Corner
SBS

Q: Oda, I prepared some piping hot winter stew right before your very eyes. Anyway, please start. --Demomo

A: Wow! Winter stew is nice. Warms a person up.
Hot? It's not hot. Not this rice cake dumpling...
I can eat it in one bite. Agh!! H-H-Hot! Argh!!
H-H-Hot!! Ack!! Th-The inside of my mouth!!
The skin peeled off!!
There. How was that for a change?

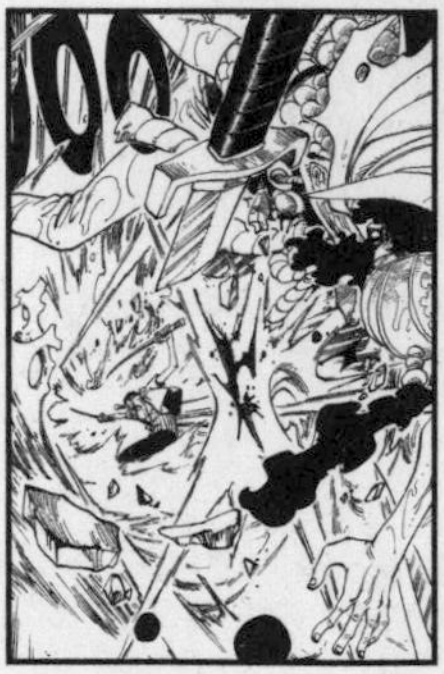

Q: I have a question for Odacchi! Recently in our house the following formula... "Bull Demon Courageous Talons" → Gyugyuzume → **Firmly Packed** "Charming Demon Sleepless Night" → Ebi mayone-zu onigiri → **Shrimp & Mayonnaise Rice Ball** ...has been theorized, but is it correct? --Hachikou

A: That's ridiculous... Uh...
I wouldn't use that kind of
word play. I-I really wouldn't.
Right, dear Zolo?
I wouldn't, right?

Zolo: N-nah. Uh... It's just
your imagination.

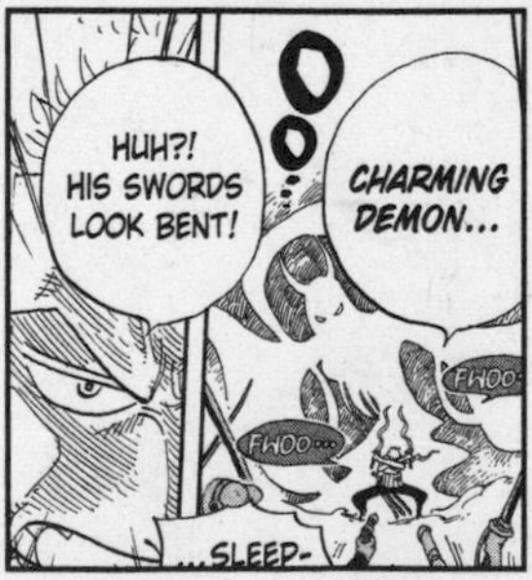
CHARMING DEMON...
HUH?! HIS SWORDS LOOK BENT!
FWOO-
FWOO...
...SLEEP-

A: You're not a good liar!

Chapter 395: OHARA VS. THE WORLD GOVERNMENT

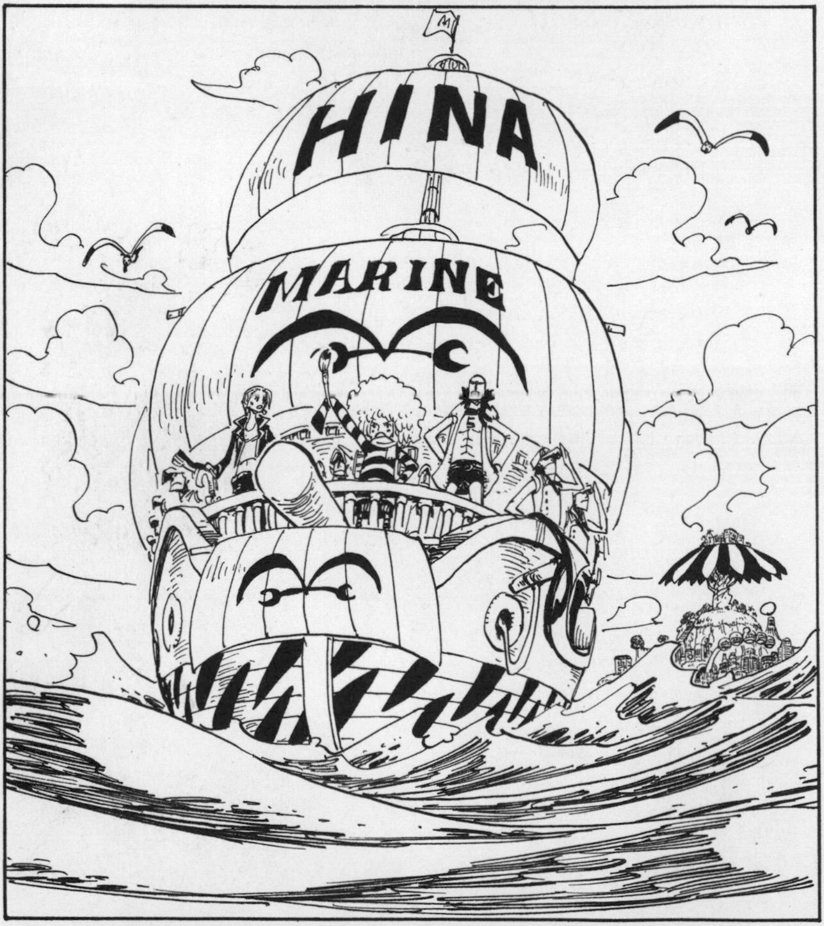
HINA
MARINE

MS. GOLDEN WEEK'S PLAN, A BAROQUE REUNION, VOL. 27:
"TAKING OVER THE SHIP WITH 'BETRAYAL BLACK'"

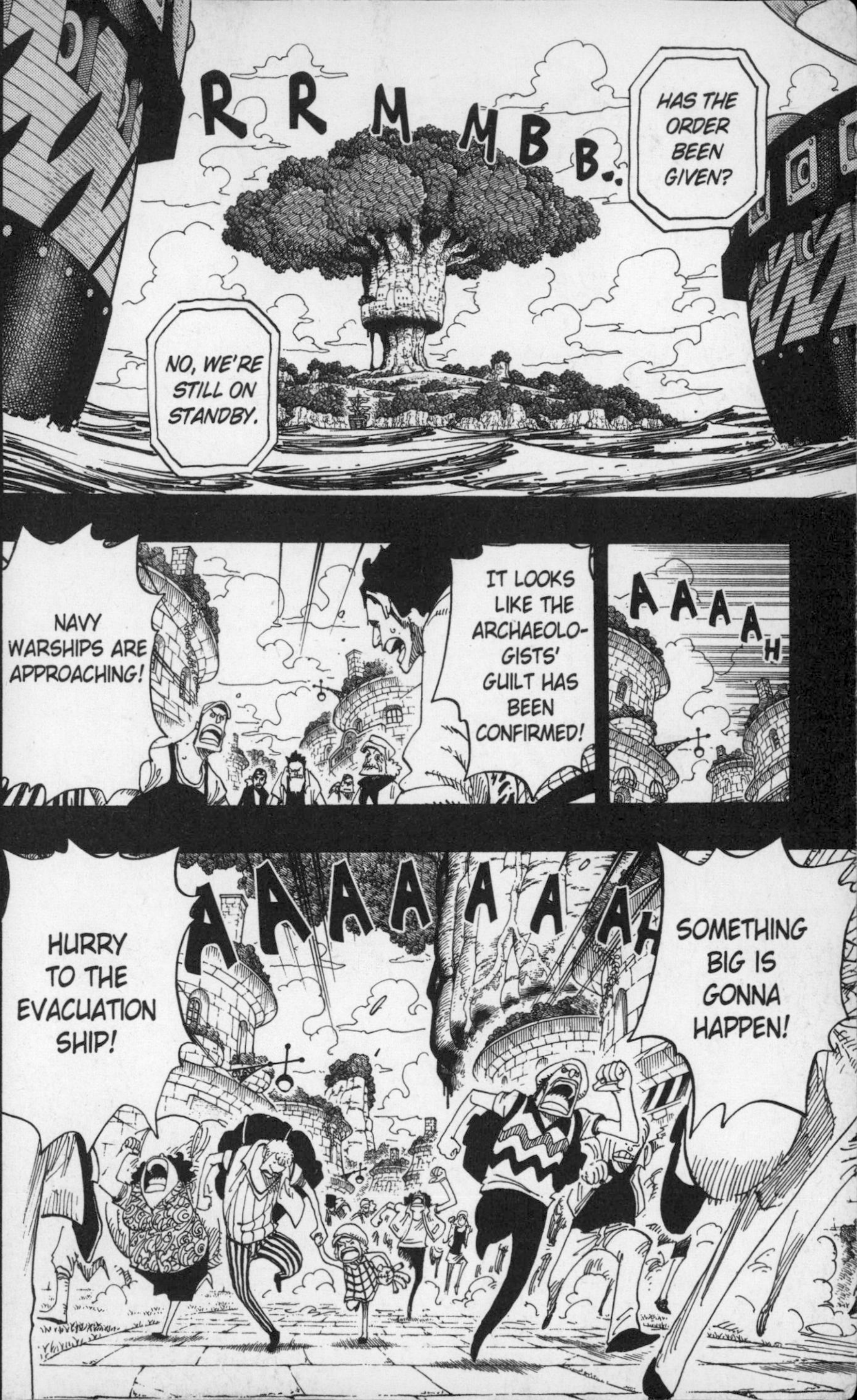
RRMMBB..
HAS THE ORDER BEEN GIVEN?
NO, WE'RE STILL ON STANDBY.
AAAAH
IT LOOKS LIKE THE ARCHAEOLO-GISTS' GUILT HAS BEEN CONFIRMED!
NAVY WARSHIPS ARE APPROACHING!
SOMETHING BIG IS GONNA HAPPEN!
AAAAAAAH
HURRY TO THE EVACUATION SHIP!

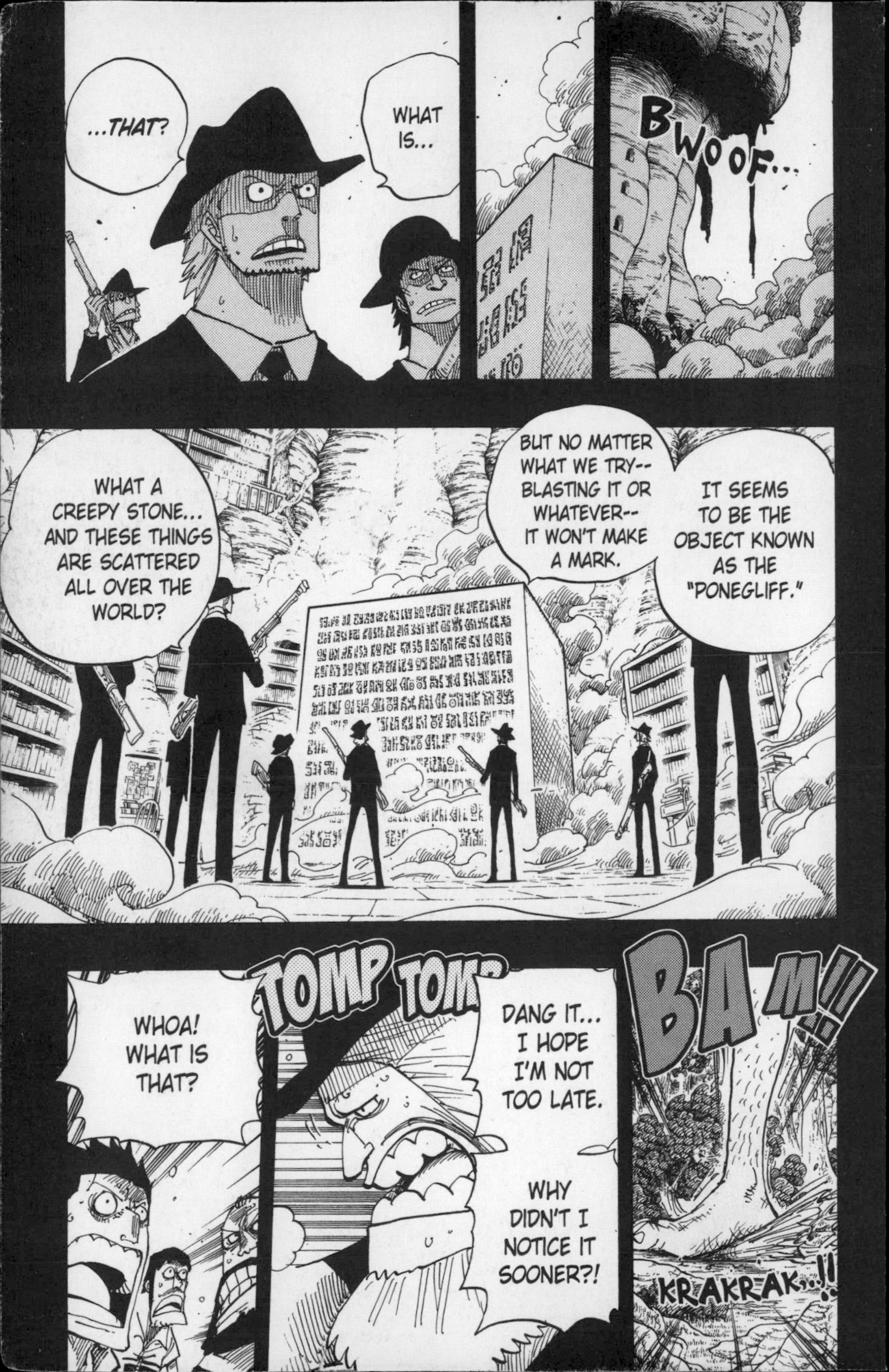
BWOOF...
WHAT IS...
...THAT?
IT SEEMS TO BE THE OBJECT KNOWN AS THE "PONEGLIFF."
BUT NO MATTER WHAT WE TRY-- BLASTING IT OR WHATEVER-- IT WON'T MAKE A MARK.
WHAT A CREEPY STONE... AND THESE THINGS ARE SCATTERED ALL OVER THE WORLD?
BAM!!
KRAKRAK...!!
TOMP TOM
DANG IT... I HOPE I'M NOT TOO LATE.
WHY DIDN'T I NOTICE IT SOONER?!
WHOA! WHAT IS THAT?

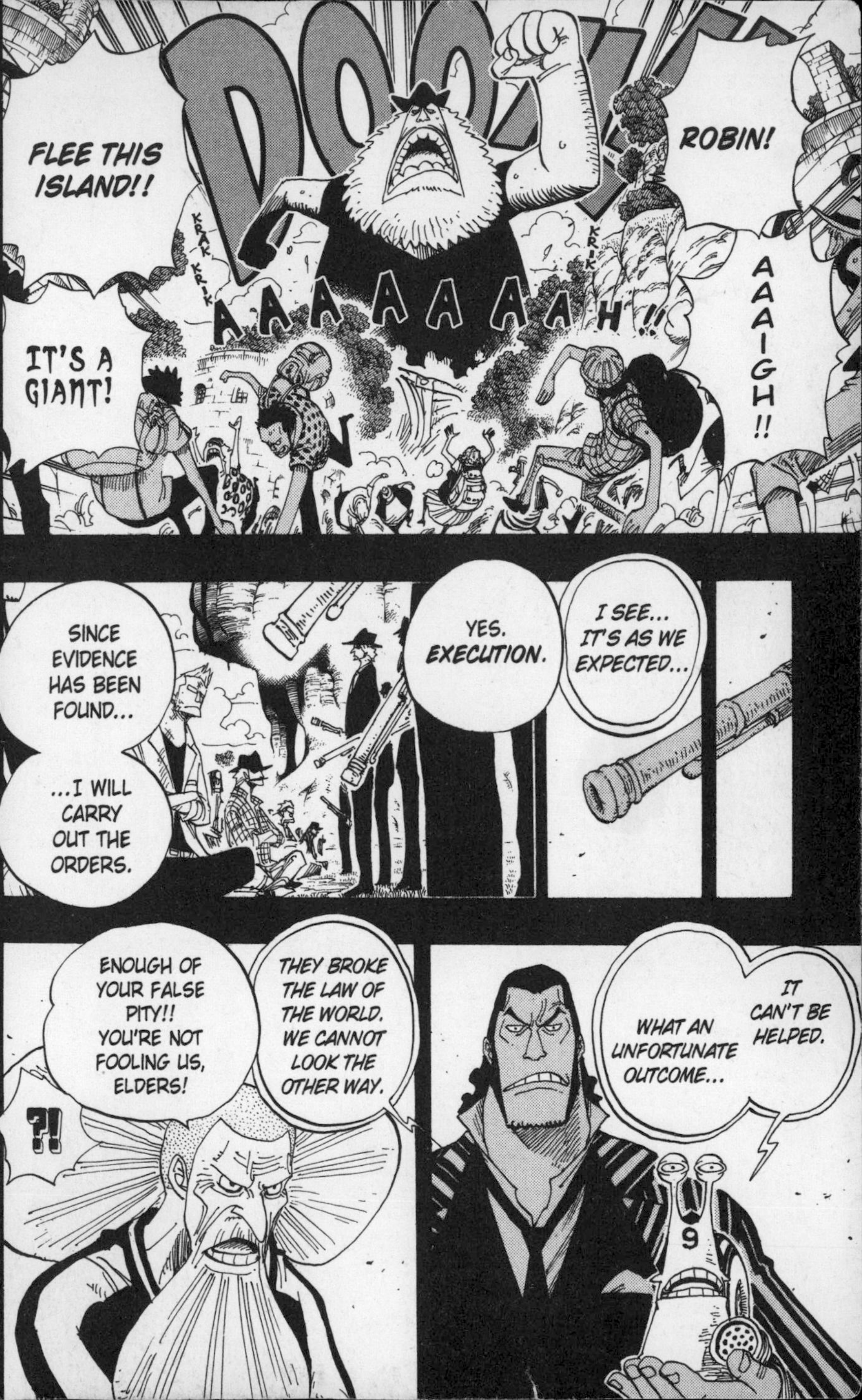
ROBIN!
FLEE THIS ISLAND!!
KRIK
KRAK KRIK
AAAAAAAAH!!
AAAIGH!!
IT'S A GIANT!
I SEE... IT'S AS WE EXPECTED...
YES. EXECUTION.
SINCE EVIDENCE HAS BEEN FOUND...
...I WILL CARRY OUT THE ORDERS.
IT CAN'T BE HELPED.
WHAT AN UNFORTUNATE OUTCOME...
THEY BROKE THE LAW OF THE WORLD. WE CANNOT LOOK THE OTHER WAY.
ENOUGH OF YOUR FALSE PITY!! YOU'RE NOT FOOLING US, ELDERS!
?!

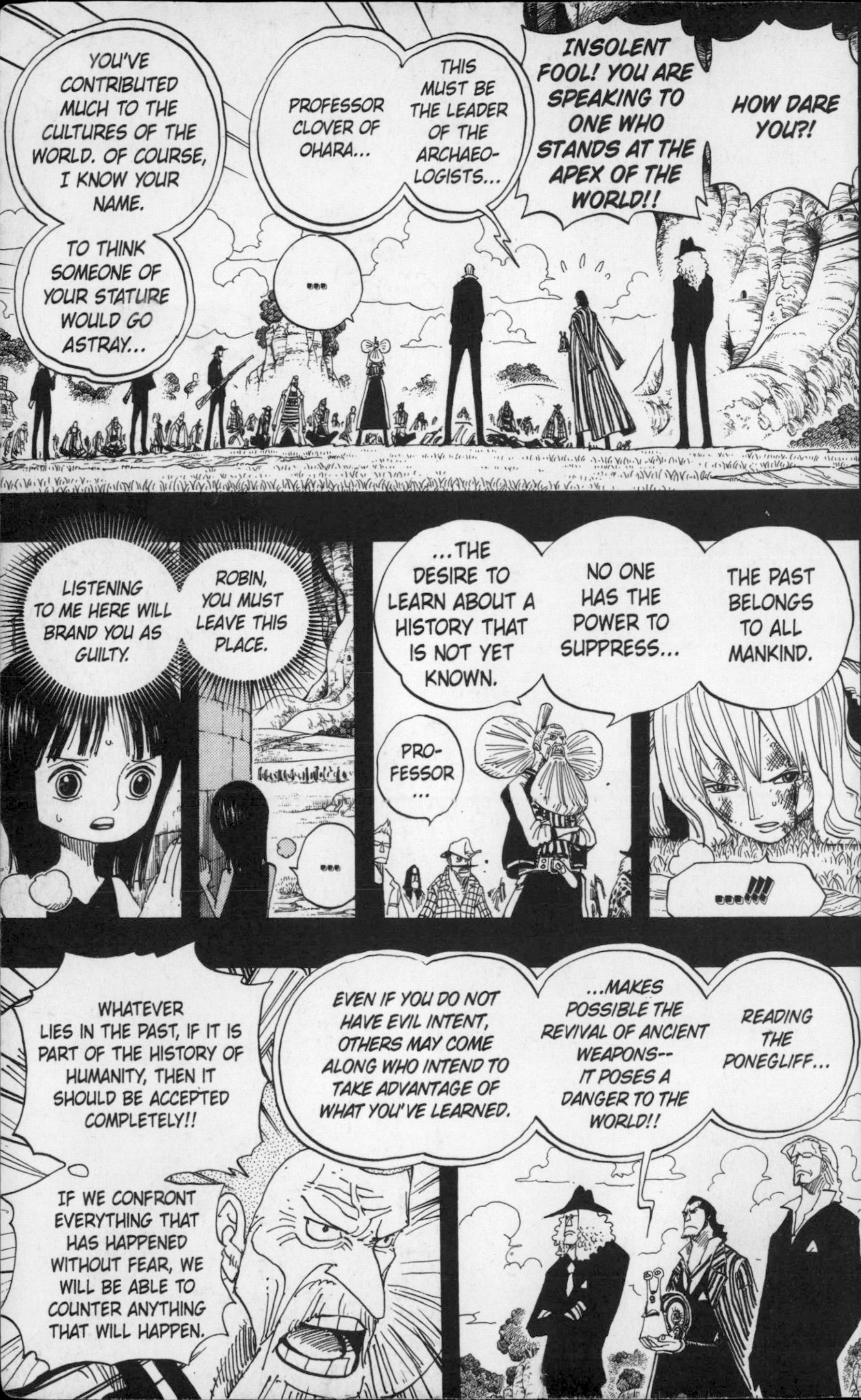
HOW DARE YOU?!
INSOLENT FOOL! YOU ARE SPEAKING TO ONE WHO STANDS AT THE APEX OF THE WORLD!!
THIS MUST BE THE LEADER OF THE ARCHAEO-LOGISTS...
PROFESSOR CLOVER OF OHARA...
...
YOU'VE CONTRIBUTED MUCH TO THE CULTURES OF THE WORLD. OF COURSE, I KNOW YOUR NAME.
TO THINK SOMEONE OF YOUR STATURE WOULD GO ASTRAY...
THE PAST BELONGS TO ALL MANKIND.
...!!!
NO ONE HAS THE POWER TO SUPPRESS...
...THE DESIRE TO LEARN ABOUT A HISTORY THAT IS NOT YET KNOWN.
PRO-FESSOR ...
ROBIN, YOU MUST LEAVE THIS PLACE.
LISTENING TO ME HERE WILL BRAND YOU AS GUILTY.
...
READING THE PONEGLIFF...
...MAKES POSSIBLE THE REVIVAL OF ANCIENT WEAPONS-- IT POSES A DANGER TO THE WORLD!!
EVEN IF YOU DO NOT HAVE EVIL INTENT, OTHERS MAY COME ALONG WHO INTEND TO TAKE ADVANTAGE OF WHAT YOU'VE LEARNED.
WHATEVER LIES IN THE PAST, IF IT IS PART OF THE HISTORY OF HUMANITY, THEN IT SHOULD BE ACCEPTED COMPLETELY!!
IF WE CONFRONT EVERYTHING THAT HAS HAPPENED WITHOUT FEAR, WE WILL BE ABLE TO COUNTER ANYTHING THAT WILL HAPPEN.

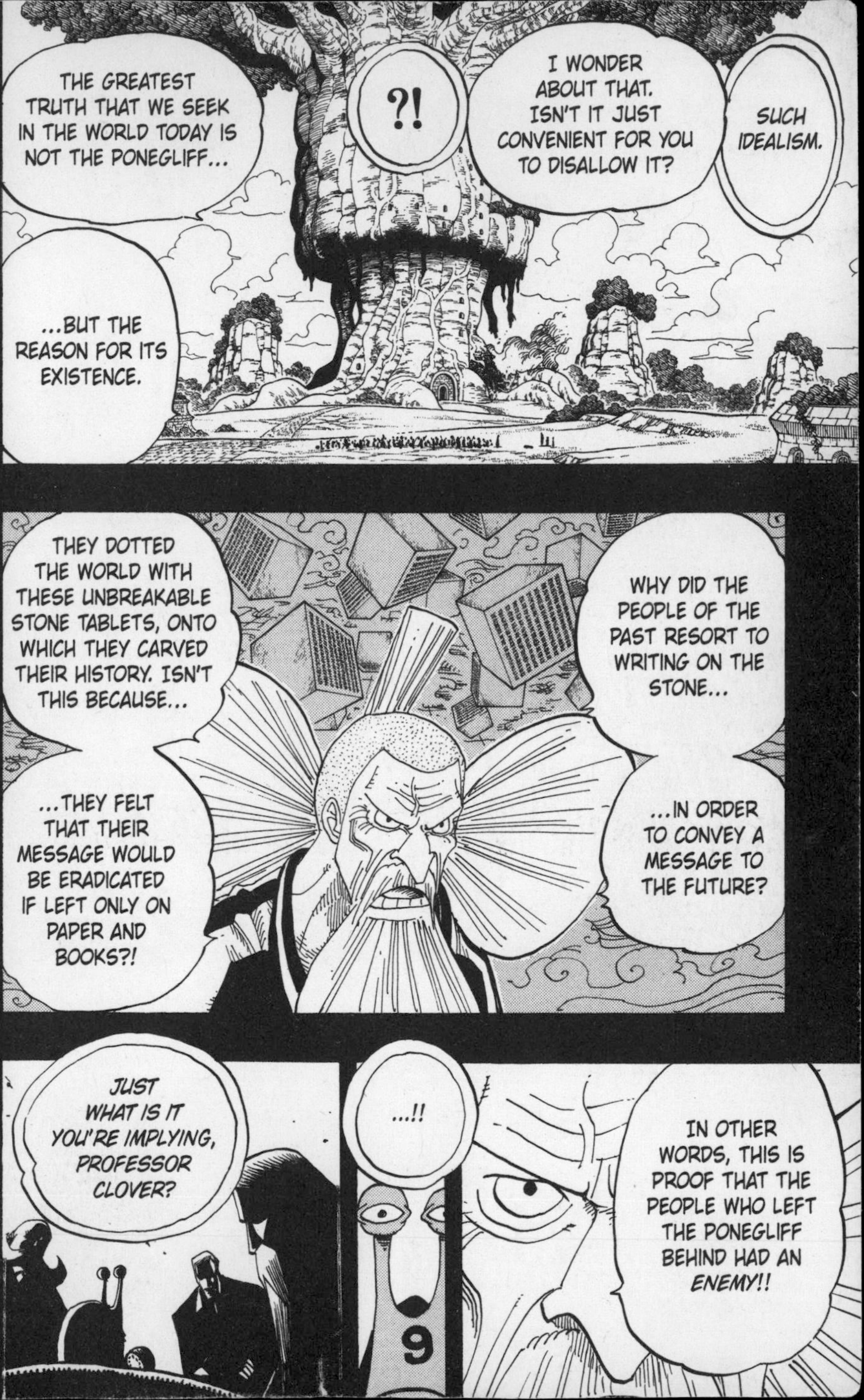
SUCH IDEALISM.
I WONDER ABOUT THAT. ISN'T IT JUST CONVENIENT FOR YOU TO DISALLOW IT?
?!
THE GREATEST TRUTH THAT WE SEEK IN THE WORLD TODAY IS NOT THE PONEGLIFF...
...BUT THE REASON FOR ITS EXISTENCE.
WHY DID THE PEOPLE OF THE PAST RESORT TO WRITING ON THE STONE...
...IN ORDER TO CONVEY A MESSAGE TO THE FUTURE?
THEY DOTTED THE WORLD WITH THESE UNBREAKABLE STONE TABLETS, ONTO WHICH THEY CARVED THEIR HISTORY. ISN'T THIS BECAUSE...
...THEY FELT THAT THEIR MESSAGE WOULD BE ERADICATED IF LEFT ONLY ON PAPER AND BOOKS?!
IN OTHER WORDS, THIS IS PROOF THAT THE PEOPLE WHO LEFT THE PONEGLIFF BEHIND HAD AN *ENEMY*!!
...!!
JUST WHAT IS IT YOU'RE IMPLYING, PROFESSOR CLOVER?

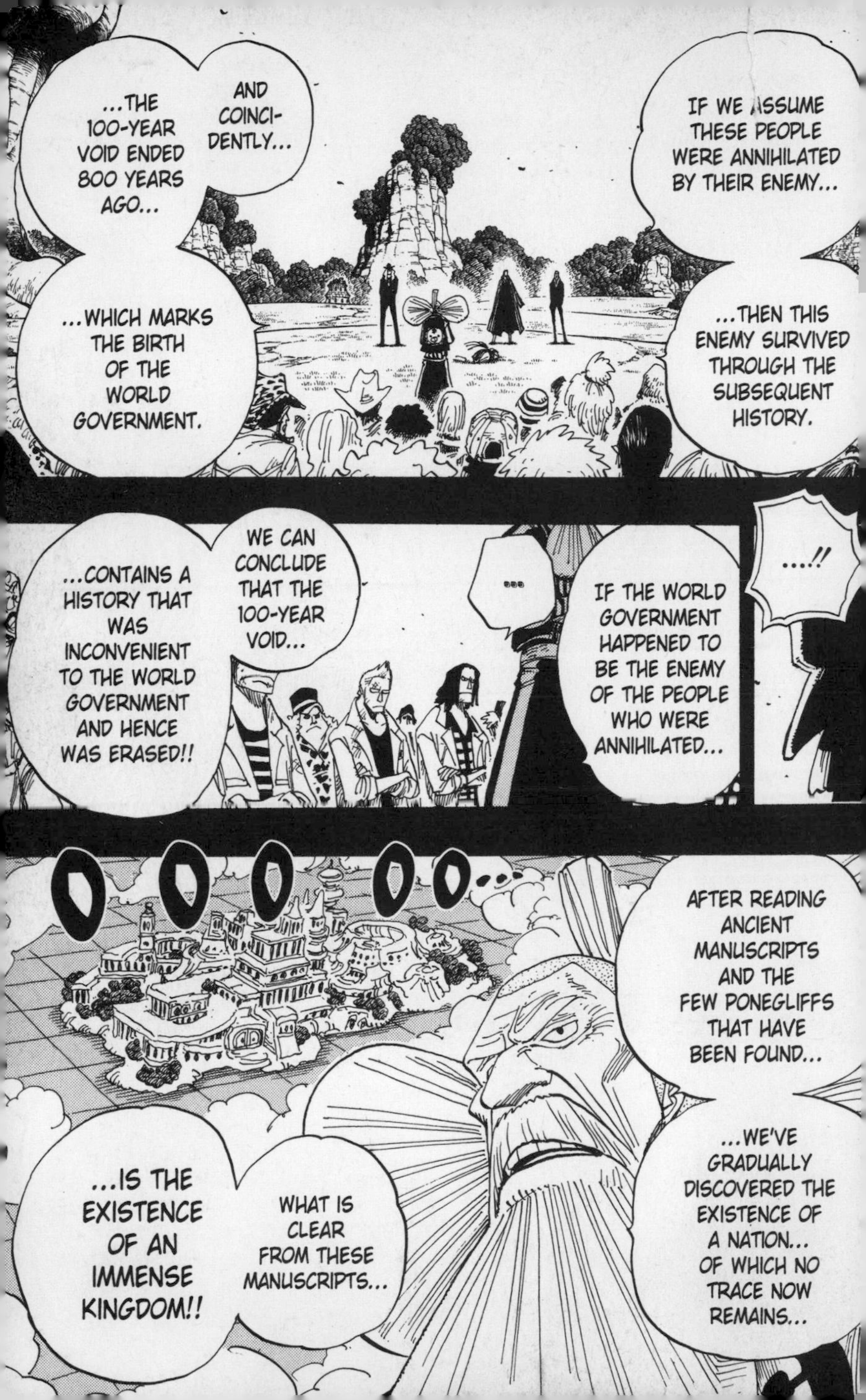

IF WE ASSUME THESE PEOPLE WERE ANNIHILATED BY THEIR ENEMY...
...THEN THIS ENEMY SURVIVED THROUGH THE SUBSEQUENT HISTORY.
AND COINCI-DENTLY...
...THE 100-YEAR VOID ENDED 800 YEARS AGO...
...WHICH MARKS THE BIRTH OF THE WORLD GOVERNMENT.
...!!
IF THE WORLD GOVERNMENT HAPPENED TO BE THE ENEMY OF THE PEOPLE WHO WERE ANNIHILATED...
...
WE CAN CONCLUDE THAT THE 100-YEAR VOID...
...CONTAINS A HISTORY THAT WAS INCONVENIENT TO THE WORLD GOVERNMENT AND HENCE WAS ERASED!!
AFTER READING ANCIENT MANUSCRIPTS AND THE FEW PONEGLIFFS THAT HAVE BEEN FOUND...
...WE'VE GRADUALLY DISCOVERED THE EXISTENCE OF A NATION... OF WHICH NO TRACE NOW REMAINS...
OOOOO...
WHAT IS CLEAR FROM THESE MANUSCRIPTS...
...IS THE EXISTENCE OF AN IMMENSE KINGDOM!!

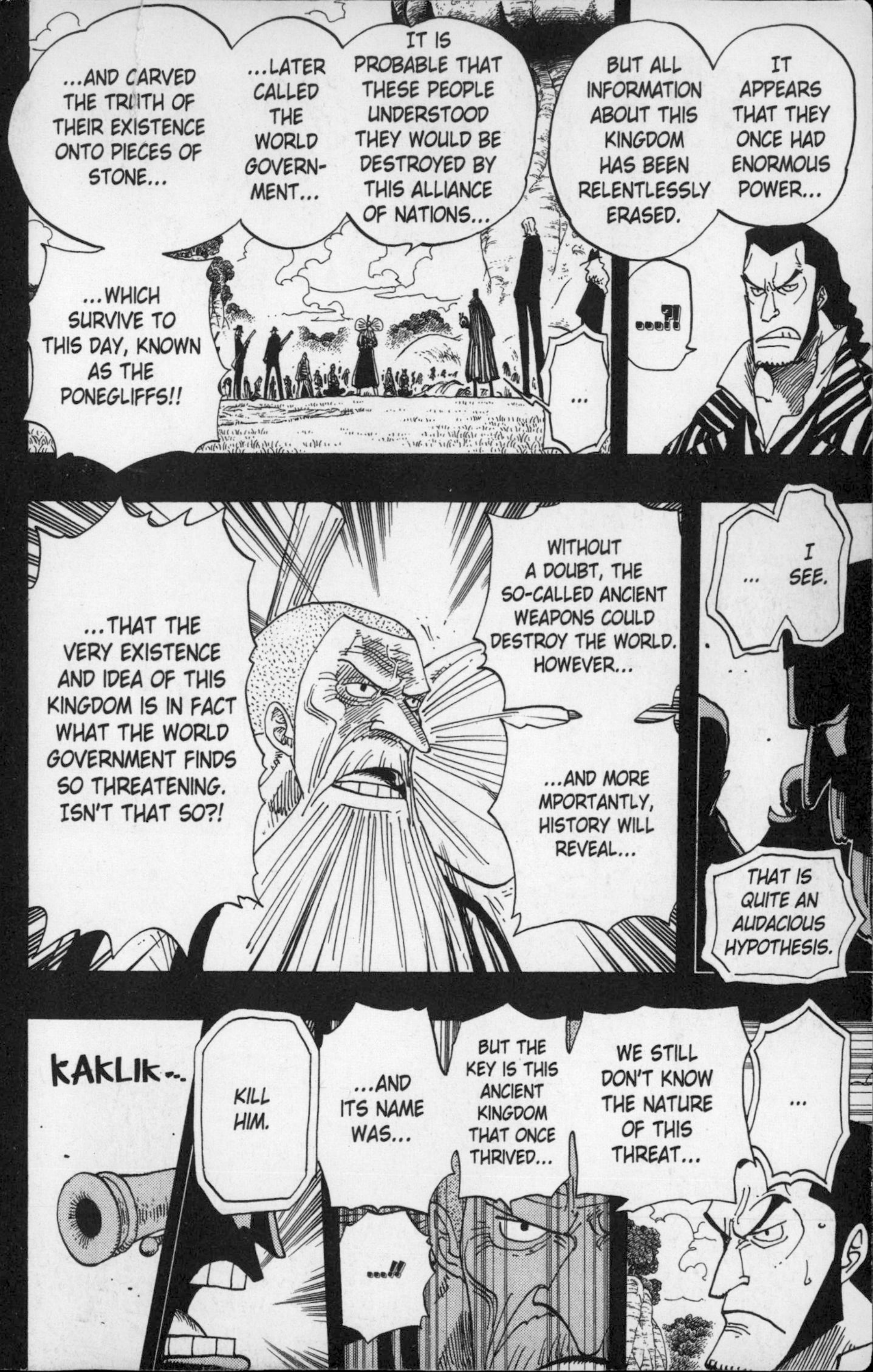
IT APPEARS THAT THEY ONCE HAD ENORMOUS POWER...
BUT ALL INFORMATION ABOUT THIS KINGDOM HAS BEEN RELENTLESSLY ERASED.
...?!
...
IT IS PROBABLE THAT THESE PEOPLE UNDERSTOOD THEY WOULD BE DESTROYED BY THIS ALLIANCE OF NATIONS...
...LATER CALLED THE WORLD GOVERNMENT...
...AND CARVED THE TRUTH OF THEIR EXISTENCE ONTO PIECES OF STONE...
...WHICH SURVIVE TO THIS DAY, KNOWN AS THE PONEGLIFFS!!
... I SEE.
THAT IS QUITE AN AUDACIOUS HYPOTHESIS.
WITHOUT A DOUBT, THE SO-CALLED ANCIENT WEAPONS COULD DESTROY THE WORLD. HOWEVER...
...AND MORE MPORTANTLY, HISTORY WILL REVEAL...
...THAT THE VERY EXISTENCE AND IDEA OF THIS KINGDOM IS IN FACT WHAT THE WORLD GOVERNMENT FINDS SO THREATENING. ISN'T THAT SO?!
...
WE STILL DON'T KNOW THE NATURE OF THIS THREAT...
BUT THE KEY IS THIS ANCIENT KINGDOM THAT ONCE THRIVED...
...AND ITS NAME WAS...
...!!
KILL HIM.
KAKLIK--

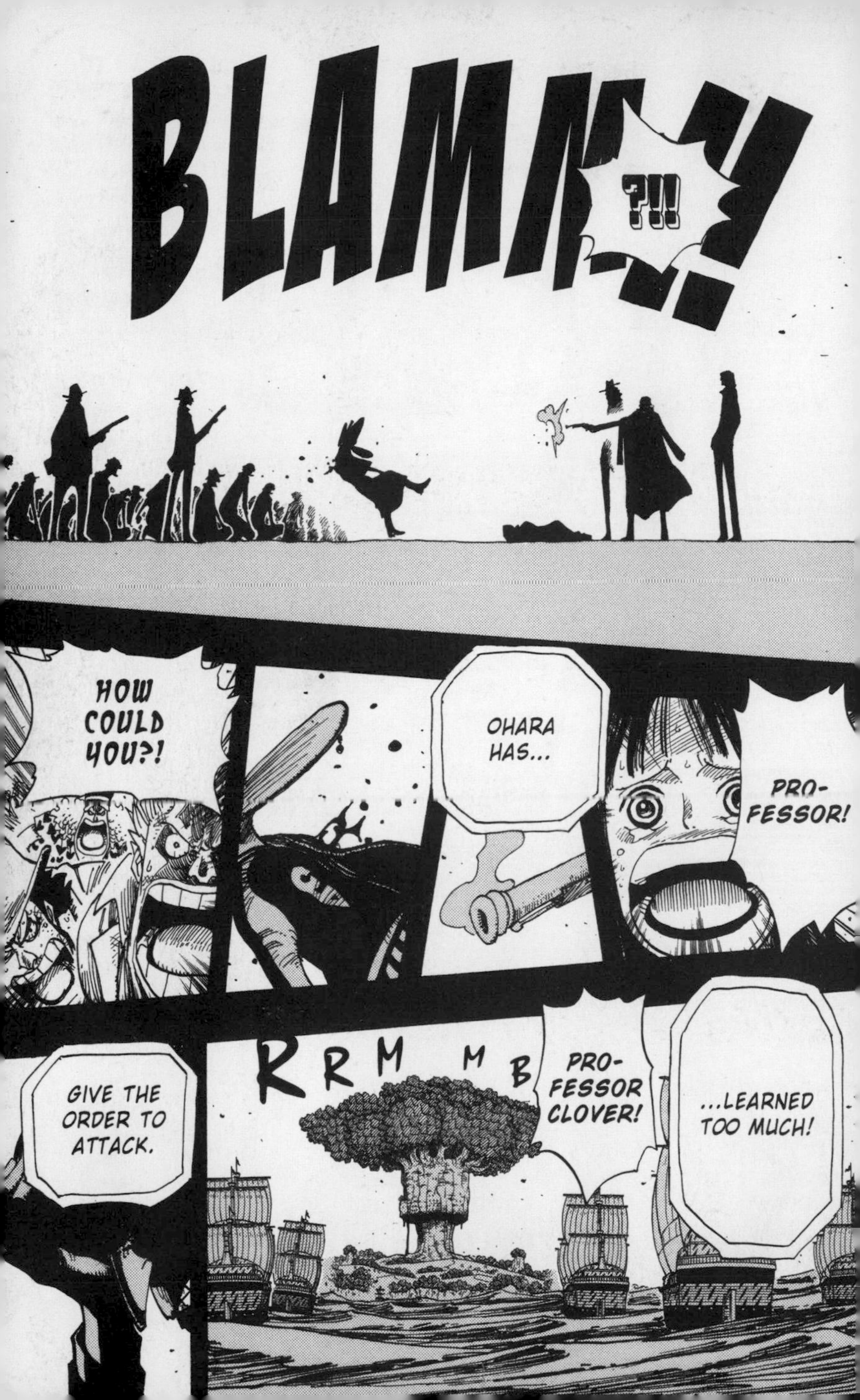
BLAMM
?!!
PRO-FESSOR!
OHARA HAS...
HOW COULD YOU?!
...LEARNED TOO MUCH!
PRO-FESSOR CLOVER!
RRMMB
GIVE THE ORDER TO ATTACK.

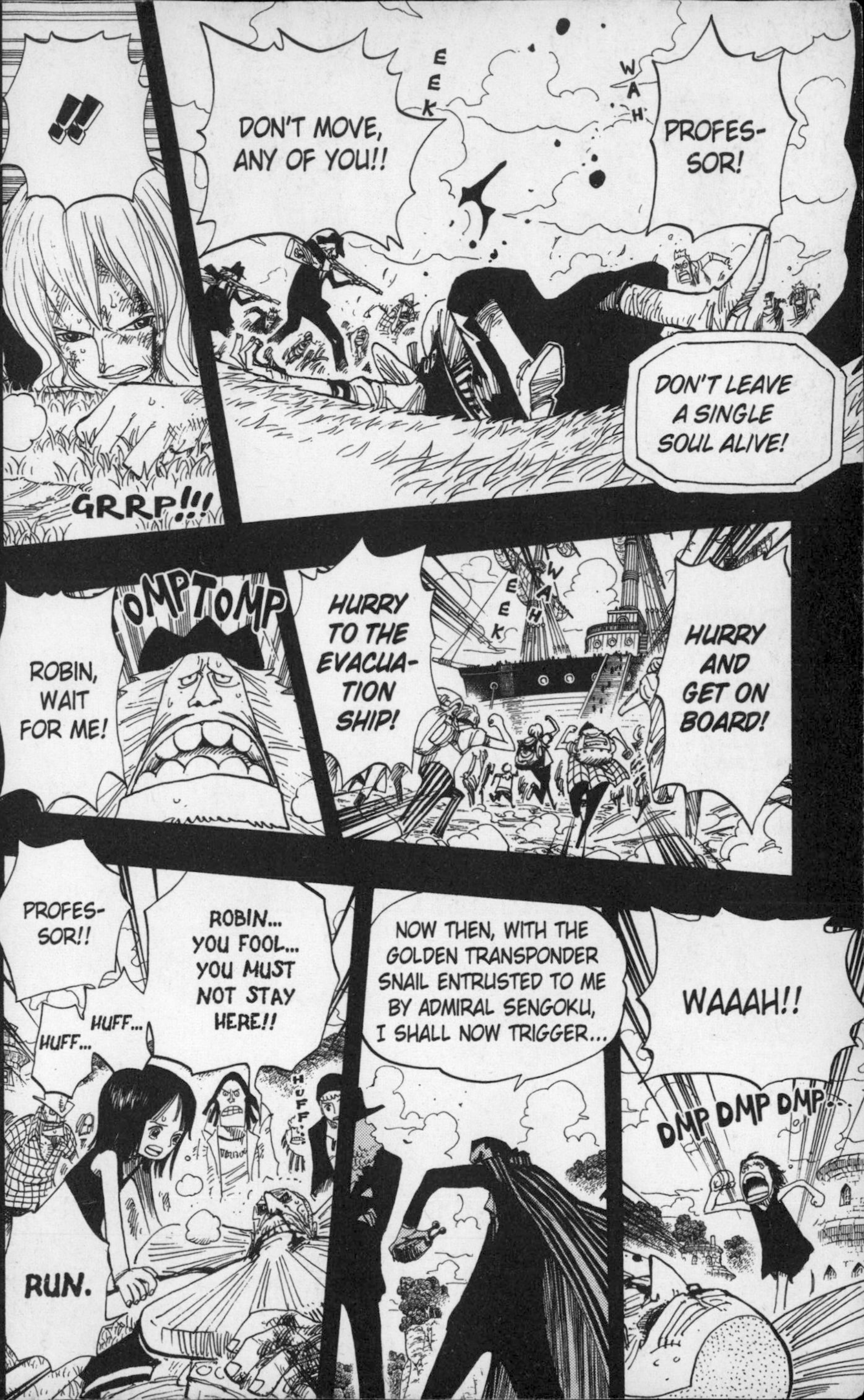
PROFES-SOR!
WAH
EEK
DON'T MOVE, ANY OF YOU!!
DON'T LEAVE A SINGLE SOUL ALIVE!
!!
GRRP!!!
HURRY AND GET ON BOARD!
WAH
EEK
HURRY TO THE EVACUATION SHIP!
OMPTOMP
ROBIN, WAIT FOR ME!
WAAAH!!
DMP DMP DMP...
NOW THEN, WITH THE GOLDEN TRANSPONDER SNAIL ENTRUSTED TO ME BY ADMIRAL SENGOKU, I SHALL NOW TRIGGER...
ROBIN... YOU FOOL... YOU MUST NOT STAY HERE!!
PROFES-SOR!!
HUFF... HUFF...
HUFF...
RUN.

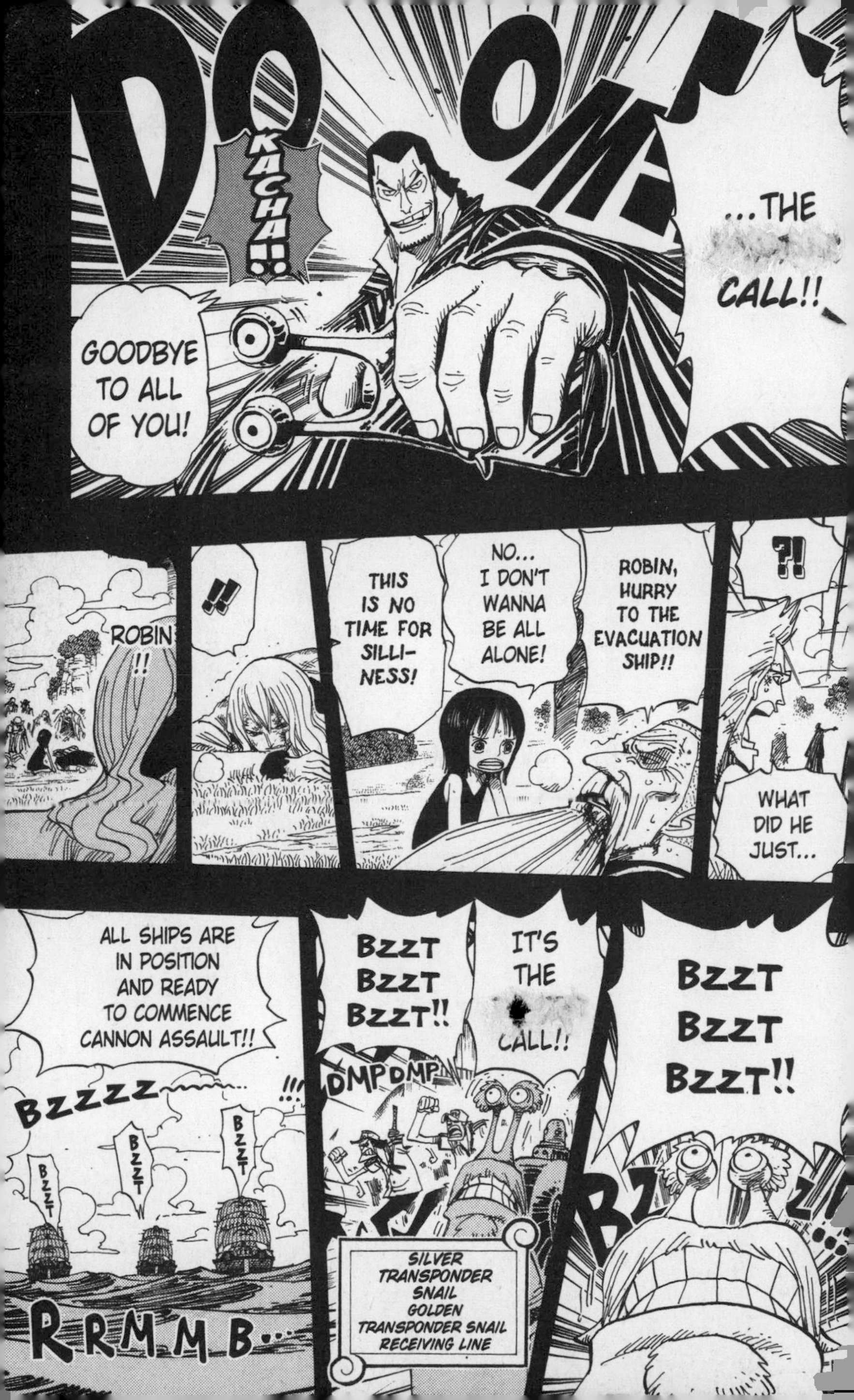
...THE
CALL!!
KACHA!!
GOODBYE TO ALL OF YOU!
?!
WHAT DID HE JUST...
ROBIN, HURRY TO THE EVACUATION SHIP!!
NO... I DON'T WANNA BE ALL ALONE!
THIS IS NO TIME FOR SILLINESS!
!!
ROBIN!!
BZZT BZZT BZZT!!
BZ...Z...
IT'S THE
CALL!!
BZZT BZZT BZZT!!
DMP DMP
SILVER TRANSPONDER SNAIL
GOLDEN TRANSPONDER SNAIL RECEIVING LINE
ALL SHIPS ARE IN POSITION AND READY TO COMMENCE CANNON ASSAULT!!
!!
BZZZZ...
BZZT
BZZT
BZZT
RRMMB...

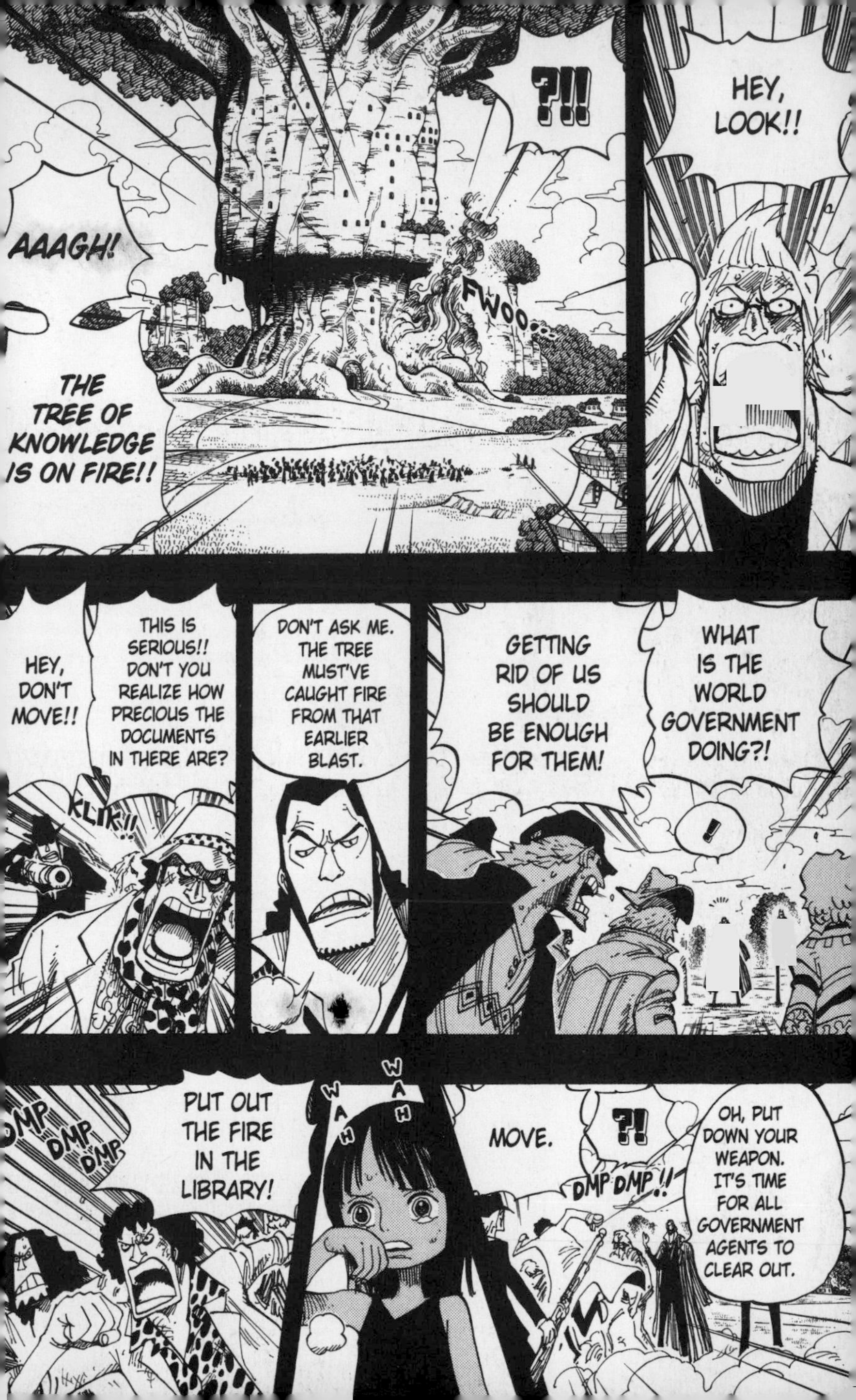
HEY, LOOK!!
?!!
AAAGH!
FWOO...
THE TREE OF KNOWLEDGE IS ON FIRE!!
WHAT IS THE WORLD GOVERNMENT DOING?!
GETTING RID OF US SHOULD BE ENOUGH FOR THEM!
!
DON'T ASK ME. THE TREE MUST'VE CAUGHT FIRE FROM THAT EARLIER BLAST.
THIS IS SERIOUS!! DON'T YOU REALIZE HOW PRECIOUS THE DOCUMENTS IN THERE ARE?
HEY, DON'T MOVE!!
KLIK!!
OH, PUT DOWN YOUR WEAPON. IT'S TIME FOR ALL GOVERNMENT AGENTS TO CLEAR OUT.
?!
DMP DMP!!
MOVE.
WAH WAH
WAH
PUT OUT THE FIRE IN THE LIBRARY!
DMP DMP DMP

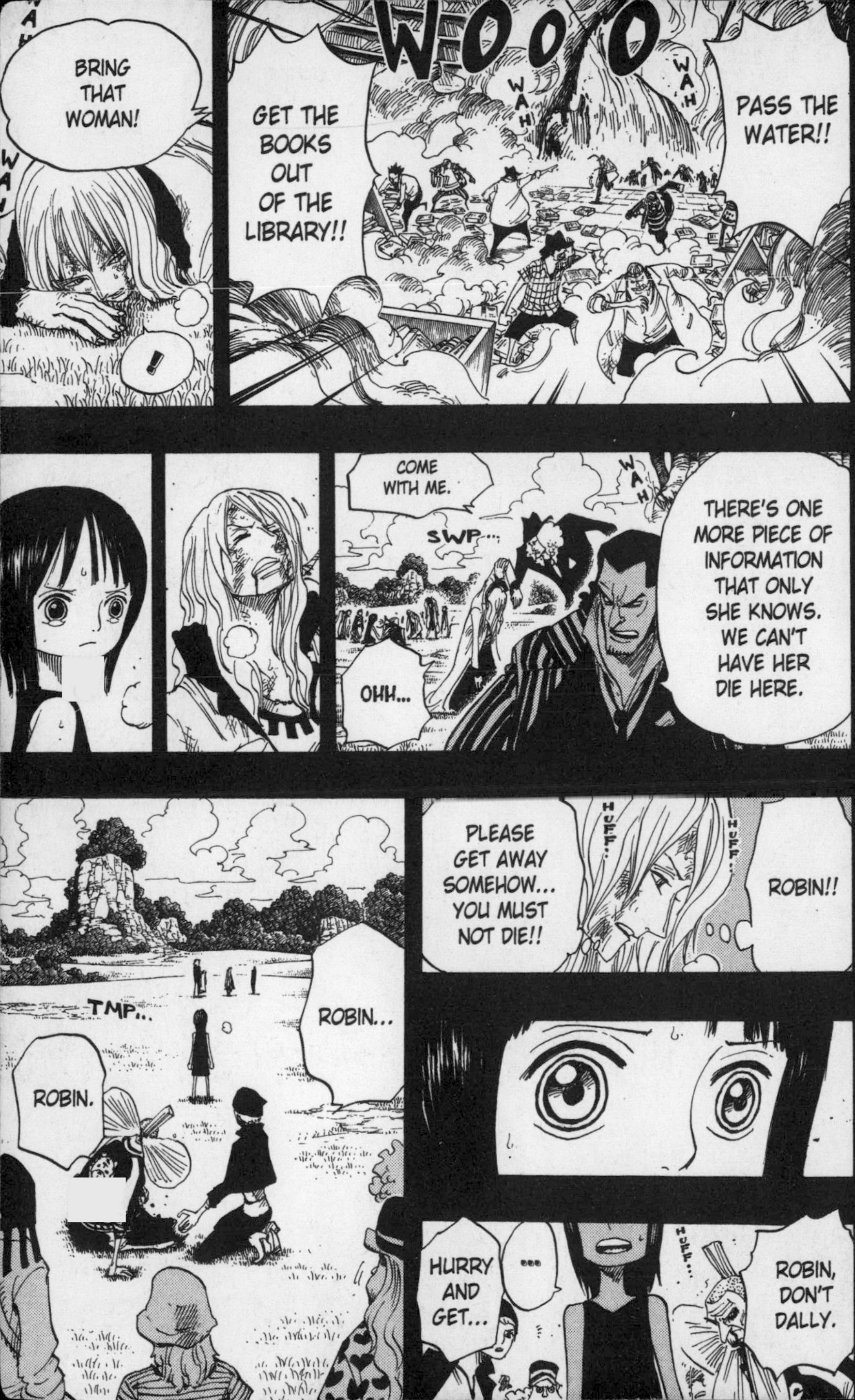
WOOO
WAH
PASS THE WATER!!
WAH
GET THE BOOKS OUT OF THE LIBRARY!!
WAH
BRING THAT WOMAN!
WAH
!
THERE'S ONE MORE PIECE OF INFORMATION THAT ONLY SHE KNOWS. WE CAN'T HAVE HER DIE HERE.
WAH
COME WITH ME.
SWP...
OHH...
ROBIN!!
HUFF...
HUFF...
PLEASE GET AWAY SOMEHOW... YOU MUST NOT DIE!!
ROBIN, DON'T DALLY.
HUFF...
...
HURRY AND GET...
ROBIN...
TMP..
ROBIN.

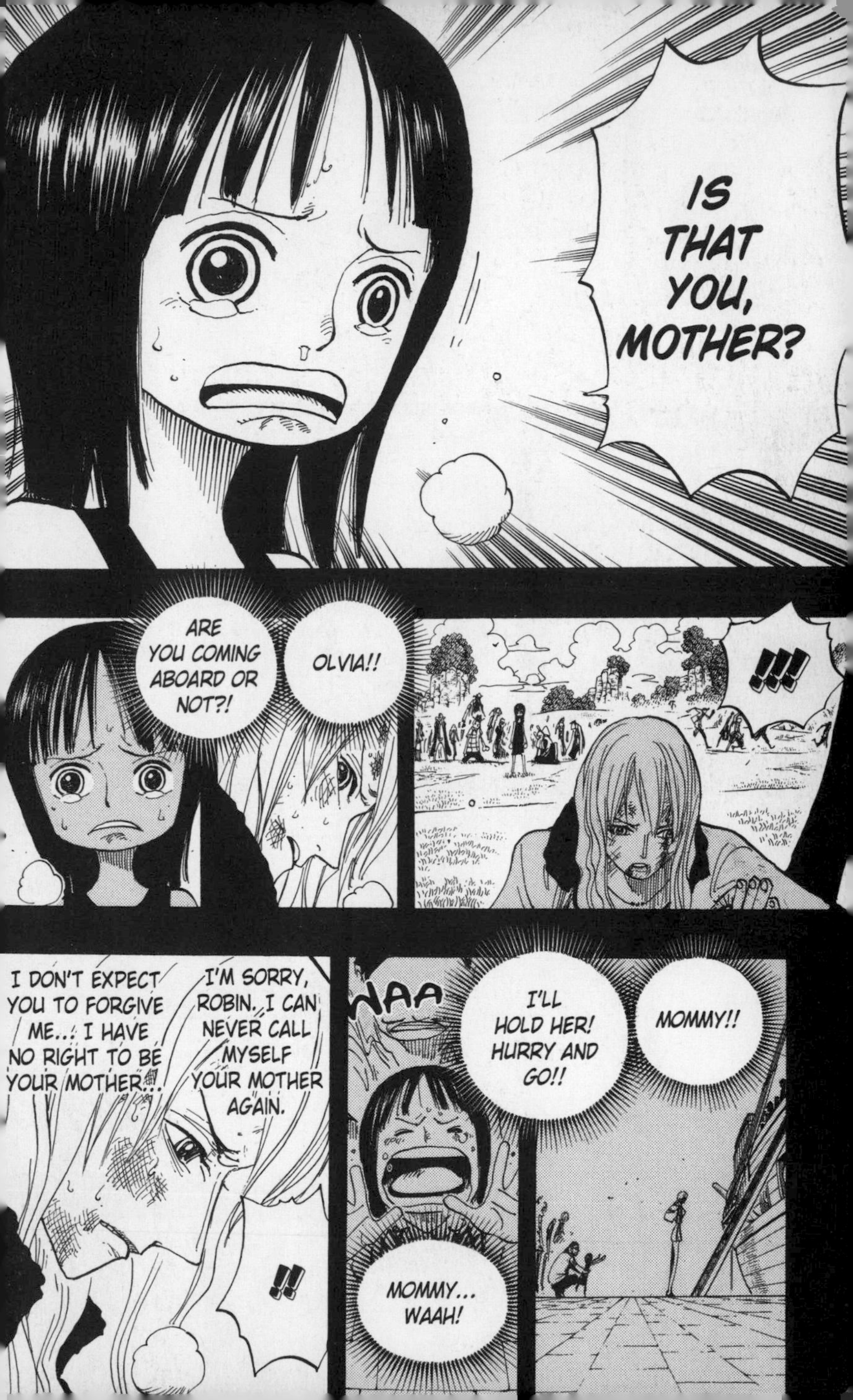
IS THAT YOU, MOTHER?
!!!
OLVIA!!
ARE YOU COMING ABOARD OR NOT?!
MOMMY!!
I'LL HOLD HER! HURRY AND GO!!
WAA
MOMMY... WAAH!
I'M SORRY, ROBIN. I CAN NEVER CALL MYSELF YOUR MOTHER AGAIN.
I DON'T EXPECT YOU TO FORGIVE ME... I HAVE NO RIGHT TO BE YOUR MOTHER...
!!

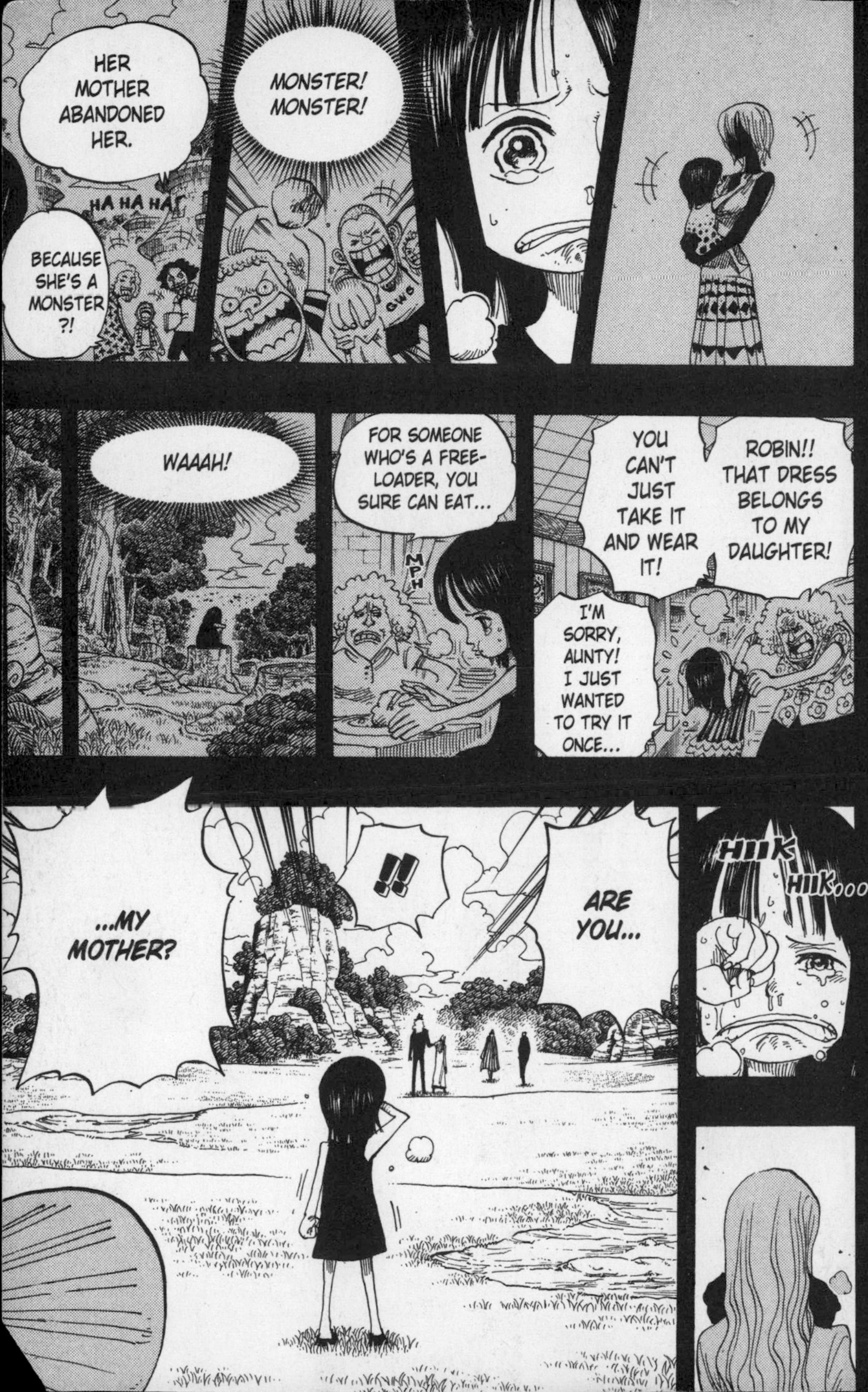
MONSTER! MONSTER!
HER MOTHER ABANDONED HER.
HA HA HA
BECAUSE SHE'S A MONSTER ?!
ROBIN!! THAT DRESS BELONGS TO MY DAUGHTER!
YOU CAN'T JUST TAKE IT AND WEAR IT!
I'M SORRY, AUNTY! I JUST WANTED TO TRY IT ONCE...
FOR SOMEONE WHO'S A FREE-LOADER, YOU SURE CAN EAT...
MPH
WAAAH!
HIIK
HIIKooo
!!
ARE YOU...
...MY MOTHER?

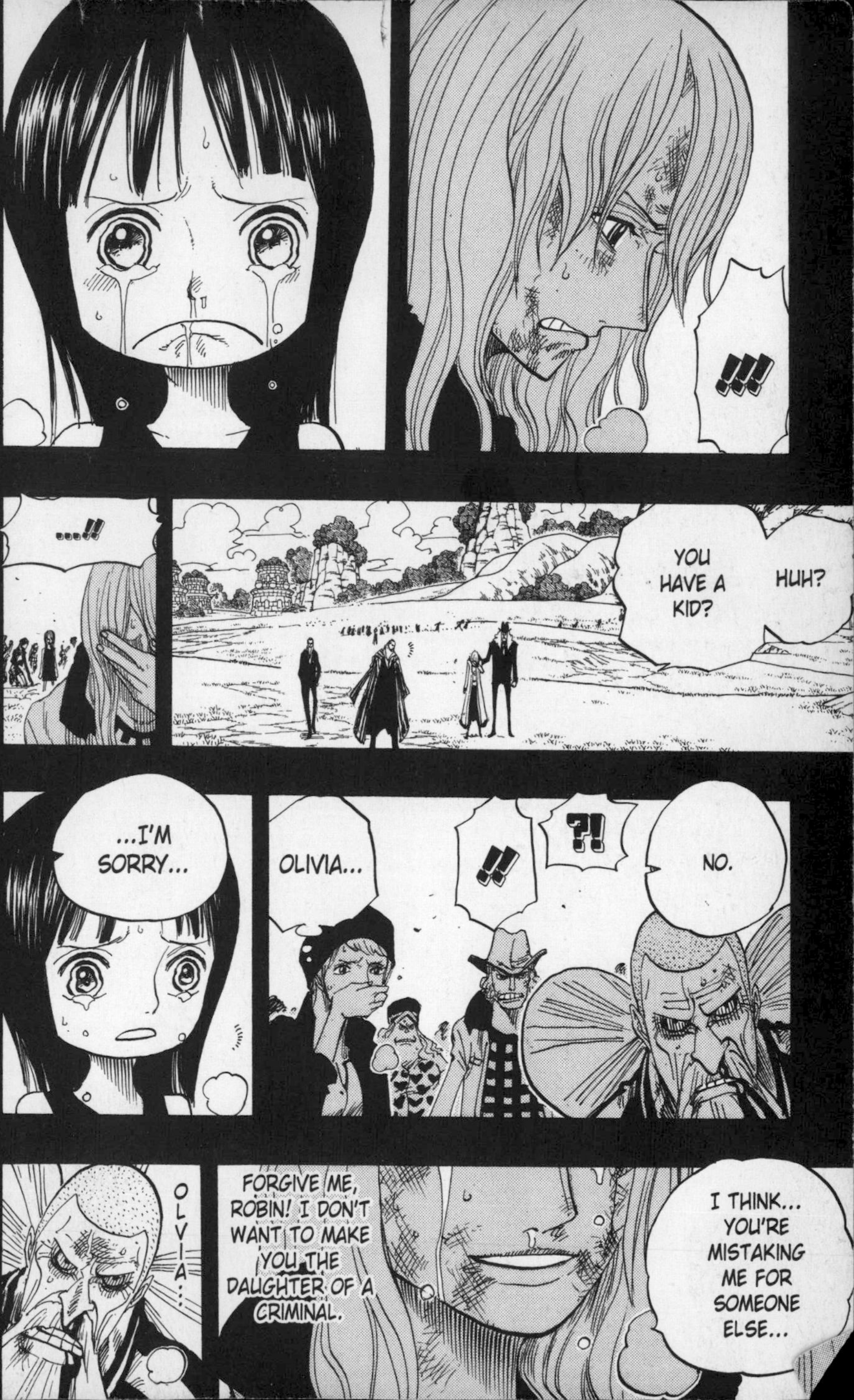
!!!
HUH?
YOU HAVE A KID?
...!!
NO.
?!
!!
OLIVIA...
...I'M SORRY...
I THINK... YOU'RE MISTAKING ME FOR SOMEONE ELSE...
FORGIVE ME, ROBIN! I DON'T WANT TO MAKE YOU THE DAUGHTER OF A CRIMINAL.
OLVIA...

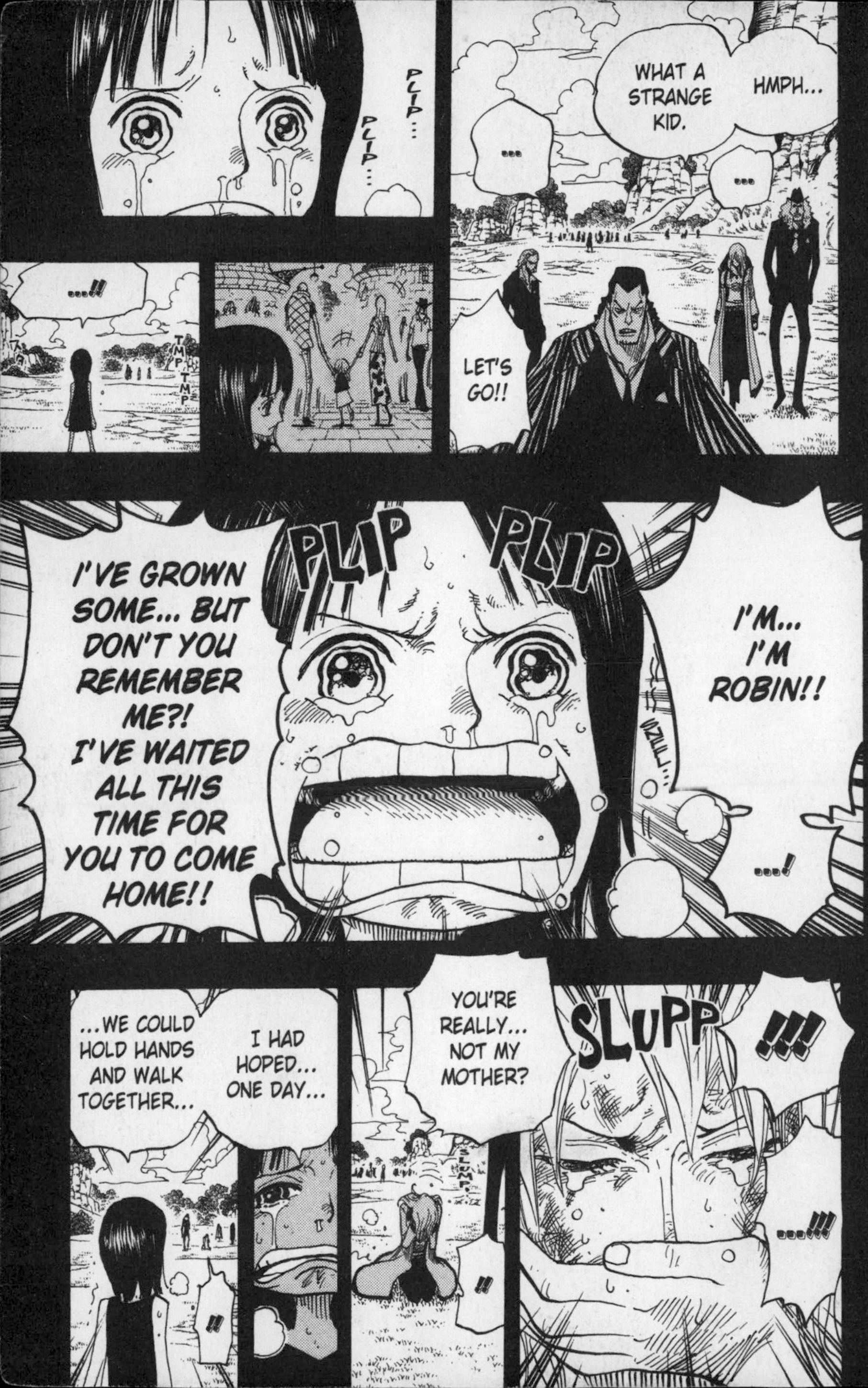
HMPH...
WHAT A STRANGE KID.
...
...
LET'S GO!!
PLIP... PLIP...
...!!
TMP TMP
I'M... I'M ROBIN!!
PLIP PLIP
...!
I'VE GROWN SOME... BUT DON'T YOU REMEMBER ME?! I'VE WAITED ALL THIS TIME FOR YOU TO COME HOME!!
SLUPP!!!
...!!!
YOU'RE REALLY... NOT MY MOTHER?
SLUMP
!!
I HAD HOPED... ONE DAY...
...WE COULD HOLD HANDS AND WALK TOGETHER...
!!

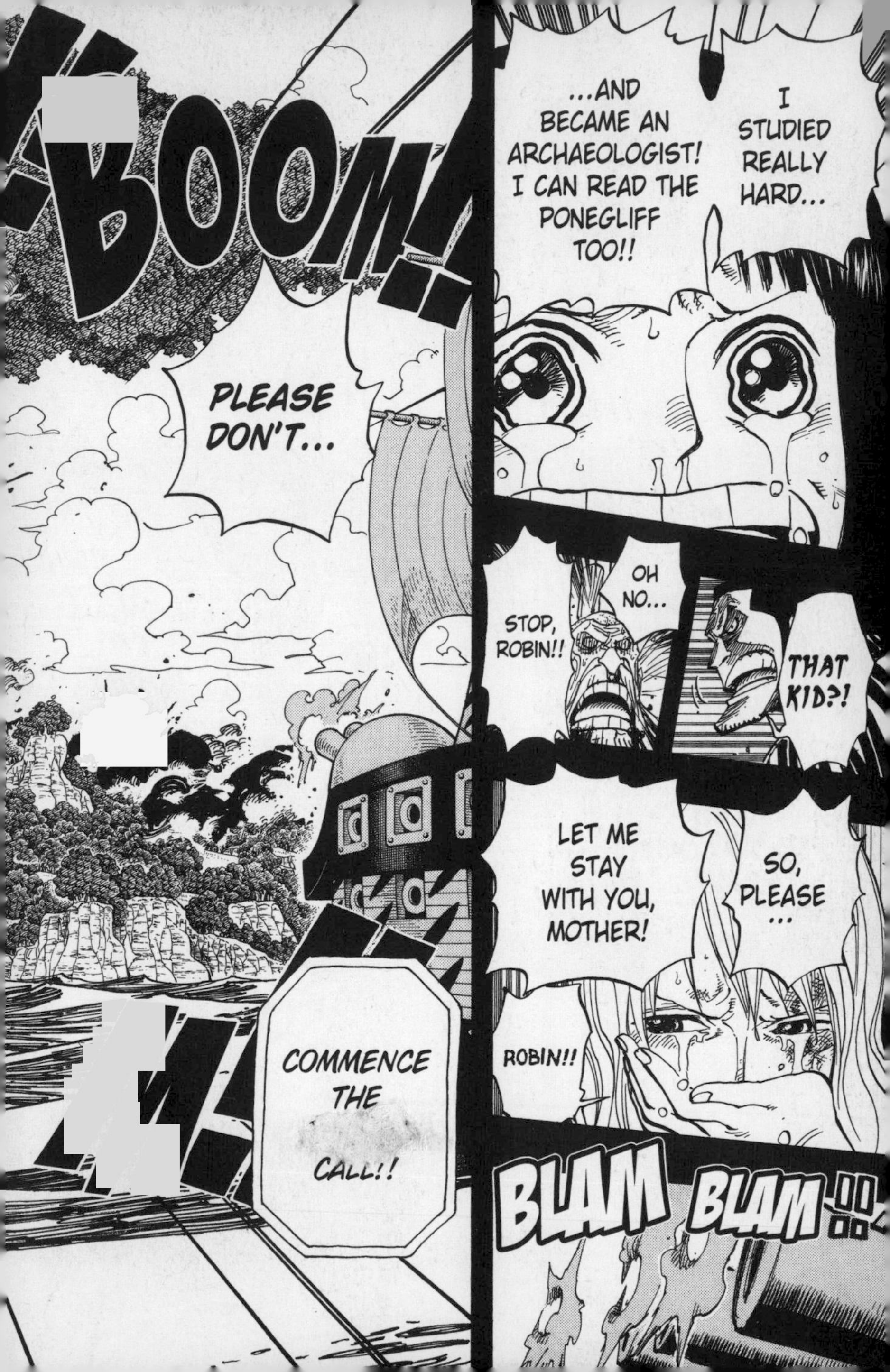
I STUDIED REALLY HARD...
...AND BECAME AN ARCHAEOLOGIST! I CAN READ THE PONEGLIFF TOO!!
THAT KID?!
OH NO...
STOP, ROBIN!!
SO, PLEASE...
LET ME STAY WITH YOU, MOTHER!
ROBIN!!
BLAM BLAM!!
BOOM!!
PLEASE DON'T...
COMMENCE THE CALL!!

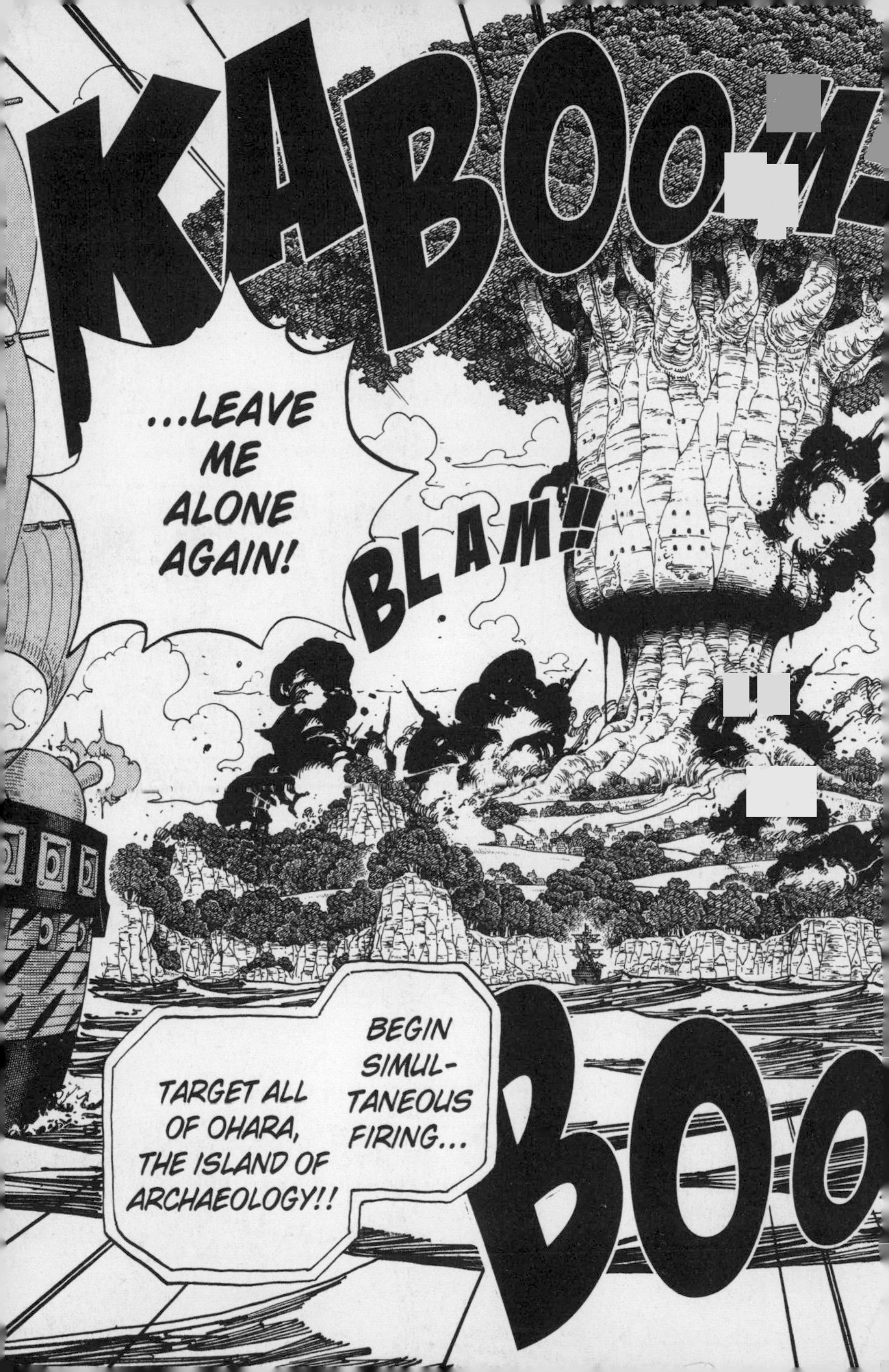
KABOO
BLAM!!
...LEAVE ME ALONE AGAIN!
BEGIN SIMUL-TANEOUS FIRING... TARGET ALL OF OHARA, THE ISLAND OF ARCHAEOLOGY!!
BOO

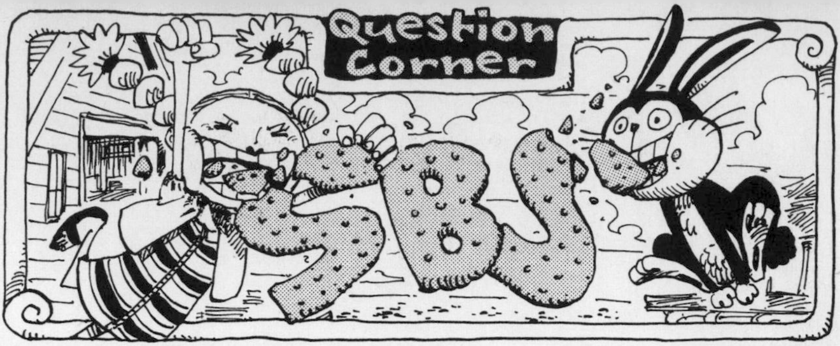
Question Corner
SBS

Q: Please massage my shoulders!

A: Massage, massage. All right, on to the next postcard.

Q: In Chapter 376: "I Get It!!" Sniper King gives Chopper an autograph, but what did it say?? Please tell me. Please. ☆

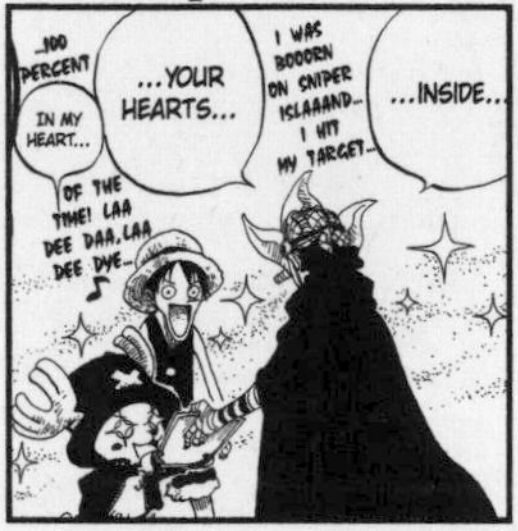
...INSIDE...
I WAS BOOORN ON SNIPER ISLAAAND... I HIT MY TARGET...
...YOUR HEARTS...
...100 PERCENT IN MY HEART... OF THE TIME! LAA DEE DAA, LAA DEE DYE...

--**T-Bone look-alike**
(Actually, the one who looks just like T-Bone is my kid sister.)

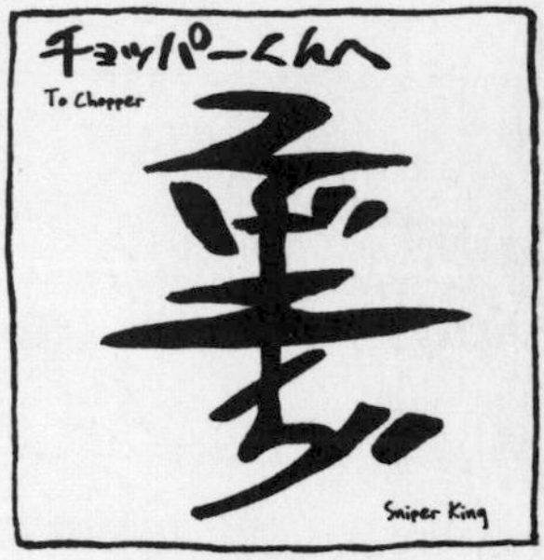
チョッパーくんへ
To Chopper
Sniper King

A: ⬆ This

Q: ☆To Odacchi☆ Do you think it's possible to will yourself to fly through the sky?

--Mutsuki☆

A: Ages ago, people did fly across the skies. One day, someone said, "You can't fly in the sky," and people lost their ability to fly. Because they lost their wings, also known as "faith." The end. (←Hey!!)

Q: What would happen if you used the **Tempest Kick** for a haircut?

--Anga the Second

A: Your head would be cut off--a real clean shave! Still, it's possible to stay alive like that. And only those who really believe that should try it.

Q: **Gum-Gum...!! 300 pound...!! Cannon...!! Boom!!**

--Man of Leisure

A: Shave!! Phew!!

Chapter 396: SAUL

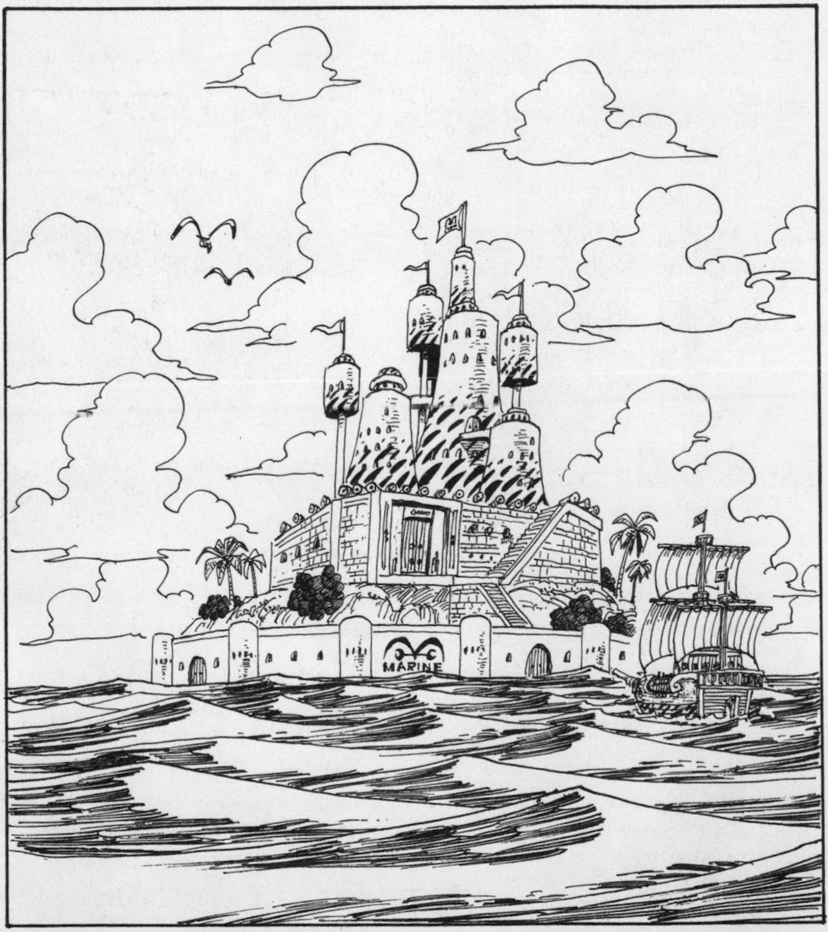
MARINE

MS. GOLDEN WEEK'S PLAN, A BAROQUE REUNION, VOL. 28:
"ONWARD TO THE NAVY PRISON"

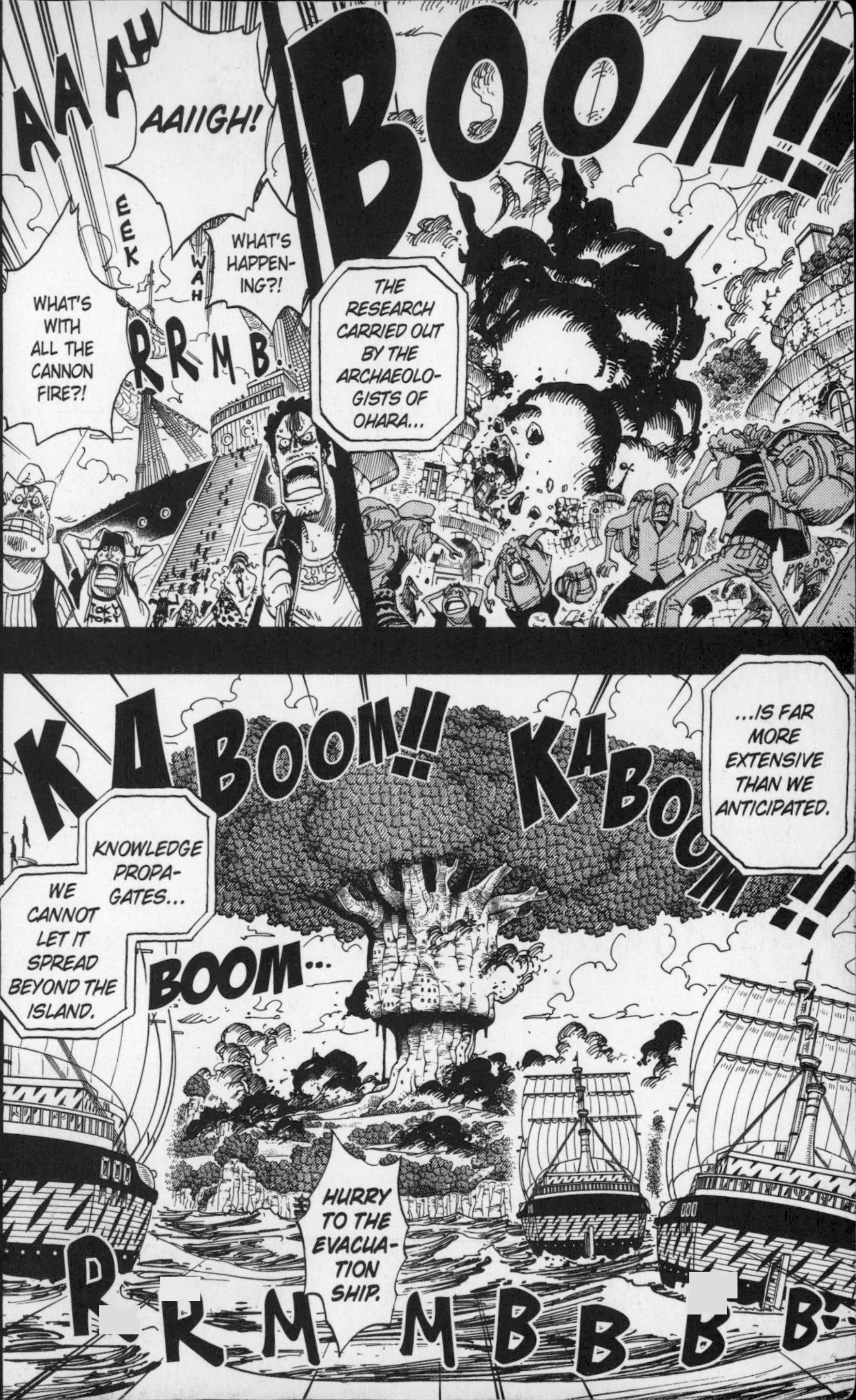
BOOM!!
THE RESEARCH CARRIED OUT BY THE ARCHAEOLOGISTS OF OHARA...
WHAT'S HAPPENING?!
WAH
EEK
AAIIGH!
AAAH
RRMB
WHAT'S WITH ALL THE CANNON FIRE?!
...IS FAR MORE EXTENSIVE THAN WE ANTICIPATED.
KABOOOM!!
KABOOM!!
KNOWLEDGE PROPAGATES...
WE CANNOT LET IT SPREAD BEYOND THE ISLAND.
BOOM...
HURRY TO THE EVACUATION SHIP.
RRMMBBBB

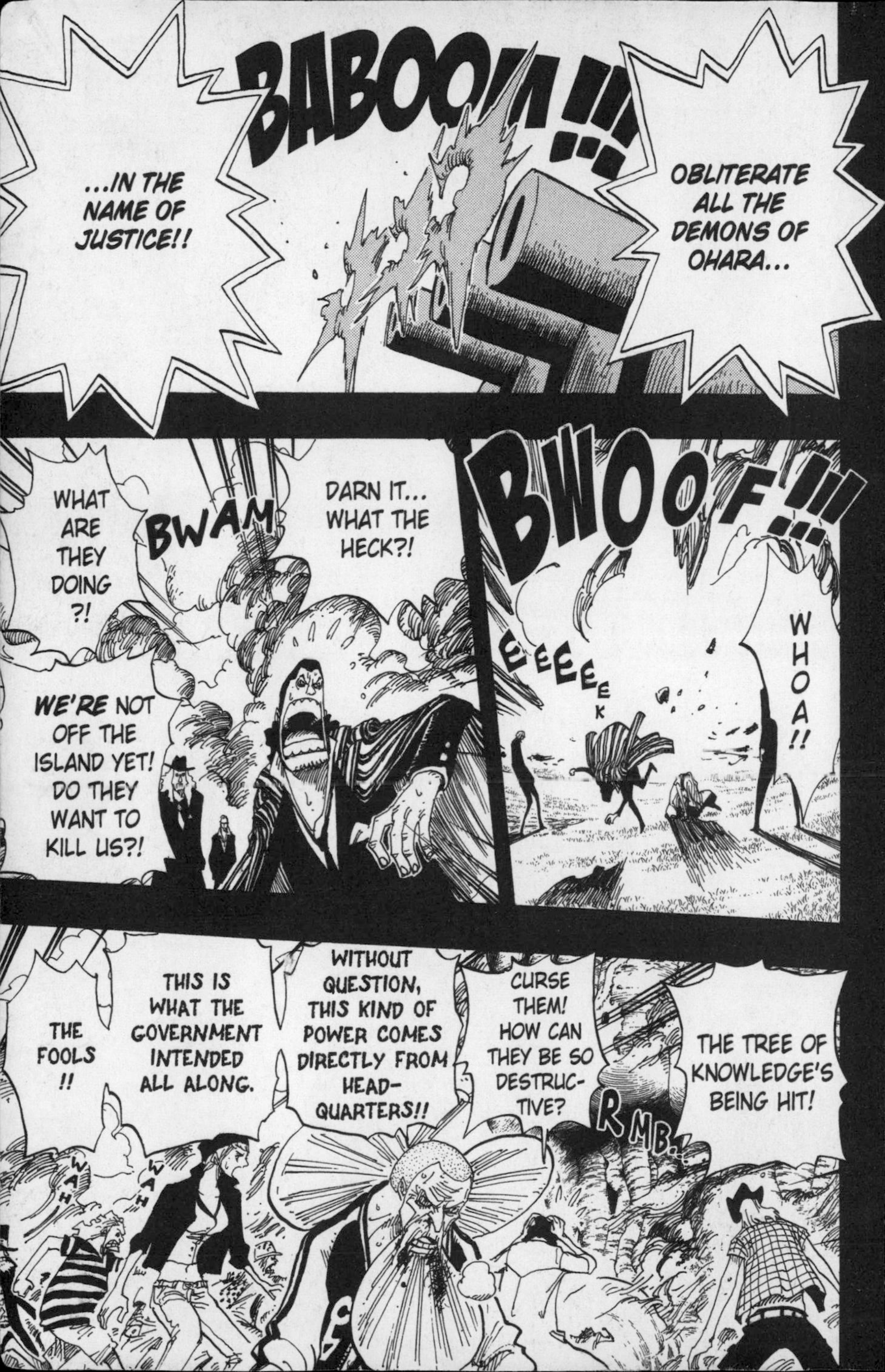
BABOOM!!!
OBLITERATE ALL THE DEMONS OF OHARA...
...IN THE NAME OF JUSTICE!!
BWOOF!!!
WHOA!!
EEEEEK
DARN IT... WHAT THE HECK?!
BWAM
WHAT ARE THEY DOING?!
WE'RE NOT OFF THE ISLAND YET! DO THEY WANT TO KILL US?!
THE TREE OF KNOWLEDGE'S BEING HIT!
RMB..
CURSE THEM! HOW CAN THEY BE SO DESTRUC-TIVE?
WITHOUT QUESTION, THIS KIND OF POWER COMES DIRECTLY FROM HEAD-QUARTERS!!
THIS IS WHAT THE GOVERNMENT INTENDED ALL ALONG.
THE FOOLS!!
WAH
WAH

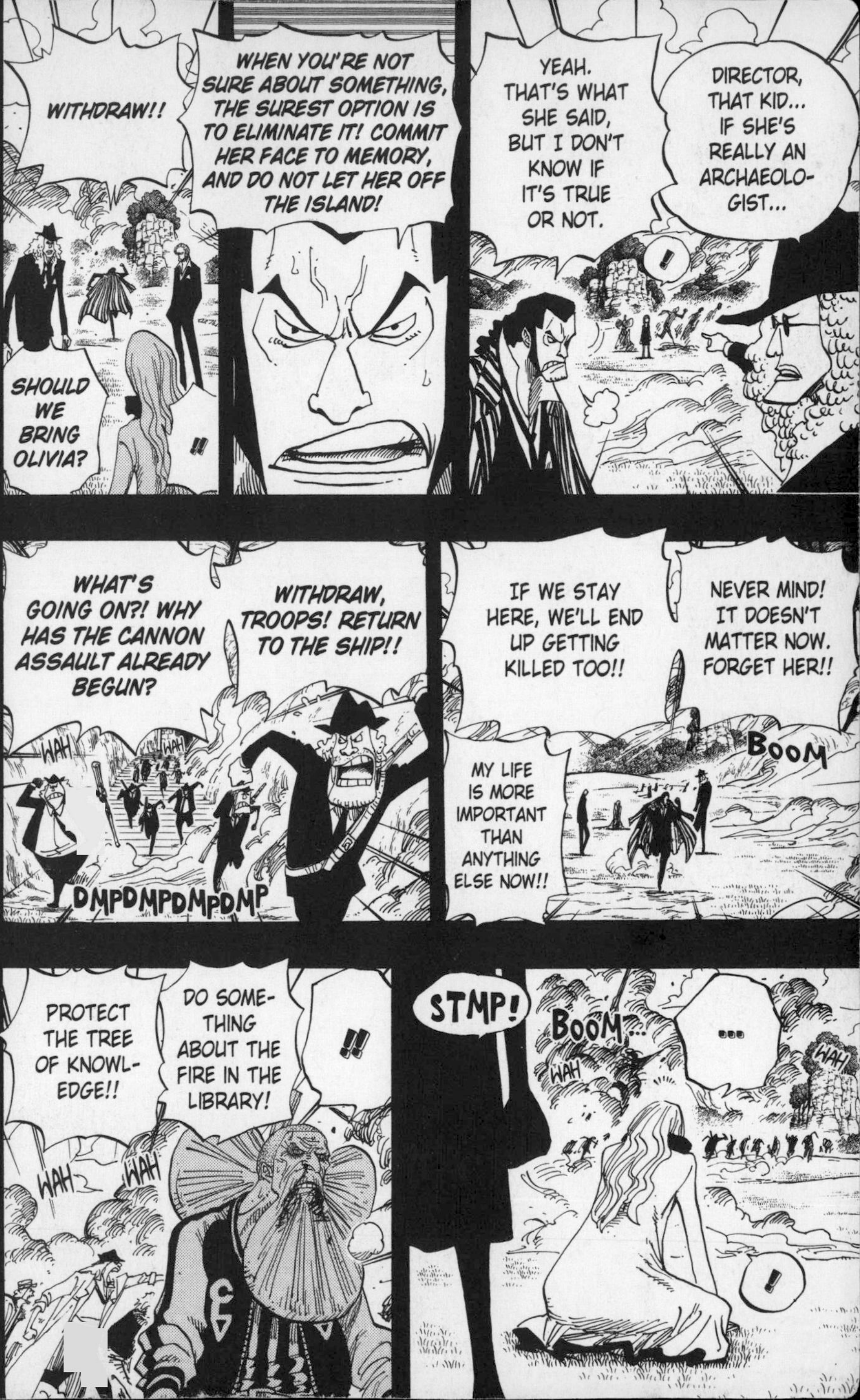
DIRECTOR, THAT KID... IF SHE'S REALLY AN ARCHAEOLOGIST...
YEAH. THAT'S WHAT SHE SAID, BUT I DON'T KNOW IF IT'S TRUE OR NOT.
!
WHEN YOU'RE NOT SURE ABOUT SOMETHING, THE SUREST OPTION IS TO ELIMINATE IT! COMMIT HER FACE TO MEMORY, AND DO NOT LET HER OFF THE ISLAND!
WITHDRAW!!
SHOULD WE BRING OLIVIA?
!!
NEVER MIND! IT DOESN'T MATTER NOW. FORGET HER!!
IF WE STAY HERE, WE'LL END UP GETTING KILLED TOO!!
BOOM
MY LIFE IS MORE IMPORTANT THAN ANYTHING ELSE NOW!!
WITHDRAW, TROOPS! RETURN TO THE SHIP!!
WHAT'S GOING ON?! WHY HAS THE CANNON ASSAULT ALREADY BEGUN?
WAH
WAH
DMPDMPDMPDMP
...
STMP!
BOOM...
WAH
WAH
!
!!
DO SOMETHING ABOUT THE FIRE IN THE LIBRARY!
PROTECT THE TREE OF KNOWLEDGE!!
WAH
WAH

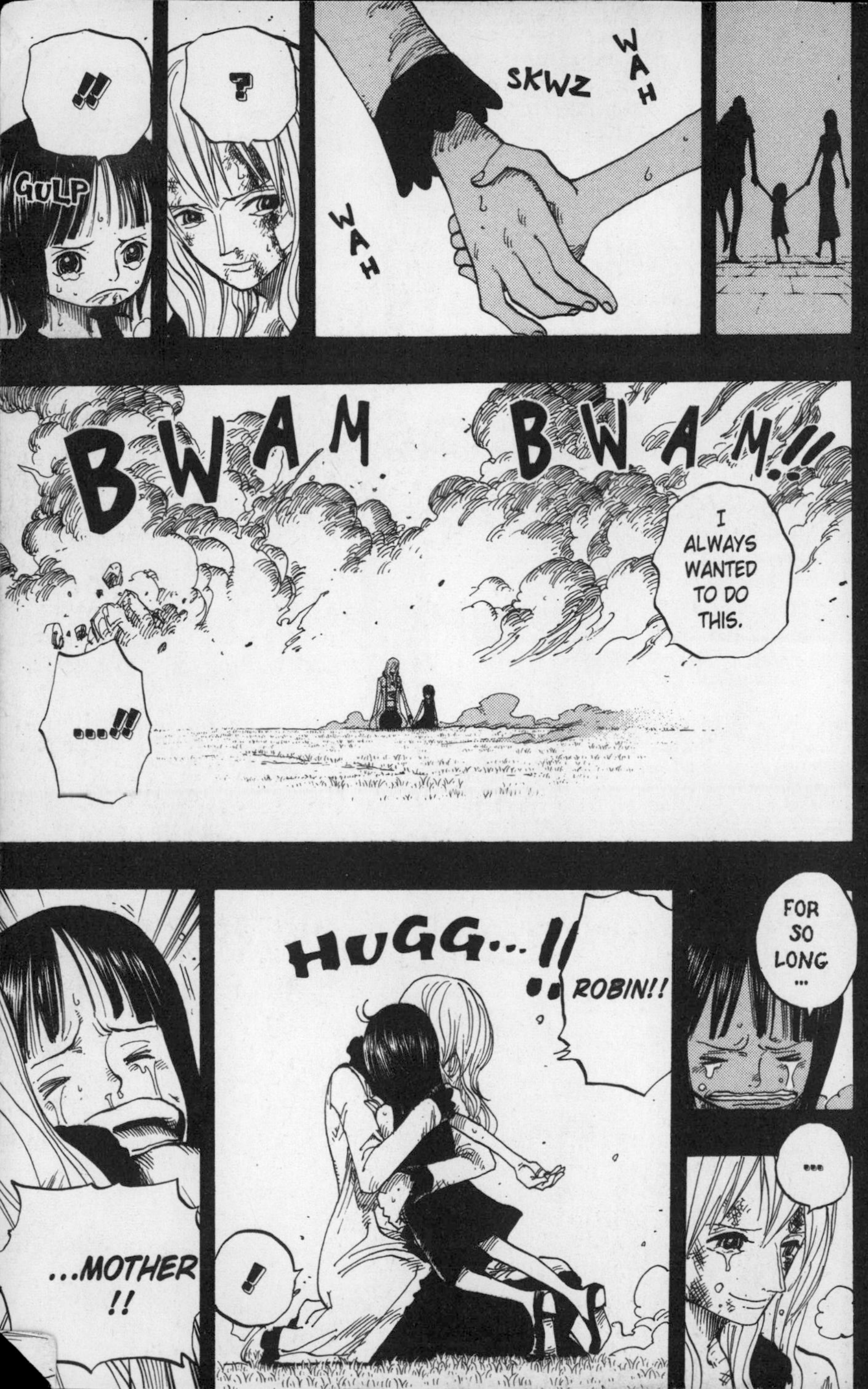
WAH
SKWZ
WAH
?
!!
GULP
BWAM BWAM!!
I ALWAYS WANTED TO DO THIS.
...!!
FOR SO LONG ...
...
HUGG...!!
.. ROBIN!!
!
...MOTHER !!

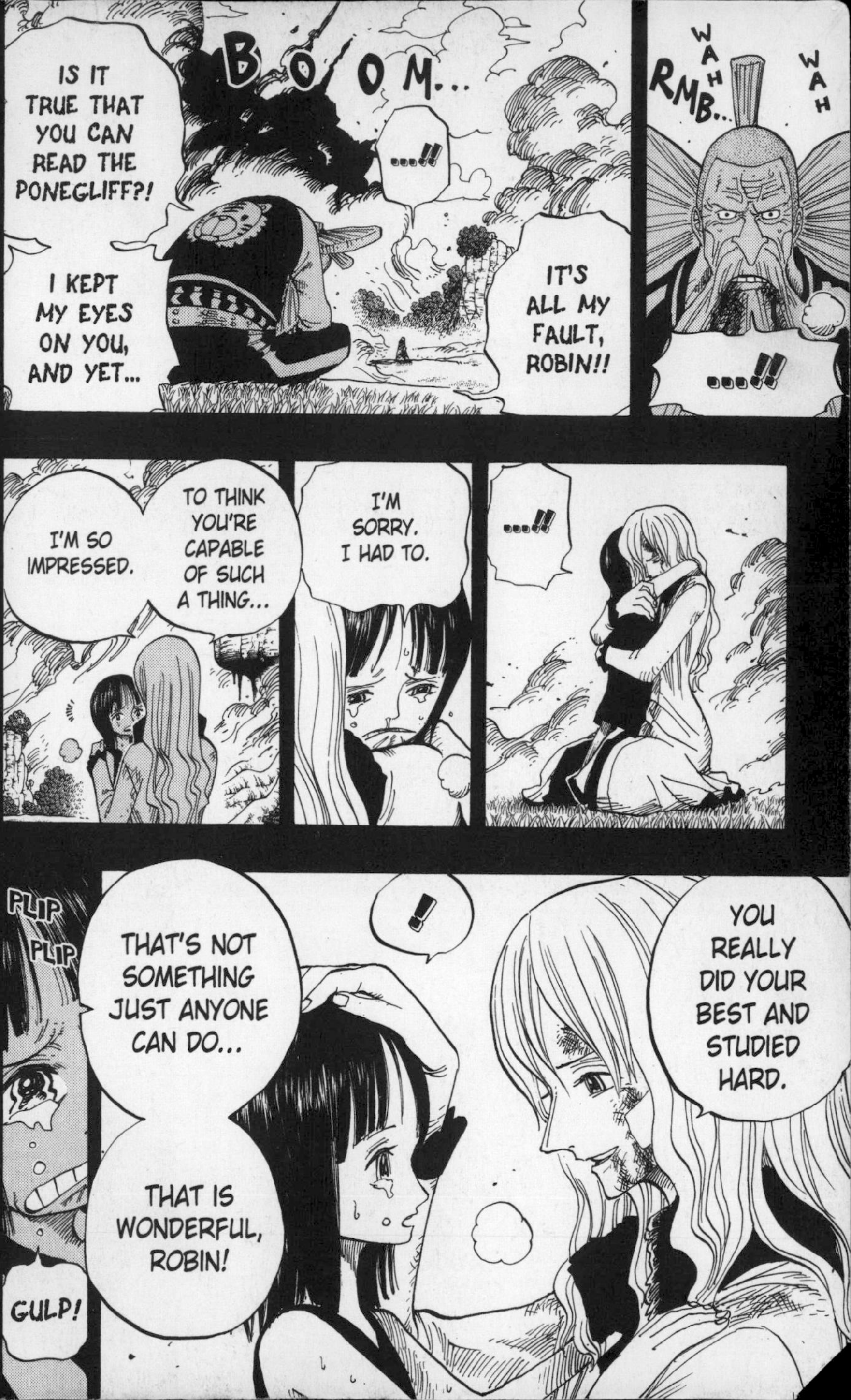
WAH
WAH
RMB...
...!!
BOOM...
...!!
IS IT TRUE THAT YOU CAN READ THE PONEGLIFF?!
I KEPT MY EYES ON YOU, AND YET...
IT'S ALL MY FAULT, ROBIN!!
...!!
I'M SORRY. I HAD TO.
TO THINK YOU'RE CAPABLE OF SUCH A THING...
I'M SO IMPRESSED.
YOU REALLY DID YOUR BEST AND STUDIED HARD.
!
THAT'S NOT SOMETHING JUST ANYONE CAN DO...
THAT IS WONDERFUL, ROBIN!
PLIP
PLIP
GULP!

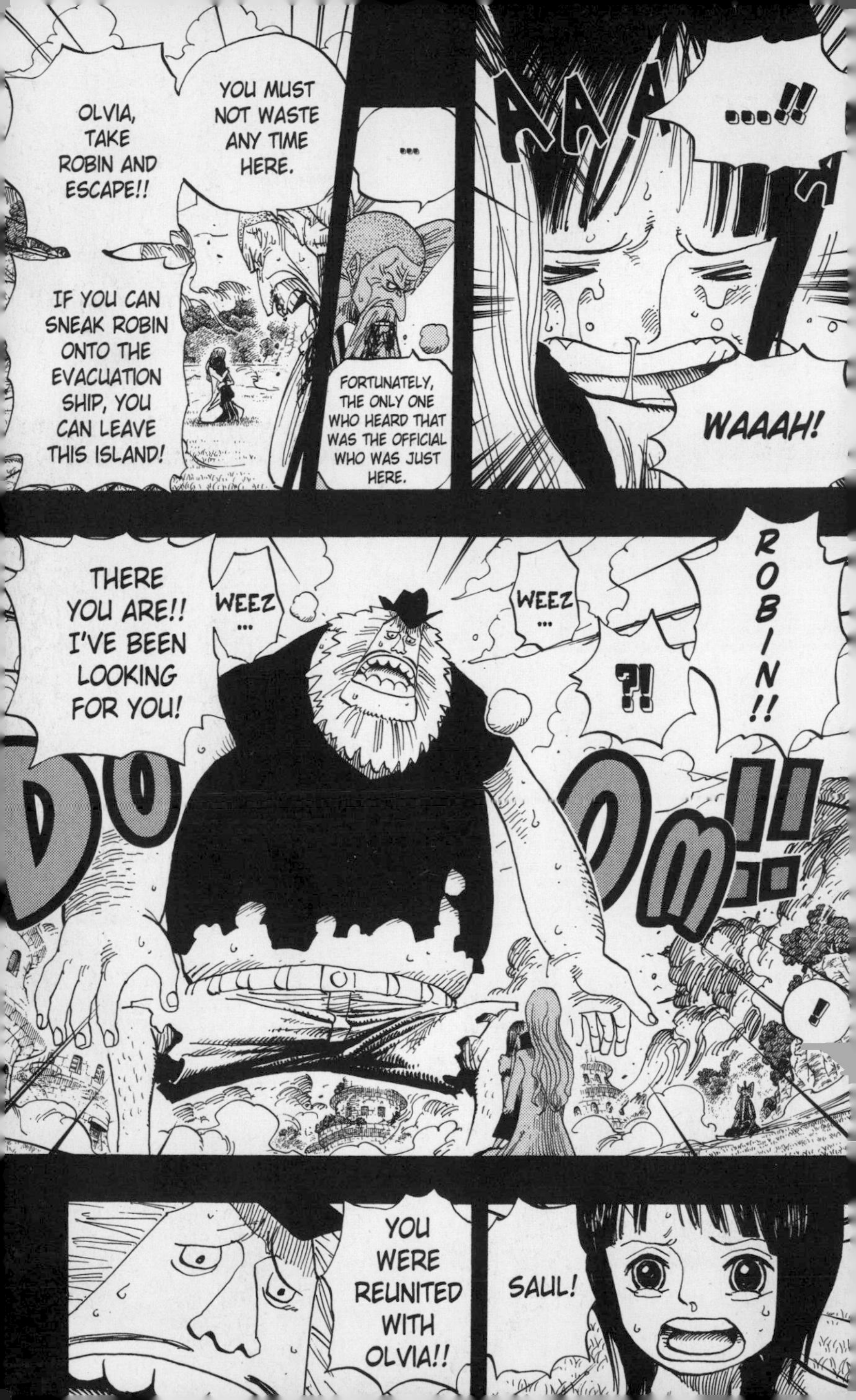
AAA
...!!
WAAAH!
...
FORTUNATELY, THE ONLY ONE WHO HEARD THAT WAS THE OFFICIAL WHO WAS JUST HERE.
YOU MUST NOT WASTE ANY TIME HERE.
OLVIA, TAKE ROBIN AND ESCAPE!!
IF YOU CAN SNEAK ROBIN ONTO THE EVACUATION SHIP, YOU CAN LEAVE THIS ISLAND!
ROBIN!!
?!
WEEZ...
WEEZ...
THERE YOU ARE!! I'VE BEEN LOOKING FOR YOU!
DOOM!!
!
SAUL!
YOU WERE REUNITED WITH OLVIA!!

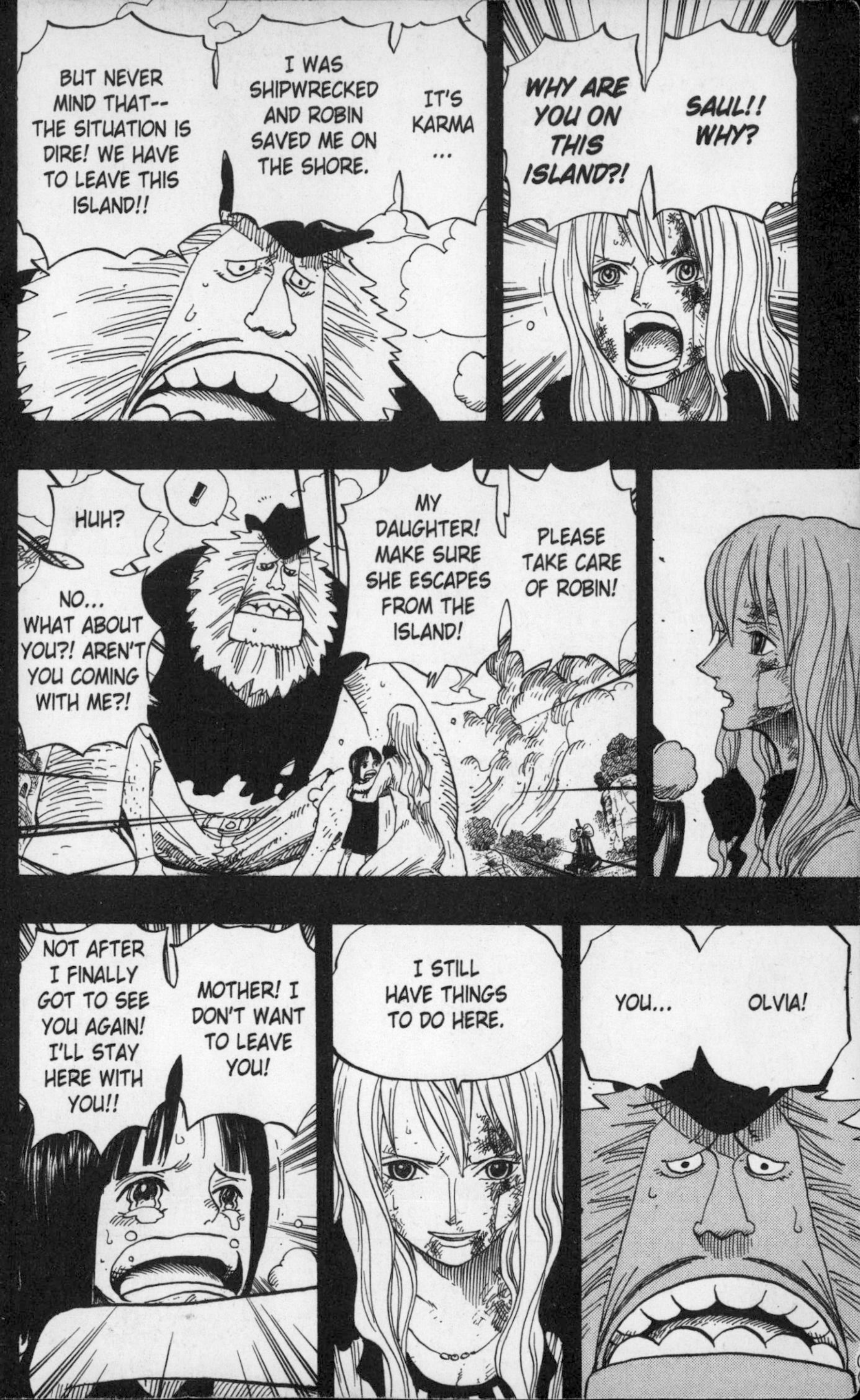
SAUL!! WHY?
WHY ARE YOU ON THIS ISLAND?!
IT'S KARMA ...
I WAS SHIPWRECKED AND ROBIN SAVED ME ON THE SHORE.
BUT NEVER MIND THAT-- THE SITUATION IS DIRE! WE HAVE TO LEAVE THIS ISLAND!!
PLEASE TAKE CARE OF ROBIN!
MY DAUGHTER! MAKE SURE SHE ESCAPES FROM THE ISLAND!
!
HUH?
NO... WHAT ABOUT YOU?! AREN'T YOU COMING WITH ME?!
YOU... OLVIA!
I STILL HAVE THINGS TO DO HERE.
MOTHER! I DON'T WANT TO LEAVE YOU!
NOT AFTER I FINALLY GOT TO SEE YOU AGAIN! I'LL STAY HERE WITH YOU!!

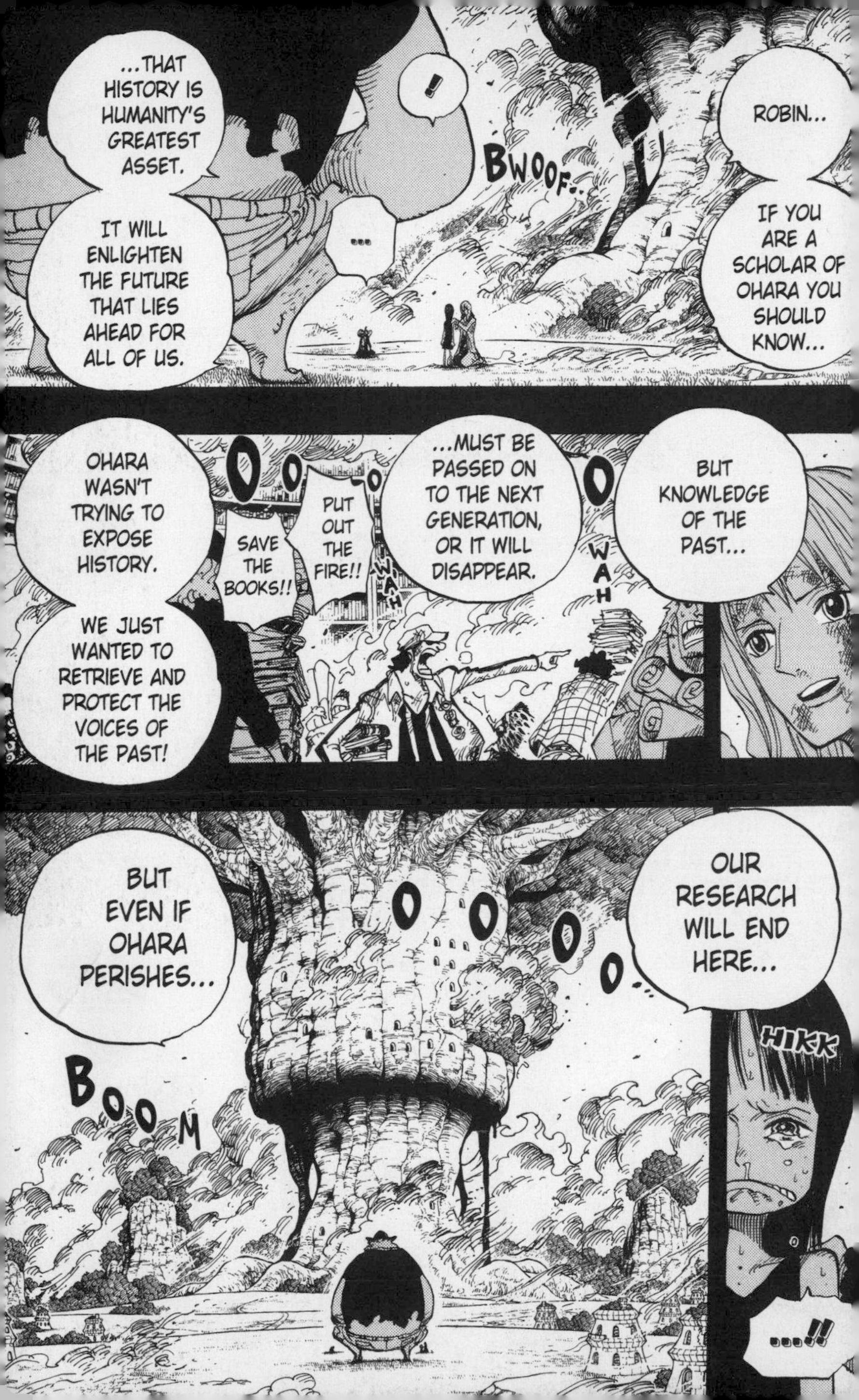
ROBIN...
IF YOU ARE A SCHOLAR OF OHARA YOU SHOULD KNOW...
BWOOF...
!
...
...THAT HISTORY IS HUMANITY'S GREATEST ASSET.
IT WILL ENLIGHTEN THE FUTURE THAT LIES AHEAD FOR ALL OF US.
BUT KNOWLEDGE OF THE PAST...
WAH
...MUST BE PASSED ON TO THE NEXT GENERATION, OR IT WILL DISAPPEAR.
O
PUT OUT THE FIRE!!
WAH
SAVE THE BOOKS!!
OO
OHARA WASN'T TRYING TO EXPOSE HISTORY.
WE JUST WANTED TO RETRIEVE AND PROTECT THE VOICES OF THE PAST!
OUR RESEARCH WILL END HERE...
HIKK
...!!
OOOO...
BUT EVEN IF OHARA PERISHES...
BOOOM

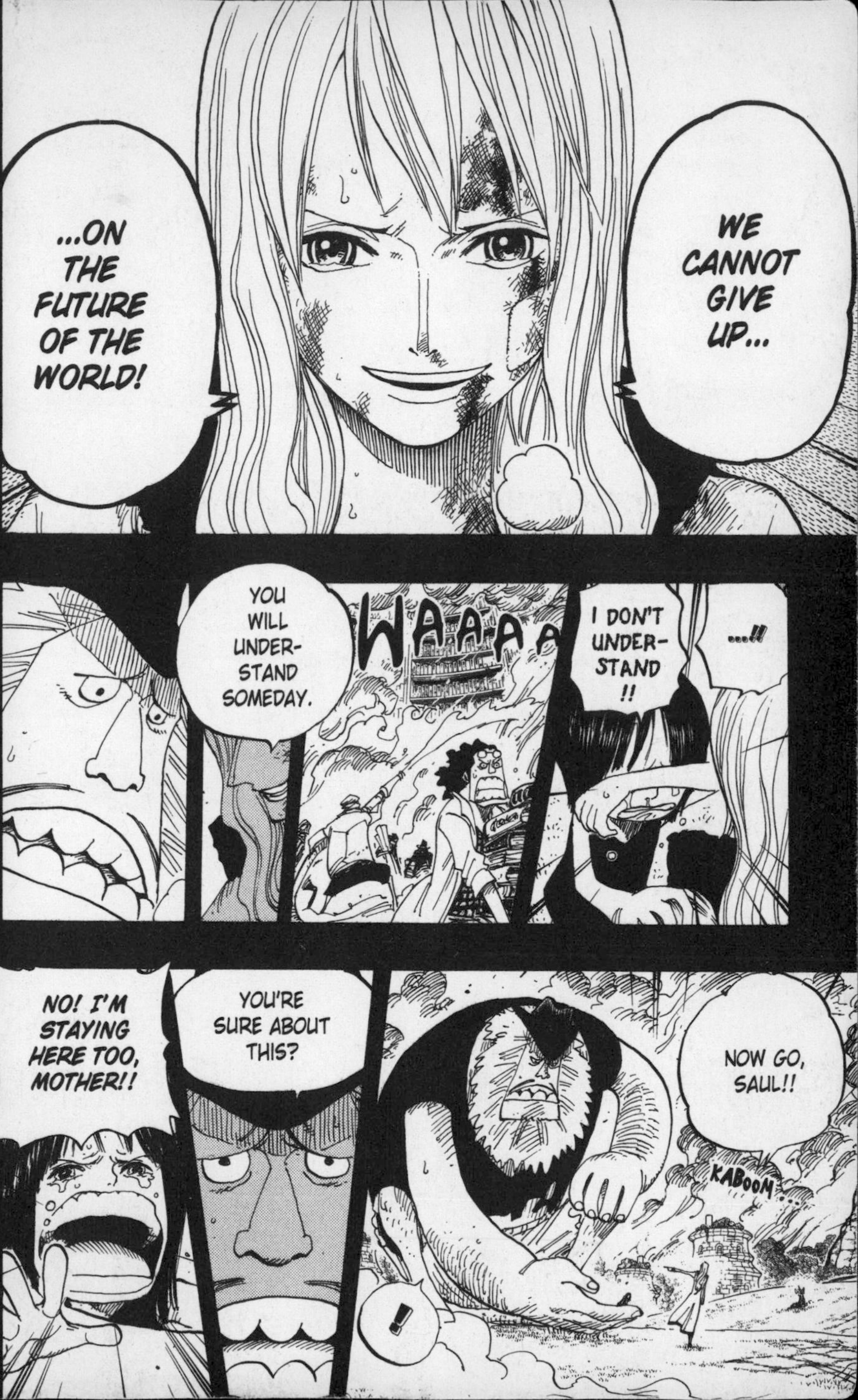

WE CANNOT GIVE UP...
...ON THE FUTURE OF THE WORLD!
...!!
I DON'T UNDER-STAND !!
WAAAA
YOU WILL UNDER-STAND SOMEDAY.
NOW GO, SAUL!!
KABOOM
!
YOU'RE SURE ABOUT THIS?
NO! I'M STAYING HERE TOO, MOTHER!!

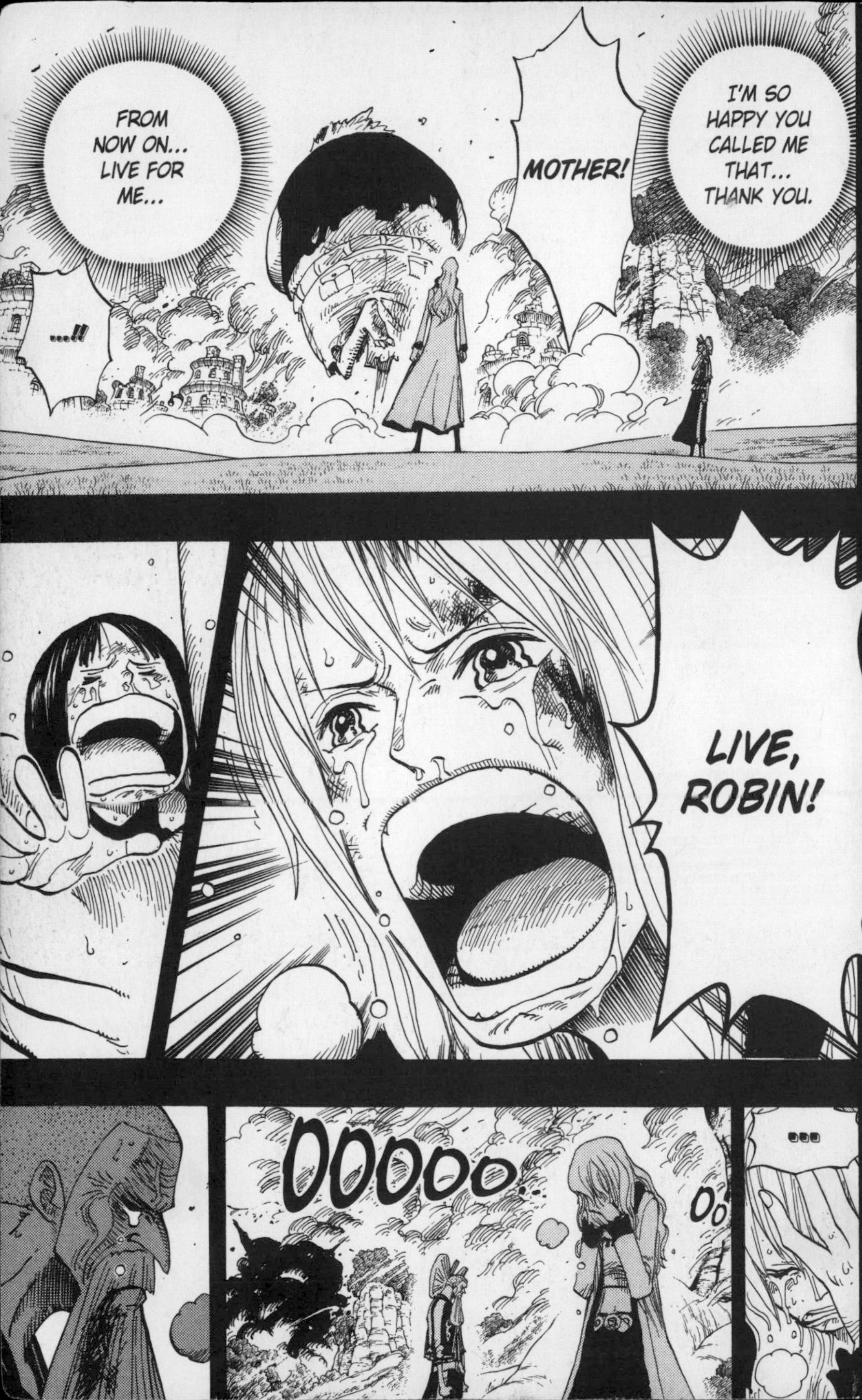
I'M SO HAPPY YOU CALLED ME THAT... THANK YOU.
MOTHER!
FROM NOW ON... LIVE FOR ME...
...!!
LIVE, ROBIN!
...
OOOOO
OO

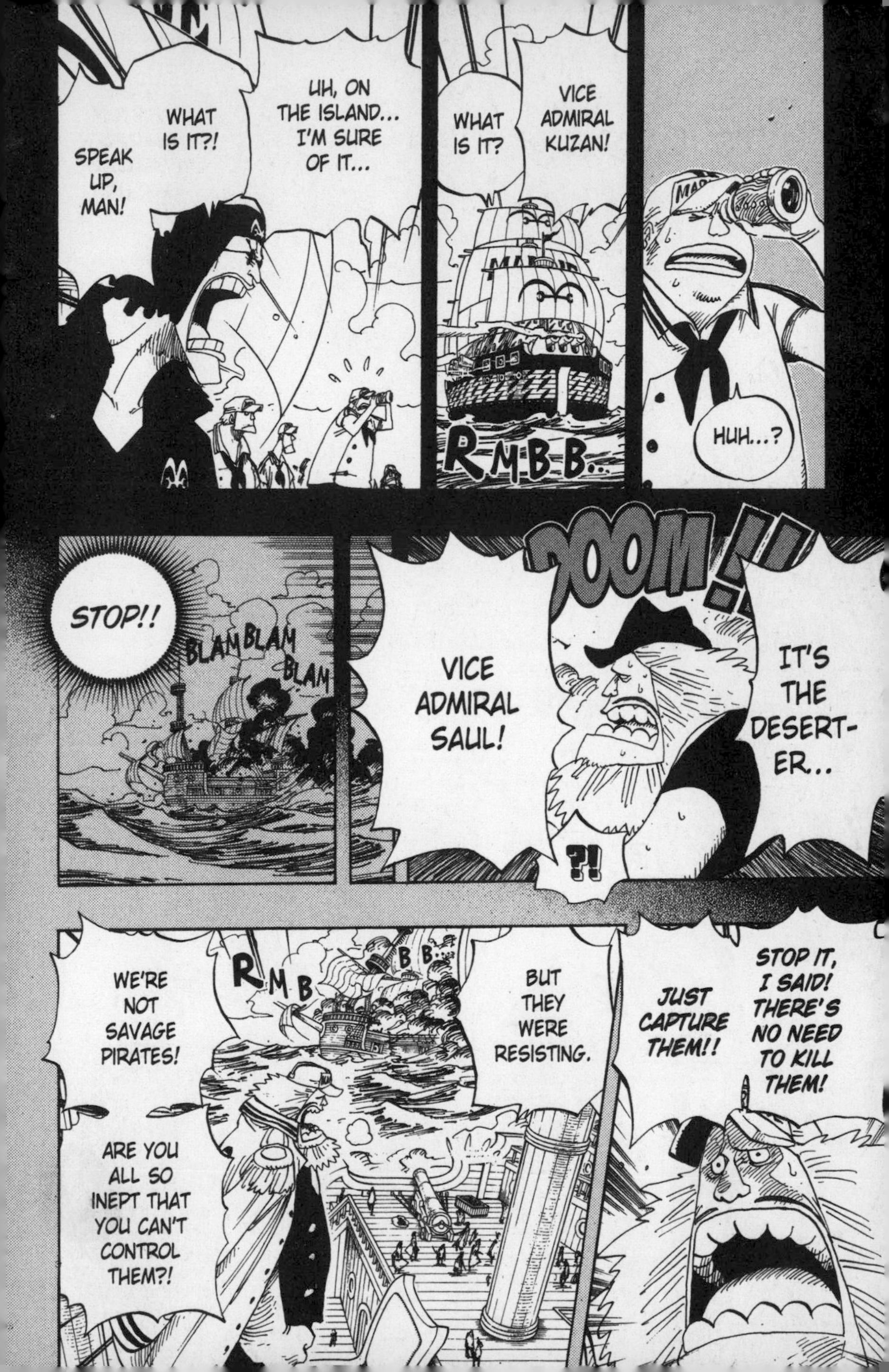
HUH...?
VICE ADMIRAL KUZAN!
WHAT IS IT?
R M B B..
UH, ON THE ISLAND... I'M SURE OF IT...
WHAT IS IT?!
SPEAK UP, MAN!
DOOM!!
IT'S THE DESERTER...
VICE ADMIRAL SAUL!
?!
STOP!!
BLAM BLAM BLAM
STOP IT, I SAID! THERE'S NO NEED TO KILL THEM!
JUST CAPTURE THEM!!
BUT THEY WERE RESISTING.
R M B B B..
WE'RE NOT SAVAGE PIRATES!
ARE YOU ALL SO INEPT THAT YOU CAN'T CONTROL THEM?!

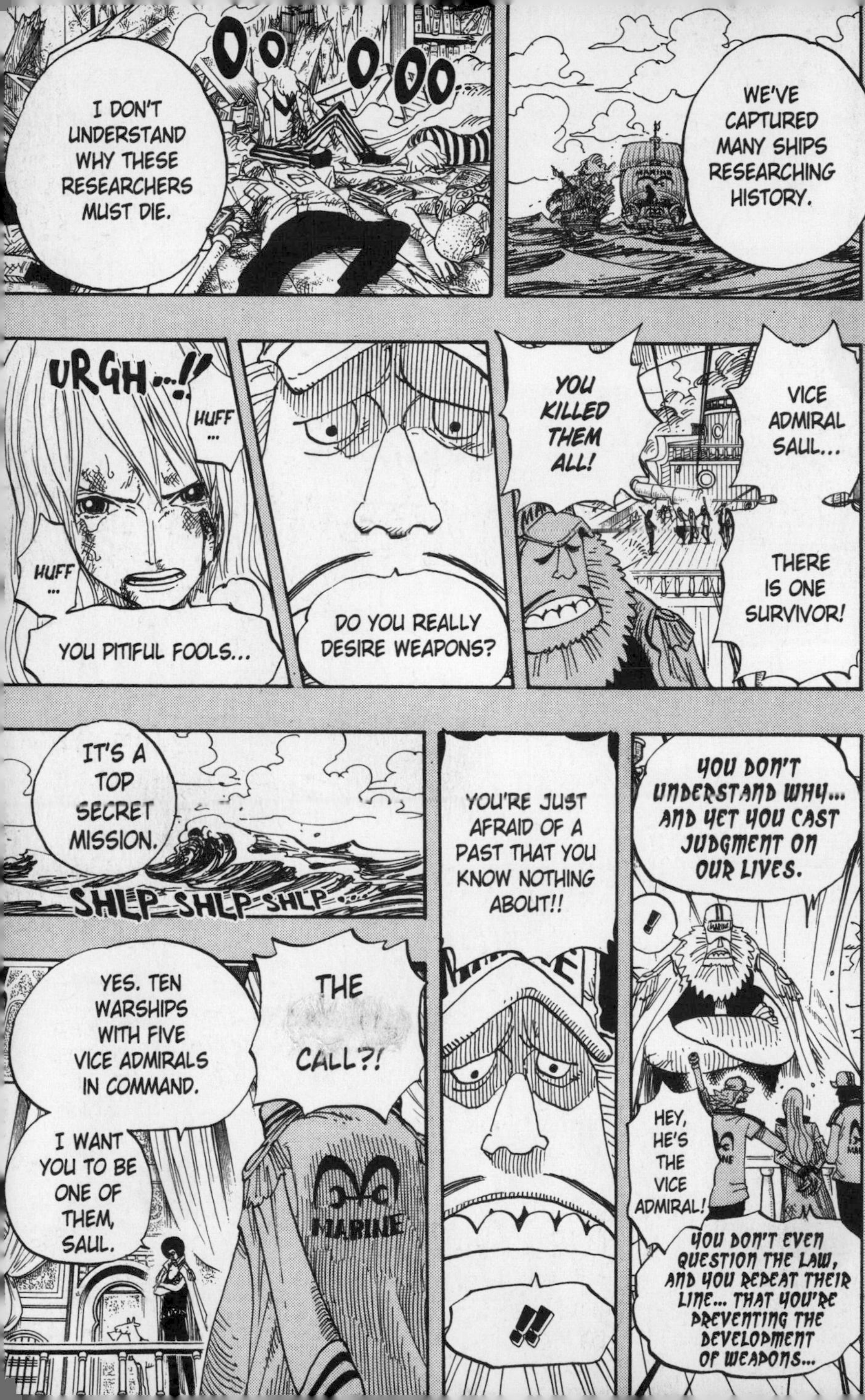
WE'VE CAPTURED MANY SHIPS RESEARCHING HISTORY.
OOOOOO...
I DON'T UNDERSTAND WHY THESE RESEARCHERS MUST DIE.
VICE ADMIRAL SAUL...
THERE IS ONE SURVIVOR!
YOU KILLED THEM ALL!
DO YOU REALLY DESIRE WEAPONS?
URGH...!!
HUFF...
HUFF...
YOU PITIFUL FOOLS...
YOU DON'T UNDERSTAND WHY... AND YET YOU CAST JUDGMENT ON OUR LIVES.
!
HEY, HE'S THE VICE ADMIRAL!
YOU DON'T EVEN QUESTION THE LAW, AND YOU REPEAT THEIR LINE... THAT YOU'RE PREVENTING THE DEVELOPMENT OF WEAPONS...
YOU'RE JUST AFRAID OF A PAST THAT YOU KNOW NOTHING ABOUT!!
!!
IT'S A TOP SECRET MISSION.
SHLP SHLP SHLP...
THE CALL?!
YES. TEN WARSHIPS WITH FIVE VICE ADMIRALS IN COMMAND.
I WANT YOU TO BE ONE OF THEM, SAUL.

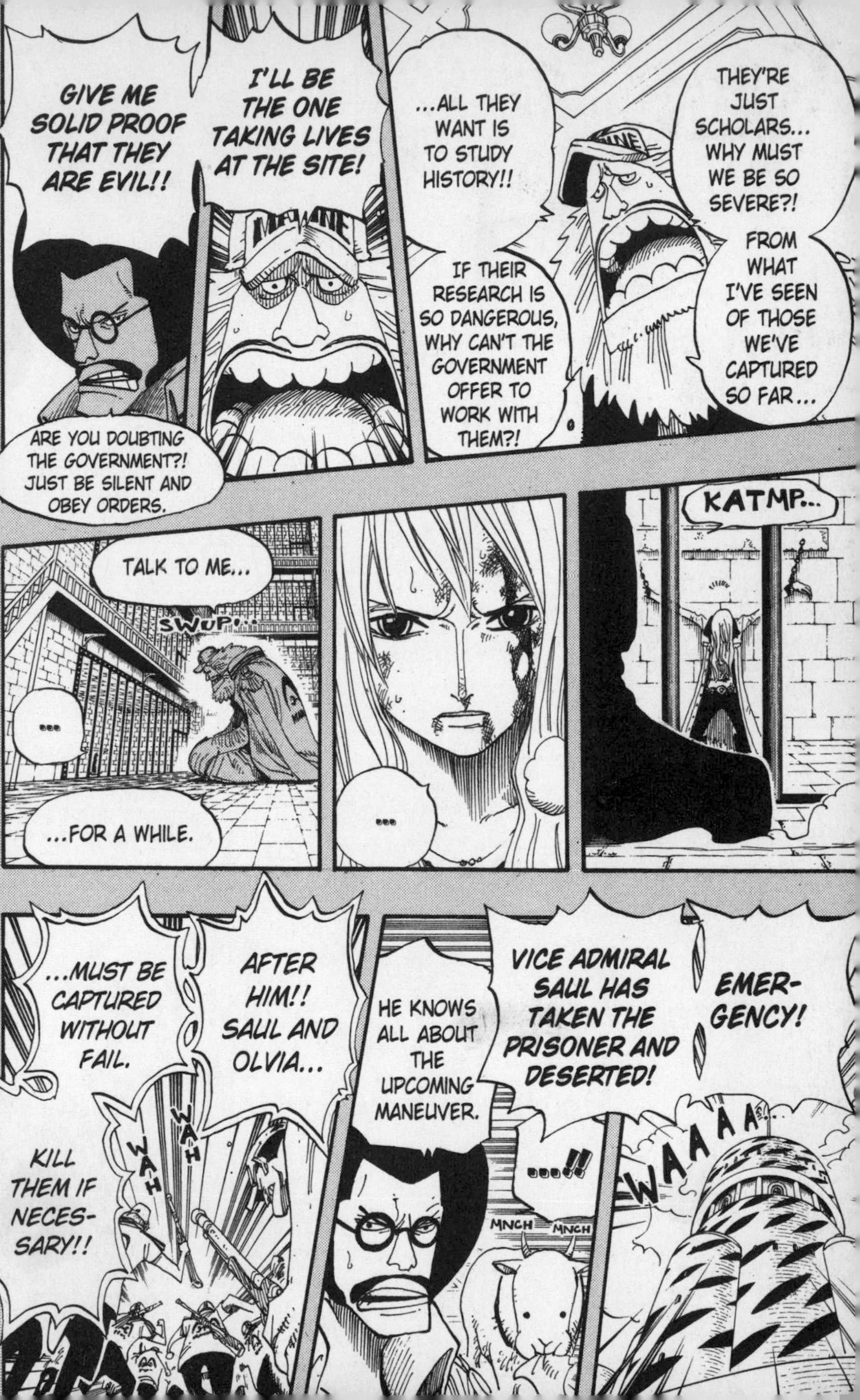
THEY'RE JUST SCHOLARS... WHY MUST WE BE SO SEVERE?!
FROM WHAT I'VE SEEN OF THOSE WE'VE CAPTURED SO FAR...
...ALL THEY WANT IS TO STUDY HISTORY!!
IF THEIR RESEARCH IS SO DANGEROUS, WHY CAN'T THE GOVERNMENT OFFER TO WORK WITH THEM?!
I'LL BE THE ONE TAKING LIVES AT THE SITE!
GIVE ME SOLID PROOF THAT THEY ARE EVIL!!
ARE YOU DOUBTING THE GOVERNMENT?! JUST BE SILENT AND OBEY ORDERS.
KATMP...
...
TALK TO ME...
SWUP!..
...
...FOR A WHILE.
EMER-GENCY!
VICE ADMIRAL SAUL HAS TAKEN THE PRISONER AND DESERTED!
WAAAAA!!...
HE KNOWS ALL ABOUT THE UPCOMING MANEUVER.
...!!
MNCH MNCH
AFTER HIM!! SAUL AND OLVIA...
...MUST BE CAPTURED WITHOUT FAIL.
WAH WAH
KILL THEM IF NECES-SARY!!

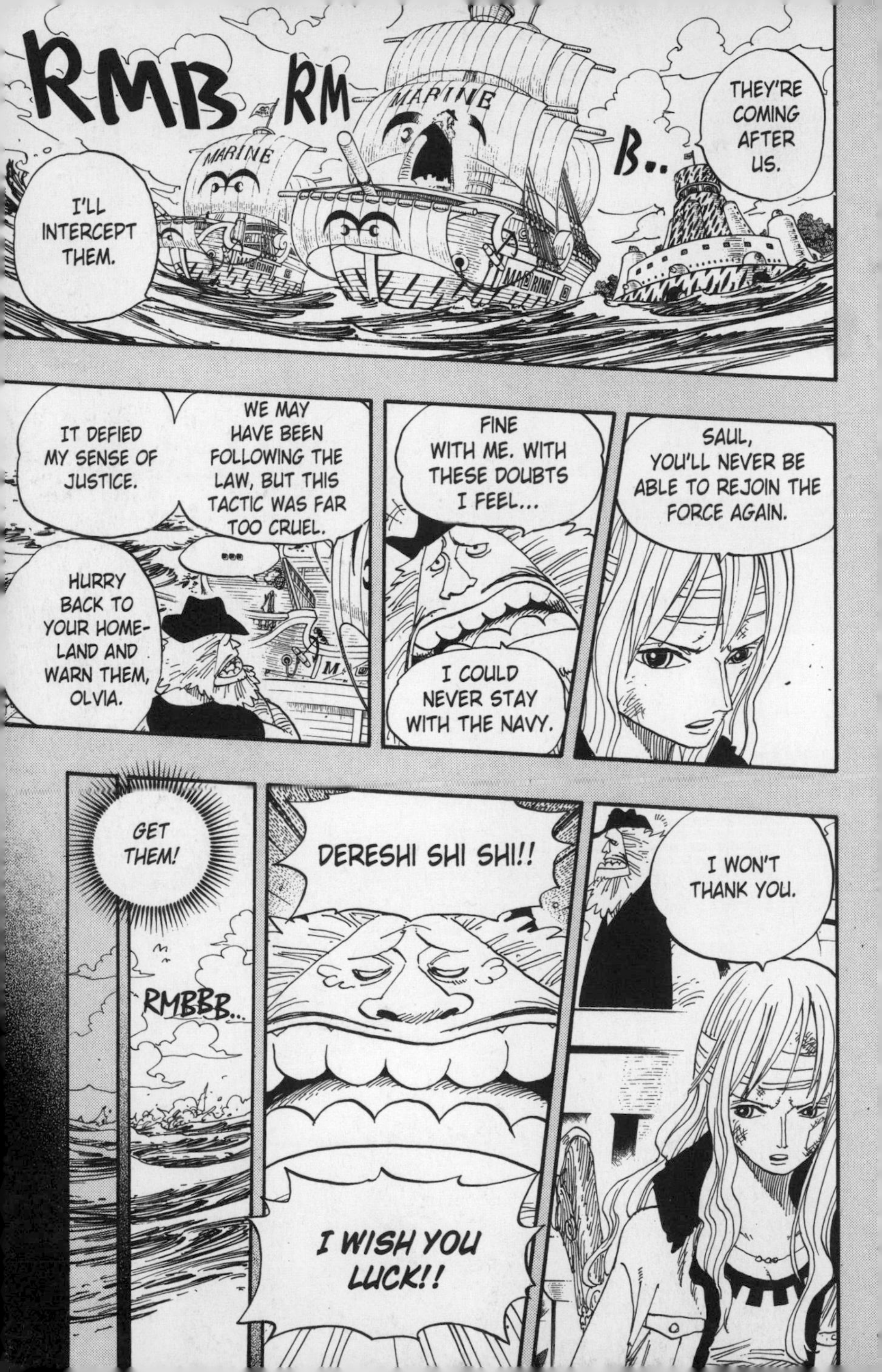
RMB RM B..
THEY'RE COMING AFTER US.
I'LL INTERCEPT THEM.
SAUL, YOU'LL NEVER BE ABLE TO REJOIN THE FORCE AGAIN.
FINE WITH ME. WITH THESE DOUBTS I FEEL...
I COULD NEVER STAY WITH THE NAVY.
WE MAY HAVE BEEN FOLLOWING THE LAW, BUT THIS TACTIC WAS FAR TOO CRUEL.
IT DEFIED MY SENSE OF JUSTICE.
...
HURRY BACK TO YOUR HOME-LAND AND WARN THEM, OLVIA.
I WON'T THANK YOU.
DERESHI SHI SHI!!
I WISH YOU LUCK!!
GET THEM!
RMBBB...

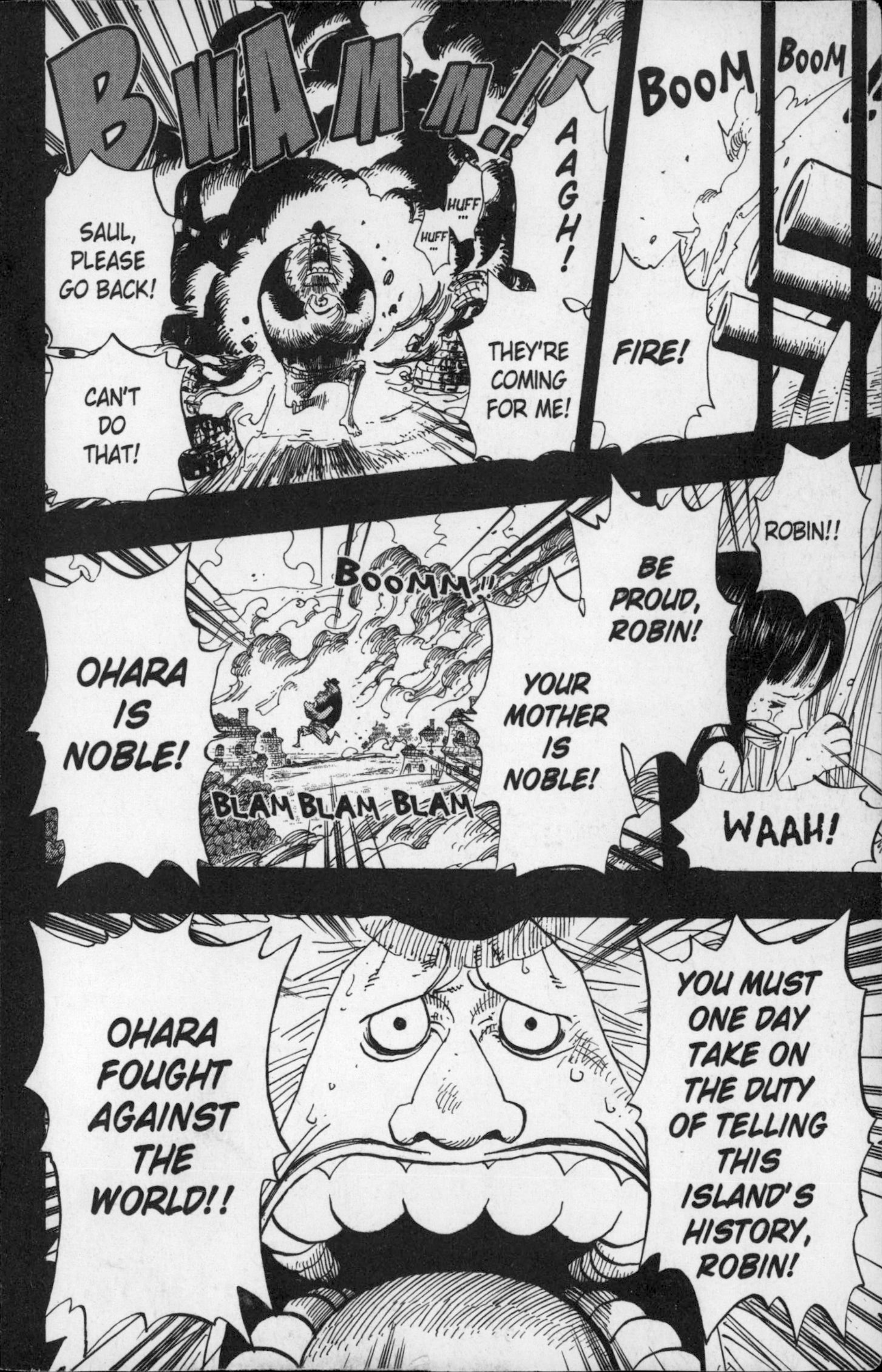
BOOM BOOM
FIRE!
BWAMM!!
AAGH!
HUFF... HUFF...
THEY'RE COMING FOR ME!
SAUL, PLEASE GO BACK!
CAN'T DO THAT!
ROBIN!!
WAAH!
BE PROUD, ROBIN!
BOOMM!!
YOUR MOTHER IS NOBLE!
OHARA IS NOBLE!
BLAM BLAM BLAM
YOU MUST ONE DAY TAKE ON THE DUTY OF TELLING THIS ISLAND'S HISTORY, ROBIN!
OHARA FOUGHT AGAINST THE WORLD!!

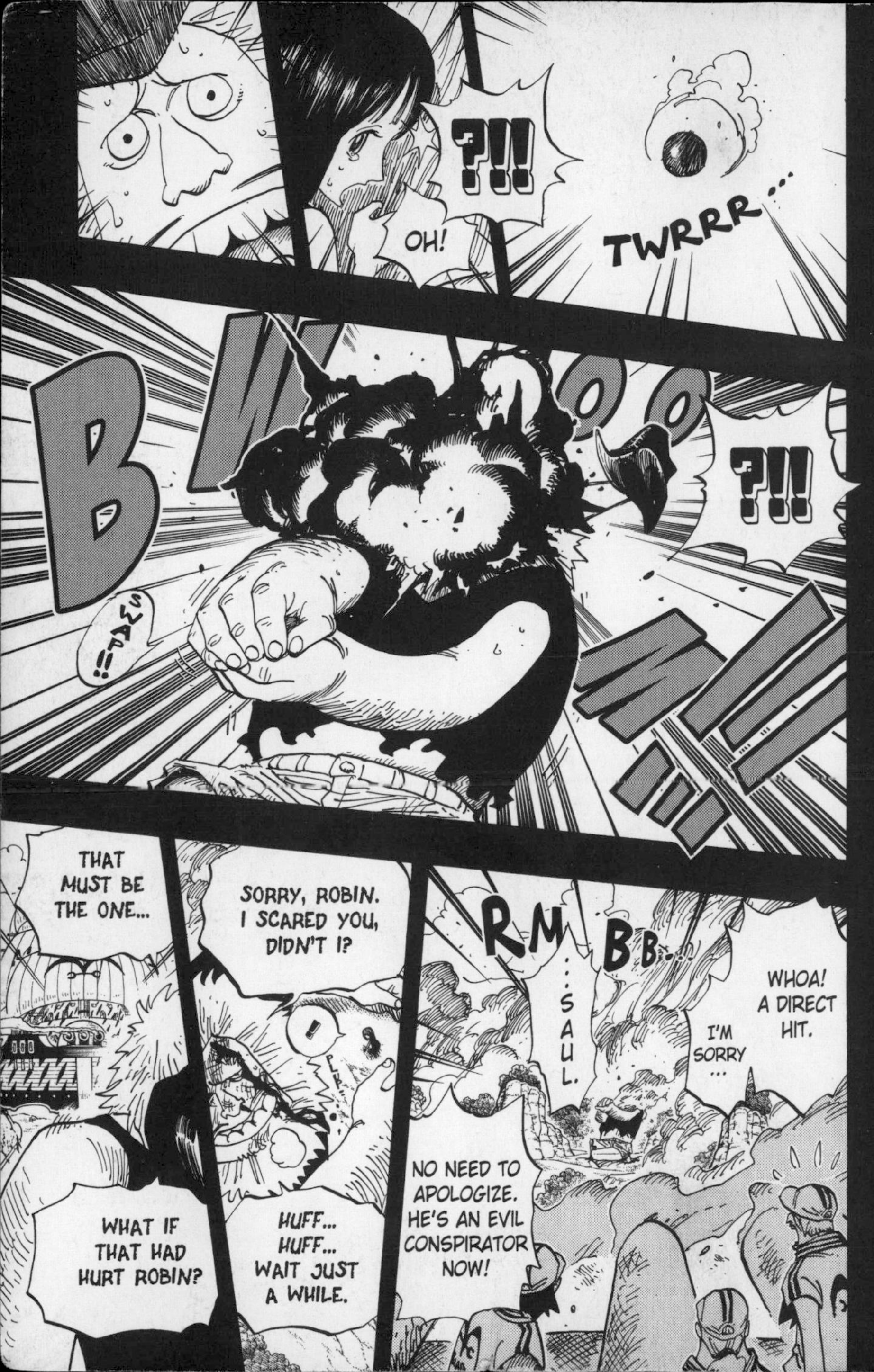
TWRRR...
?!!
OH!
BWOOOM
?!!
SWAP!!
RMBB...
WHOA! A DIRECT HIT.
I'M SORRY...
...SAUL.
NO NEED TO APOLOGIZE. HE'S AN EVIL CONSPIRATOR NOW!
SORRY, ROBIN. I SCARED YOU, DIDN'T I?
!
HUFF... HUFF... WAIT JUST A WHILE.
THAT MUST BE THE ONE...
WHAT IF THAT HAD HURT ROBIN?

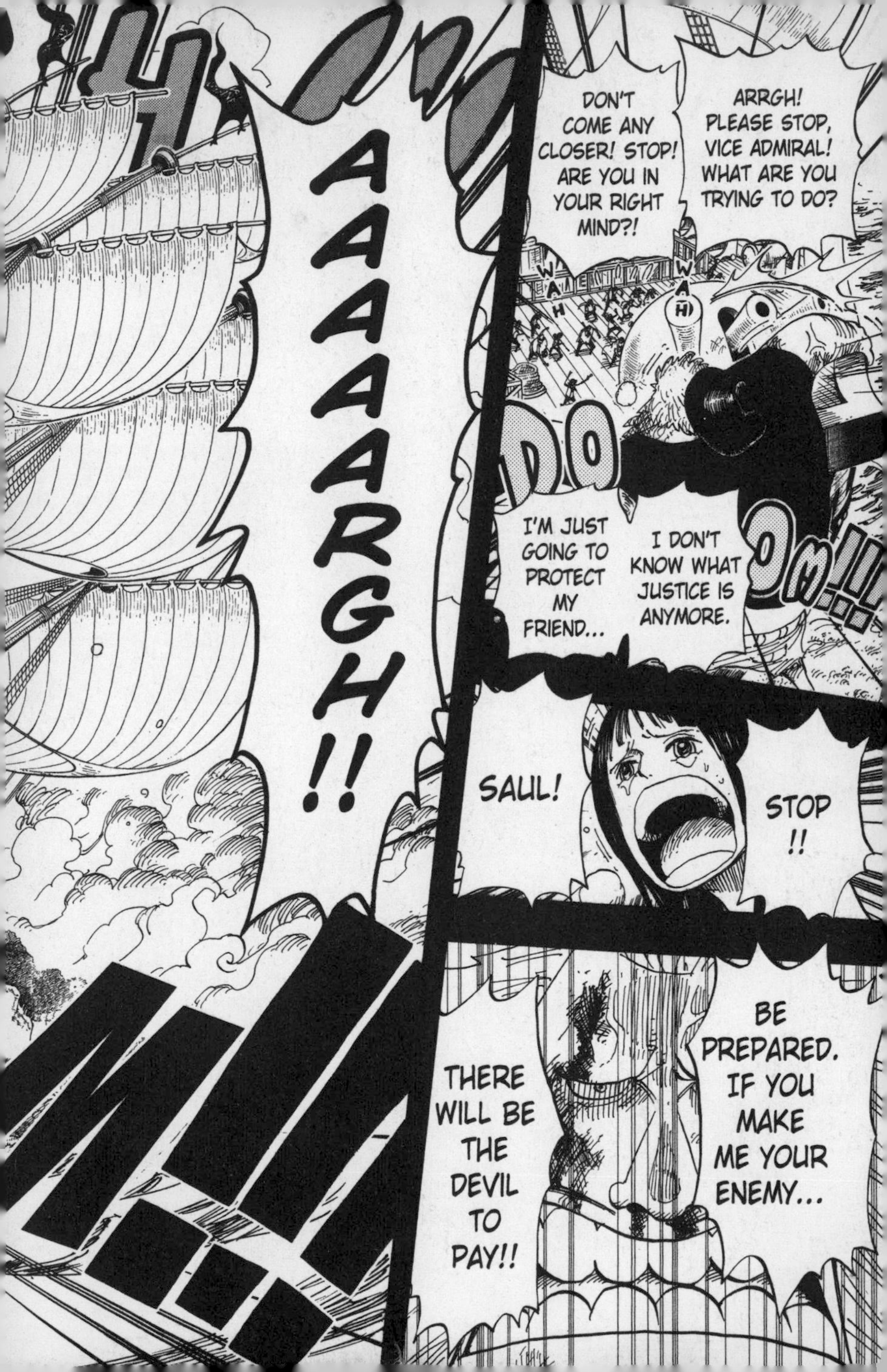
ARRGH! PLEASE STOP, VICE ADMIRAL! WHAT ARE YOU TRYING TO DO?
DON'T COME ANY CLOSER! STOP! ARE YOU IN YOUR RIGHT MIND?!
WAH
WAH
DOOM!!!
I DON'T KNOW WHAT JUSTICE IS ANYMORE.
I'M JUST GOING TO PROTECT MY FRIEND...
STOP!!
SAUL!
BE PREPARED. IF YOU MAKE ME YOUR ENEMY...
THERE WILL BE THE DEVIL TO PAY!!
AAAAARGH!!

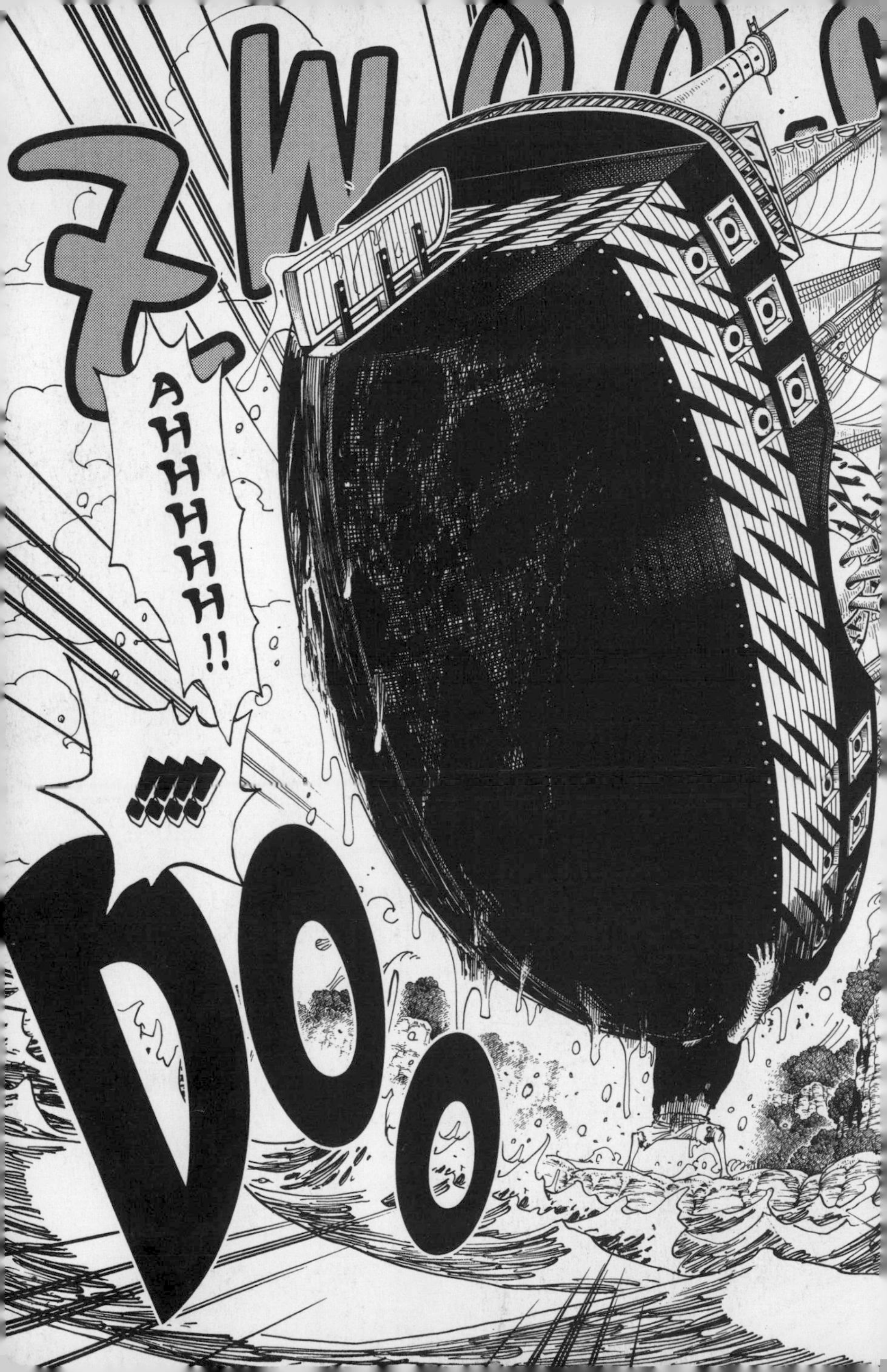
ZWOOO
AHHHHHH!!
DOOO

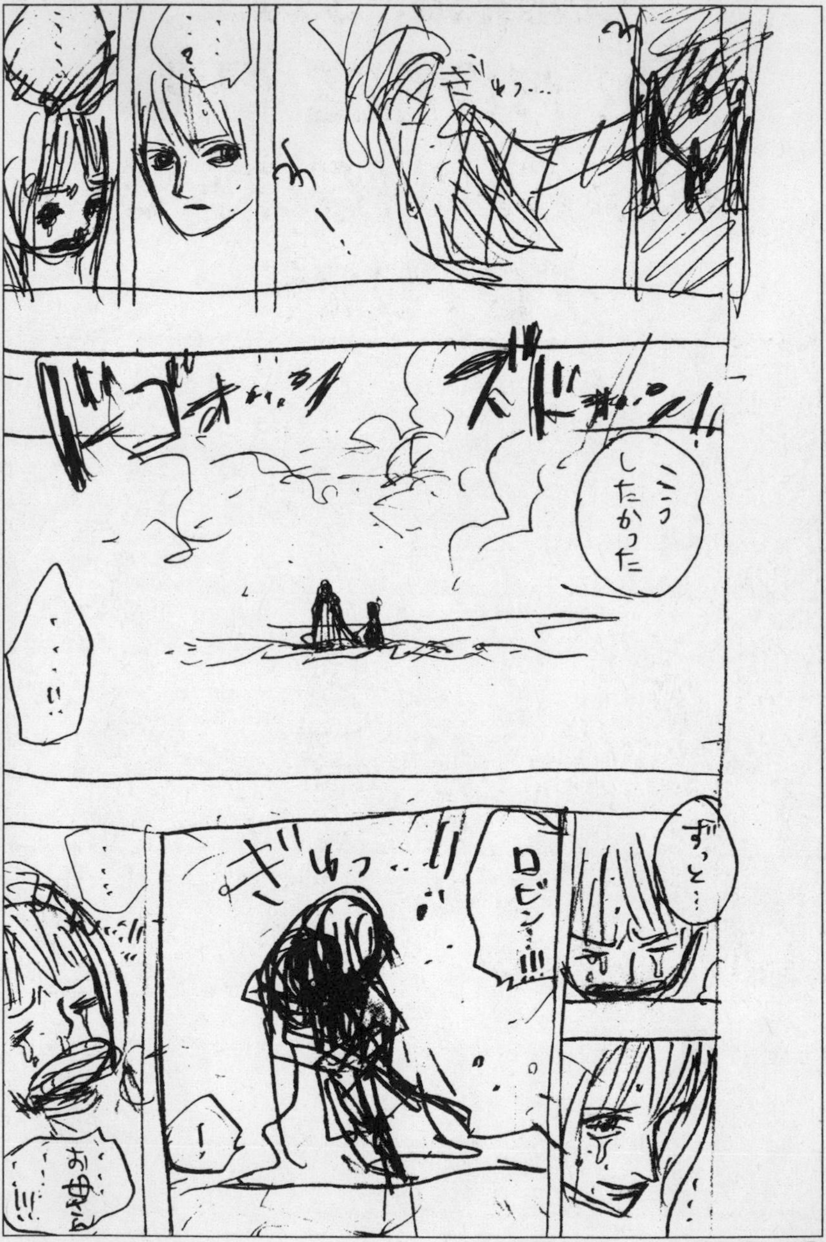
ぎゅっ…
こうしたかった
ずっと…
ロビン…!!!
ぎゅっ…!!
お母さん…!!!

FROM VOL. 41, PAGE 151 --ED.

Chapter 397:

IN HOPES OF REACHING THE FUTURE

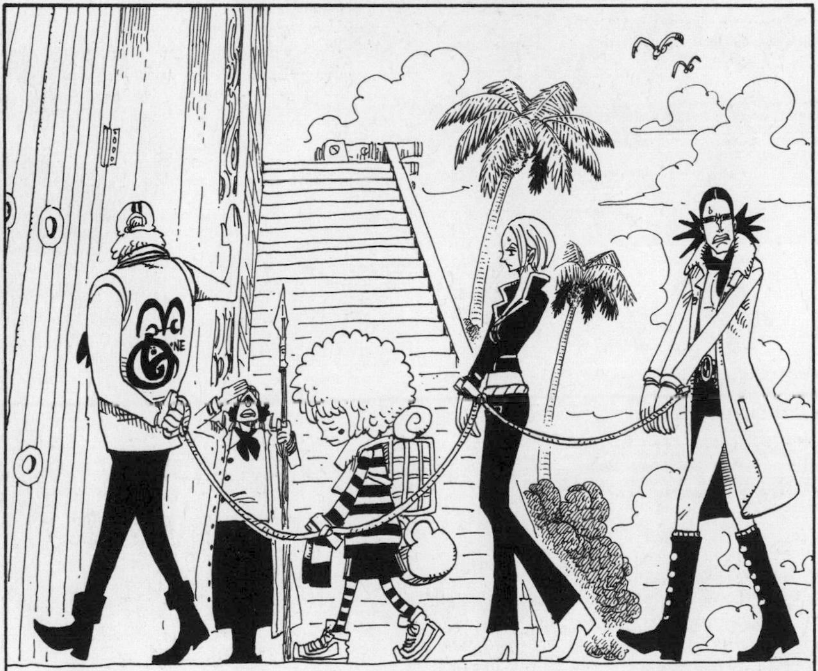

MS. GOLDEN WEEK'S PLAN, A BAROQUE REUNION, VOL. 29:
"PRETENDING TO BE CAPTURED TO INFILTRATE THE PRISON"

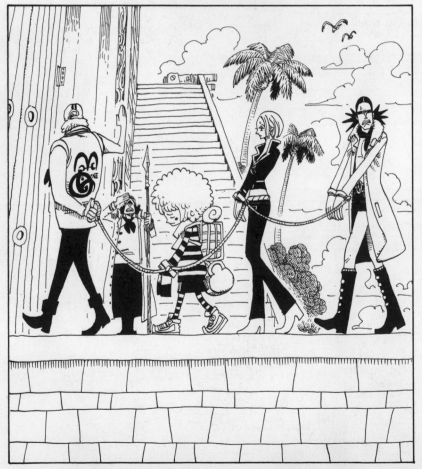

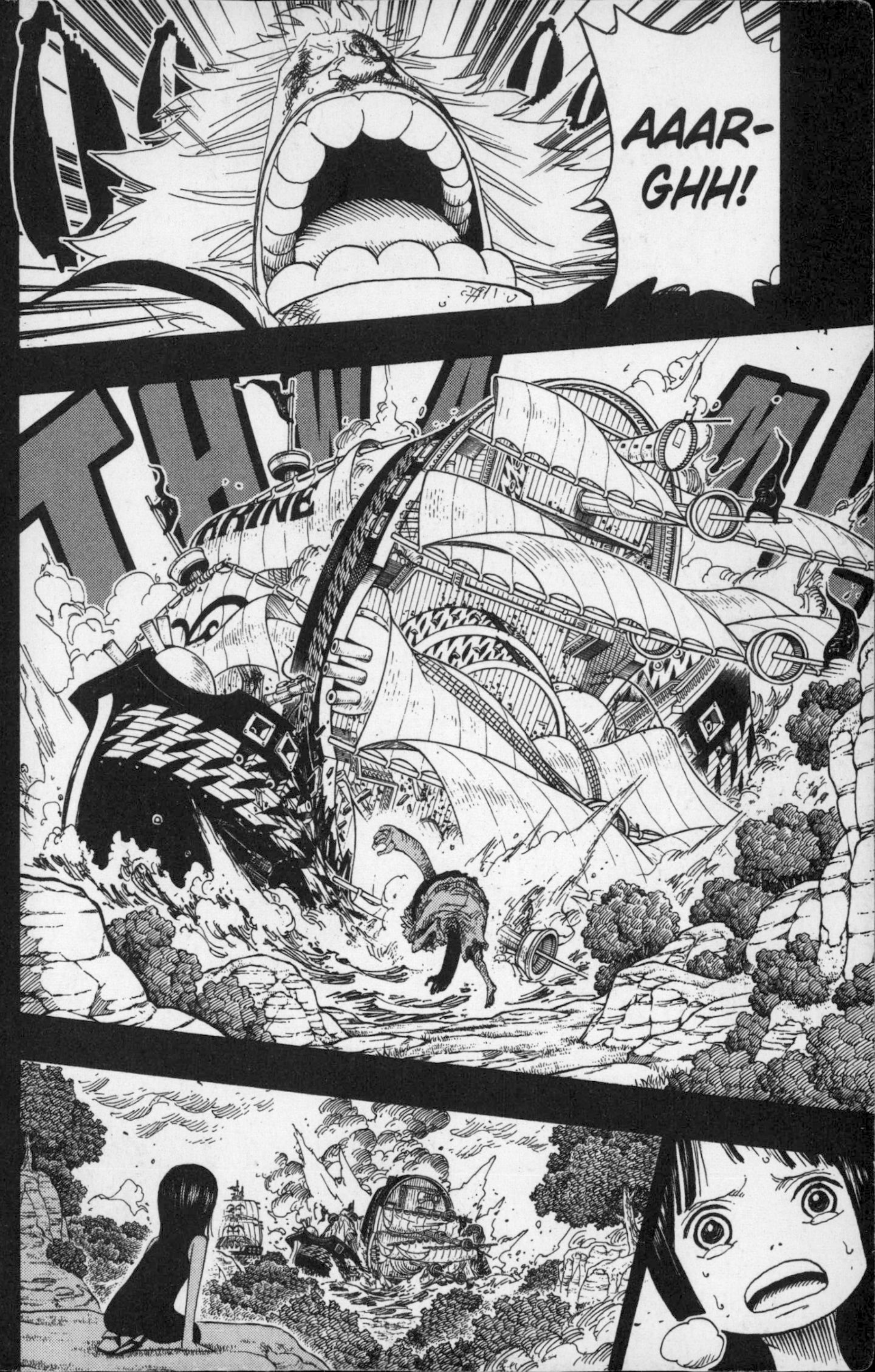
AAAR-
GHH!
ARINE

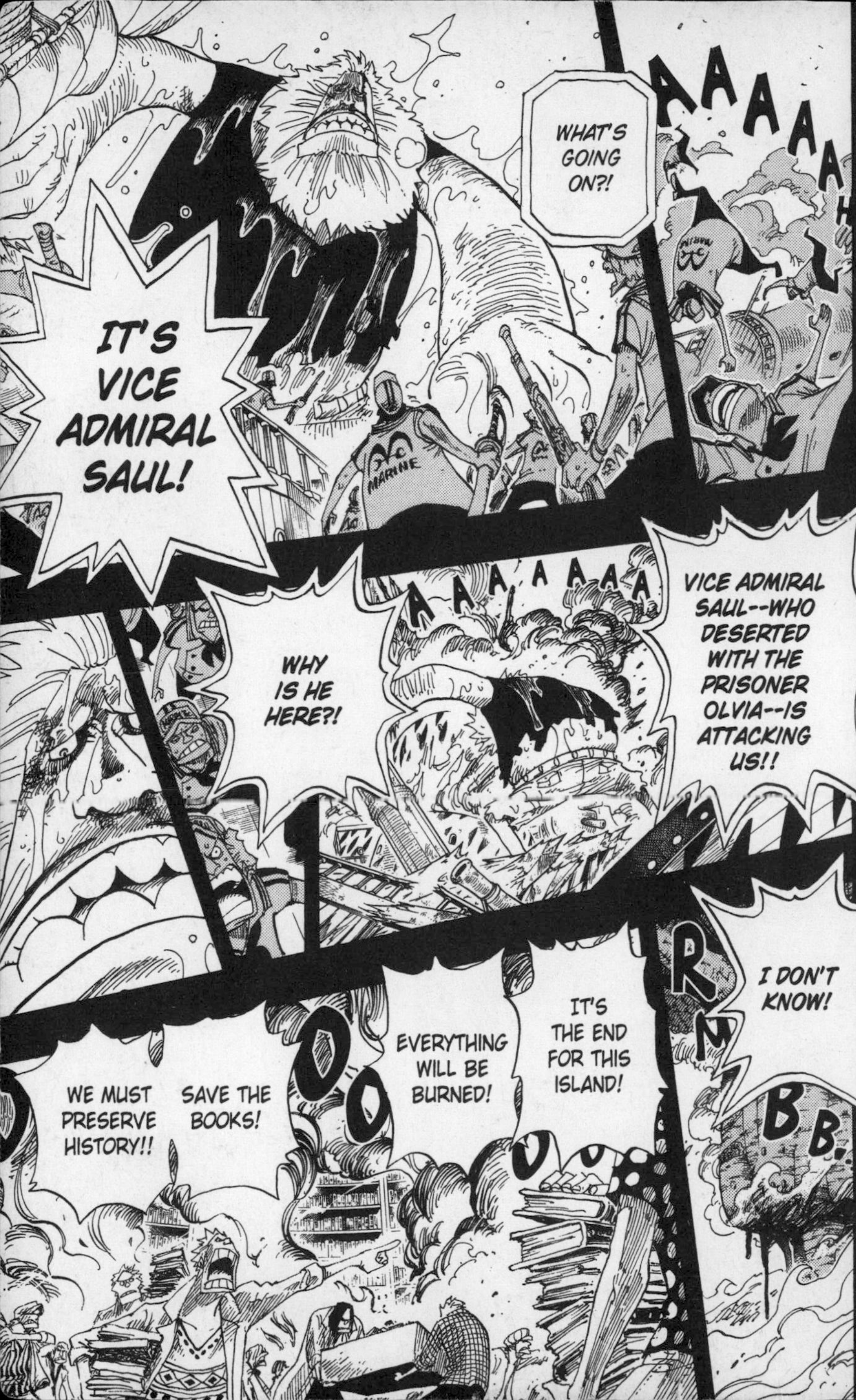
AAAAAAH
WHAT'S GOING ON?!
IT'S VICE ADMIRAL SAUL!
AAAAAAA
VICE ADMIRAL SAUL--WHO DESERTED WITH THE PRISONER OLVIA--IS ATTACKING US!!
WHY IS HE HERE?!
R M BB.
I DON'T KNOW!
IT'S THE END FOR THIS ISLAND!
EVERYTHING WILL BE BURNED!
SAVE THE BOOKS!
WE MUST PRESERVE HISTORY!!

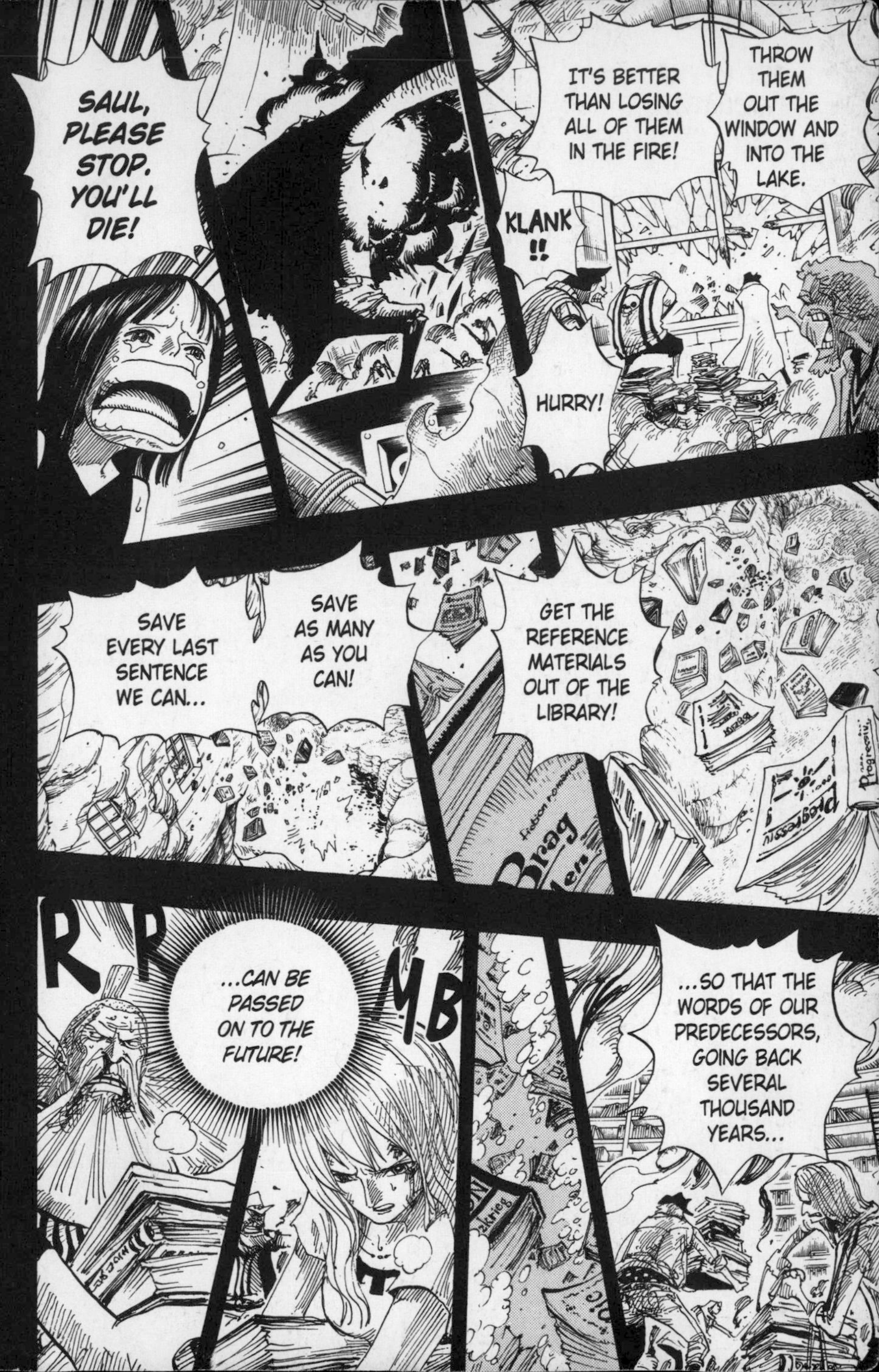
THROW THEM OUT THE WINDOW AND INTO THE LAKE.
IT'S BETTER THAN LOSING ALL OF THEM IN THE FIRE!
KLANK!!
HURRY!
SAUL, PLEASE STOP. YOU'LL DIE!
GET THE REFERENCE MATERIALS OUT OF THE LIBRARY!
SAVE AS MANY AS YOU CAN!
SAVE EVERY LAST SENTENCE WE CAN...
...SO THAT THE WORDS OF OUR PREDECESSORS, GOING BACK SEVERAL THOUSAND YEARS...
...CAN BE PASSED ON TO THE FUTURE!
RRMB

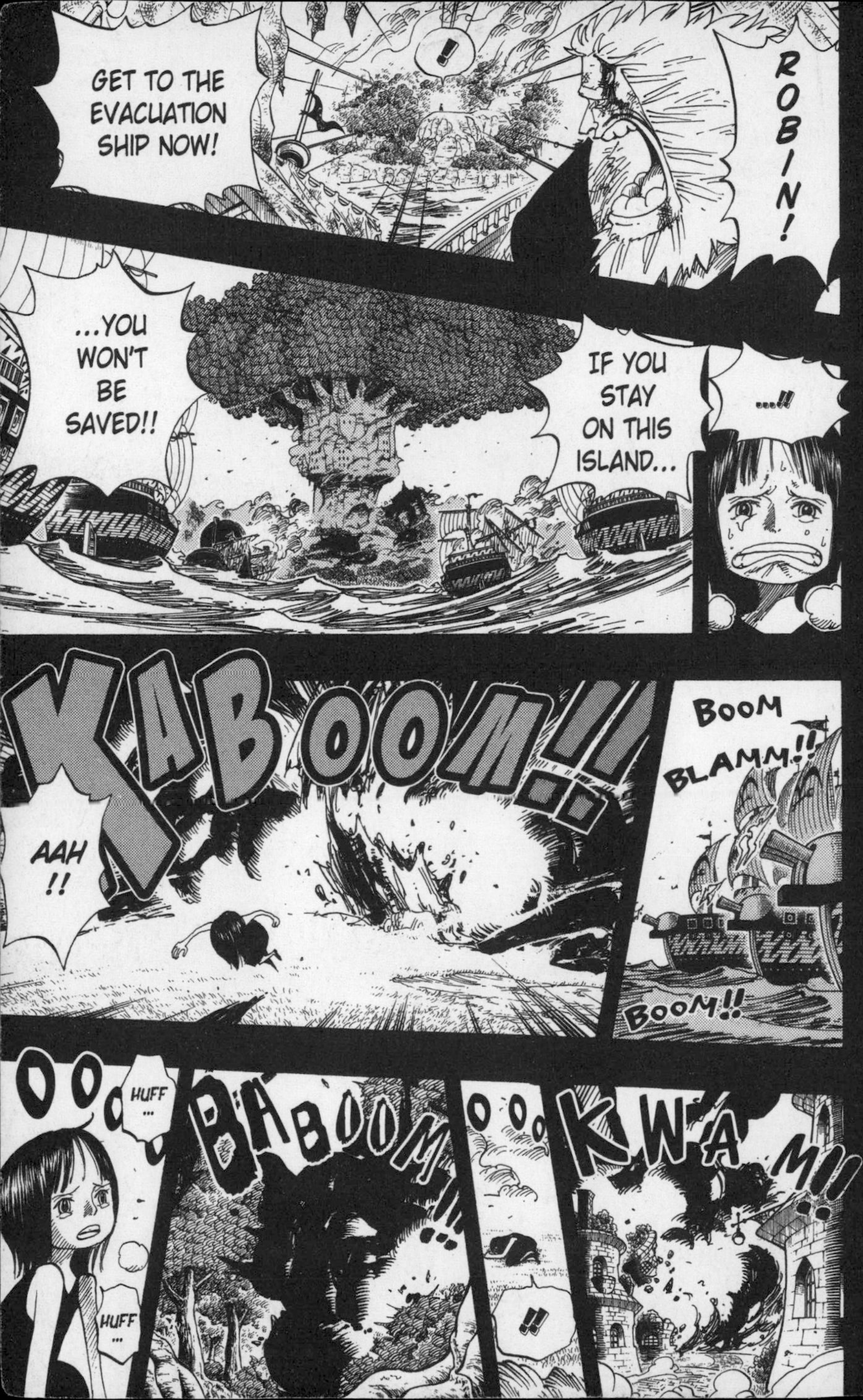
ROBIN!
!
GET TO THE EVACUATION SHIP NOW!
...!!
IF YOU STAY ON THIS ISLAND...
...YOU WON'T BE SAVED!!
BOOM
BLAMM!!
BOOM!!
KABOOM!!
AAH!!
KWAM!!
!!
BABOOM!!
HUFF...
HUFF...

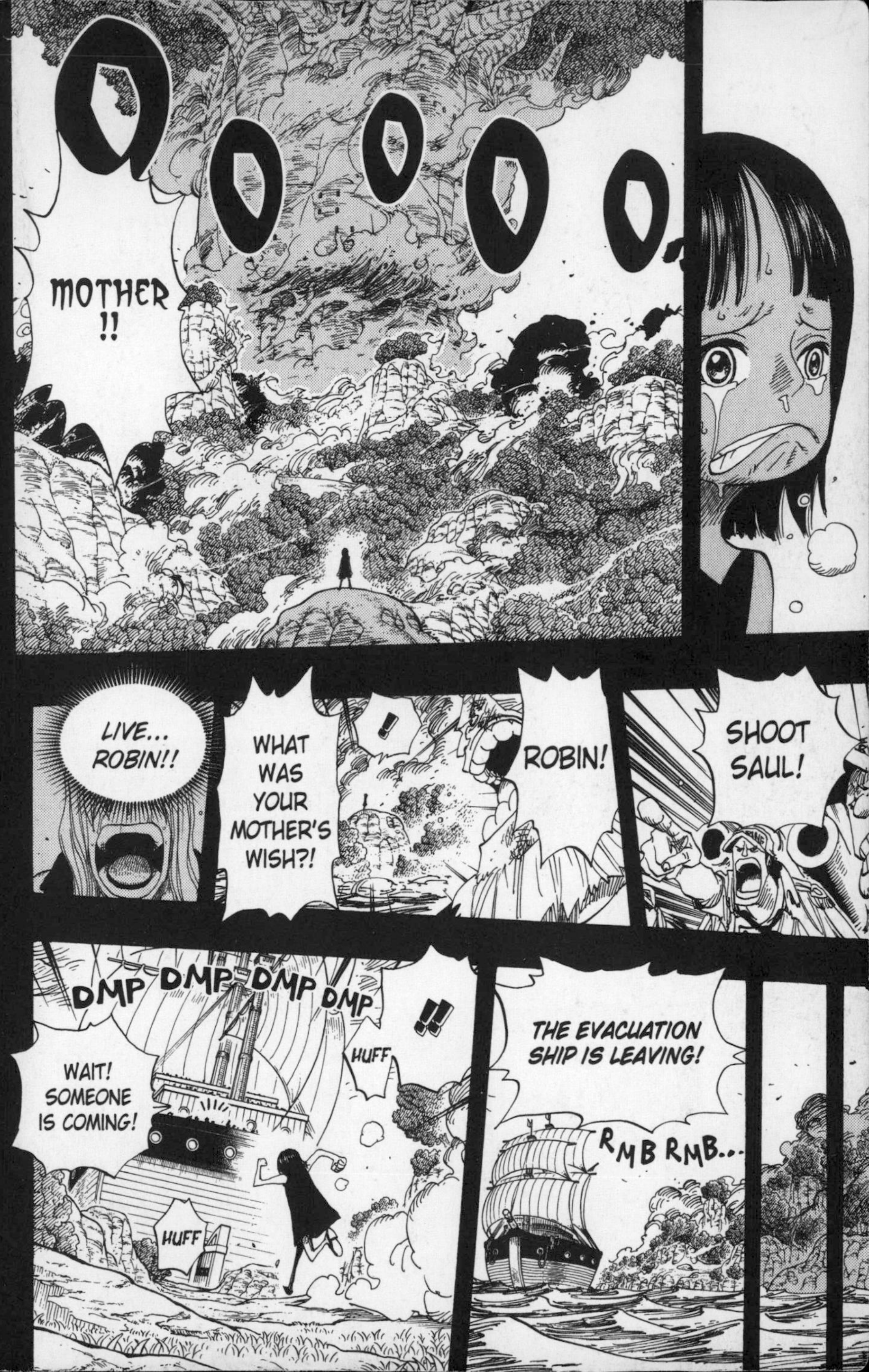
MOTHER !!
SHOOT SAUL!
ROBIN!
WHAT WAS YOUR MOTHER'S WISH?!
LIVE... ROBIN!!
THE EVACUATION SHIP IS LEAVING!
RMB RMB...
DMP DMP DMP DMP
!!
HUFF
WAIT! SOMEONE IS COMING!
HUFF

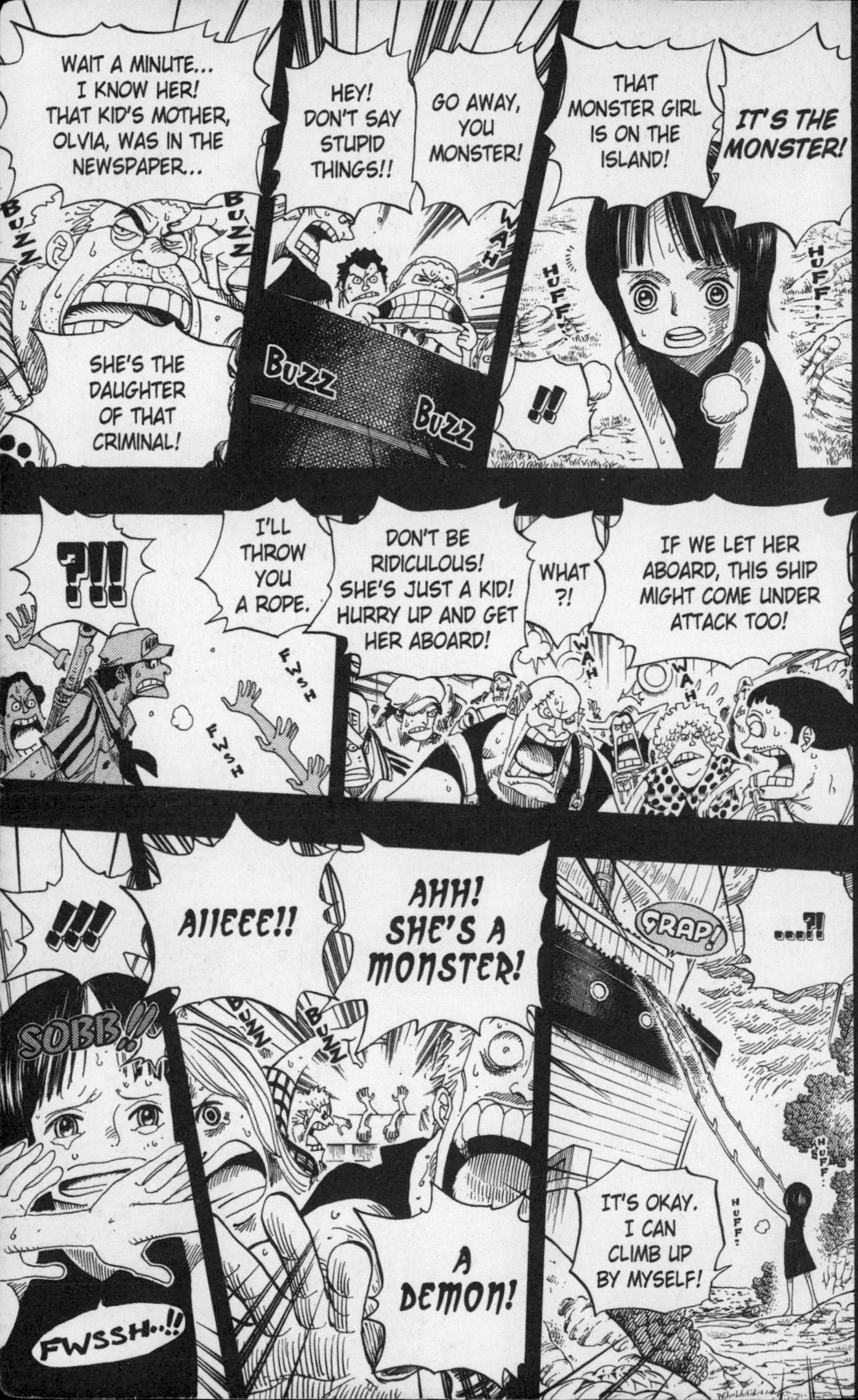
IT'S THE MONSTER!
THAT MONSTER GIRL IS ON THE ISLAND!
HUFF
HUFF
!!
GO AWAY, YOU MONSTER!
HEY! DON'T SAY STUPID THINGS!!
WAH
BUZZ
BUZZ
WAIT A MINUTE... I KNOW HER! THAT KID'S MOTHER, OLVIA, WAS IN THE NEWSPAPER...
BUZZ
BUZZ
SHE'S THE DAUGHTER OF THAT CRIMINAL!
IF WE LET HER ABOARD, THIS SHIP MIGHT COME UNDER ATTACK TOO!
WHAT ?!
DON'T BE RIDICULOUS! SHE'S JUST A KID! HURRY UP AND GET HER ABOARD!
WAH
WAH
I'LL THROW YOU A ROPE.
?!!
FWSH
FWSH
...?!
GRAP!
HUFF
IT'S OKAY. I CAN CLIMB UP BY MYSELF!
HUFF
AHH! SHE'S A MONSTER!
BUZZ
A DEMON!
AIIEEE!!
!!!
SOBB!!
FWSSH..!!

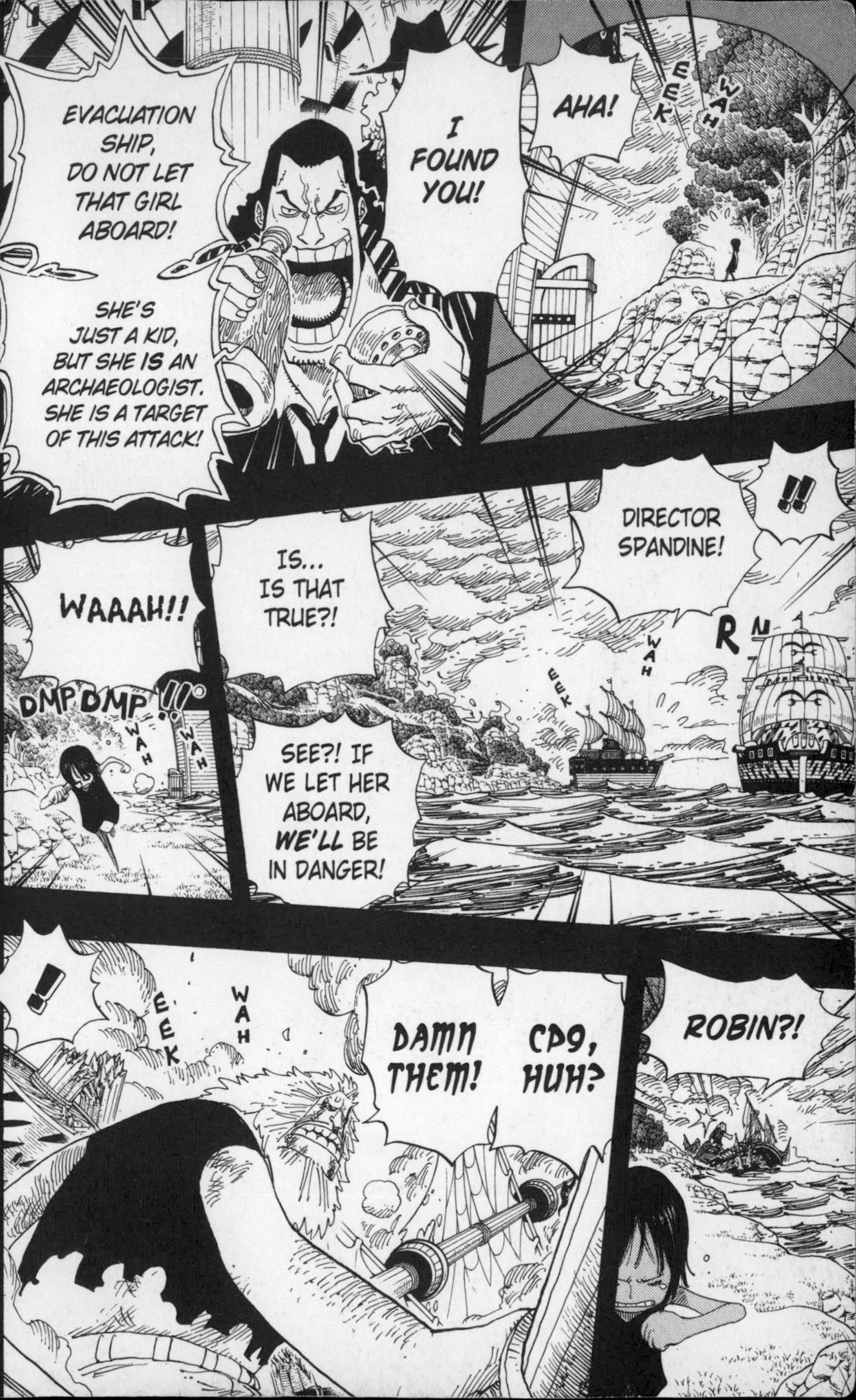
EEK
WAH
AHA!
I FOUND YOU!
EVACUATION SHIP, DO NOT LET THAT GIRL ABOARD!
SHE'S JUST A KID, BUT SHE IS AN ARCHAEOLOGIST. SHE IS A TARGET OF THIS ATTACK!
!!
DIRECTOR SPANDINE!
RN
WAH
EEK
IS... IS THAT TRUE?!
SEE?! IF WE LET HER ABOARD, WE'LL BE IN DANGER!
WAAAH!!
DMP DMP
!!!
WAH
WAH
ROBIN?!
CP9, HUH?
DAMN THEM!
WAH
EEK
!

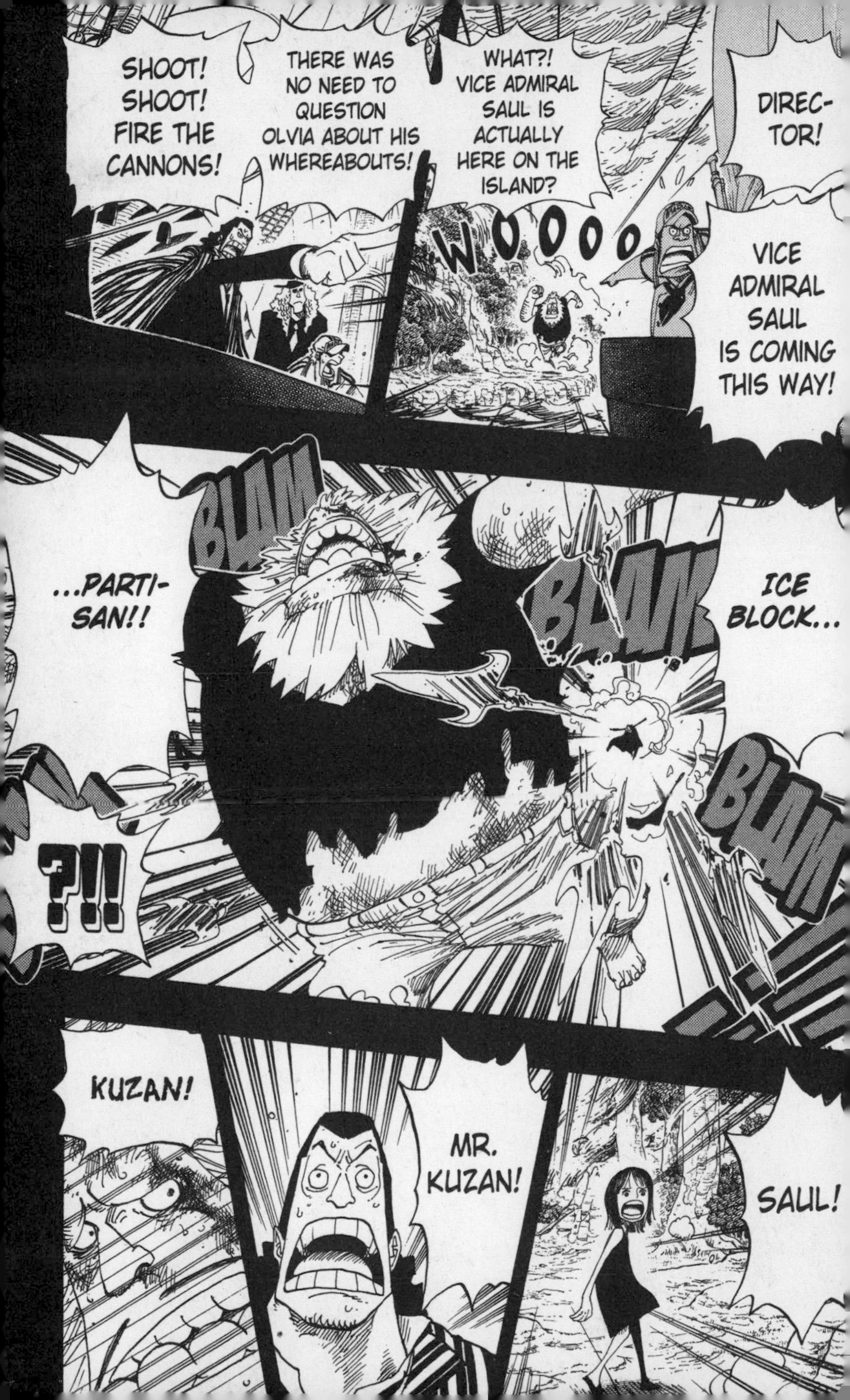
DIREC-
TOR!
VICE ADMIRAL SAUL IS COMING THIS WAY!
WOOOO
WHAT?! VICE ADMIRAL SAUL IS ACTUALLY HERE ON THE ISLAND?
THERE WAS NO NEED TO QUESTION OLVIA ABOUT HIS WHEREABOUTS!
SHOOT! SHOOT! FIRE THE CANNONS!
ICE BLOCK...
BLAM
BLAM
BLAM
...PARTI-
SAN!!
?!!
SAUL!
MR. KUZAN!
KUZAN!

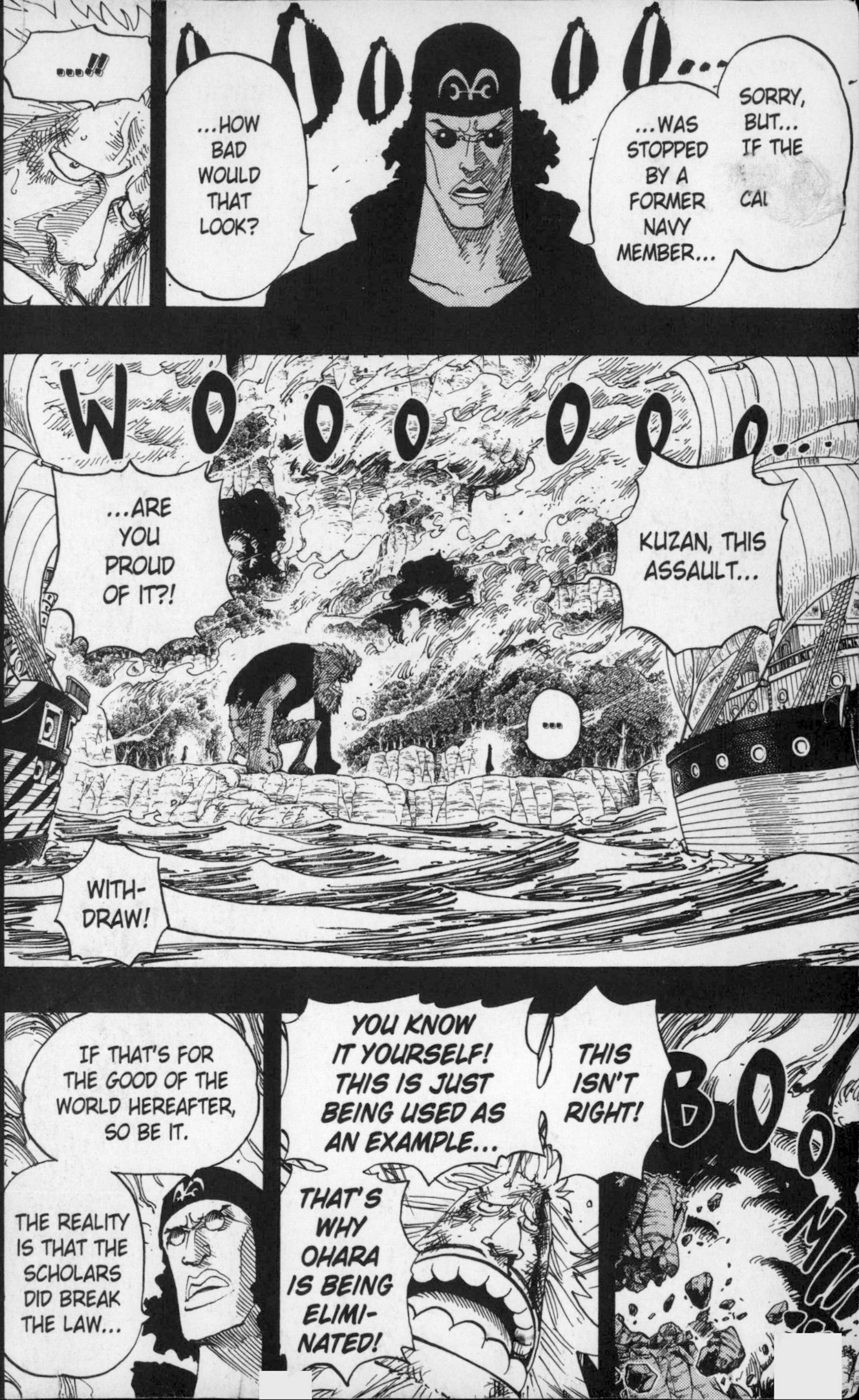
OOOOO...
SORRY, BUT... IF THE
CA
...WAS STOPPED BY A FORMER NAVY MEMBER...
...HOW BAD WOULD THAT LOOK?
...!!
WOOOOO...
KUZAN, THIS ASSAULT...
...ARE YOU PROUD OF IT?!
...
WITH-DRAW!
BOO
M
THIS ISN'T RIGHT!
YOU KNOW IT YOURSELF! THIS IS JUST BEING USED AS AN EXAMPLE...
THAT'S WHY OHARA IS BEING ELIMI-NATED!
IF THAT'S FOR THE GOOD OF THE WORLD HEREAFTER, SO BE IT.
THE REALITY IS THAT THE SCHOLARS DID BREAK THE LAW...

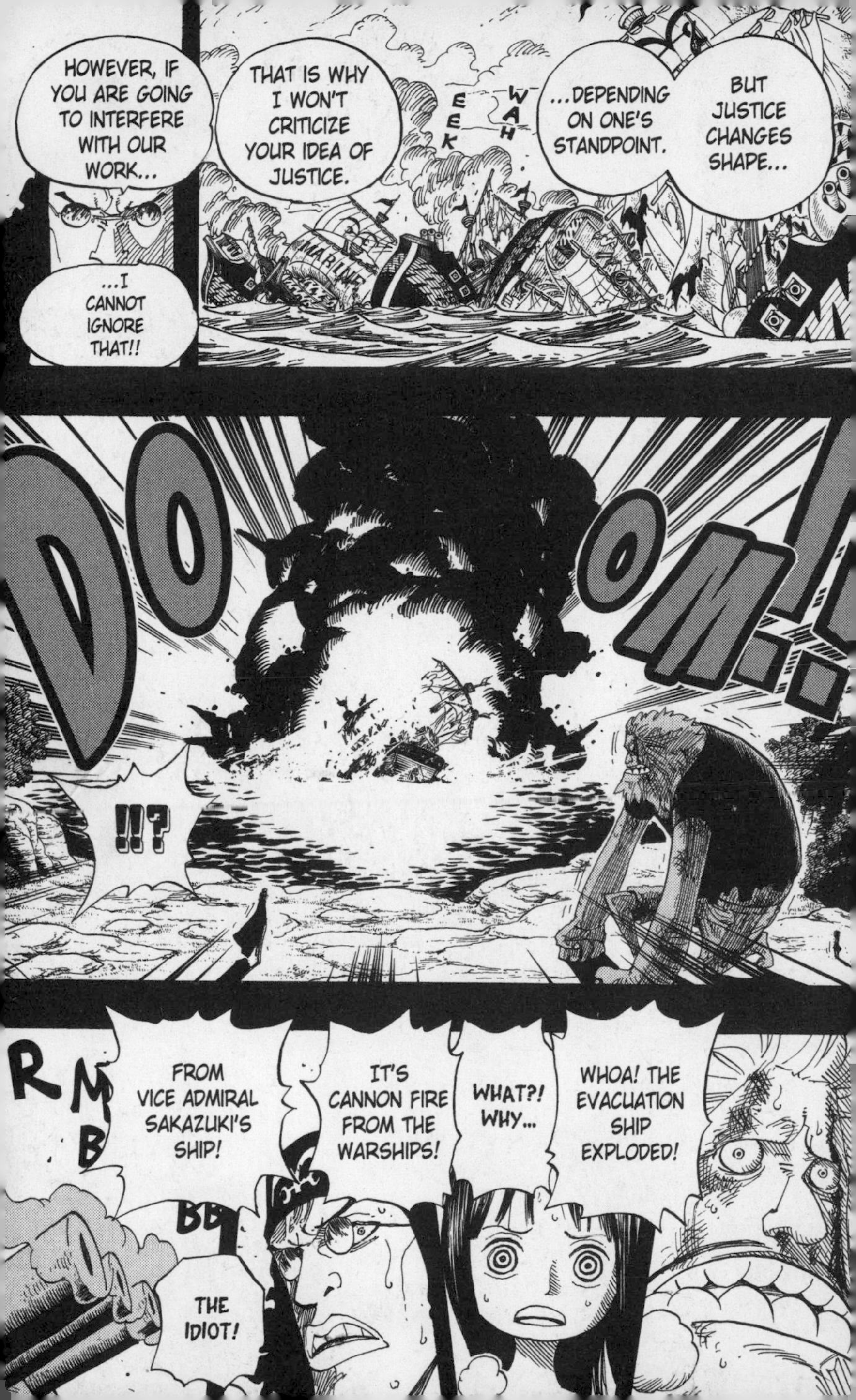
BUT JUSTICE CHANGES SHAPE...
...DEPENDING ON ONE'S STANDPOINT.
WAH
EEK
THAT IS WHY I WON'T CRITICIZE YOUR IDEA OF JUSTICE.
HOWEVER, IF YOU ARE GOING TO INTERFERE WITH OUR WORK...
...I CANNOT IGNORE THAT!!
DOOM..!!
!!?
WHOA! THE EVACUATION SHIP EXPLODED!
WHAT?! WHY...
IT'S CANNON FIRE FROM THE WARSHIPS!
FROM VICE ADMIRAL SAKAZUKI'S SHIP!
RMB
BB
THE IDIOT!

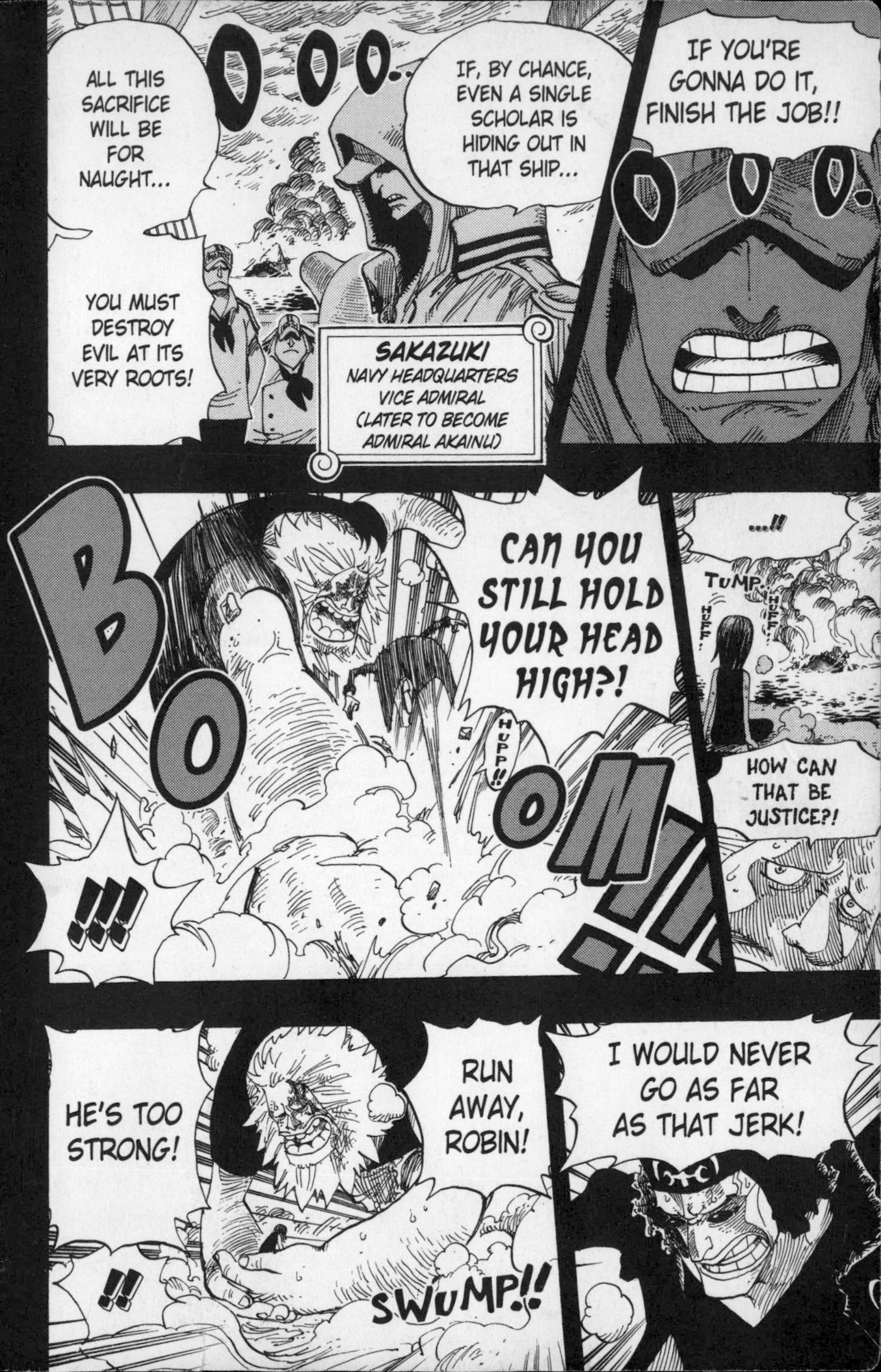

IF YOU'RE GONNA DO IT, FINISH THE JOB!!
IF, BY CHANCE, EVEN A SINGLE SCHOLAR IS HIDING OUT IN THAT SHIP...
ALL THIS SACRIFICE WILL BE FOR NAUGHT...
SAKAZUKI
NAVY HEADQUARTERS VICE ADMIRAL (LATER TO BECOME ADMIRAL AKAINU)
YOU MUST DESTROY EVIL AT ITS VERY ROOTS!
...!!
TUMP
HUFF HUFF
HOW CAN THAT BE JUSTICE?!
CAN YOU STILL HOLD YOUR HEAD HIGH?!
HUPP!!
BOOOM
!!!
I WOULD NEVER GO AS FAR AS THAT JERK!
RUN AWAY, ROBIN!
HE'S TOO STRONG!
!!
SWUMP!!

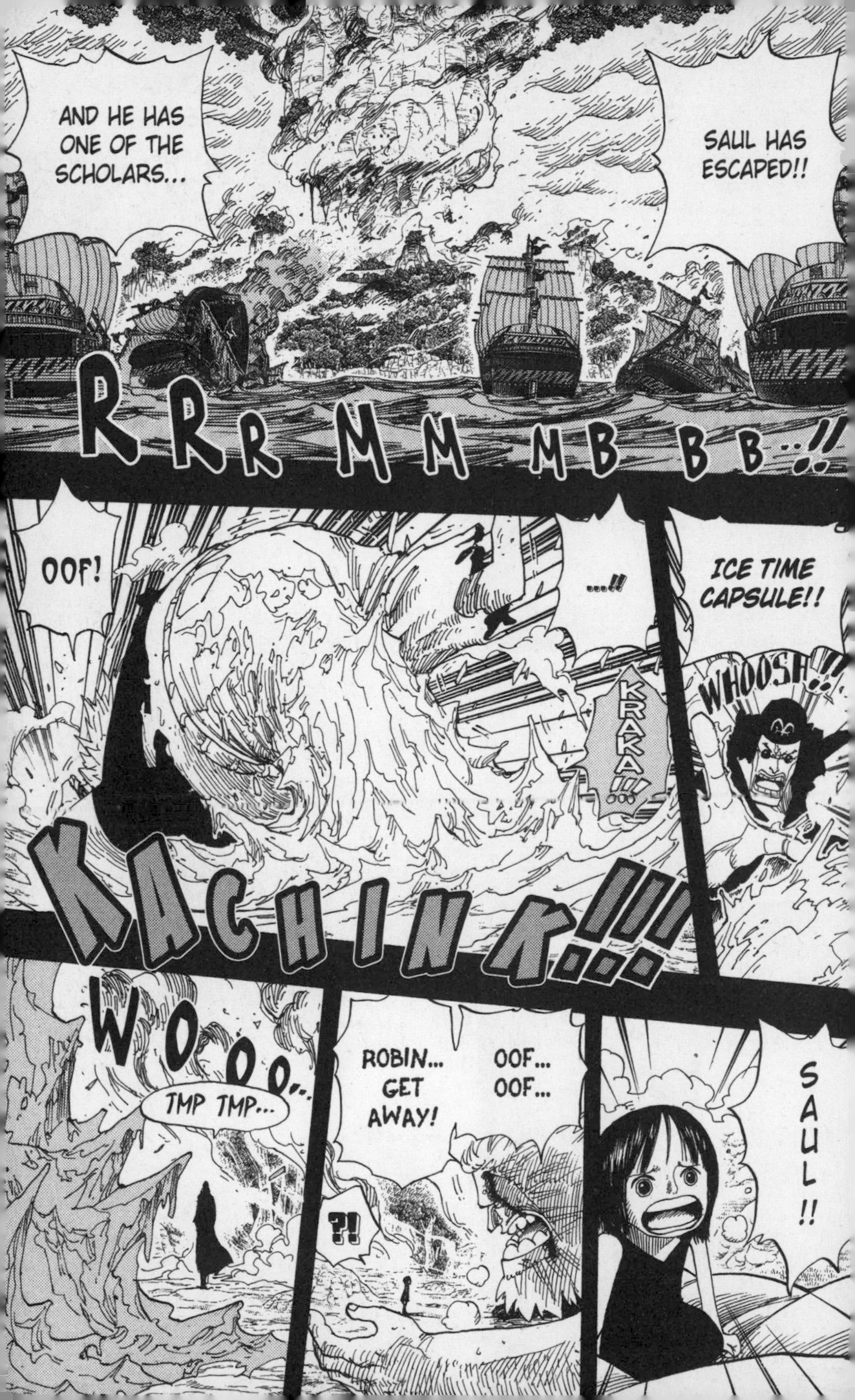
SAUL HAS ESCAPED!!
AND HE HAS ONE OF THE SCHOLARS...
RRRMMMBBB..!!
ICE TIME CAPSULE!!
WHOOSH!!
...!!
KRAKA!!
OOF!
KACHINK!!!
SAUL!!
OOF... OOF...
ROBIN... GET AWAY!
?!
WOOO..
TMP TMP...

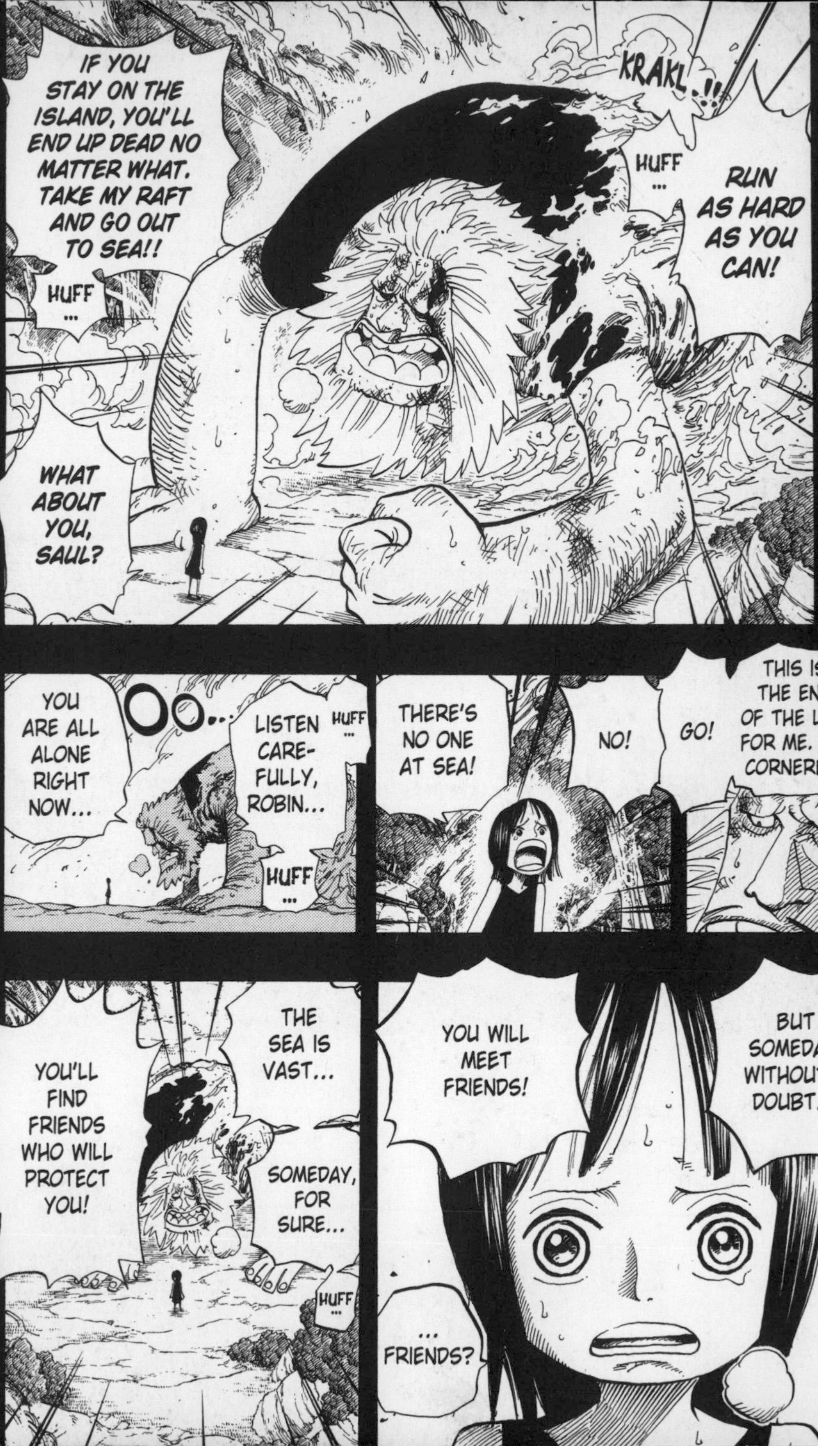
KRAKL..!!
HUFF ...
RUN AS HARD AS YOU CAN!
IF YOU STAY ON THE ISLAND, YOU'LL END UP DEAD NO MATTER WHAT. TAKE MY RAFT AND GO OUT TO SEA!!
HUFF ...
WHAT ABOUT YOU, SAUL?
THIS IS THE END OF THE LINE FOR ME. I'M CORNERED!
GO!
NO!
THERE'S NO ONE AT SEA!
HUFF ...
LISTEN CAREFULLY, ROBIN...
OO...
YOU ARE ALL ALONE RIGHT NOW...
HUFF ...
BUT SOMEDAY, WITHOUT A DOUBT...
YOU WILL MEET FRIENDS!
... FRIENDS?
THE SEA IS VAST...
SOMEDAY, FOR SURE...
YOU'LL FIND FRIENDS WHO WILL PROTECT YOU!
HUFF ...

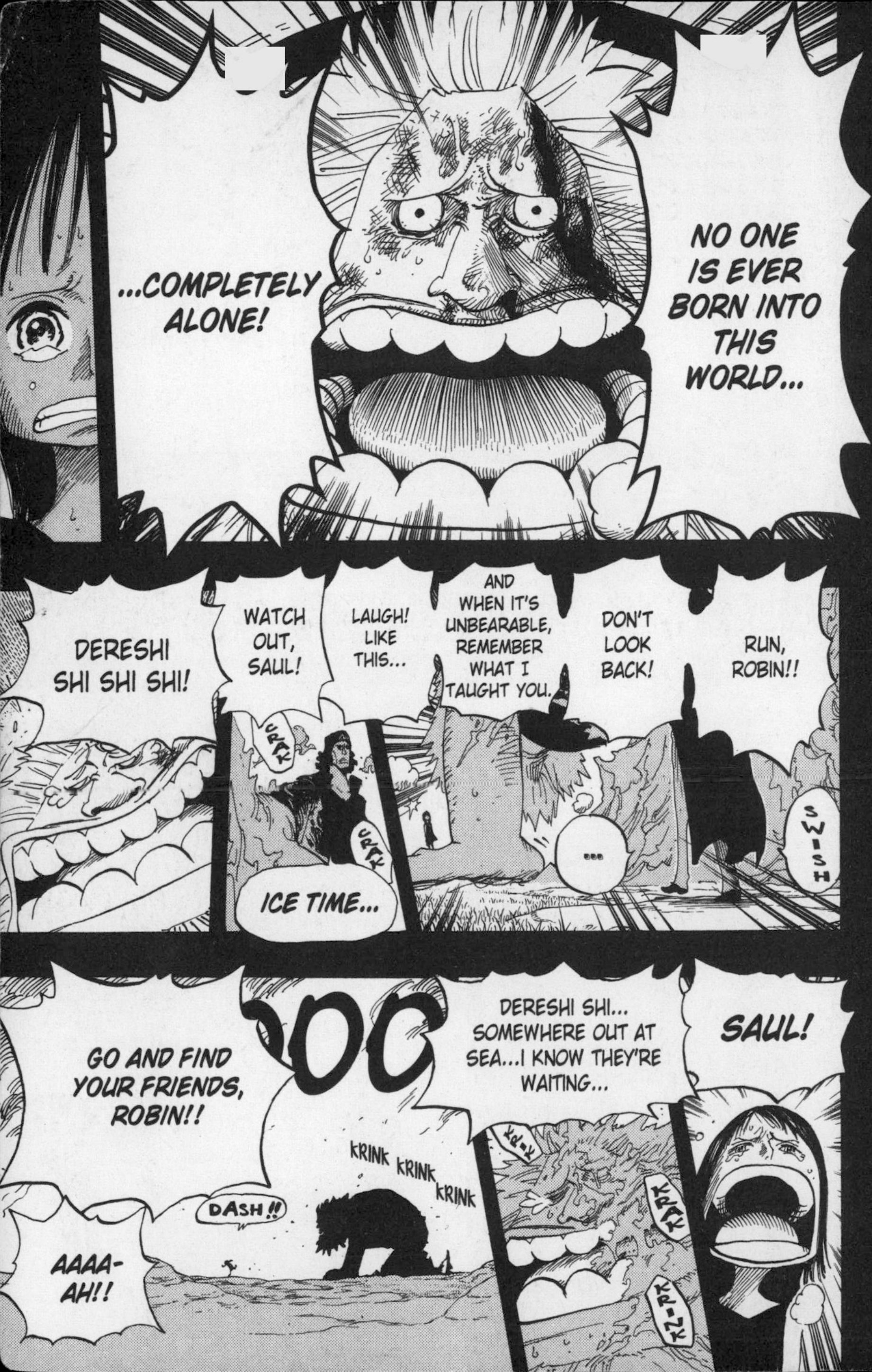
NO ONE IS EVER BORN INTO THIS WORLD...
...COMPLETELY ALONE!
RUN, ROBIN!!
DON'T LOOK BACK!
SWISH
...
AND WHEN IT'S UNBEARABLE, REMEMBER WHAT I TAUGHT YOU.
LAUGH! LIKE THIS...
WATCH OUT, SAUL!
CRAK
CRAK
ICE TIME...
DERESHI SHI SHI SHI!
SAUL!
DERESHI SHI... SOMEWHERE OUT AT SEA...I KNOW THEY'RE WAITING...
KRAK
KRINK
GO AND FIND YOUR FRIENDS, ROBIN!!
KRINK KRINK KRINK
DASH!!
AAAA-AH!!

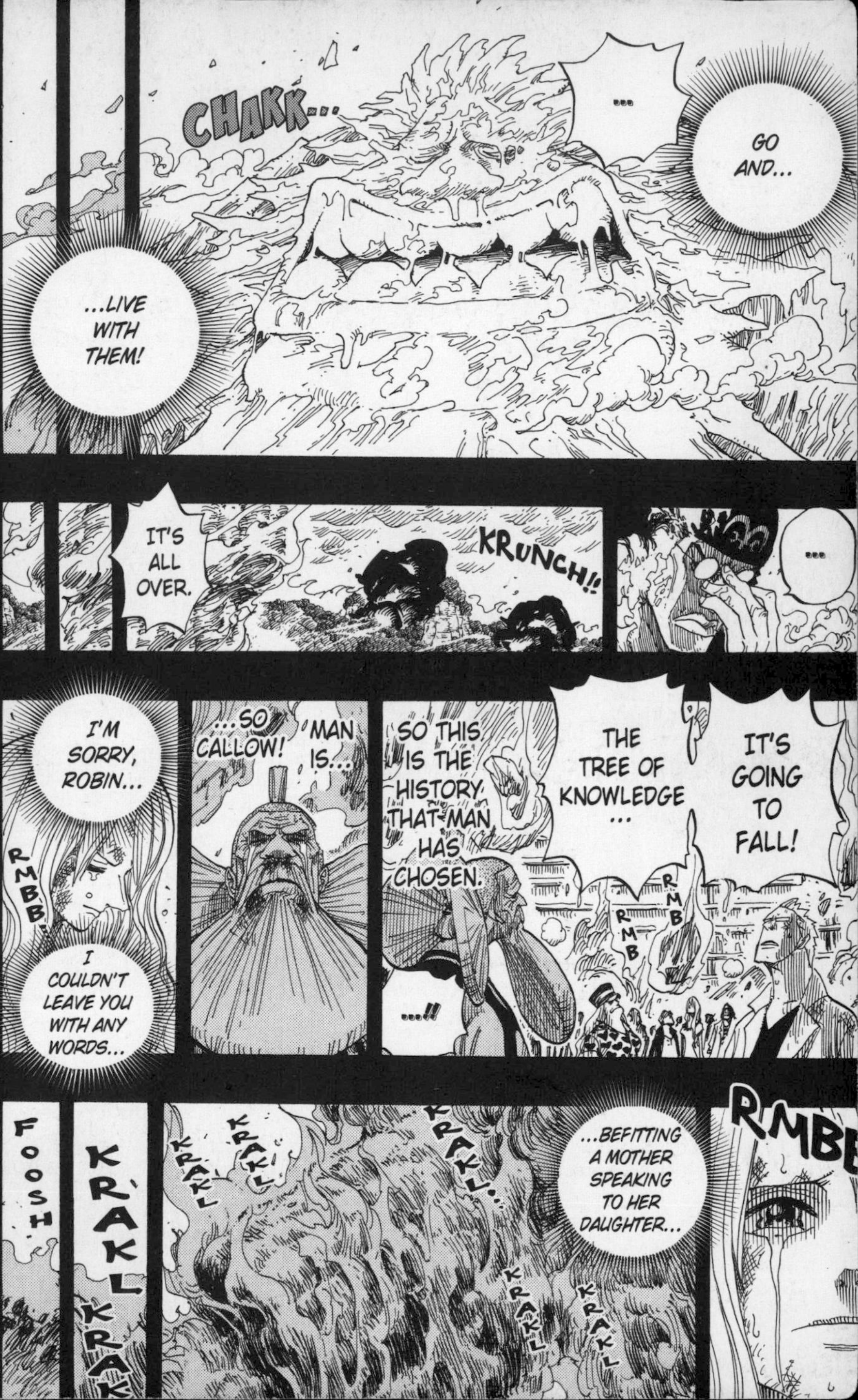
...
GO AND...
CHAKK...
...LIVE WITH THEM!
...
KRUNCH!!
IT'S ALL OVER.
IT'S GOING TO FALL!
THE TREE OF KNOWLEDGE ...
SO THIS IS THE HISTORY THAT MAN HAS CHOSEN.
RMB
RMB
...!!
MAN IS...
...SO CALLOW!
I'M SORRY, ROBIN...
RMBB
I COULDN'T LEAVE YOU WITH ANY WORDS...
RMBB
...BEFITTING A MOTHER SPEAKING TO HER DAUGHTER...
KRAKL...
KRAKL
KRAKL
KRAKL
KRAKL
KRAKL
KRAKL
FOOSH
KRAK

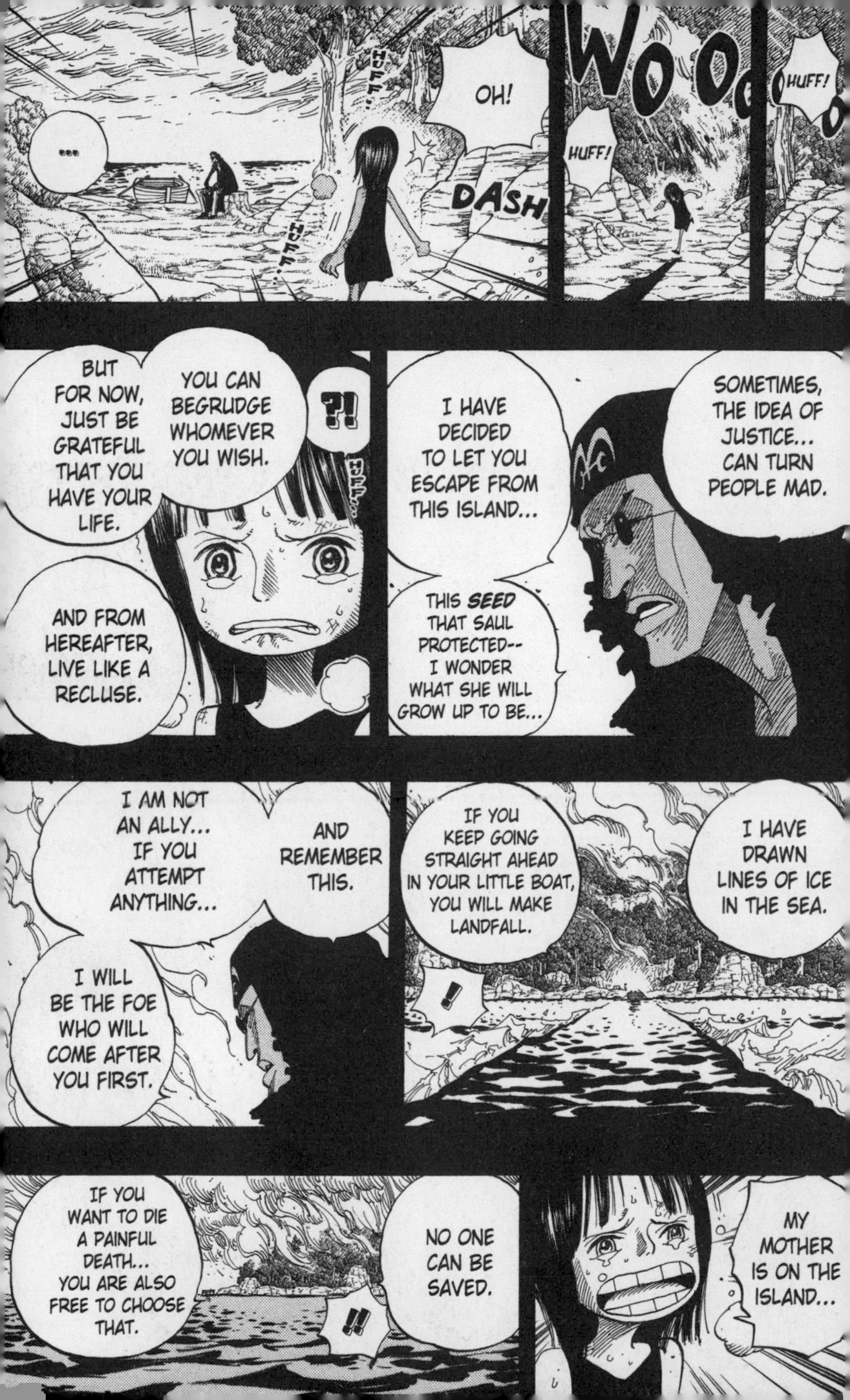
HUFF!
WOOOO
HUFF!
OH!
HUFF HUFF...
DASH
HUFF HUFF...
...
SOMETIMES, THE IDEA OF JUSTICE... CAN TURN PEOPLE MAD.
I HAVE DECIDED TO LET YOU ESCAPE FROM THIS ISLAND...
THIS SEED THAT SAUL PROTECTED-- I WONDER WHAT SHE WILL GROW UP TO BE...
?!
HUFF...
YOU CAN BEGRUDGE WHOMEVER YOU WISH.
BUT FOR NOW, JUST BE GRATEFUL THAT YOU HAVE YOUR LIFE.
AND FROM HEREAFTER, LIVE LIKE A RECLUSE.
I HAVE DRAWN LINES OF ICE IN THE SEA.
IF YOU KEEP GOING STRAIGHT AHEAD IN YOUR LITTLE BOAT, YOU WILL MAKE LANDFALL.
!
AND REMEMBER THIS.
I AM NOT AN ALLY... IF YOU ATTEMPT ANYTHING...
I WILL BE THE FOE WHO WILL COME AFTER YOU FIRST.
MY MOTHER IS ON THE ISLAND...
NO ONE CAN BE SAVED.
!!
IF YOU WANT TO DIE A PAINFUL DEATH... YOU ARE ALSO FREE TO CHOOSE THAT.

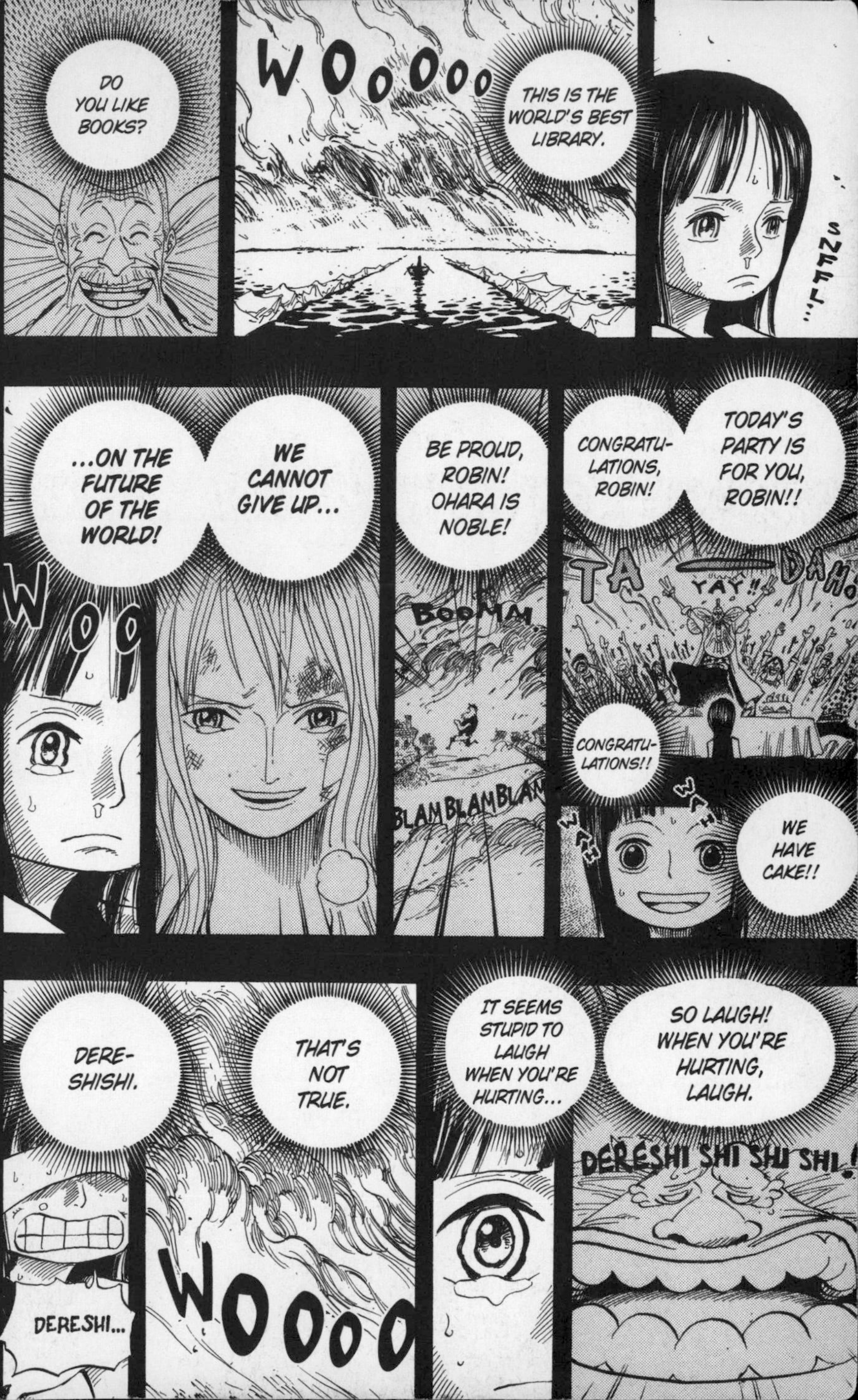
SNFFL...
THIS IS THE WORLD'S BEST LIBRARY.
WOOOOO
DO YOU LIKE BOOKS?
TODAY'S PARTY IS FOR YOU, ROBIN!!
CONGRATU-LATIONS, ROBIN!
TA DAH
YAY!!
CONGRATU-LATIONS!!
WE HAVE CAKE!!
WAH WAH
BE PROUD, ROBIN! OHARA IS NOBLE!
BOOM
BLAMBLAMBLAM
WE CANNOT GIVE UP...
...ON THE FUTURE OF THE WORLD!
WOO
SO LAUGH! WHEN YOU'RE HURTING, LAUGH.
DERESHI SHI SHI SHI!
IT SEEMS STUPID TO LAUGH WHEN YOU'RE HURTING...
THAT'S NOT TRUE.
WOOOO
DERE-SHISHI.
DERESHI...

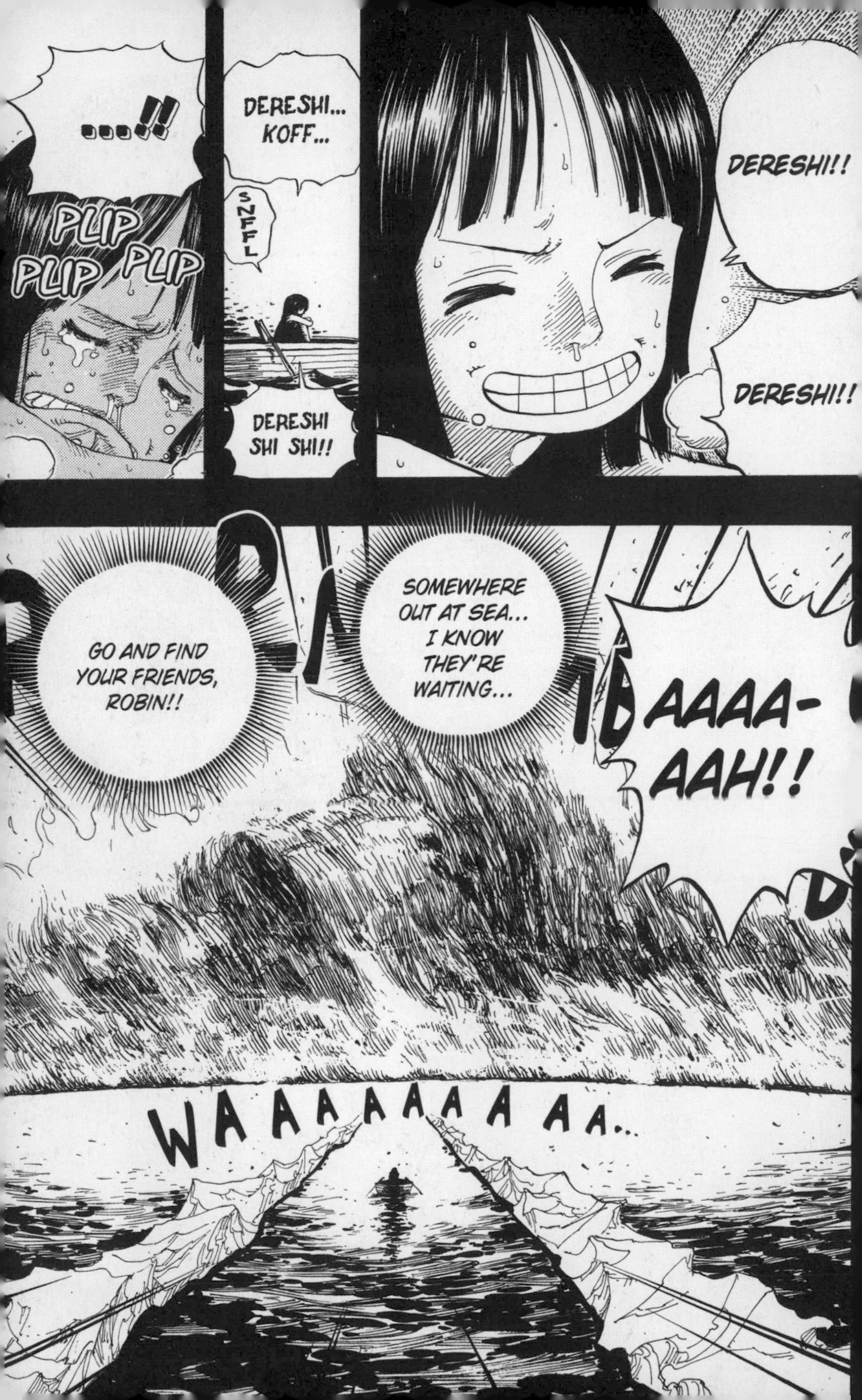
DERESHI!!
DERESHI!!
DERESHI... KOFF...
SNFFL
DERESHI SHI SHI!!
...!!
PLIP PLIP PLIP
AAAA-AAH!!
SOMEWHERE OUT AT SEA... I KNOW THEY'RE WAITING...
GO AND FIND YOUR FRIENDS, ROBIN!!
WAAAAAAAA...

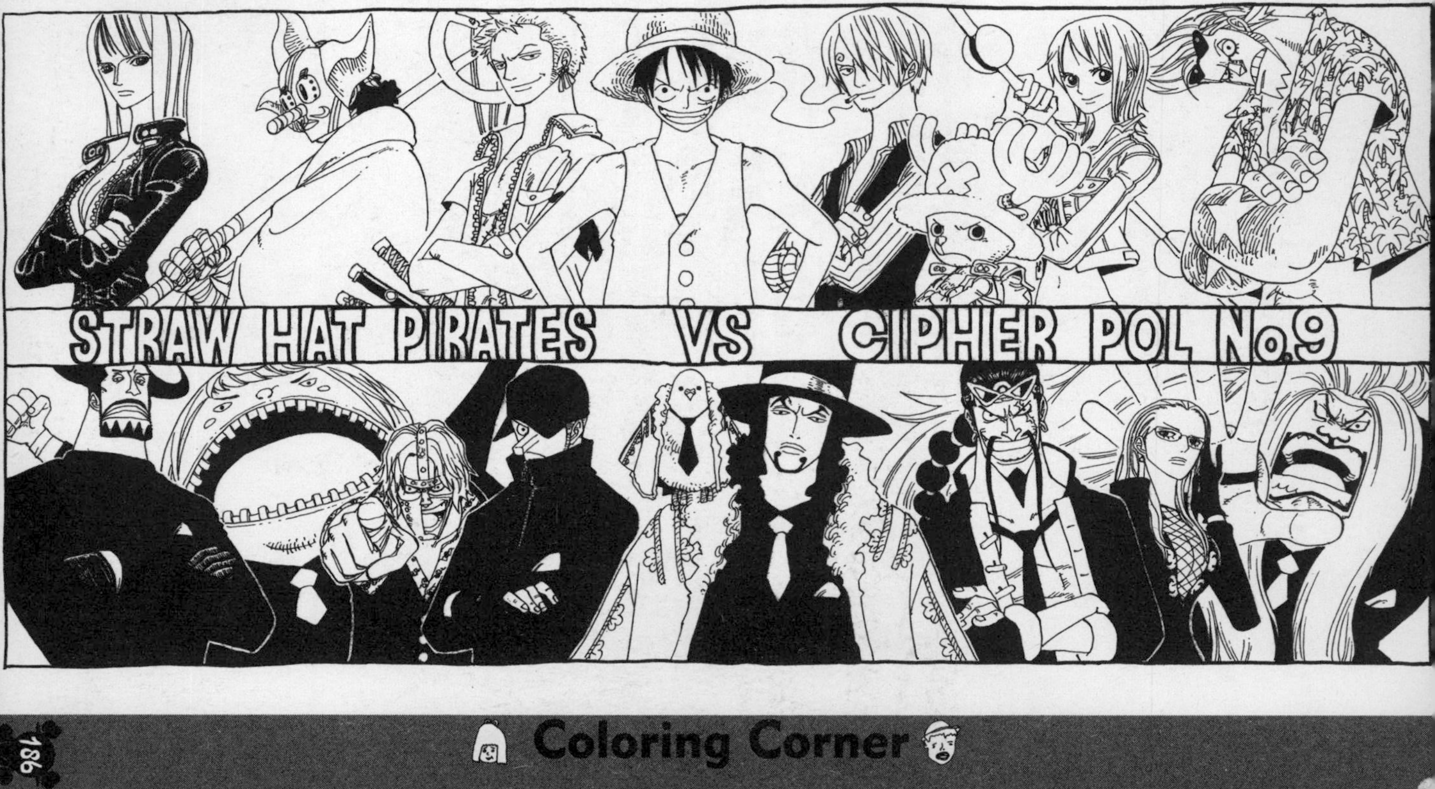
STRAW HAT PIRATES VS CIPHER POL No.9

Coloring Corner

Chapter 398:
DECLARATION OF WAR

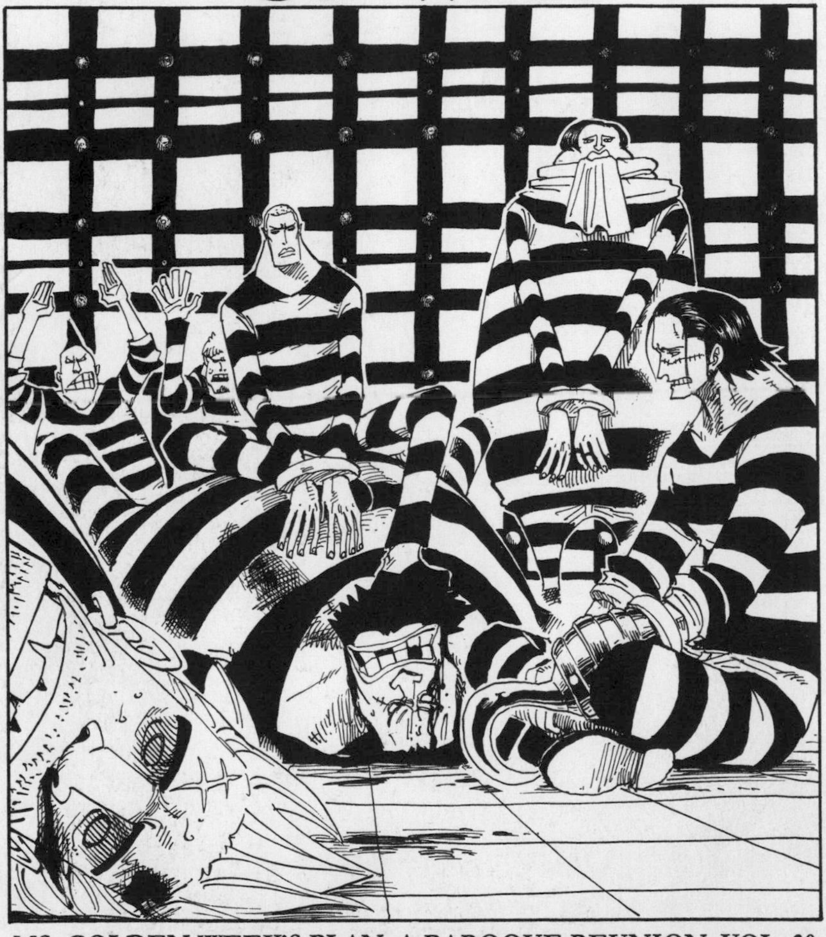

MS. GOLDEN WEEK'S PLAN, A BAROQUE REUNION, VOL. 30:
"THE STRONGEST SUSPECTS"

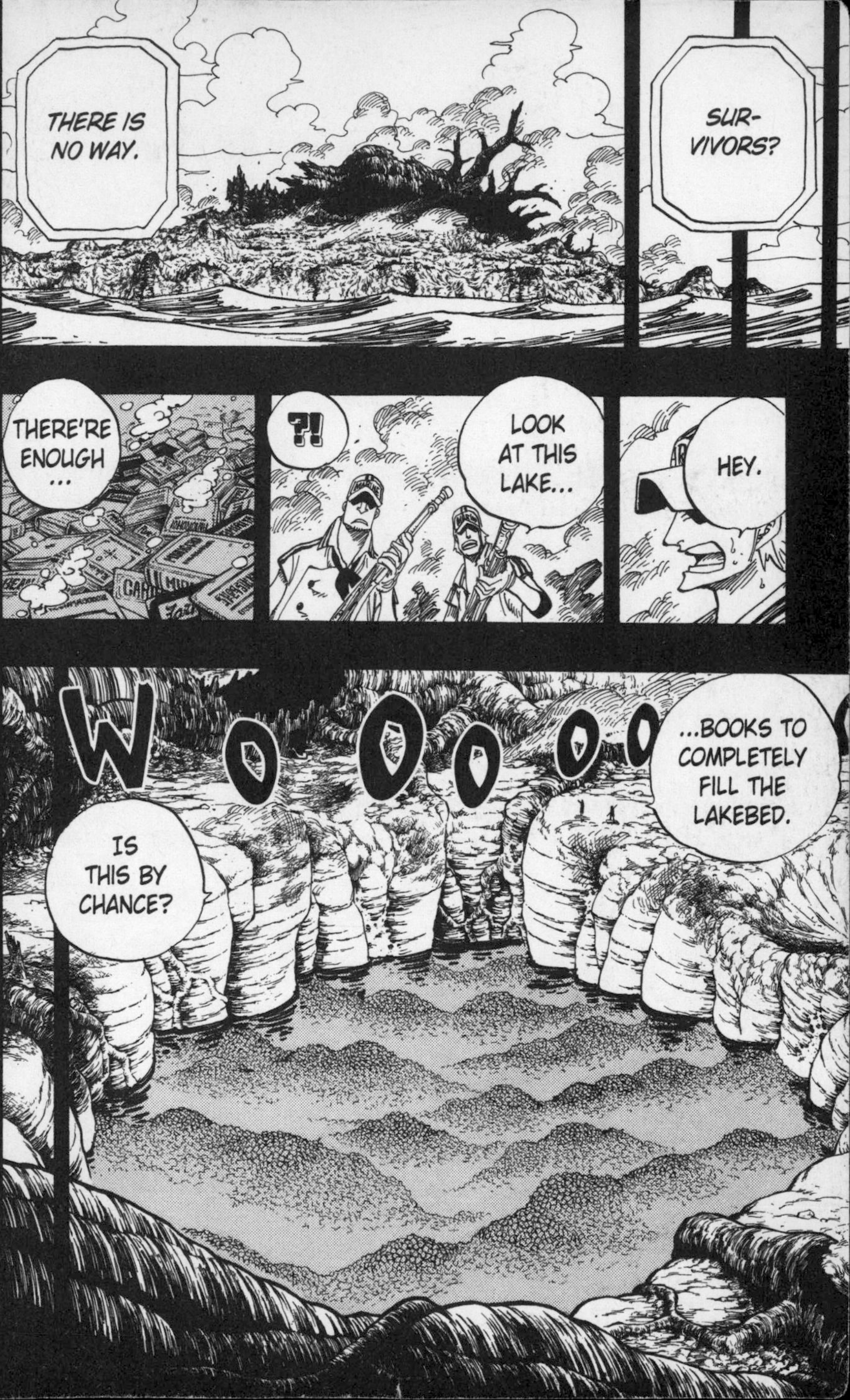
SUR-VIVORS?
THERE IS NO WAY.
HEY.
LOOK AT THIS LAKE...
?!
THERE'RE ENOUGH ...
...BOOKS TO COMPLETELY FILL THE LAKEBED.
WOOOOO
IS THIS BY CHANCE?

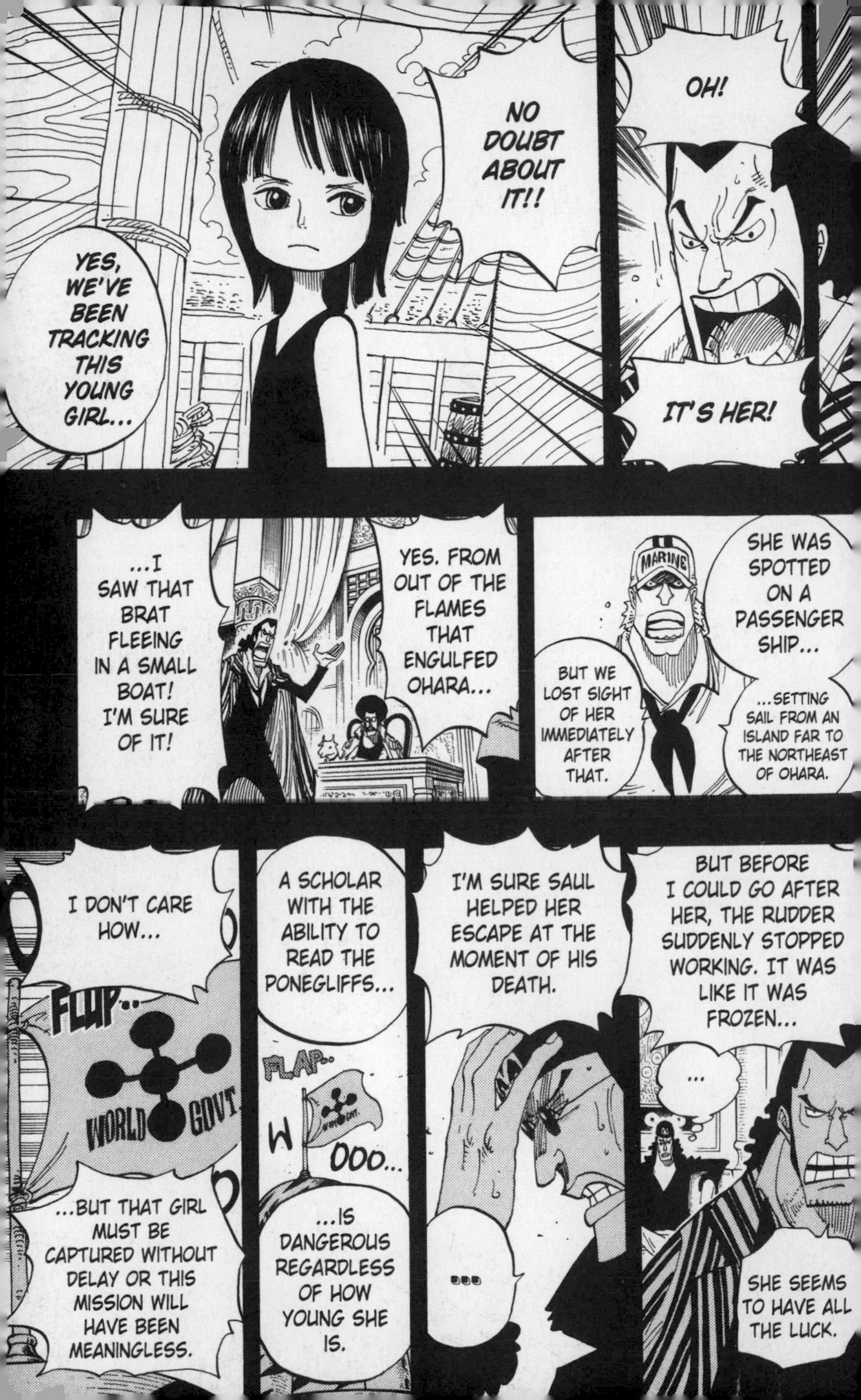
OH!
IT'S HER!
NO DOUBT ABOUT IT!!
YES, WE'VE BEEN TRACKING THIS YOUNG GIRL...
SHE WAS SPOTTED ON A PASSENGER SHIP...
...SETTING SAIL FROM AN ISLAND FAR TO THE NORTHEAST OF OHARA.
BUT WE LOST SIGHT OF HER IMMEDIATELY AFTER THAT.
YES. FROM OUT OF THE FLAMES THAT ENGULFED OHARA...
...I SAW THAT BRAT FLEEING IN A SMALL BOAT! I'M SURE OF IT!
BUT BEFORE I COULD GO AFTER HER, THE RUDDER SUDDENLY STOPPED WORKING. IT WAS LIKE IT WAS FROZEN...
...
SHE SEEMS TO HAVE ALL THE LUCK.
I'M SURE SAUL HELPED HER ESCAPE AT THE MOMENT OF HIS DEATH.
...
A SCHOLAR WITH THE ABILITY TO READ THE PONEGLIFFS...
FLAP..
WOOO...
...IS DANGEROUS REGARDLESS OF HOW YOUNG SHE IS.
I DON'T CARE HOW...
FLUP..
WORLD GOVT
...BUT THAT GIRL MUST BE CAPTURED WITHOUT DELAY OR THIS MISSION WILL HAVE BEEN MEANINGLESS.

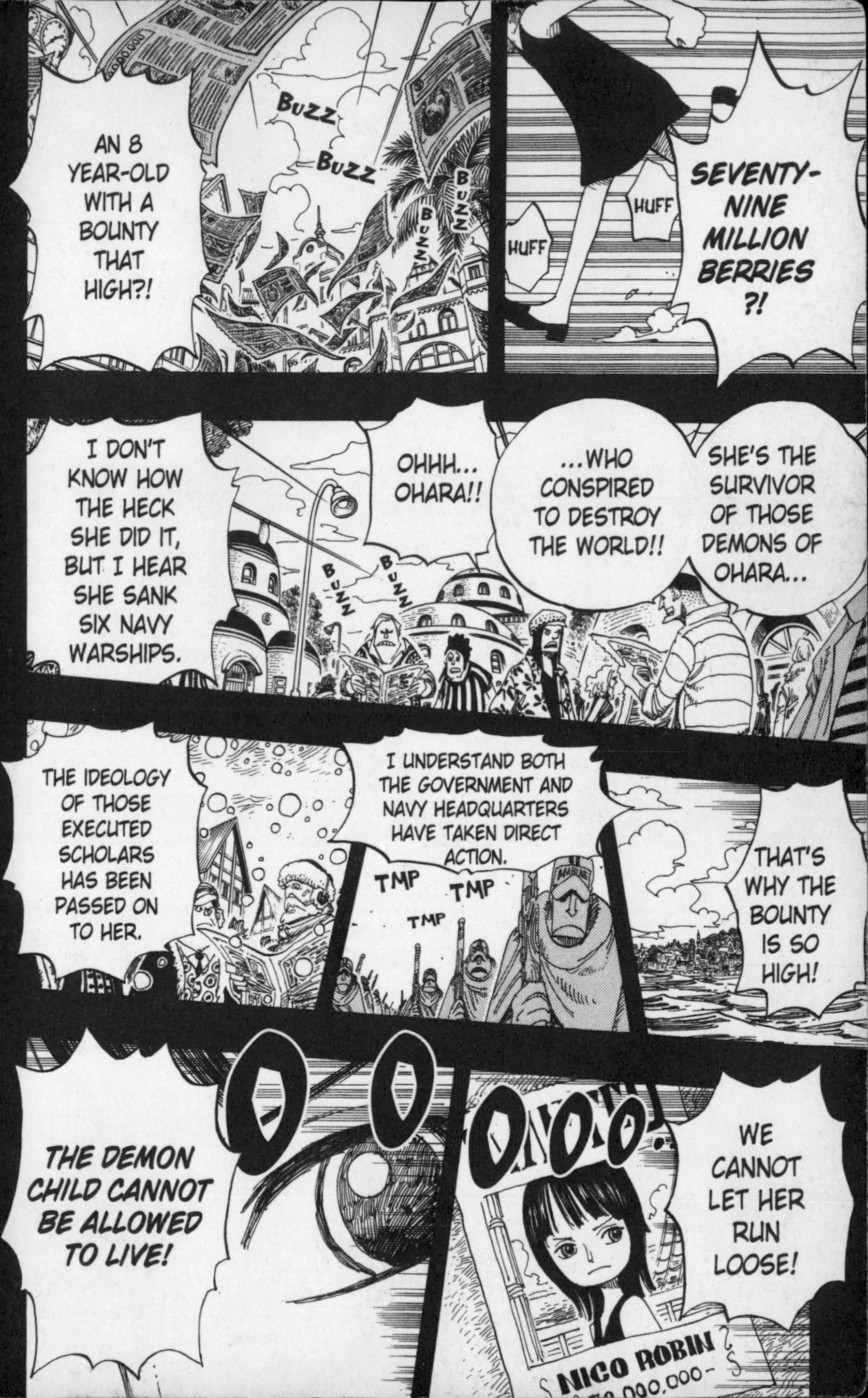

HUFF
HUFF
SEVENTY-NINE MILLION BERRIES?!
BUZZ
BUZZ
BUZZ
BUZZ
AN 8 YEAR-OLD WITH A BOUNTY THAT HIGH?!
SHE'S THE SURVIVOR OF THOSE DEMONS OF OHARA...
...WHO CONSPIRED TO DESTROY THE WORLD!!
OHHH... OHARA!!
BUZZ
BUZZ
I DON'T KNOW HOW THE HECK SHE DID IT, BUT I HEAR SHE SANK SIX NAVY WARSHIPS.
THAT'S WHY THE BOUNTY IS SO HIGH!
I UNDERSTAND BOTH THE GOVERNMENT AND NAVY HEADQUARTERS HAVE TAKEN DIRECT ACTION.
TMP
TMP
TMP
THE IDEOLOGY OF THOSE EXECUTED SCHOLARS HAS BEEN PASSED ON TO HER.
WE CANNOT LET HER RUN LOOSE!
NICO ROBIN
THE DEMON CHILD CANNOT BE ALLOWED TO LIVE!

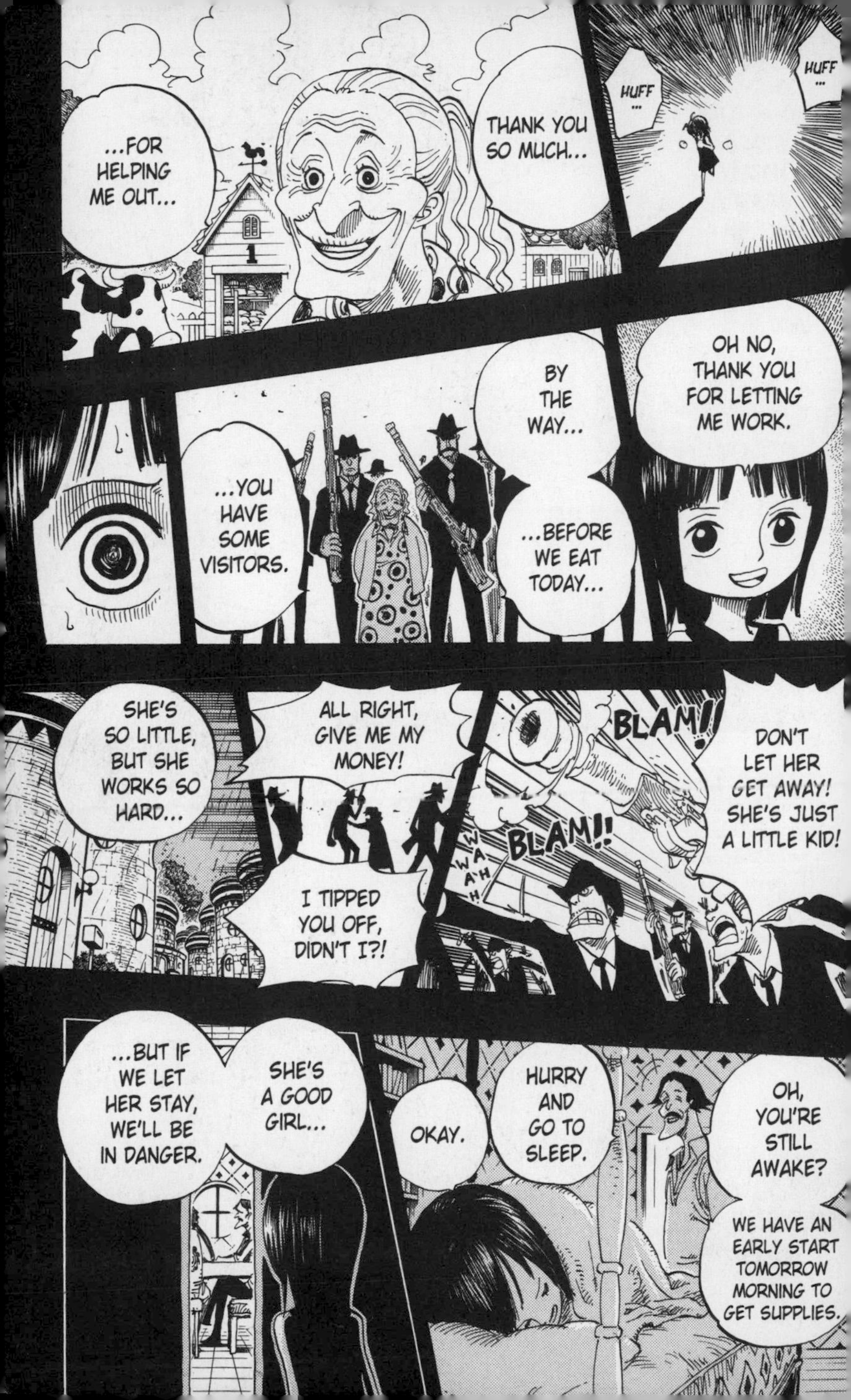
HUFF ...
HUFF ...
THANK YOU SO MUCH...
...FOR HELPING ME OUT...
OH NO, THANK YOU FOR LETTING ME WORK.
BY THE WAY...
...BEFORE WE EAT TODAY...
...YOU HAVE SOME VISITORS.
DON'T LET HER GET AWAY! SHE'S JUST A LITTLE KID!
BLAM!
BLAM!!
ALL RIGHT, GIVE ME MY MONEY!
I TIPPED YOU OFF, DIDN'T I?!
SHE'S SO LITTLE, BUT SHE WORKS SO HARD...
OH, YOU'RE STILL AWAKE?
WE HAVE AN EARLY START TOMORROW MORNING TO GET SUPPLIES.
HURRY AND GO TO SLEEP.
OKAY.
SHE'S A GOOD GIRL...
...BUT IF WE LET HER STAY, WE'LL BE IN DANGER.

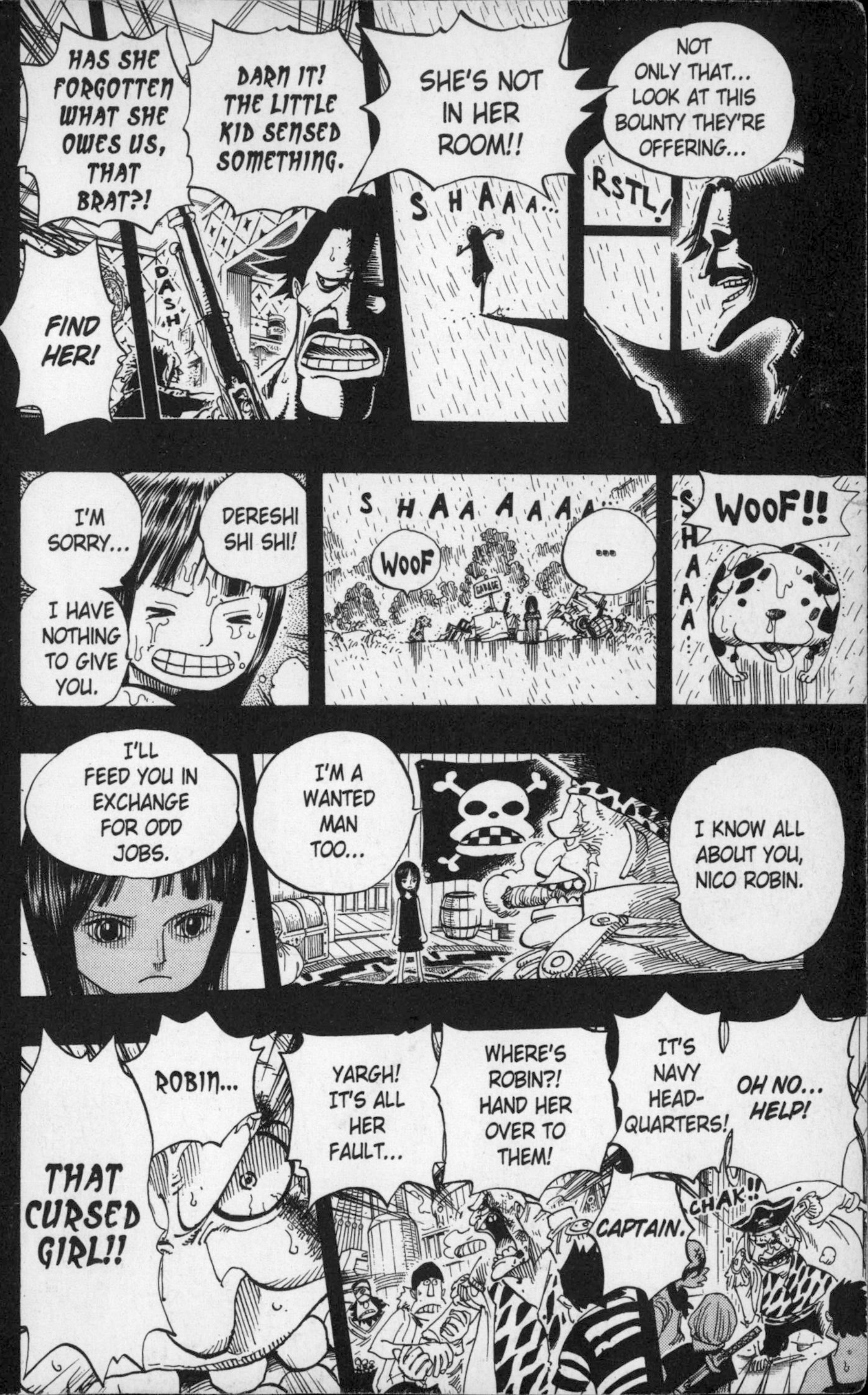
NOT ONLY THAT... LOOK AT THIS BOUNTY THEY'RE OFFERING...
RSTL!
SHE'S NOT IN HER ROOM!!
SHAAA...
DARN IT! THE LITTLE KID SENSED SOMETHING.
HAS SHE FORGOTTEN WHAT SHE OWES US, THAT BRAT?!
DASH
FIND HER!
WOOF!!
SHAAAA...
SHAAAAAAA...
...
WOOF
DERESHI SHI SHI!
I'M SORRY...
I HAVE NOTHING TO GIVE YOU.
I KNOW ALL ABOUT YOU, NICO ROBIN.
I'M A WANTED MAN TOO...
I'LL FEED YOU IN EXCHANGE FOR ODD JOBS.
OH NO... HELP!
IT'S NAVY HEADQUARTERS!
CHAK!!
CAPTAIN.
WHERE'S ROBIN?! HAND HER OVER TO THEM!
YARGH! IT'S ALL HER FAULT...
ROBIN...
THAT CURSED GIRL!!

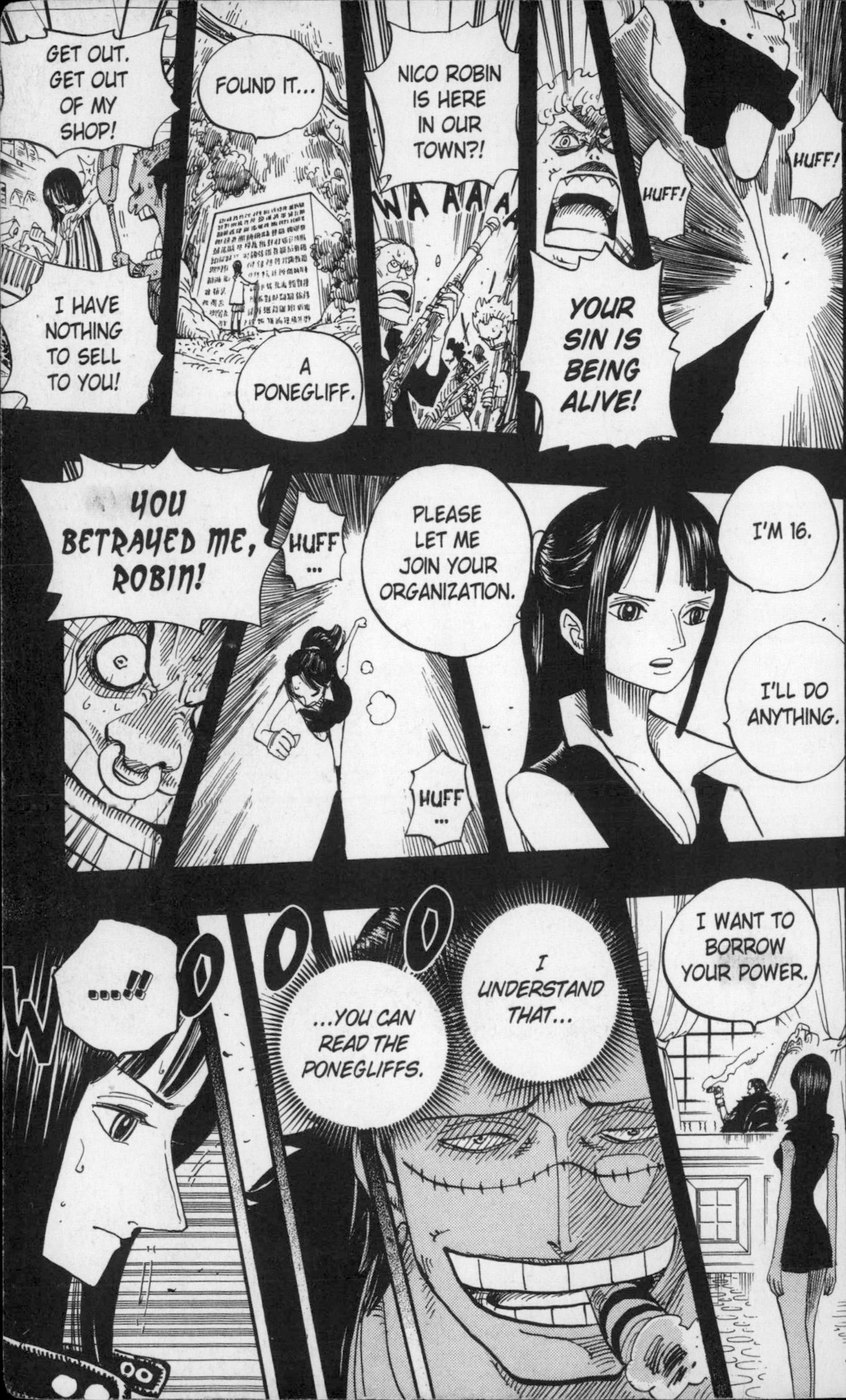
HUFF!
HUFF!
YOUR SIN IS BEING ALIVE!
NICO ROBIN IS HERE IN OUR TOWN?!
WAAAA
FOUND IT...
A PONEGLIFF.
GET OUT. GET OUT OF MY SHOP!
I HAVE NOTHING TO SELL TO YOU!
I'M 16.
I'LL DO ANYTHING.
HUFF...
PLEASE LET ME JOIN YOUR ORGANIZATION.
HUFF...
YOU BETRAYED ME, ROBIN!
I WANT TO BORROW YOUR POWER.
I UNDERSTAND THAT...
...YOU CAN READ THE PONEGLIFFS.
...!!

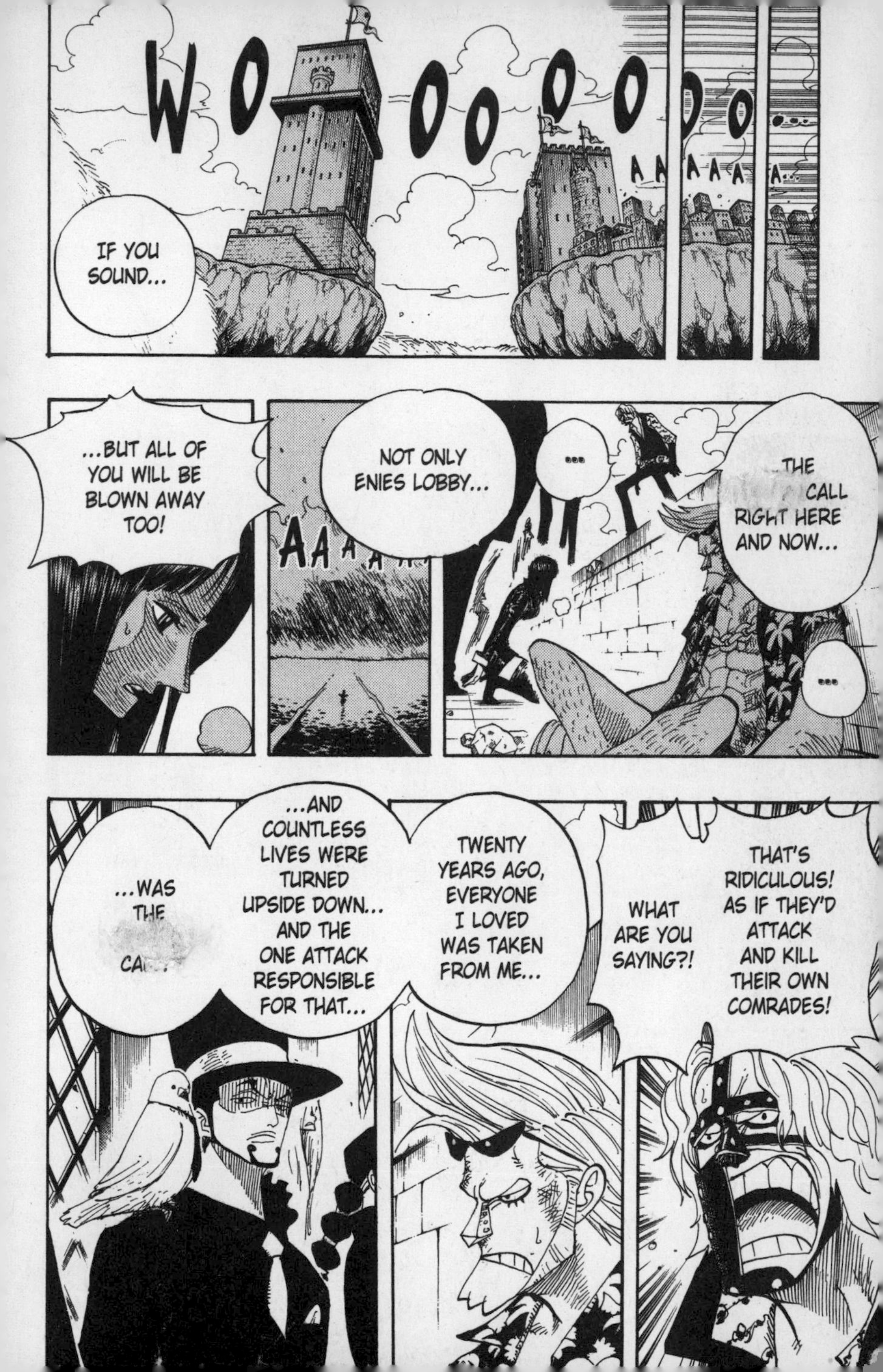
WOOOOOOO...
AAAAAA...
IF YOU SOUND...
...THE CALL RIGHT HERE AND NOW...
...
...
NOT ONLY ENIES LOBBY...
AAAAA
...BUT ALL OF YOU WILL BE BLOWN AWAY TOO!
THAT'S RIDICULOUS! AS IF THEY'D ATTACK AND KILL THEIR OWN COMRADES!
WHAT ARE YOU SAYING?!
TWENTY YEARS AGO, EVERYONE I LOVED WAS TAKEN FROM ME...
...AND COUNTLESS LIVES WERE TURNED UPSIDE DOWN... AND THE ONE ATTACK RESPONSIBLE FOR THAT...
...WAS THE CA...

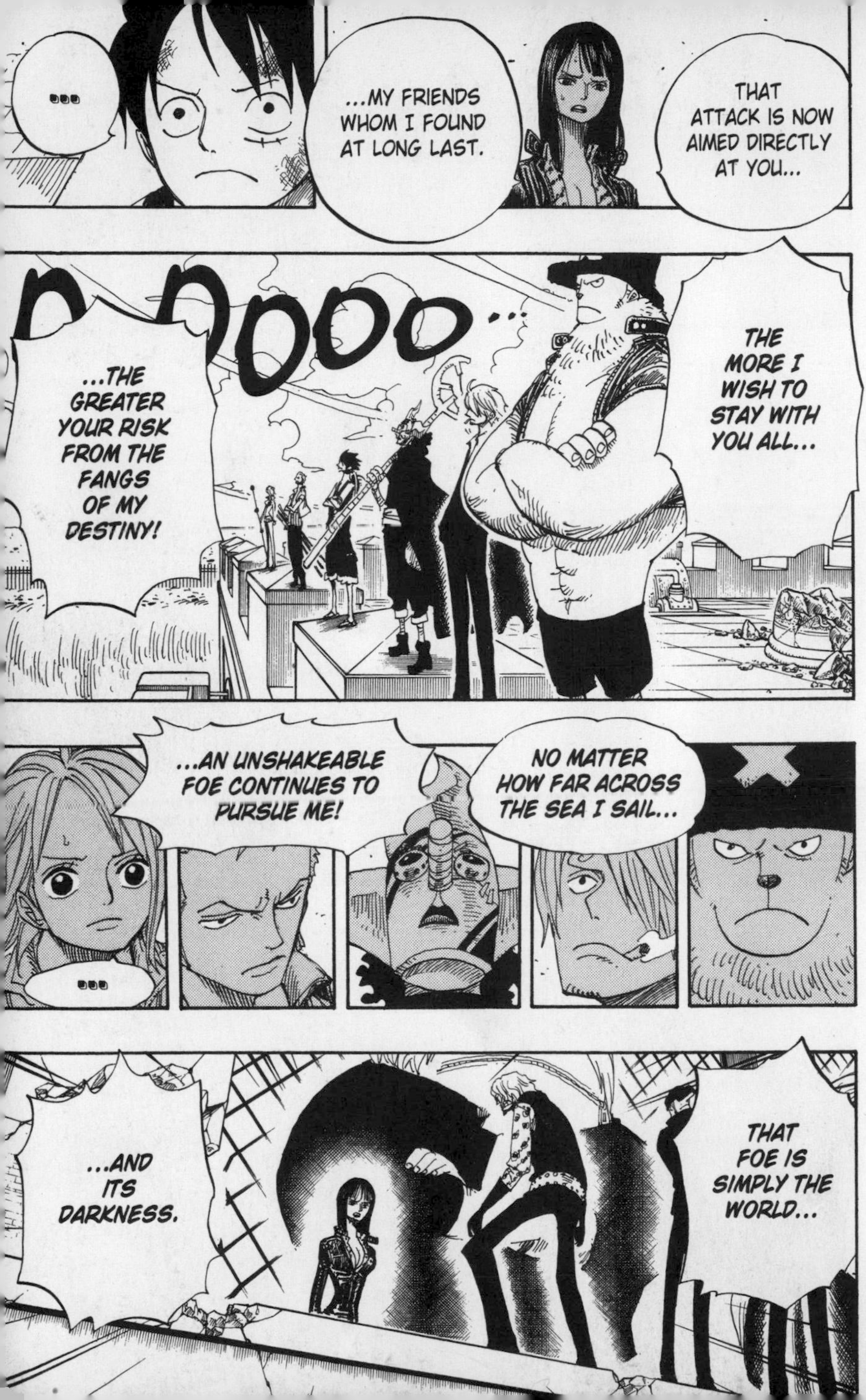
THAT ATTACK IS NOW AIMED DIRECTLY AT YOU...
...MY FRIENDS WHOM I FOUND AT LONG LAST.
...
THE MORE I WISH TO STAY WITH YOU ALL...
DOOOO...
...THE GREATER YOUR RISK FROM THE FANGS OF MY DESTINY!
NO MATTER HOW FAR ACROSS THE SEA I SAIL...
...AN UNSHAKEABLE FOE CONTINUES TO PURSUE ME!
...
THAT FOE IS SIMPLY THE WORLD...
...AND ITS DARKNESS.

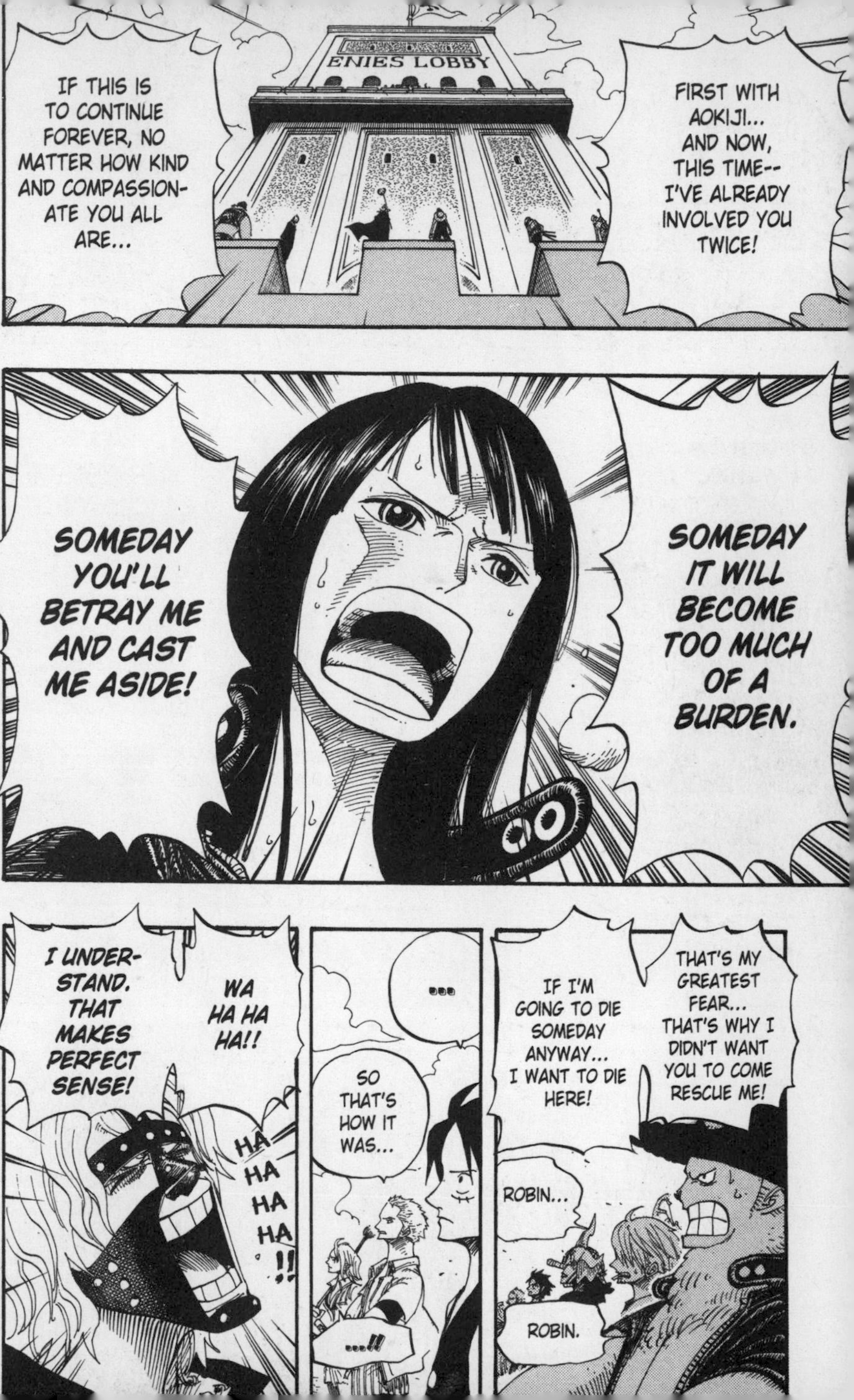
ENIES LOBBY
FIRST WITH AOKIJI... AND NOW, THIS TIME-- I'VE ALREADY INVOLVED YOU TWICE!
IF THIS IS TO CONTINUE FOREVER, NO MATTER HOW KIND AND COMPASSION-ATE YOU ALL ARE...
SOMEDAY IT WILL BECOME TOO MUCH OF A BURDEN.
SOMEDAY YOU'LL BETRAY ME AND CAST ME ASIDE!
THAT'S MY GREATEST FEAR... THAT'S WHY I DIDN'T WANT YOU TO COME RESCUE ME!
IF I'M GOING TO DIE SOMEDAY ANYWAY... I WANT TO DIE HERE!
ROBIN...
ROBIN.
...
SO THAT'S HOW IT WAS...
...!!
WA HA HA HA!!
I UNDER-STAND. THAT MAKES PERFECT SENSE!
HA HA HA HA!!

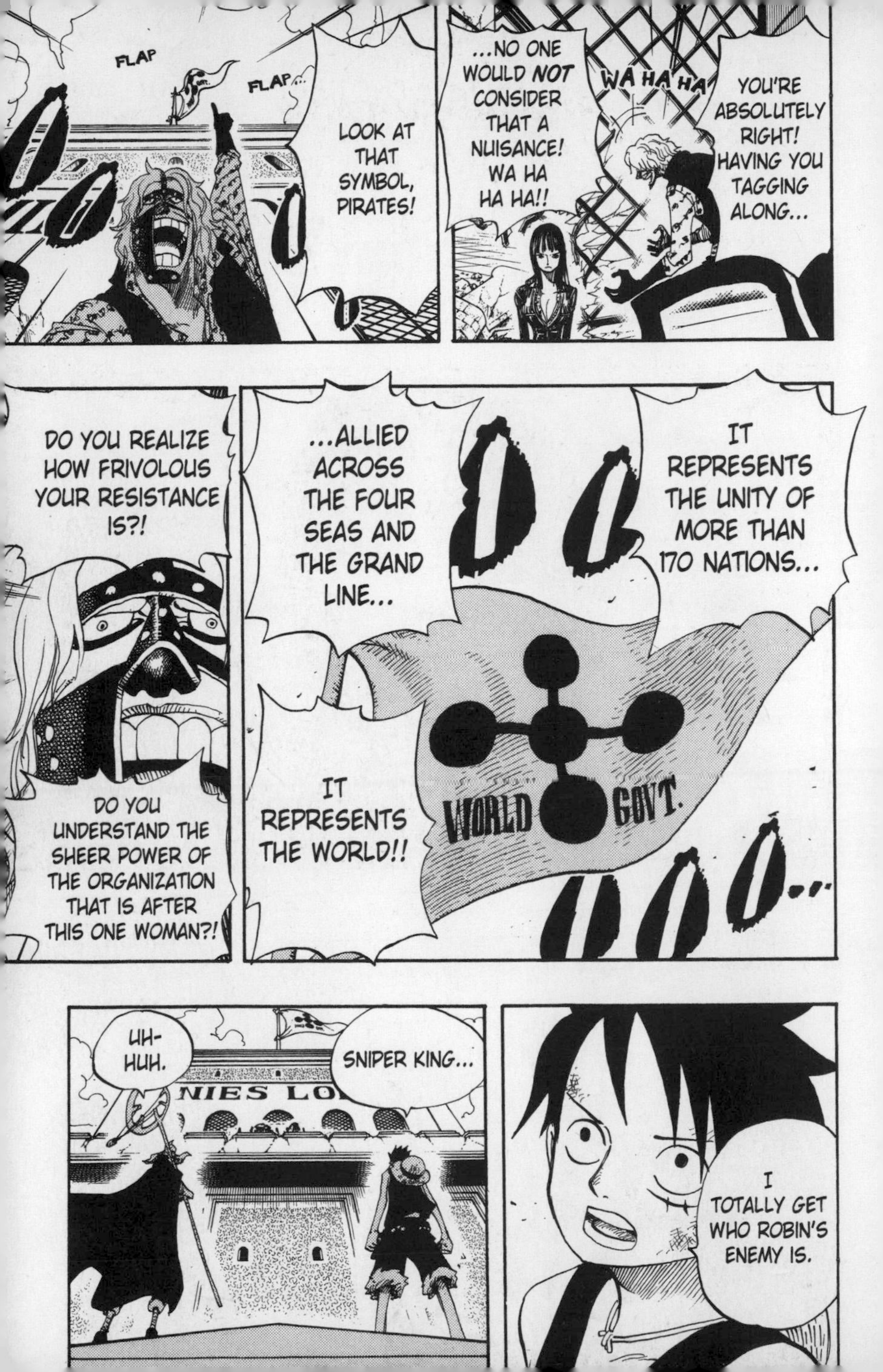
YOU'RE ABSOLUTELY RIGHT! HAVING YOU TAGGING ALONG...
WA HA HA
...NO ONE WOULD NOT CONSIDER THAT A NUISANCE! WA HA HA HA!!
FLAP
FLAP...
LOOK AT THAT SYMBOL, PIRATES!
IT REPRESENTS THE UNITY OF MORE THAN 170 NATIONS...
...ALLIED ACROSS THE FOUR SEAS AND THE GRAND LINE...
WORLD GOVT.
IT REPRESENTS THE WORLD!!
DO YOU REALIZE HOW FRIVOLOUS YOUR RESISTANCE IS?!
DO YOU UNDERSTAND THE SHEER POWER OF THE ORGANIZATION THAT IS AFTER THIS ONE WOMAN?!
I TOTALLY GET WHO ROBIN'S ENEMY IS.
SNIPER KING...
UH-HUH.

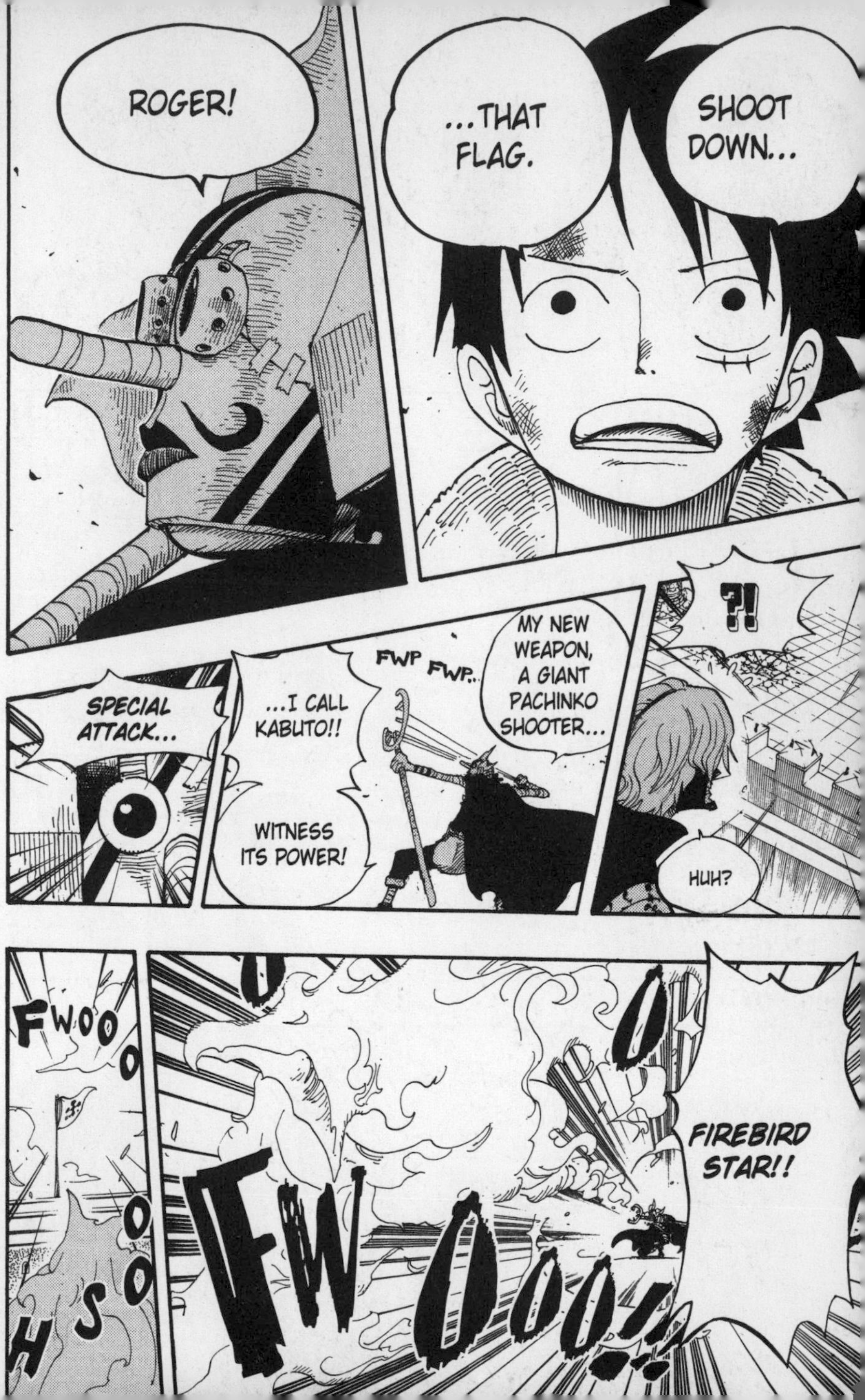
SHOOT DOWN...
...THAT FLAG.
ROGER!
?!
HUH?
MY NEW WEAPON, A GIANT PACHINKO SHOOTER...
FWP FWP...
...I CALL KABUTO!!
WITNESS ITS POWER!
SPECIAL ATTACK...
FIREBIRD STAR!!
FWOOOO!!
FWOOOOOSH

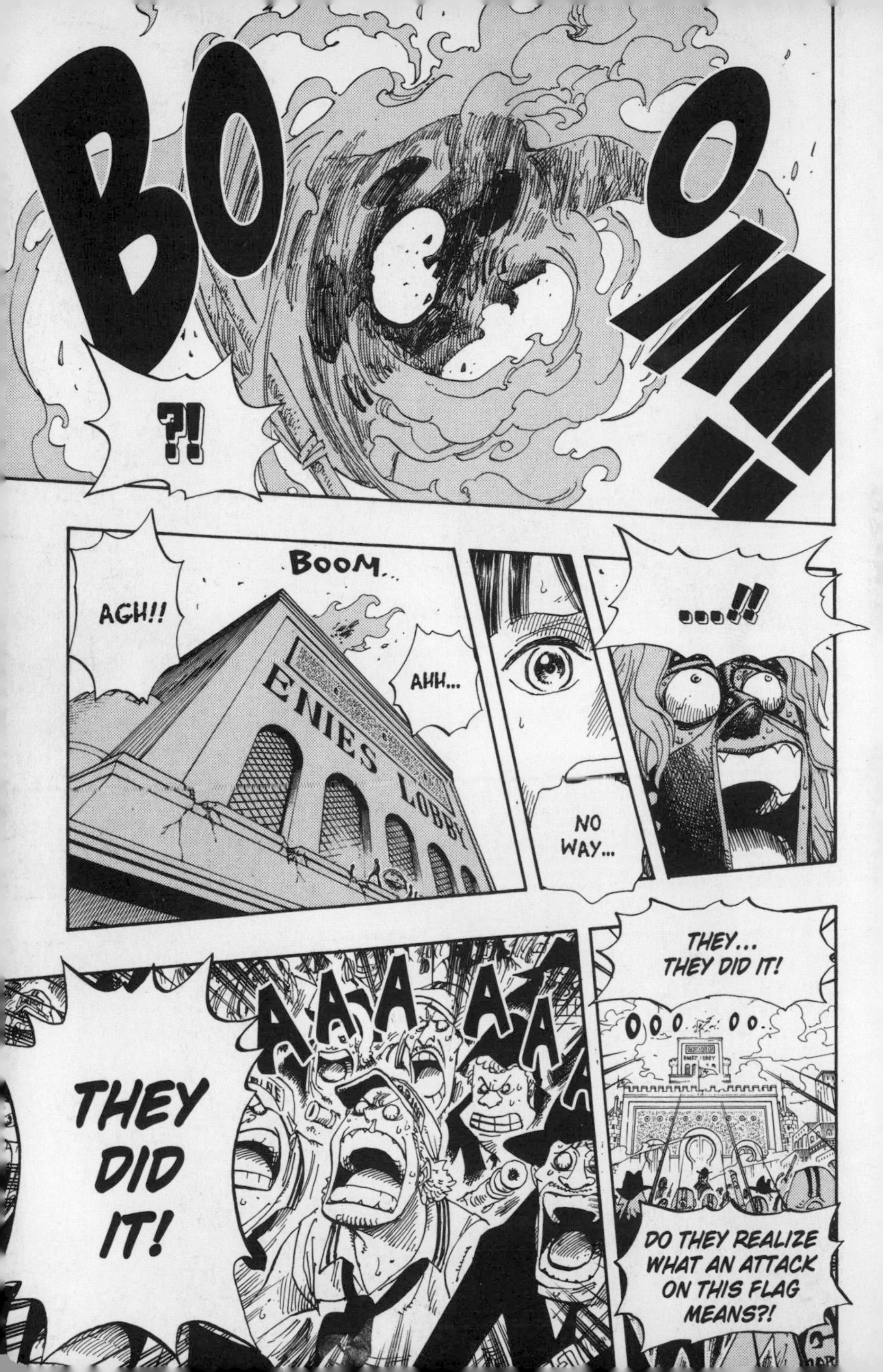
BOOOM!!
?!
...!!
NO WAY...
BOOM...
AGH!!
AHH...
THEY... THEY DID IT!
OOO... OO..
DO THEY REALIZE WHAT AN ATTACK ON THIS FLAG MEANS?!
AAAAA
THEY DID IT!

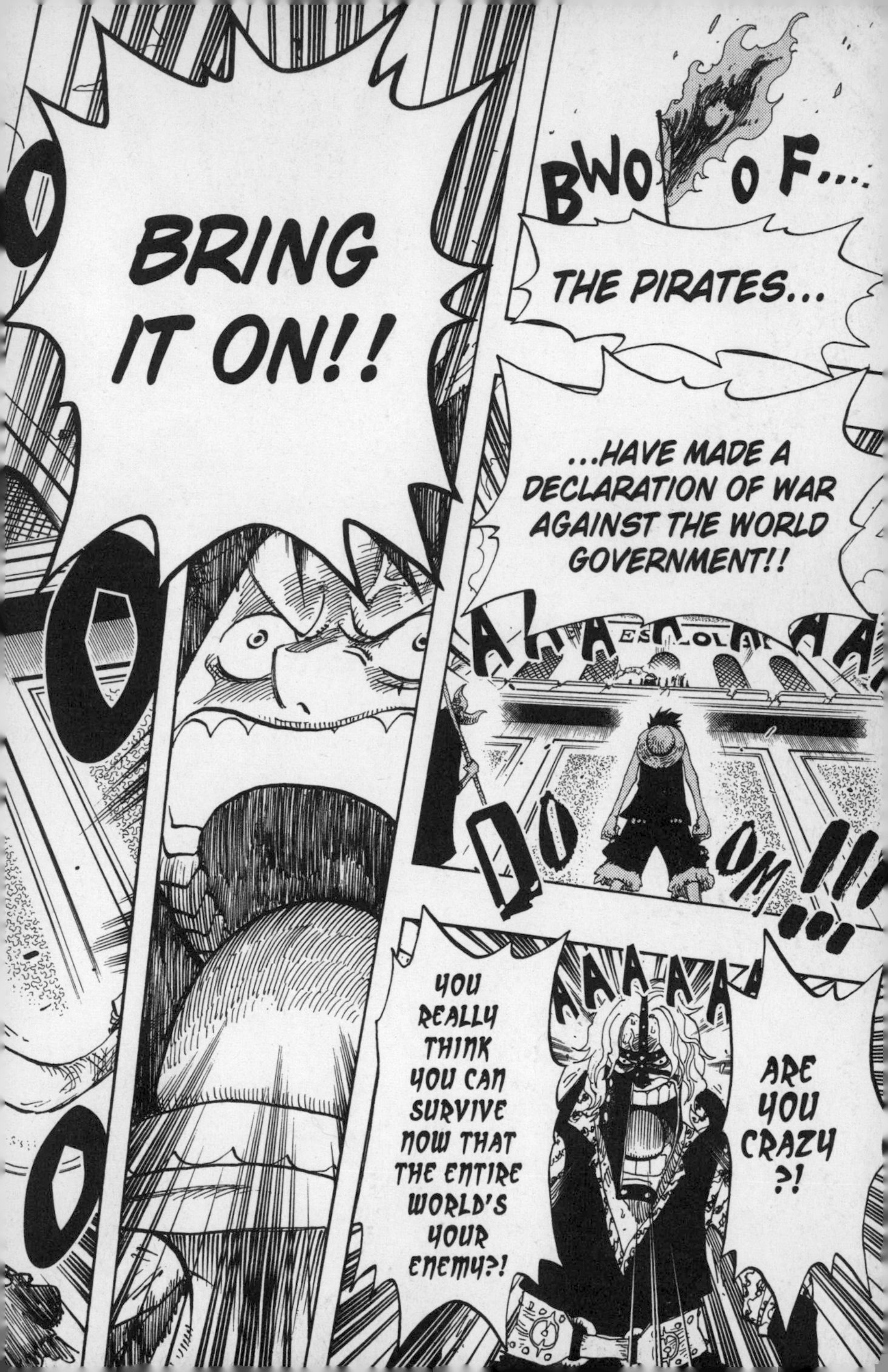
BWO OF....
THE PIRATES...
...HAVE MADE A DECLARATION OF WAR AGAINST THE WORLD GOVERNMENT!!
DOOM!!!
ARE YOU CRAZY?!
YOU REALLY THINK YOU CAN SURVIVE NOW THAT THE ENTIRE WORLD'S YOUR ENEMY?!
BRING IT ON!!

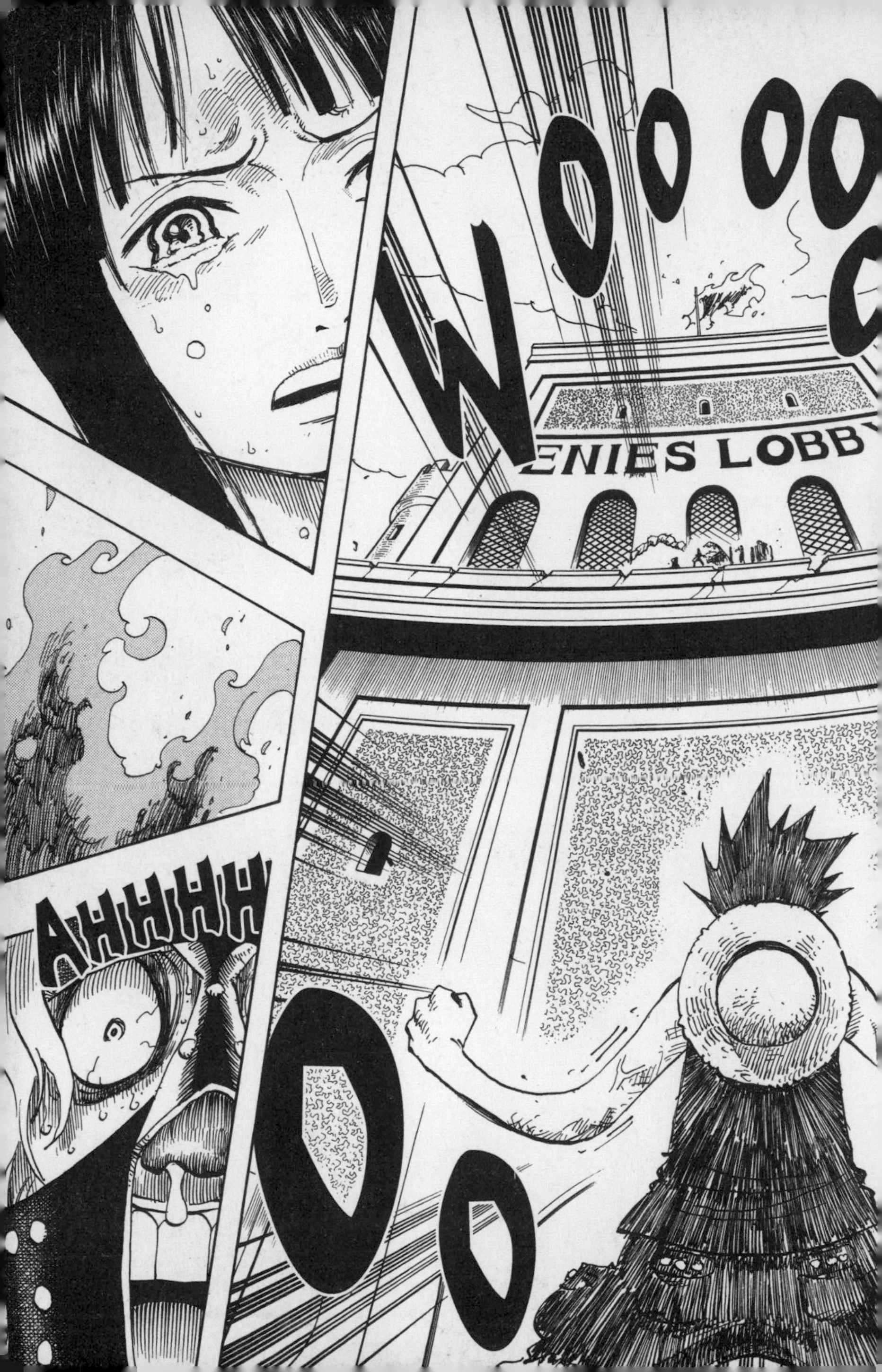
WOOOOO
ENIES LOBBY
OO
AHHHHH

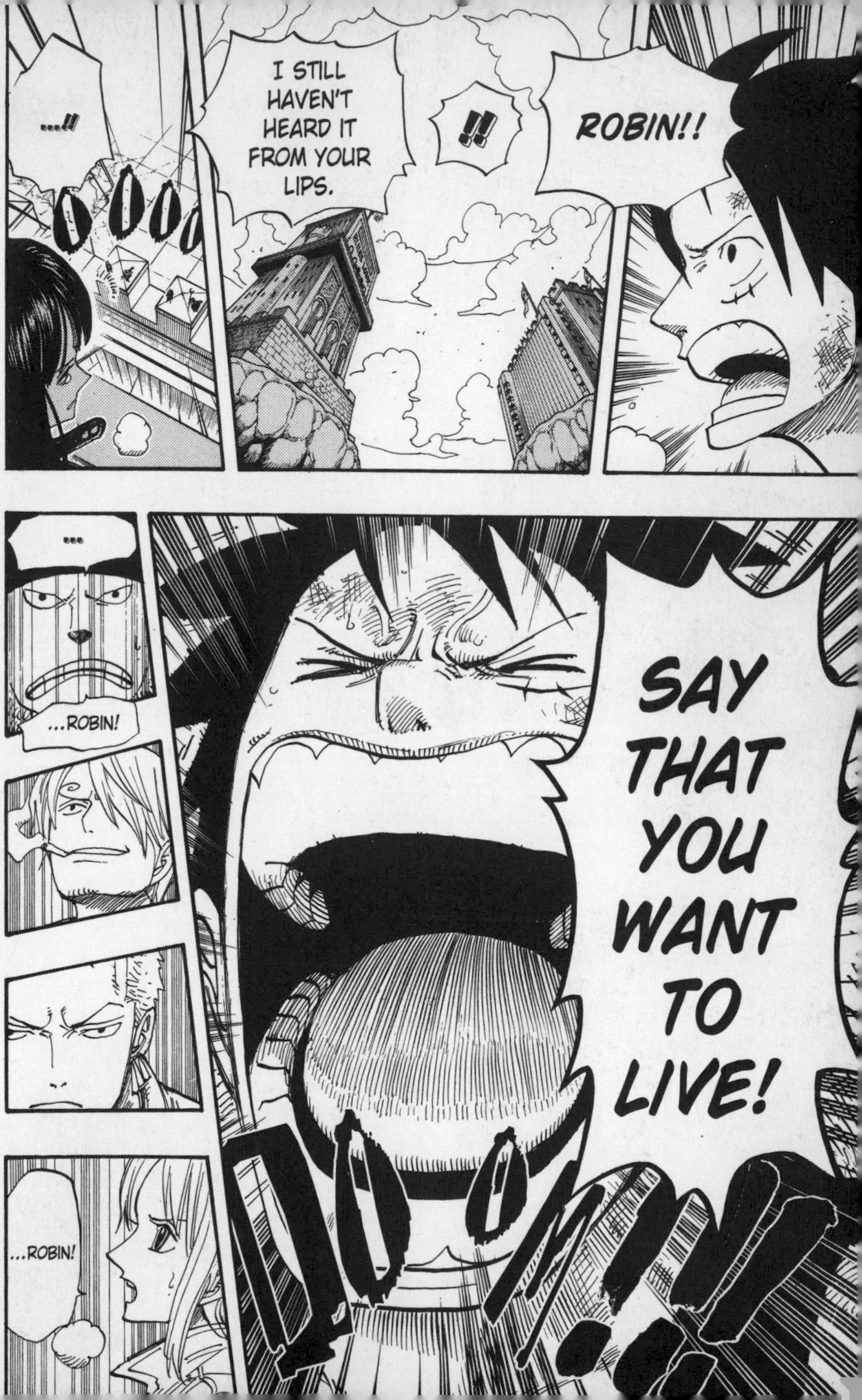
ROBIN!!
!!
I STILL HAVEN'T HEARD IT FROM YOUR LIPS.
...!!
SAY THAT YOU WANT TO LIVE!
...
...ROBIN!
...ROBIN!

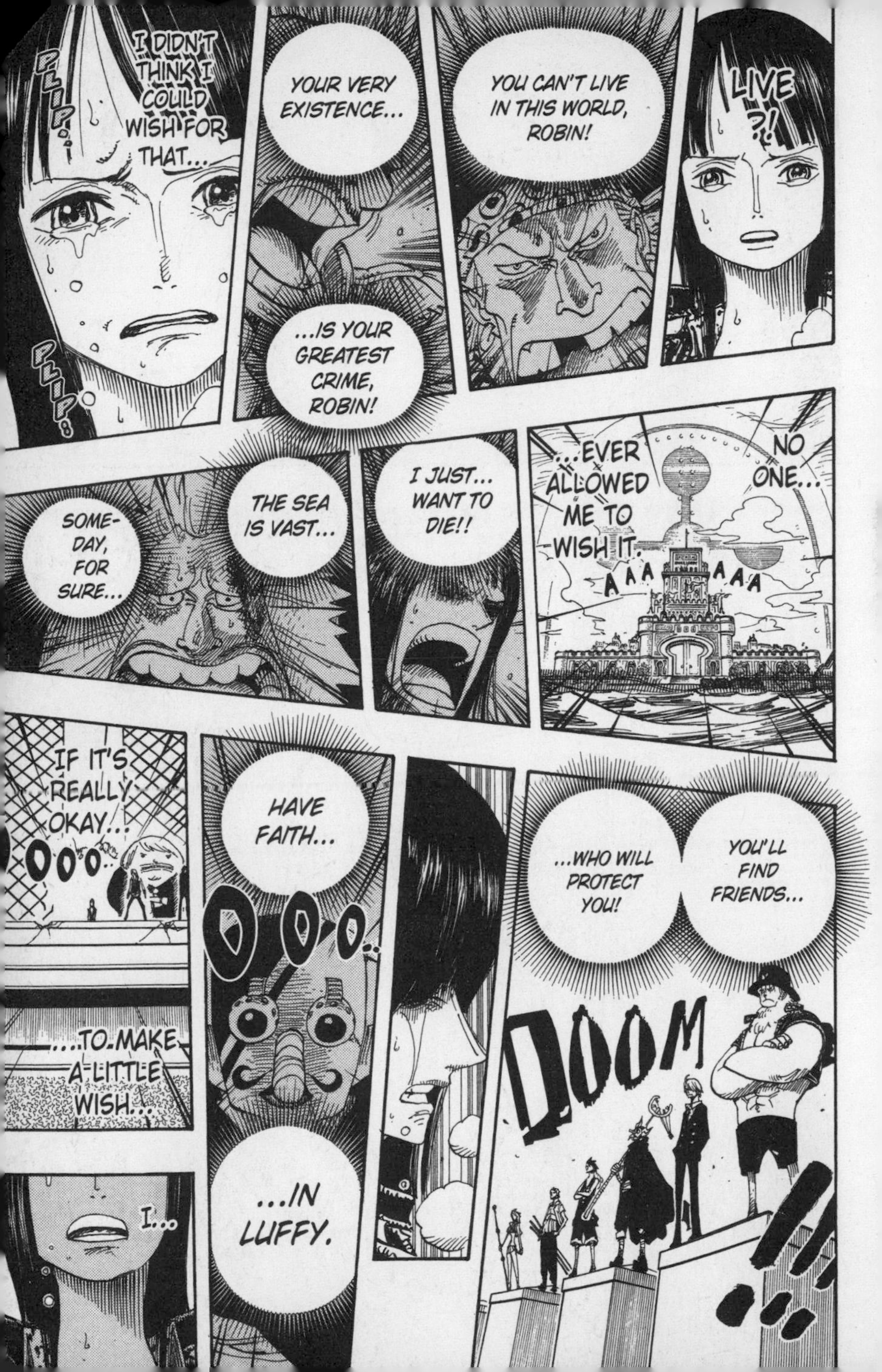
LIVE?!
YOU CAN'T LIVE IN THIS WORLD, ROBIN!
YOUR VERY EXISTENCE...
...IS YOUR GREATEST CRIME, ROBIN!
I DIDN'T THINK I COULD WISH FOR THAT...
PLIP
PLIP
NO ONE...
...EVER ALLOWED ME TO WISH IT.
AAA
AAA
I JUST... WANT TO DIE!!
THE SEA IS VAST...
SOME-DAY, FOR SURE...
YOU'LL FIND FRIENDS...
...WHO WILL PROTECT YOU!
DOOM
HAVE FAITH...
OOO..
...IN LUFFY.
IF IT'S REALLY OKAY...
OOO..
...TO MAKE A LITTLE WISH...
I...

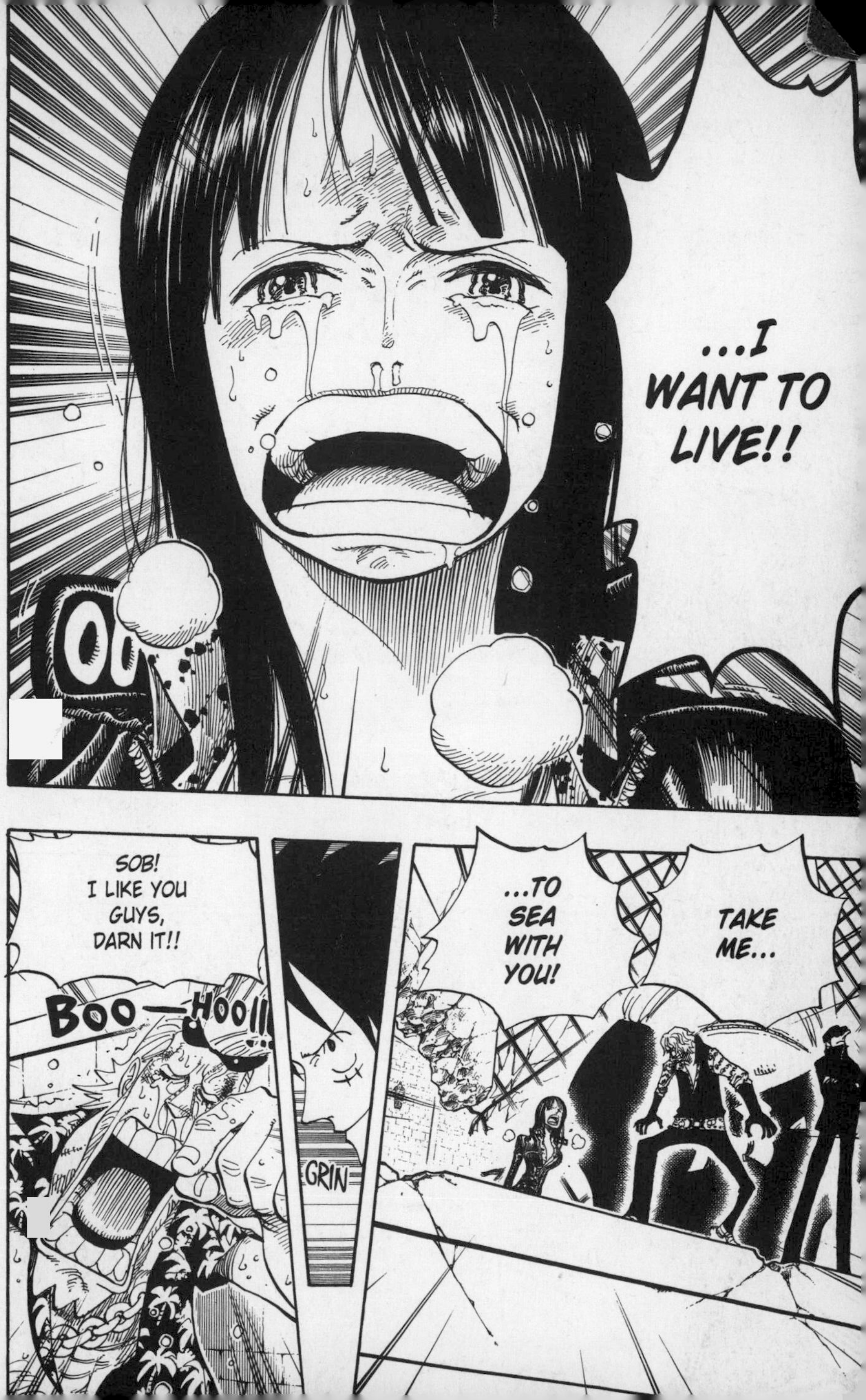
...I WANT TO LIVE!!
TAKE ME...
...TO SEA WITH YOU!
GRIN
SOB! I LIKE YOU GUYS, DARN IT!!
BOO-HOO!!!

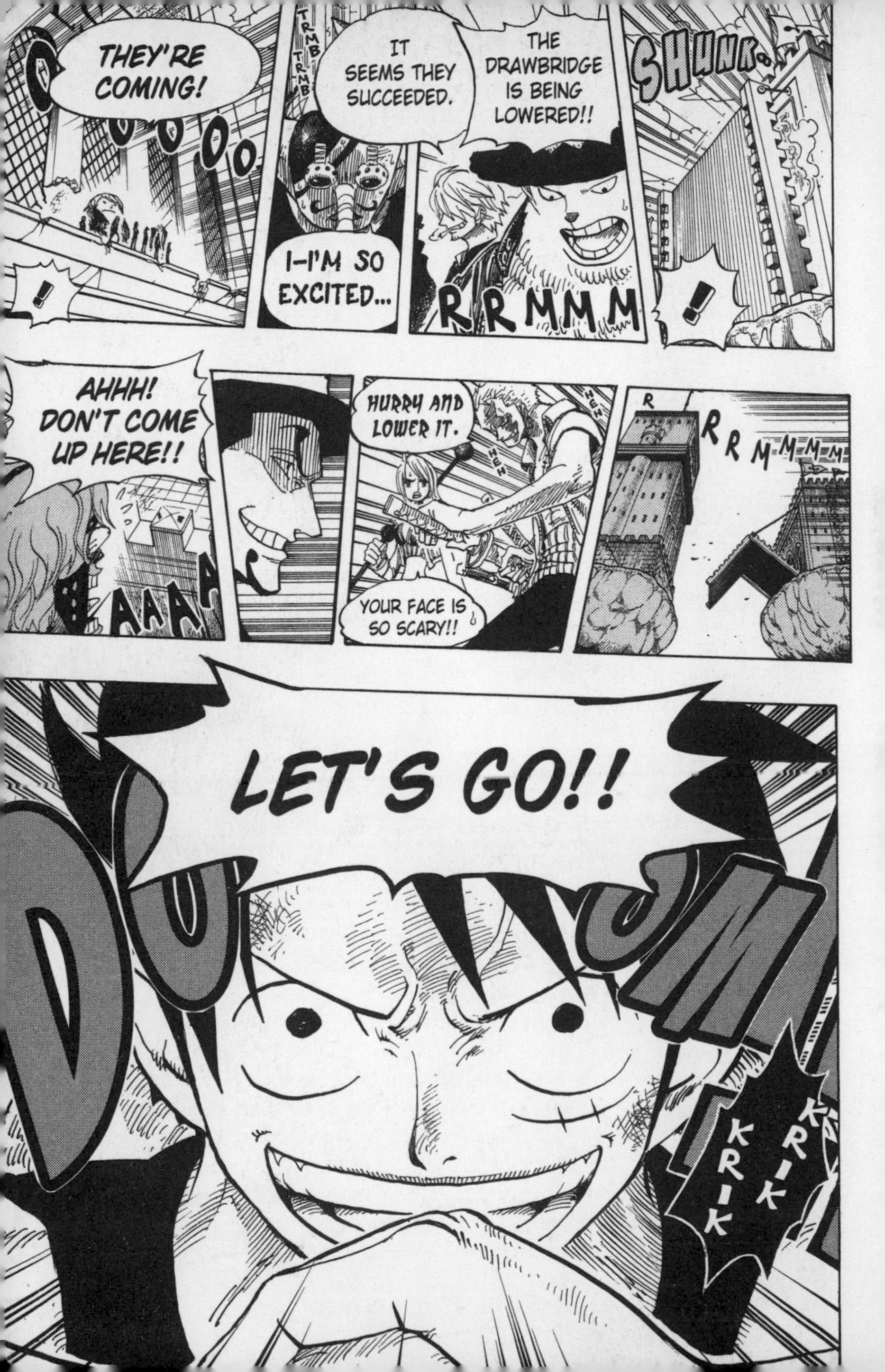
SHUNK
!
THE DRAWBRIDGE IS BEING LOWERED!!
RRMMM
IT SEEMS THEY SUCCEEDED.
TRMB TRMB
I-I'M SO EXCITED...
THEY'RE COMING!
!
R R RMMMMM
HURRY AND LOWER IT.
HEH HEH
YOUR FACE IS SO SCARY!!
AHHH! DON'T COME UP HERE!!
AAAA
LET'S GO!!
KRIK KRIK

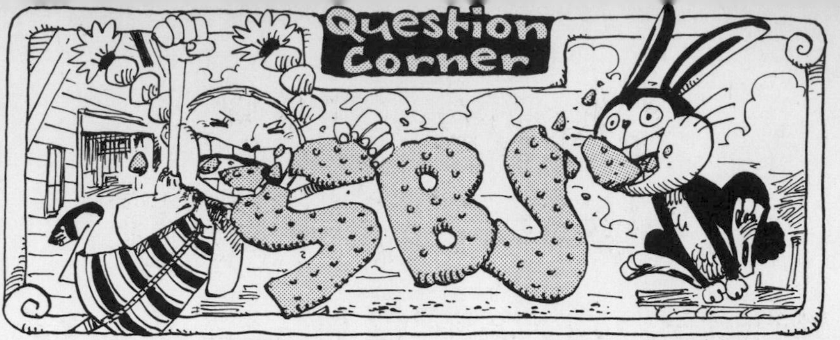
Question Corner
SBS

Q: Yo, Oda!! I know this is out of the blue, but what does Wanze use these (→) for? --Nappe

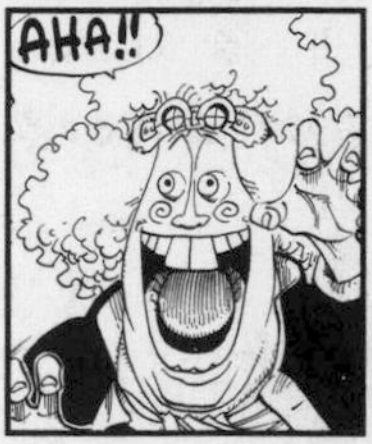
AHA!!

A: Those are "pop-up goggles"! Specially made! Wanze is a headwaiter, so naturally he uses them for cooking. Like for when he chops onions!! The goggles keep his eyes from tearing up, so he really values them. What's more, he only uses them for chopping onions!!

Q: Odacchi! I know it's sudden, but I have a question! Crocodile is made of sand, so he can't tolerate water, right? So how does he bathe?! He doesn't?! That's disgusting, isn't it?! Odacchi, do you bathe?
--Crocodile's mother ♡

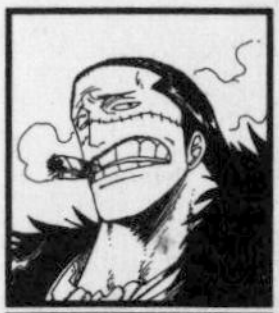

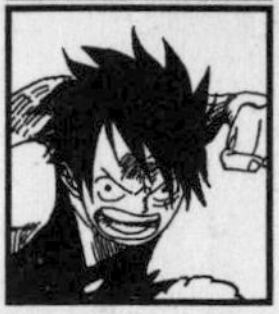

A: Well, first of all, let's deal with the bathroom issues of "those with powers." When one eats a Devil Fruit, the sea rejects that person and their bodies become unable to swim. The "sea" here includes rivers, pools, baths...everything that holds a pool of water. Seen in terms of the earth, everything is a "sea." So when one with powers enters such places, naturally their powers don't work as well as expected. They can struggle to use them, but it doesn't do much. That's if their entire bodies are submerged into the "sea." If it's just half their bodies, their arms and legs, the effect is lessened. Water that washes off, like rain, has no effect at all. So usually, they'll just submerge halfway or take showers. And in the case of Crocodile, since water itself weakens his powers, even showers will take away his ability. Still, he would only shower when there's no danger of being attacked, so he probably showers even though he momentarily loses his powers, don't you think?
And finally, to the question of whether I take baths...
I bathe twice. Annually.
And so, we'll see you in the Question Corner in the next volume!!

Chapter 399:

JUMP TOWARD THE WATERFALL!!

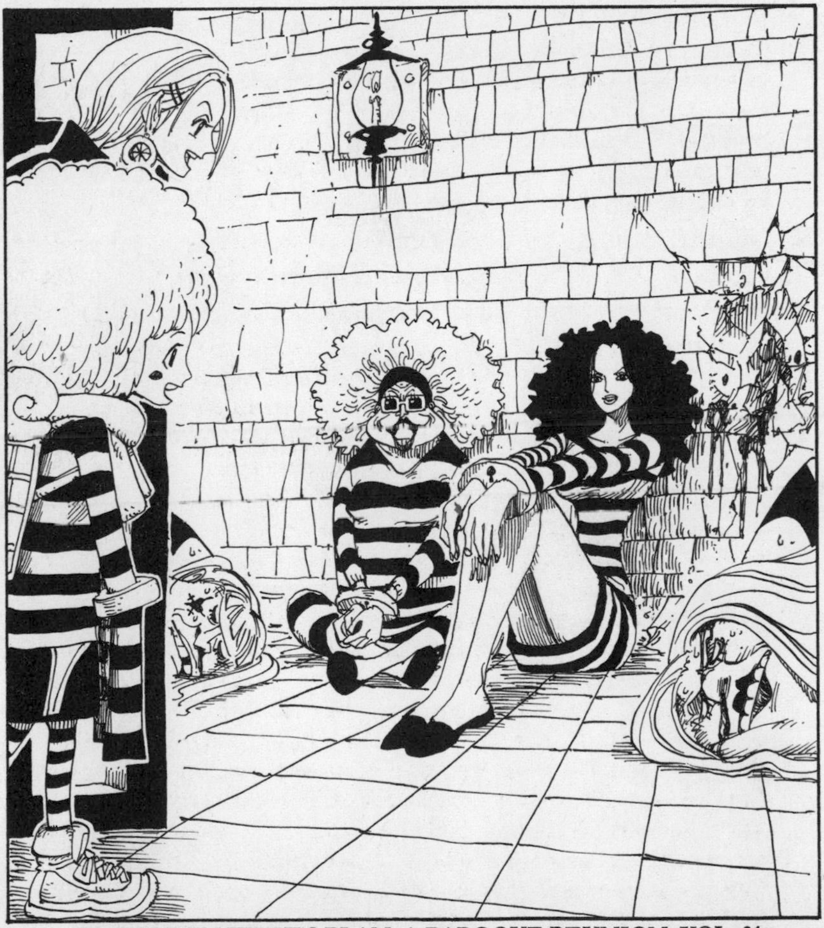

MS. GOLDEN WEEK'S PLAN, A BAROQUE REUNION, VOL. 31:
"LONG TIME NO SEE!! (THE OLD WOMAN NOT SEEN IN A LONG TIME) AND THE YOUNG LADY I'M MEETING FOR THE FIRST TIME"

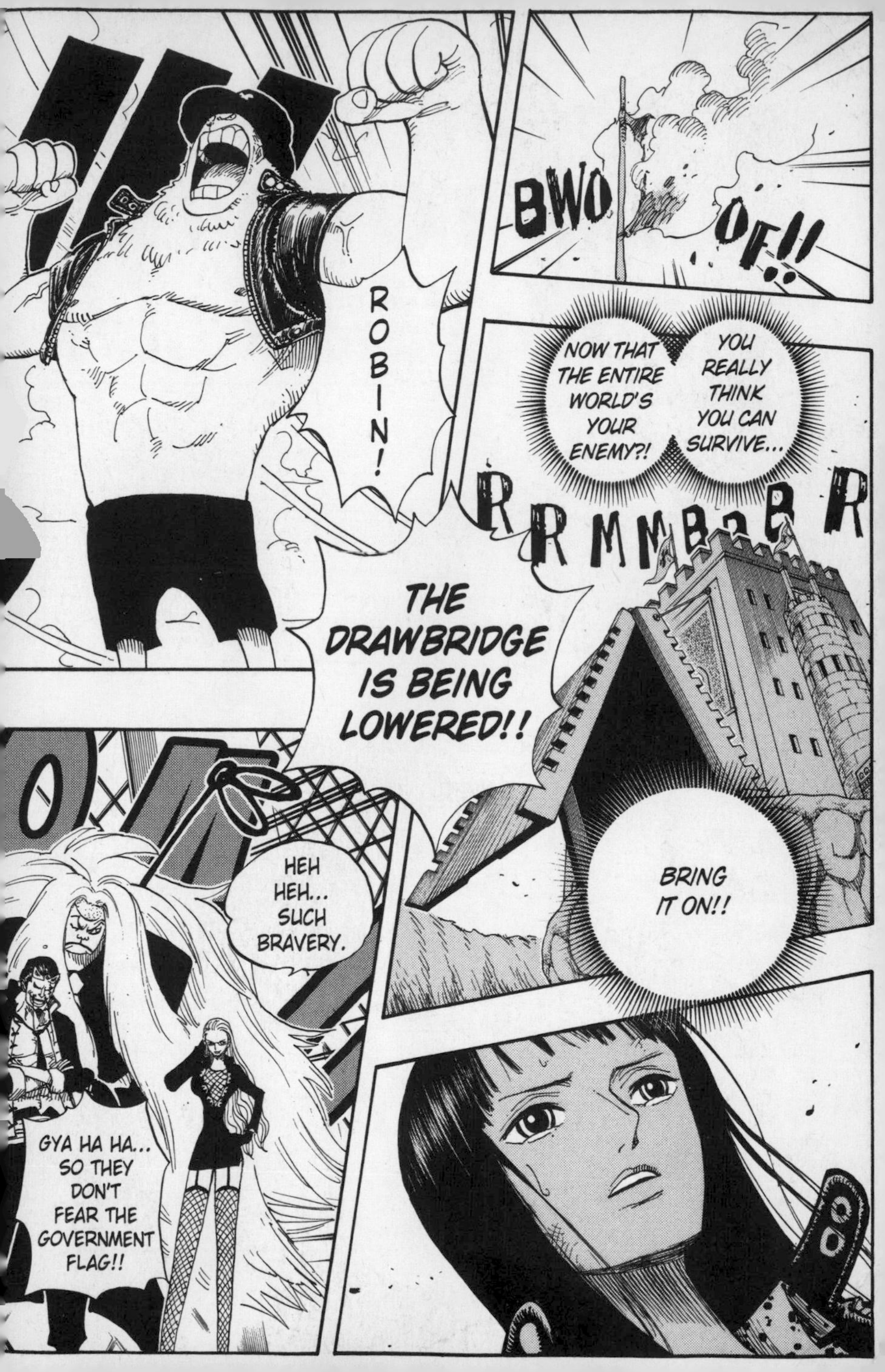

BWOOF!!
YOU REALLY THINK YOU CAN SURVIVE...
NOW THAT THE ENTIRE WORLD'S YOUR ENEMY?!
RRMMBBR
THE DRAWBRIDGE IS BEING LOWERED!!
ROBIN!
BRING IT ON!!
HEH HEH... SUCH BRAVERY.
GYA HA HA... SO THEY DON'T FEAR THE GOVERNMENT FLAG!!

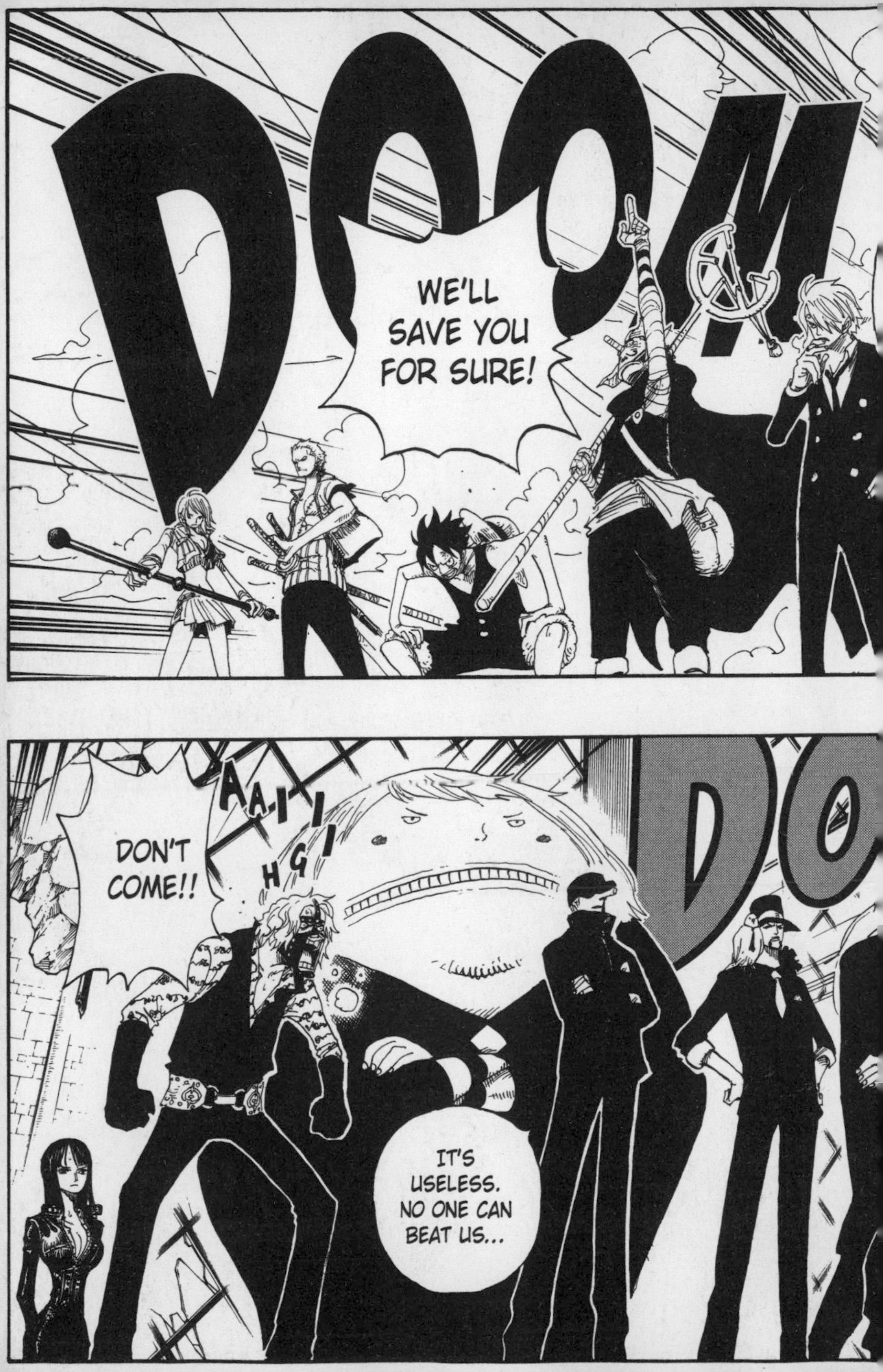
DOOM
WE'LL SAVE YOU FOR SURE!
DO
AAIIIGH
DON'T COME!!
IT'S USELESS. NO ONE CAN BEAT US...

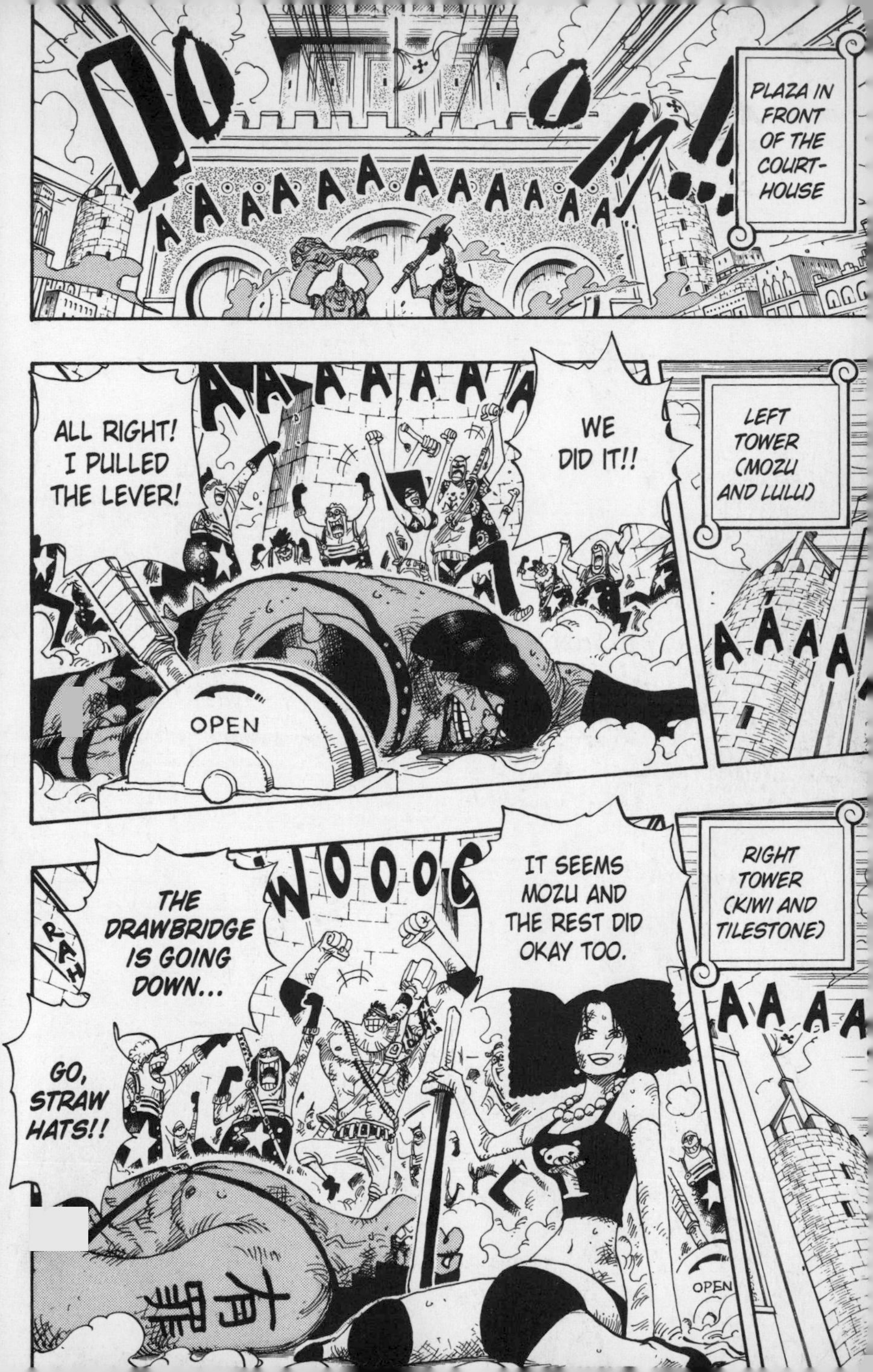
PLAZA IN FRONT OF THE COURT-HOUSE
DOOOM!!
AAAAAAAAAAAA
LEFT TOWER (MOZU AND LULU)
AAAA
WE DID IT!!
AAAAAAAA
ALL RIGHT! I PULLED THE LEVER!
OPEN
RIGHT TOWER (KIWI AND TILESTONE)
AAAA
IT SEEMS MOZU AND THE REST DID OKAY TOO.
WOOOO
THE DRAWBRIDGE IS GOING DOWN...
RAH
GO, STRAW HATS!!
OPEN

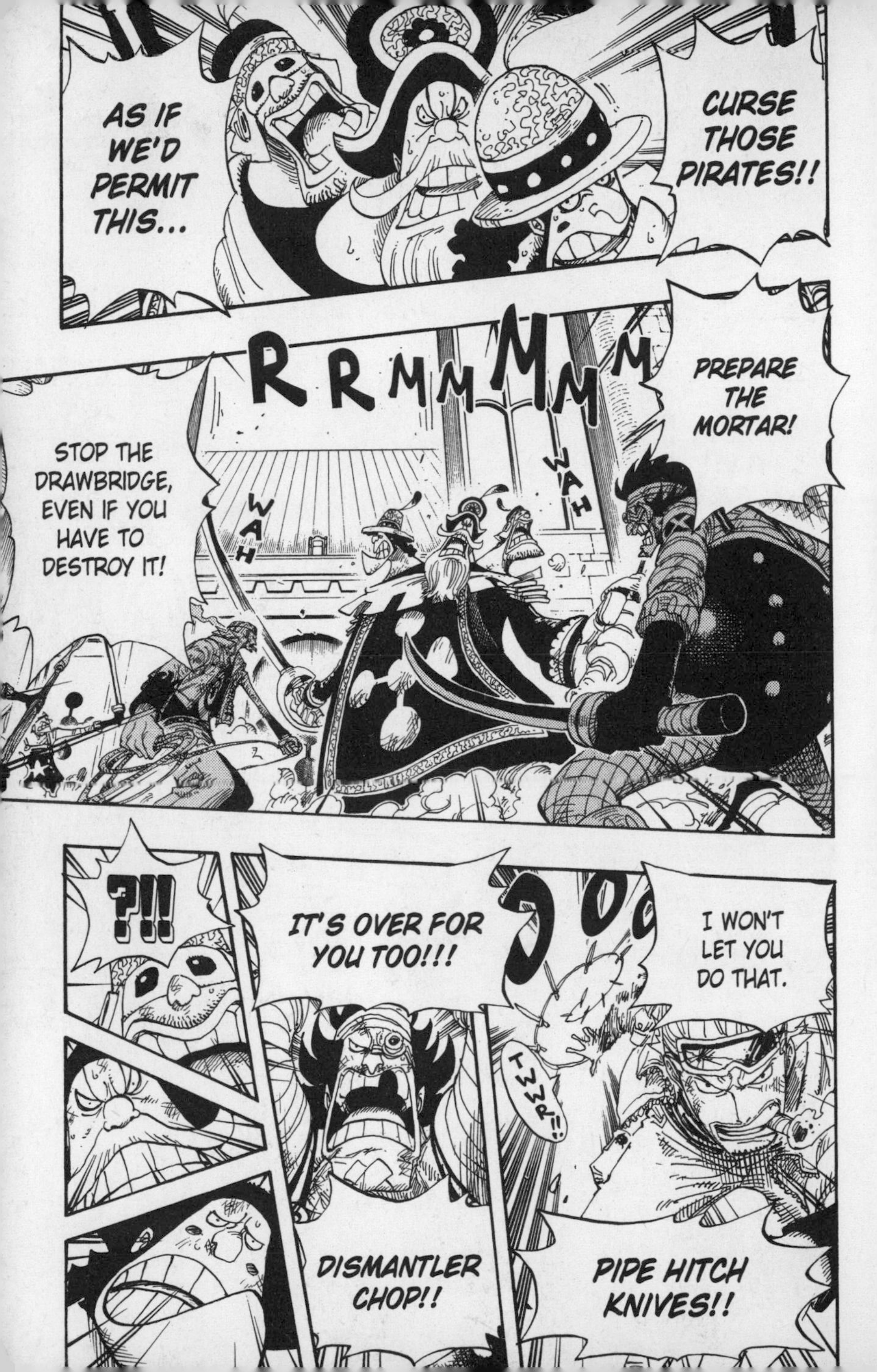
CURSE THOSE PIRATES!!
AS IF WE'D PERMIT THIS...
RRMMMMM
PREPARE THE MORTAR!
WAH
WAH
STOP THE DRAWBRIDGE, EVEN IF YOU HAVE TO DESTROY IT!
I WON'T LET YOU DO THAT.
TWWR!!
PIPE HITCH KNIVES!!
IT'S OVER FOR YOU TOO!!!
DISMANTLER CHOP!!
?!!

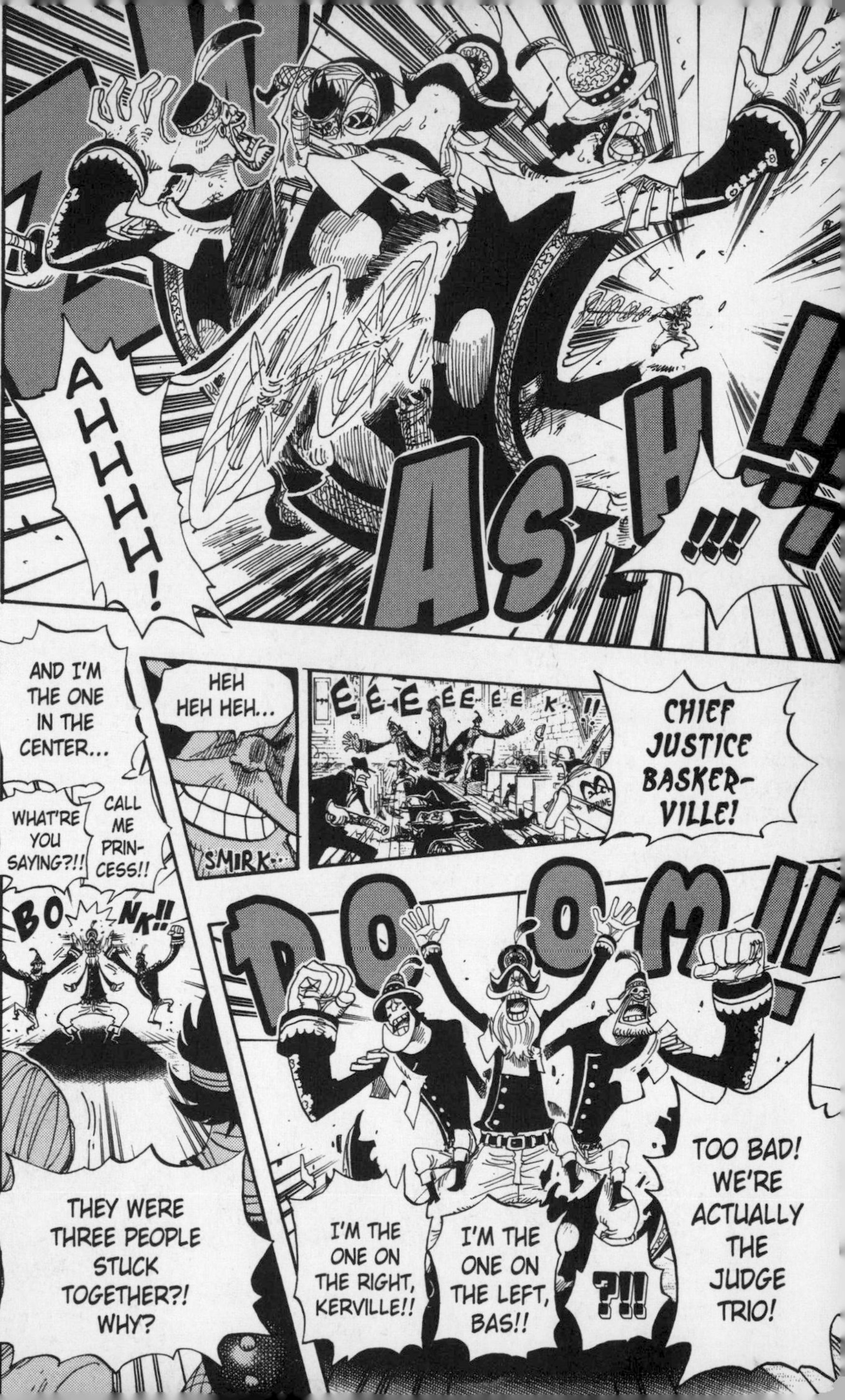
ASH!!!
AHHHH!
CHIEF JUSTICE BASKER-VILLE!
EEEEEEEK..!!
HEH HEH HEH...
SMIRK..
DOOM!!
TOO BAD! WE'RE ACTUALLY THE JUDGE TRIO!
?!!
I'M THE ONE ON THE LEFT, BAS!!
I'M THE ONE ON THE RIGHT, KERVILLE!!
THEY WERE THREE PEOPLE STUCK TOGETHER?! WHY?
AND I'M THE ONE IN THE CENTER...
CALL ME PRIN-CESS!!
WHAT'RE YOU SAYING?!!
BONK!!

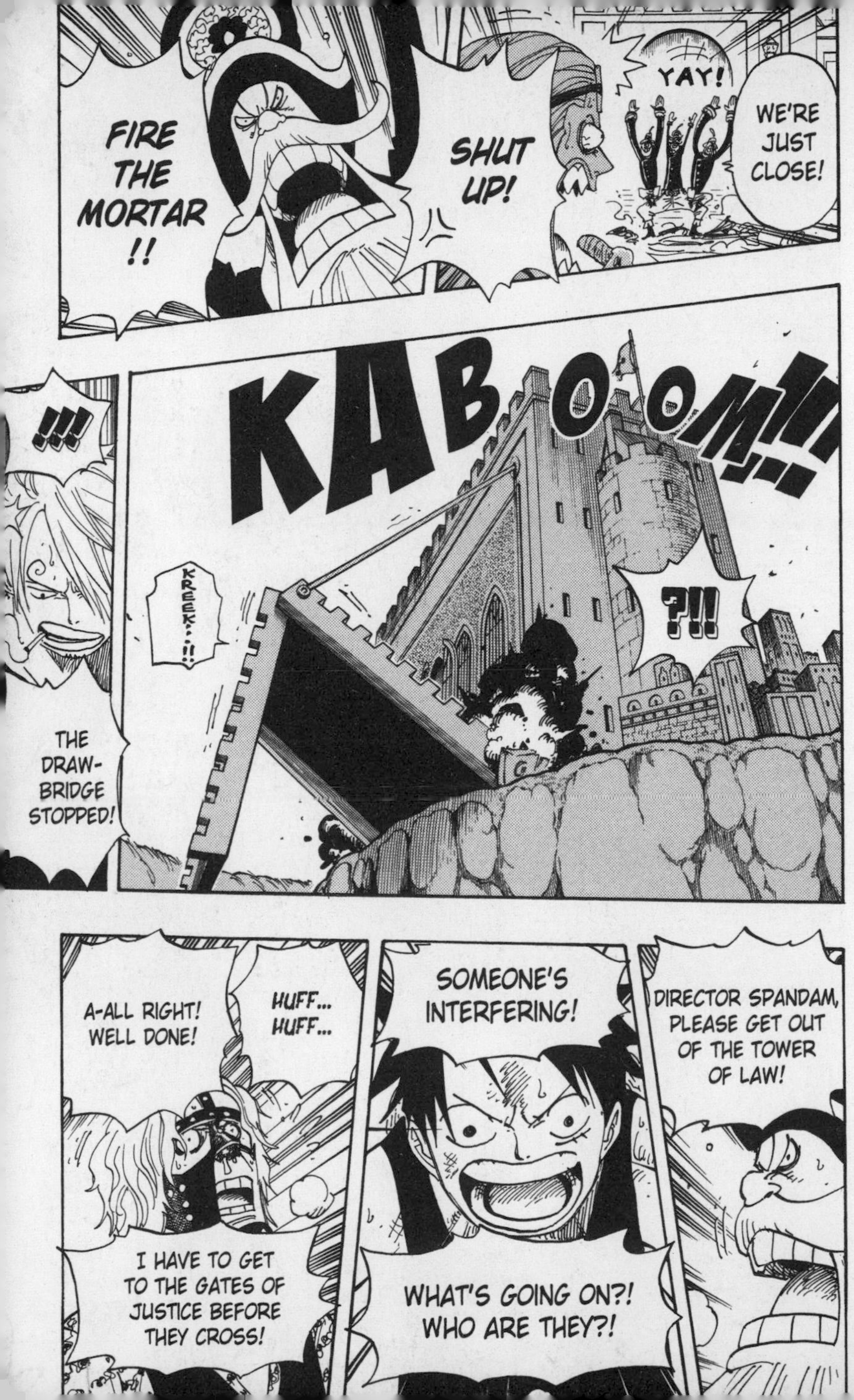
YAY!
WE'RE JUST CLOSE!
SHUT UP!
FIRE THE MORTAR !!
KABOOM!!!
KREEK..!!
?!!
!!!
THE DRAW-BRIDGE STOPPED!
DIRECTOR SPANDAM, PLEASE GET OUT OF THE TOWER OF LAW!
SOMEONE'S INTERFERING!
WHAT'S GOING ON?! WHO ARE THEY?!
HUFF... HUFF...
A-ALL RIGHT! WELL DONE!
I HAVE TO GET TO THE GATES OF JUSTICE BEFORE THEY CROSS!

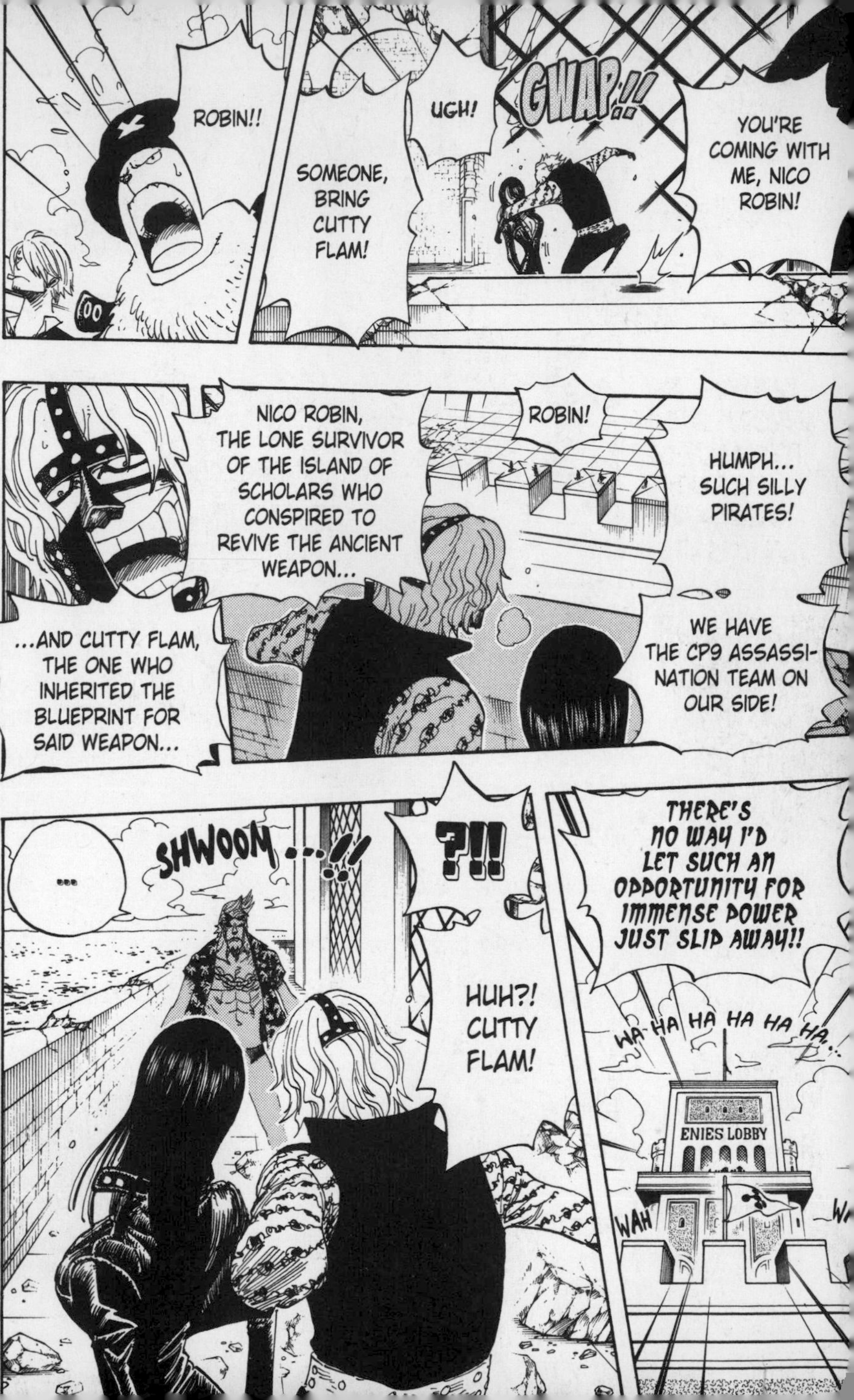
GWAP!!
YOU'RE COMING WITH ME, NICO ROBIN!
UGH!
SOMEONE, BRING CUTTY FLAM!
ROBIN!!
HUMPH... SUCH SILLY PIRATES!
WE HAVE THE CP9 ASSASSI-NATION TEAM ON OUR SIDE!
ROBIN!
NICO ROBIN, THE LONE SURVIVOR OF THE ISLAND OF SCHOLARS WHO CONSPIRED TO REVIVE THE ANCIENT WEAPON...
...AND CUTTY FLAM, THE ONE WHO INHERITED THE BLUEPRINT FOR SAID WEAPON...
THERE'S NO WAY I'D LET SUCH AN OPPORTUNITY FOR IMMENSE POWER JUST SLIP AWAY!!
WA HA HA HA HA HA...
ENIES LOBBY
WAH
?!!
HUH?! CUTTY FLAM!
SHWOOM...!!
...

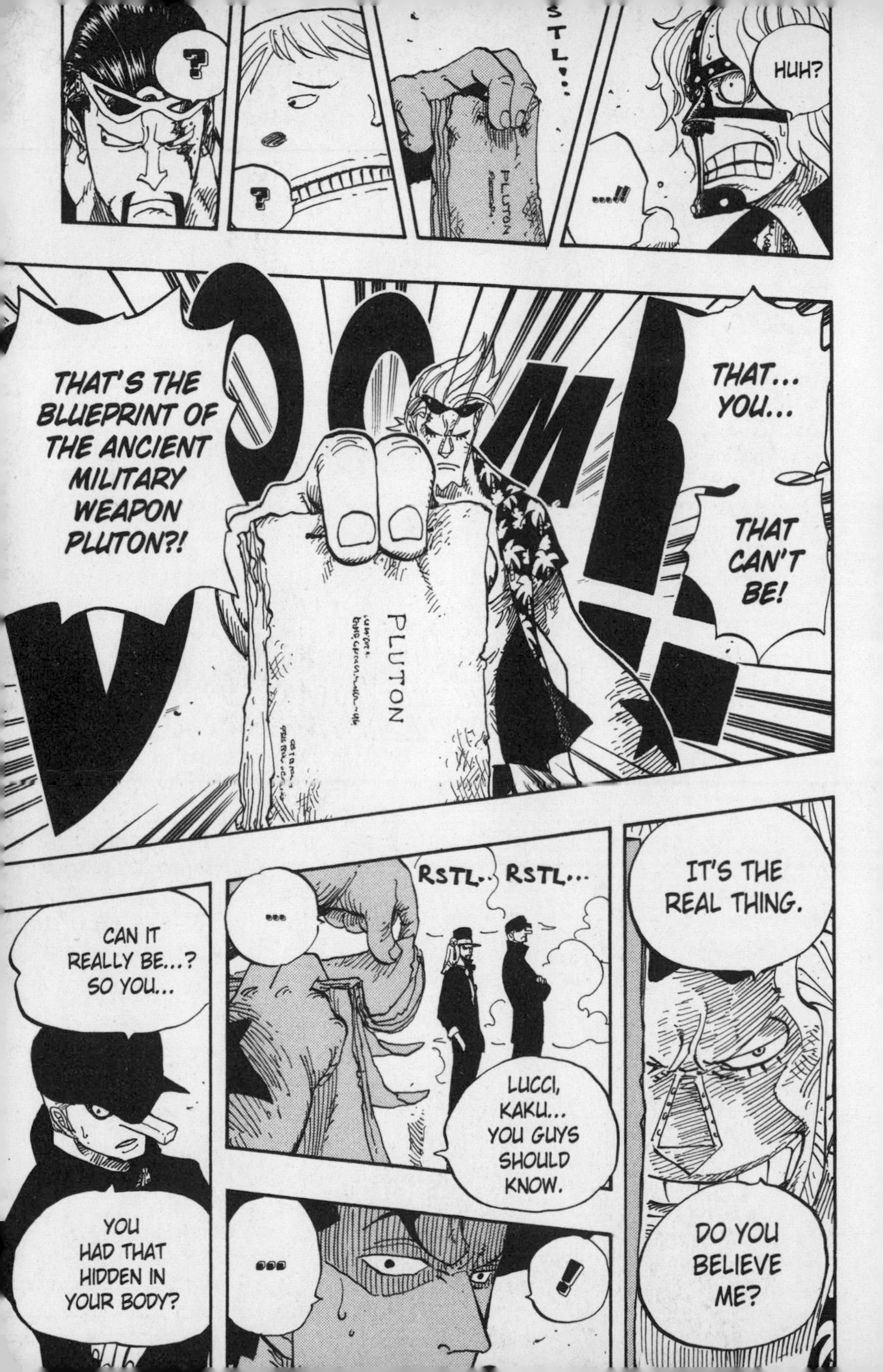
HUH?
...!!
RSTL...
PLUTON
?
?
THAT... YOU...
THAT CAN'T BE!
THAT'S THE BLUEPRINT OF THE ANCIENT MILITARY WEAPON PLUTON?!
PLUTON
IT'S THE REAL THING.
DO YOU BELIEVE ME?
RSTL... RSTL...
...
LUCCI, KAKU... YOU GUYS SHOULD KNOW.
!
...
CAN IT REALLY BE...? SO YOU...
YOU HAD THAT HIDDEN IN YOUR BODY?

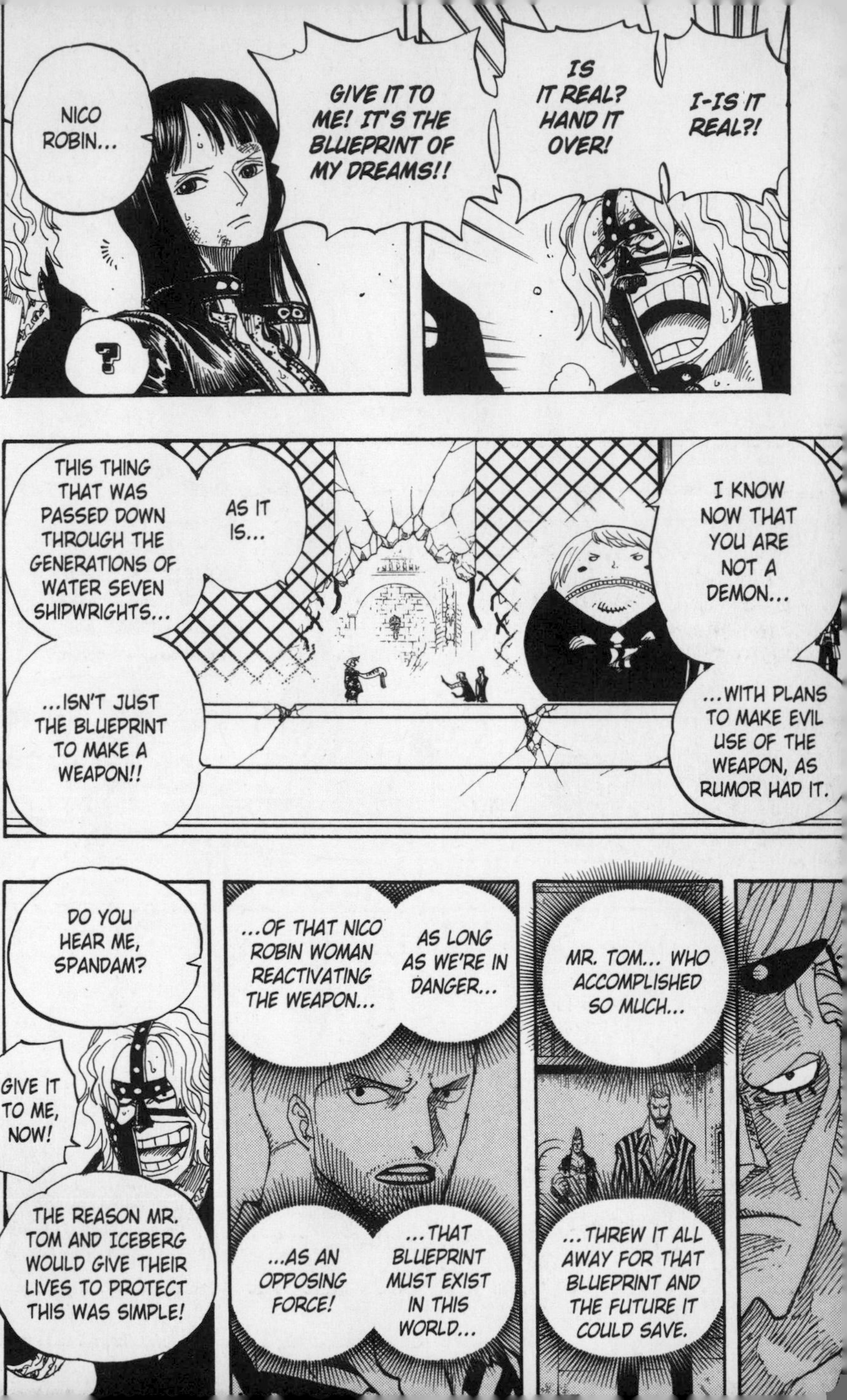
I-IS IT REAL?!
IS IT REAL? HAND IT OVER!
GIVE IT TO ME! IT'S THE BLUEPRINT OF MY DREAMS!!
NICO ROBIN...
?
I KNOW NOW THAT YOU ARE NOT A DEMON...
...WITH PLANS TO MAKE EVIL USE OF THE WEAPON, AS RUMOR HAD IT.
AS IT IS...
THIS THING THAT WAS PASSED DOWN THROUGH THE GENERATIONS OF WATER SEVEN SHIPWRIGHTS...
...ISN'T JUST THE BLUEPRINT TO MAKE A WEAPON!!
MR. TOM... WHO ACCOMPLISHED SO MUCH...
...THREW IT ALL AWAY FOR THAT BLUEPRINT AND THE FUTURE IT COULD SAVE.
AS LONG AS WE'RE IN DANGER...
...OF THAT NICO ROBIN WOMAN REACTIVATING THE WEAPON...
...THAT BLUEPRINT MUST EXIST IN THIS WORLD...
...AS AN OPPOSING FORCE!
DO YOU HEAR ME, SPANDAM?
GIVE IT TO ME, NOW!
THE REASON MR. TOM AND ICEBERG WOULD GIVE THEIR LIVES TO PROTECT THIS WAS SIMPLE!

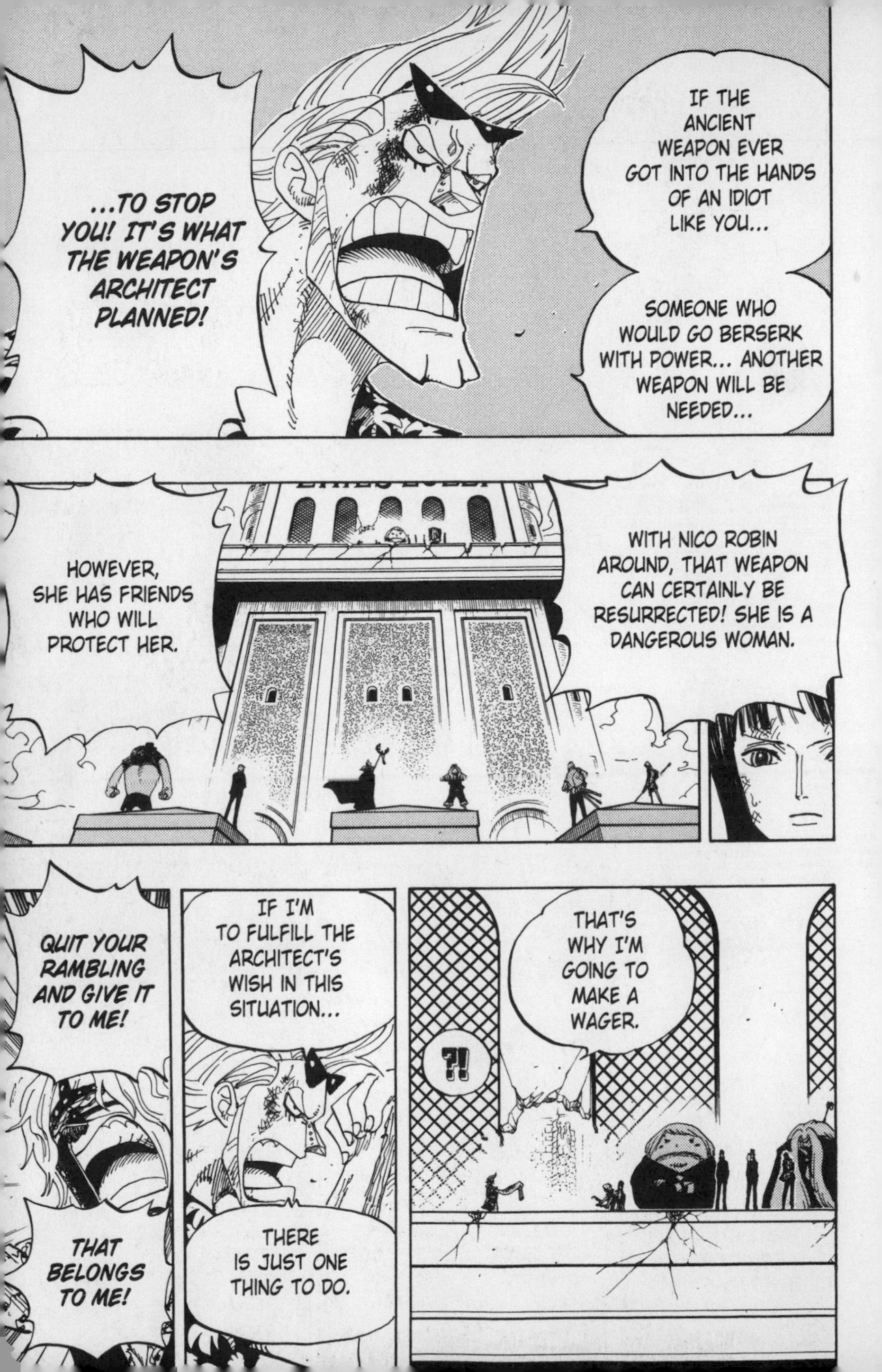
IF THE ANCIENT WEAPON EVER GOT INTO THE HANDS OF AN IDIOT LIKE YOU...
SOMEONE WHO WOULD GO BERSERK WITH POWER... ANOTHER WEAPON WILL BE NEEDED...
...TO STOP YOU! IT'S WHAT THE WEAPON'S ARCHITECT PLANNED!
WITH NICO ROBIN AROUND, THAT WEAPON CAN CERTAINLY BE RESURRECTED! SHE IS A DANGEROUS WOMAN.
HOWEVER, SHE HAS FRIENDS WHO WILL PROTECT HER.
THAT'S WHY I'M GOING TO MAKE A WAGER.
?!
IF I'M TO FULFILL THE ARCHITECT'S WISH IN THIS SITUATION...
THERE IS JUST ONE THING TO DO.
QUIT YOUR RAMBLING AND GIVE IT TO ME!
THAT BELONGS TO ME!

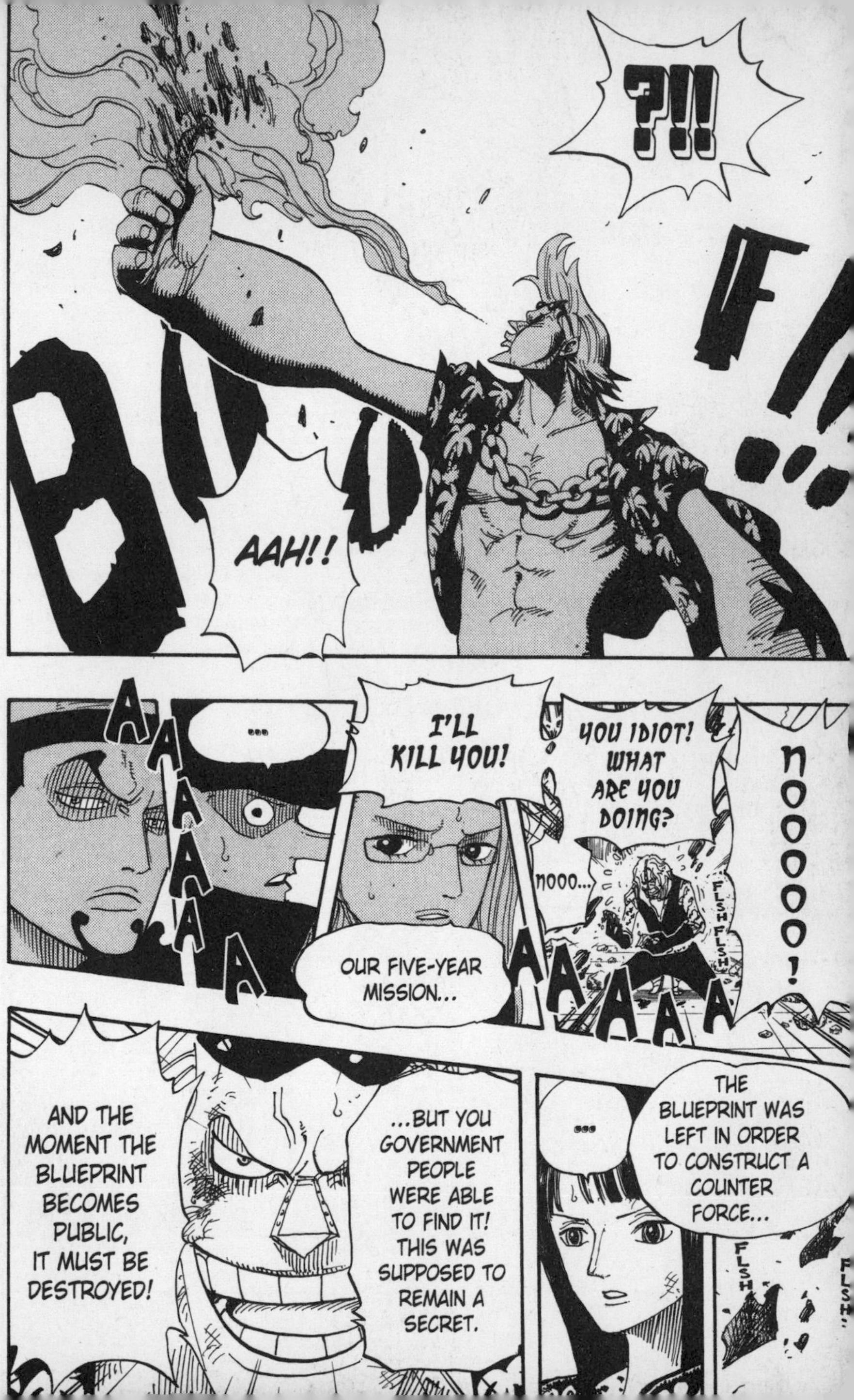
?!!
AAH!!
FLSH..
nOOOOOO!
YOU IDIOT! WHAT ARE YOU DOING?
nooo...
FLSH FLSH
I'LL KILL YOU!
OUR FIVE-YEAR MISSION...
...
THE BLUEPRINT WAS LEFT IN ORDER TO CONSTRUCT A COUNTER FORCE...
...
FLSH
...BUT YOU GOVERNMENT PEOPLE WERE ABLE TO FIND IT! THIS WAS SUPPOSED TO REMAIN A SECRET.
AND THE MOMENT THE BLUEPRINT BECOMES PUBLIC, IT MUST BE DESTROYED!

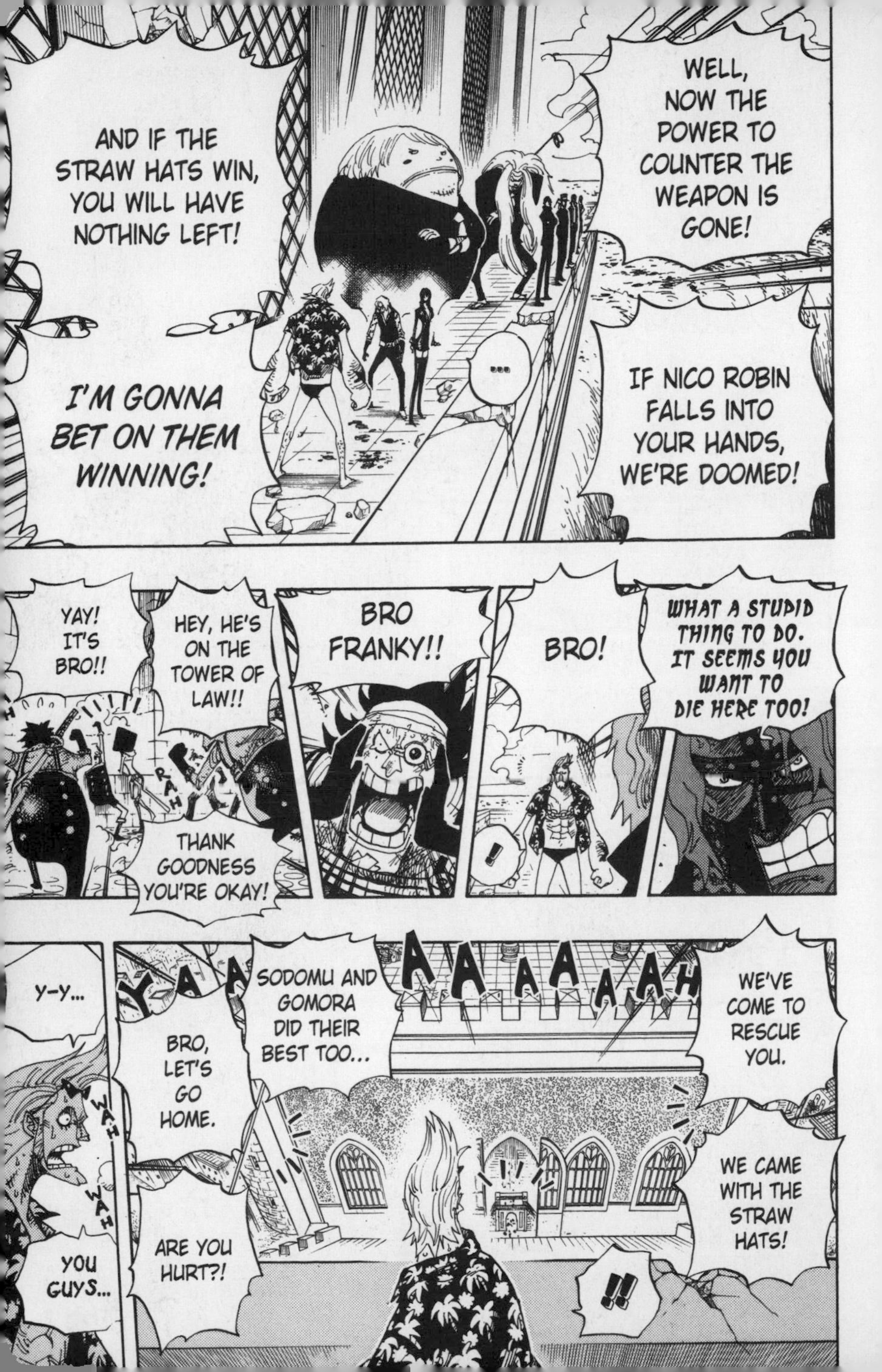
WELL, NOW THE POWER TO COUNTER THE WEAPON IS GONE!
IF NICO ROBIN FALLS INTO YOUR HANDS, WE'RE DOOMED!
...
AND IF THE STRAW HATS WIN, YOU WILL HAVE NOTHING LEFT!
I'M GONNA BET ON THEM WINNING!
WHAT A STUPID THING TO DO. IT SEEMS YOU WANT TO DIE HERE TOO!
BRO!
!
BRO FRANKY!!
HEY, HE'S ON THE TOWER OF LAW!!
YAY! IT'S BRO!!
RAH
THANK GOODNESS YOU'RE OKAY!
WE'VE COME TO RESCUE YOU.
YAAAAAAAAAAH
SODOMU AND GOMORA DID THEIR BEST TOO...
BRO, LET'S GO HOME.
WE CAME WITH THE STRAW HATS!
!!
ARE YOU HURT?!
Y-Y...
WAH
WAH
YOU GUYS...

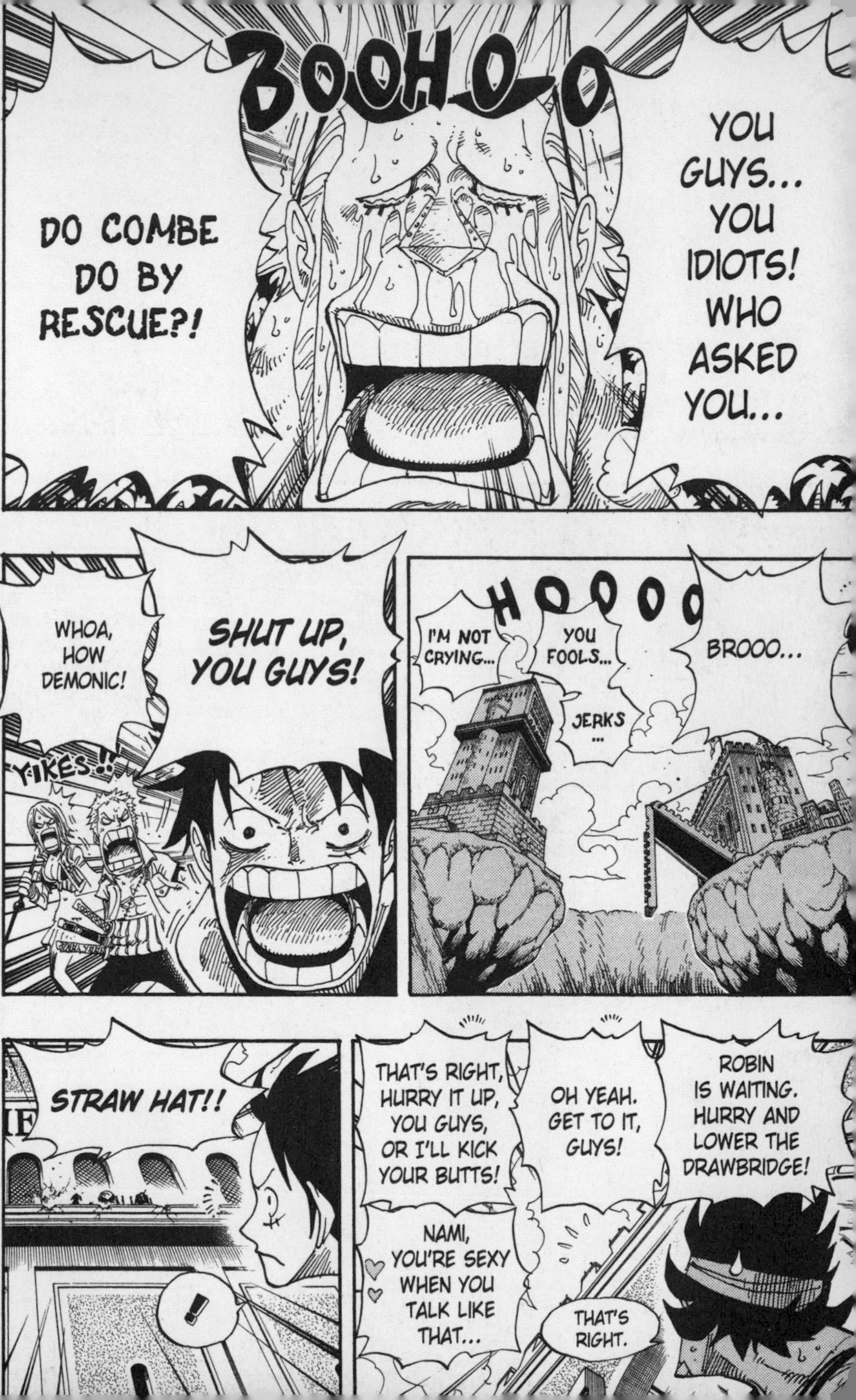
BOOHOOO
YOU GUYS... YOU IDIOTS! WHO ASKED YOU...
DO COMBE DO BY RESCUE?!
HOOOO
BROOO...
YOU FOOLS...
JERKS ...
I'M NOT CRYING...
SHUT UP, YOU GUYS!
WHOA, HOW DEMONIC!
YIKES!!
ROBIN IS WAITING. HURRY AND LOWER THE DRAWBRIDGE!
OH YEAH. GET TO IT, GUYS!
THAT'S RIGHT, HURRY IT UP, YOU GUYS, OR I'LL KICK YOUR BUTTS!
THAT'S RIGHT.
NAMI, YOU'RE SEXY WHEN YOU TALK LIKE THAT...
STRAW HAT!!
!

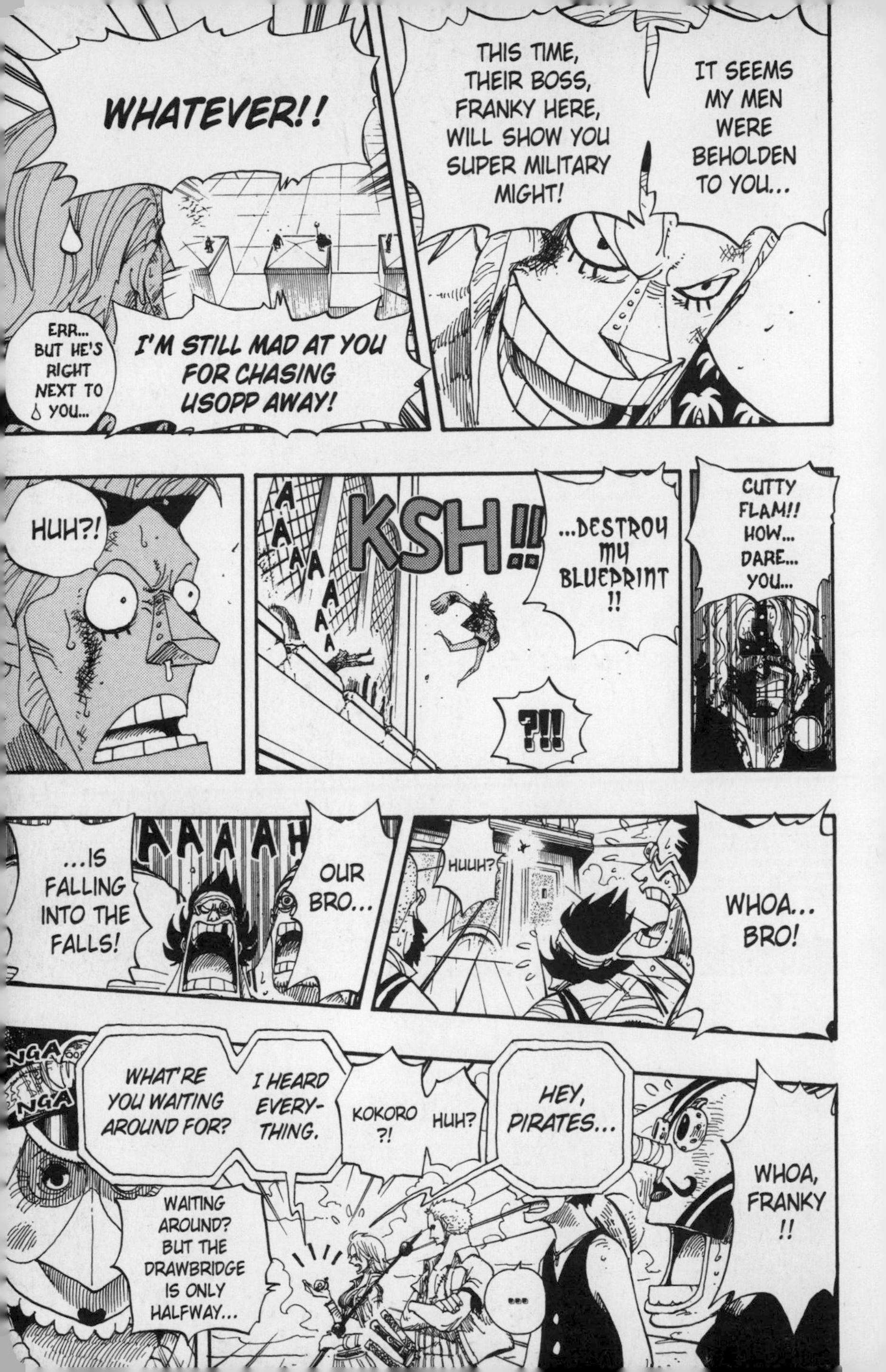
IT SEEMS MY MEN WERE BEHOLDEN TO YOU...
THIS TIME, THEIR BOSS, FRANKY HERE, WILL SHOW YOU SUPER MILITARY MIGHT!
WHATEVER!!
I'M STILL MAD AT YOU FOR CHASING USOPP AWAY!
ERR... BUT HE'S RIGHT NEXT TO YOU...
CUTTY FLAM!! HOW... DARE... YOU...
...DESTROY MY BLUEPRINT!!
?!!
KSH!!
AAAAAAAA
HUH?!
WHOA... BRO!
HUUH?
OUR BRO...
AAAAAH
...IS FALLING INTO THE FALLS!
WHOA, FRANKY!!
HEY, PIRATES...
HUH?
KOKORO?!
I HEARD EVERYTHING.
WHAT'RE YOU WAITING AROUND FOR?
...
WAITING AROUND? BUT THE DRAWBRIDGE IS ONLY HALFWAY...
NGA
NGA

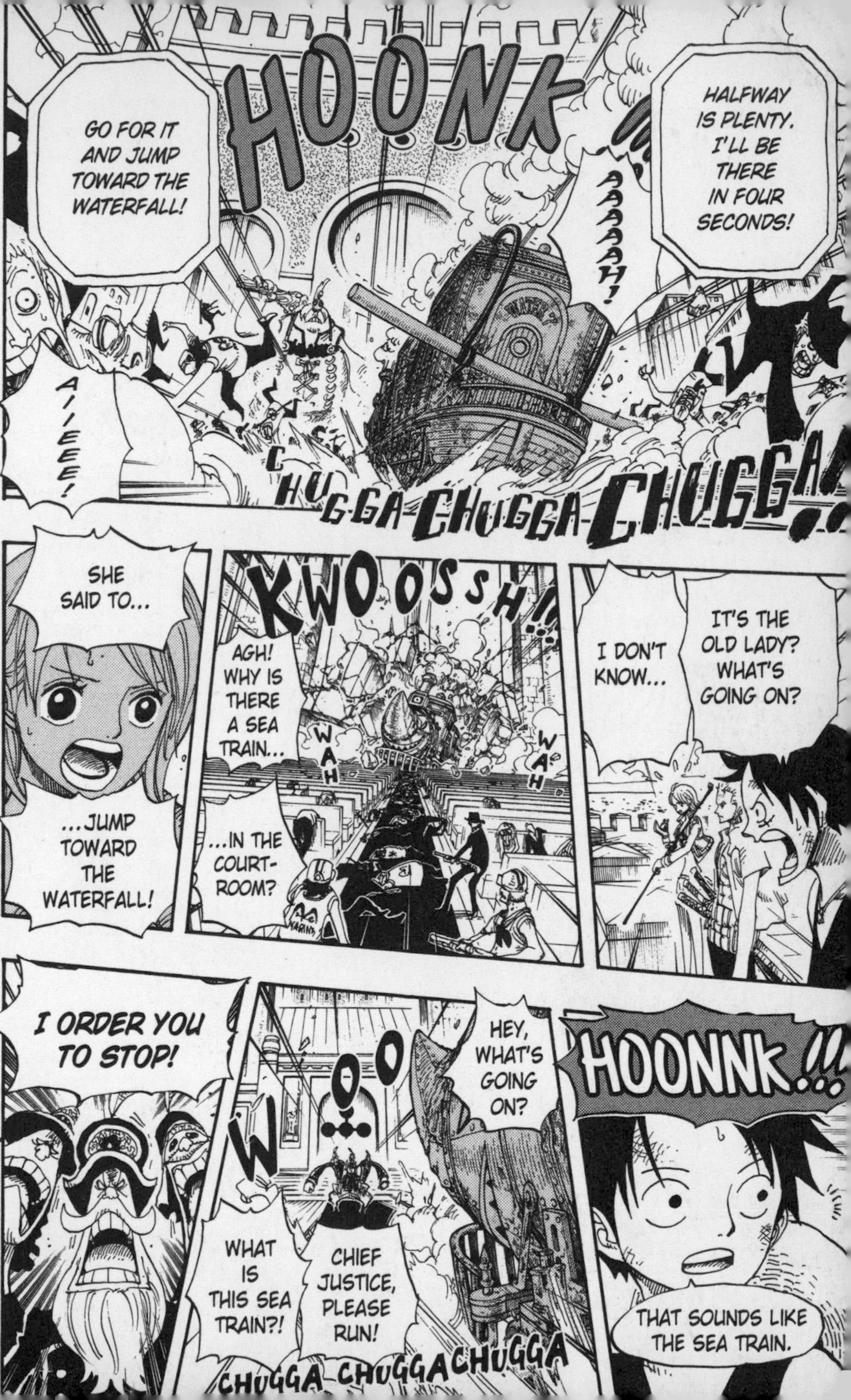
HALFWAY IS PLENTY. I'LL BE THERE IN FOUR SECONDS!
AAAAAAH!
HOONK
GO FOR IT AND JUMP TOWARD THE WATERFALL!
AIIEEE!
CHUGGA CHUGGA CHUGGA!!
IT'S THE OLD LADY? WHAT'S GOING ON?
I DON'T KNOW...
KWOOSSH!!
AGH! WHY IS THERE A SEA TRAIN...
WAH
WAH
...IN THE COURTROOM?
SHE SAID TO...
...JUMP TOWARD THE WATERFALL!
HOONNK!!
THAT SOUNDS LIKE THE SEA TRAIN.
HEY, WHAT'S GOING ON?
WOOO
CHIEF JUSTICE, PLEASE RUN!
WHAT IS THIS SEA TRAIN?!
CHUGGA CHUGGA CHUGGA
I ORDER YOU TO STOP!

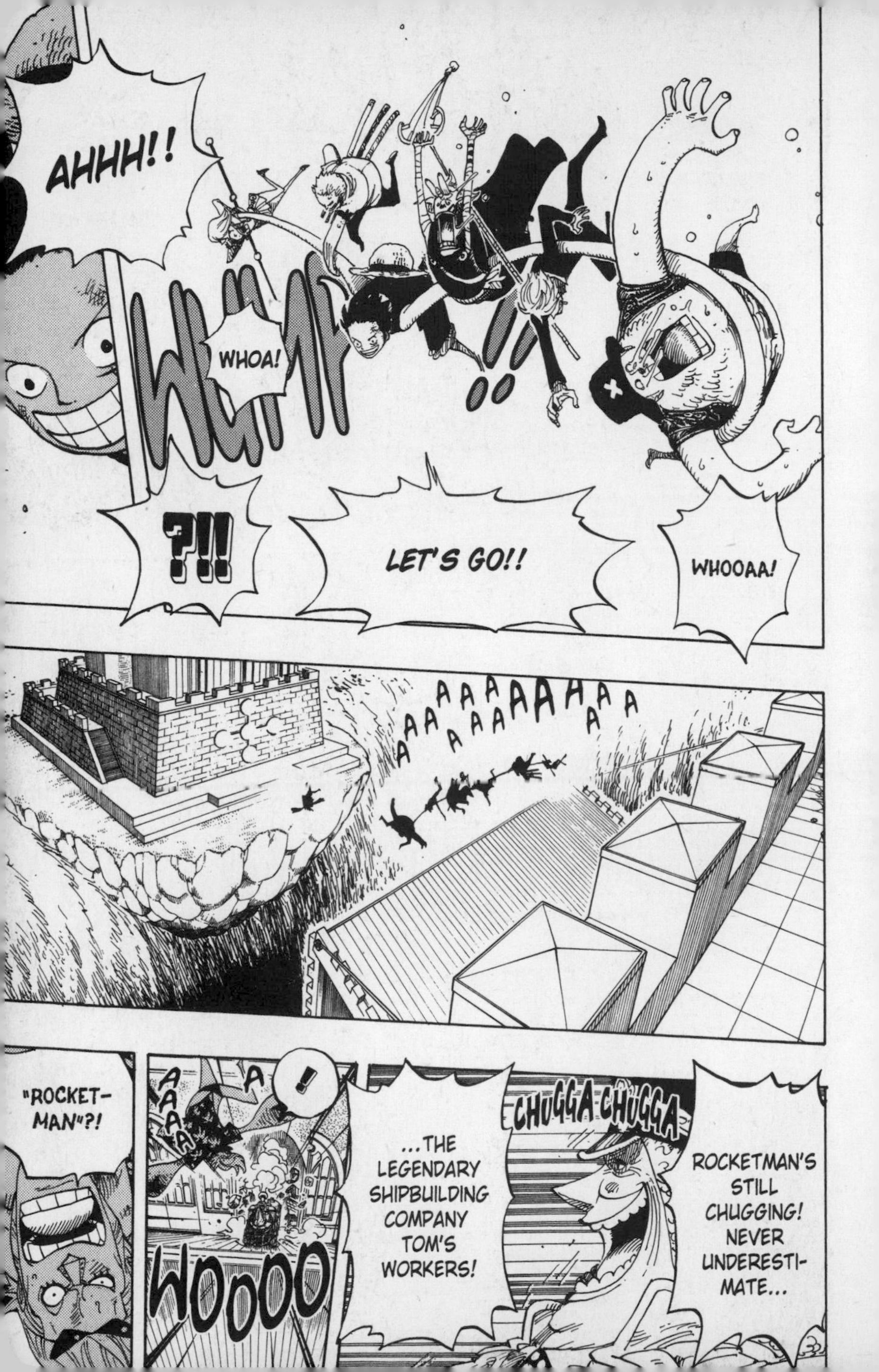
WHOOAA!
LET'S GO!!
?!!
WHOA!
AHHH!!
CHUGGA CHUGGA
ROCKETMAN'S STILL CHUGGING! NEVER UNDERESTI-MATE...
...THE LEGENDARY SHIPBUILDING COMPANY TOM'S WORKERS!
!
A
WOOOO
"ROCKET-MAN"?!

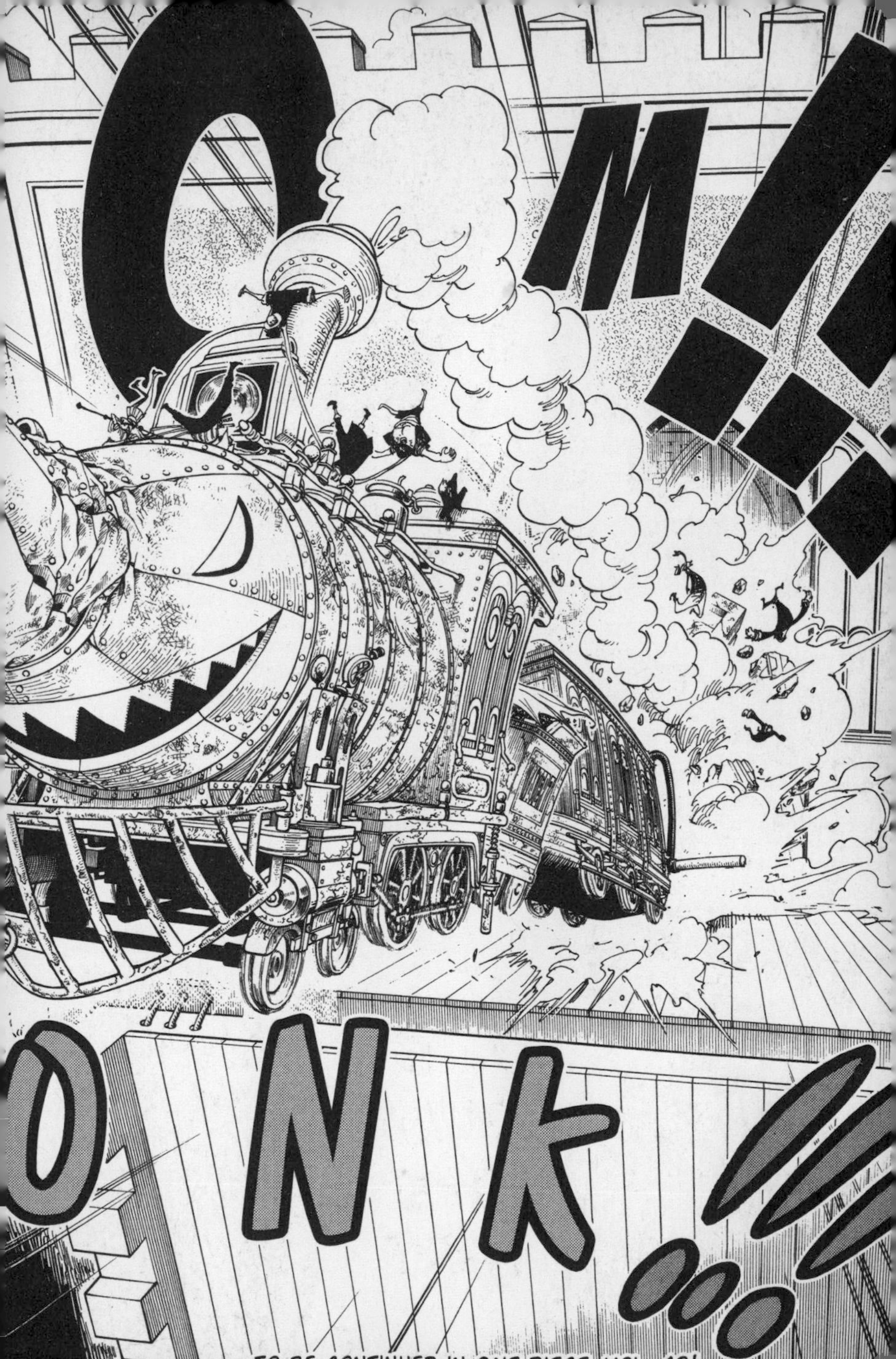
OM!!
ONK...!!

TO BE CONTINUED IN ONE PIECE, VOL. 42!

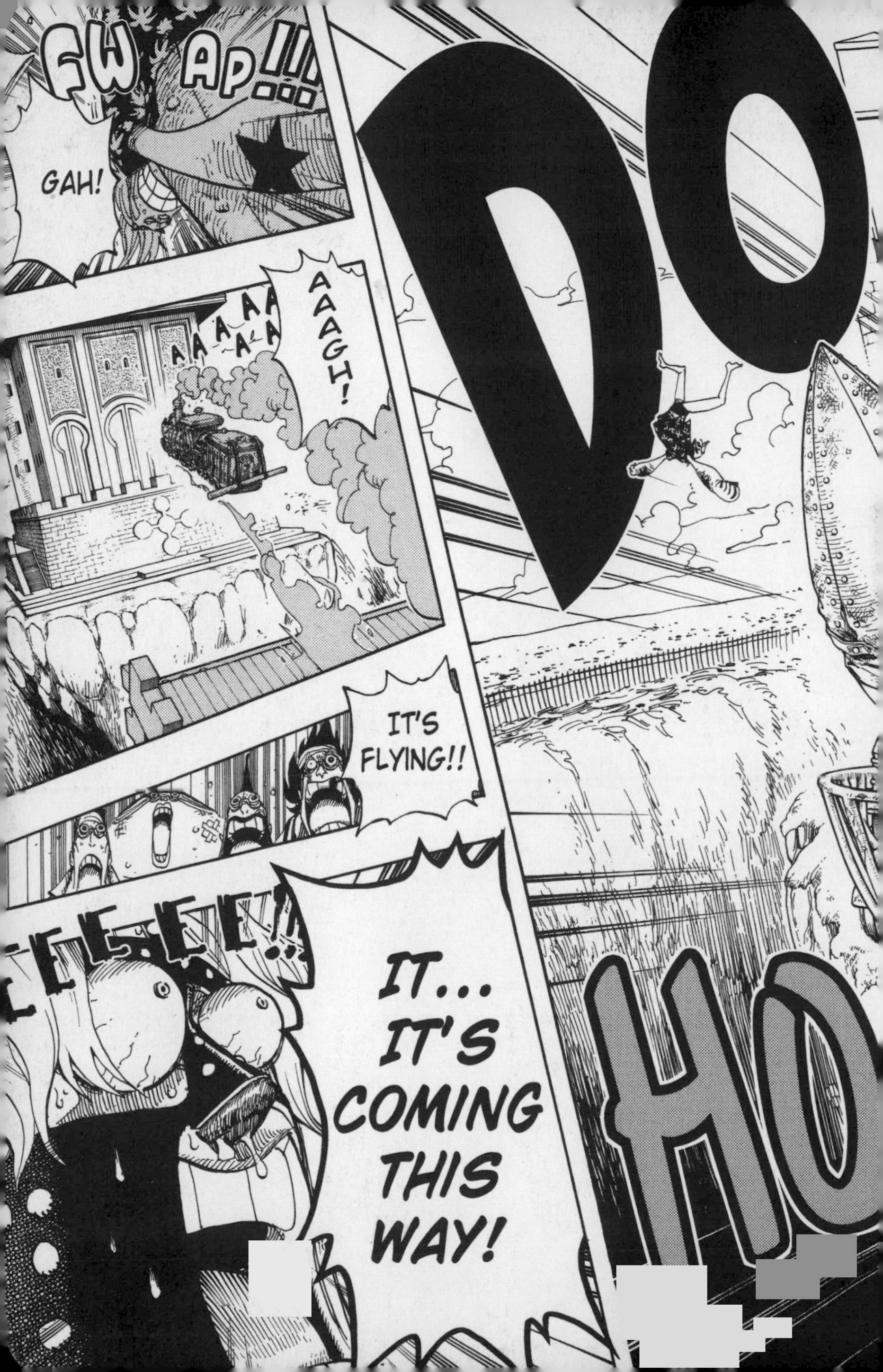
DO
HO
FWAP!!!
GAH!
AAAAAAA
AAAGH!
IT'S FLYING!!
EEEEE!!
IT... IT'S COMING THIS WAY!

COMING NEXT VOLUME:

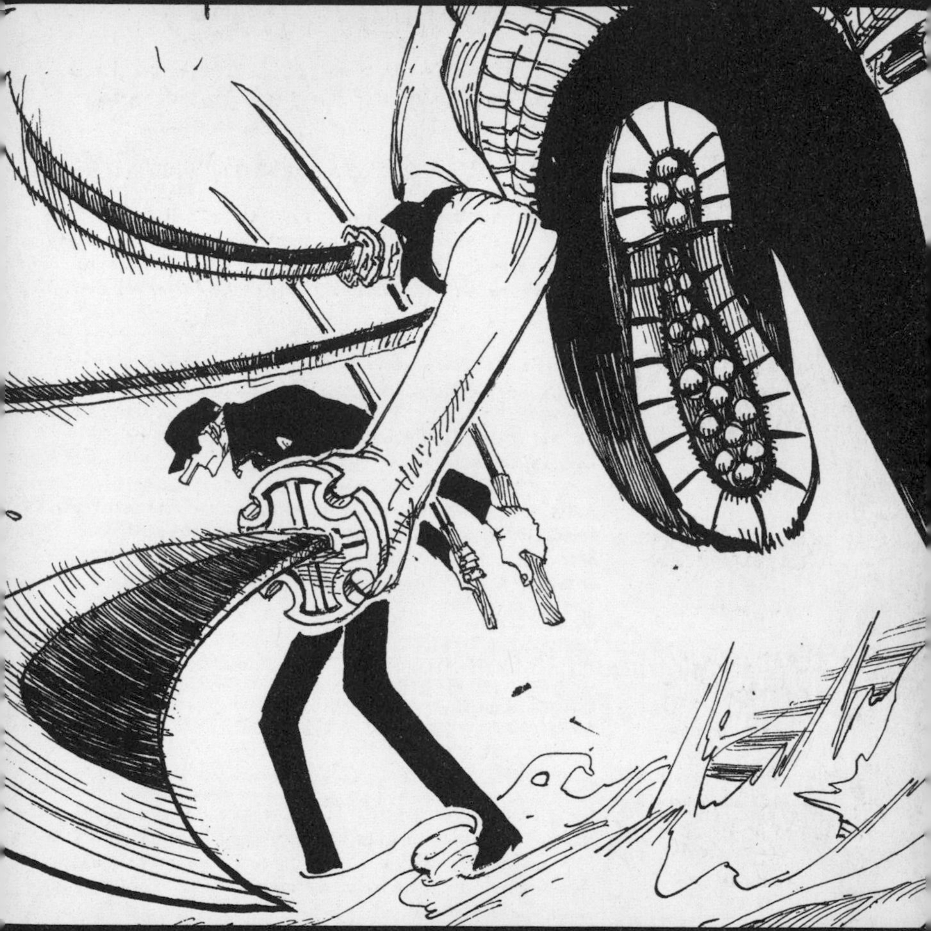

The Straw Hats have infiltrated the Tower of Law to save Robin, but they still need a special key to release her. One of the CP9 assassins holds the right key, but Luffy and his crew may have to defeat them all. Can the Straw Hats conquer CP9 and rescue Robin?

ON SALE NOW!

Set Sail with

Read all about **MONKEY D. LUFFY**'s adventures as he sails around the world assembling a motley crew to join him on his search for the legendary treasure "**ONE PIECE.**" For more information, check out **onepiece.viz.com.**

EAST BLUE
(Vols. 1-12)
Available now!

See where it all began! One man, a dinghy and a dream. Or rather… a rubber man who can't swim, setting out in a tiny boat on the vast seas without any navigational skills. What are the odds that his dream of becoming King of the Pirates will ever come true?

BAROQUE WORKS
(Vols. 12-24)
Available now!

Friend or foe? Ms. Wednesday is part of a group of bounty hunters—or isn't she? The Straw Hats get caught up in a civil war when they find a princess in their midst. But can they help her stop the revolution in her home country before the evil Crocodile gets his way?!

SKYPIEA
(Vols. 24-32)
Available now!

Luffy's quest to become King of the Pirates and find the elusive treasure known as "One Piece" continues…in the sky! The Straw Hats sail to Skypiea, an airborne island in the midst of a territorial war and ruled by a short-fused megalomaniac!

WATER SEVEN
(Vols. 32-46)
Available from February 2010!

The *Merry Go* has been a stalwart for the Straw Hats since the beginning, but countless battles have taken their toll on the ship. Luckily, their next stop is Water Seven, where a rough-and-tumble crew of shipwrights awaits their arrival!

THRILLER BARK
(Vols. 46-50)
Available from May 2010!

Luffy and crew get more than they bargained for when their ship is drawn toward haunted Thriller Bark. When Gecko Moria, one of the Warlords of the Sea, steals the crew's shadows, they'll have to get them back before the sun rises or else they'll all turn into zombies!

SABAODY
(Vols. 50-54)
Available from June 2010!

On the way to Fish-Man Island, the Straw Hats disembark on the Sabaody archipelago to get soaped up for their undersea adventure! But it's not too long before they get caught up in trouble! Luffy's made an enemy of an exalted World Noble when he saves Camie the mermaid from being sold on the slave market, and now he's got the Navy after him too!

IMPEL DOWN
(from Vol. 54)
Available from July 2010!

Luffy's brother Ace is about to be executed! Held in the Navy's maximum security prison Impel Down, Luffy needs to find a way to break in to help Ace escape. But with murderous fiends for guards inside, the notorious prisoners start to seem not so bad. Some are even friendly enough to give Luffy a helping hand!

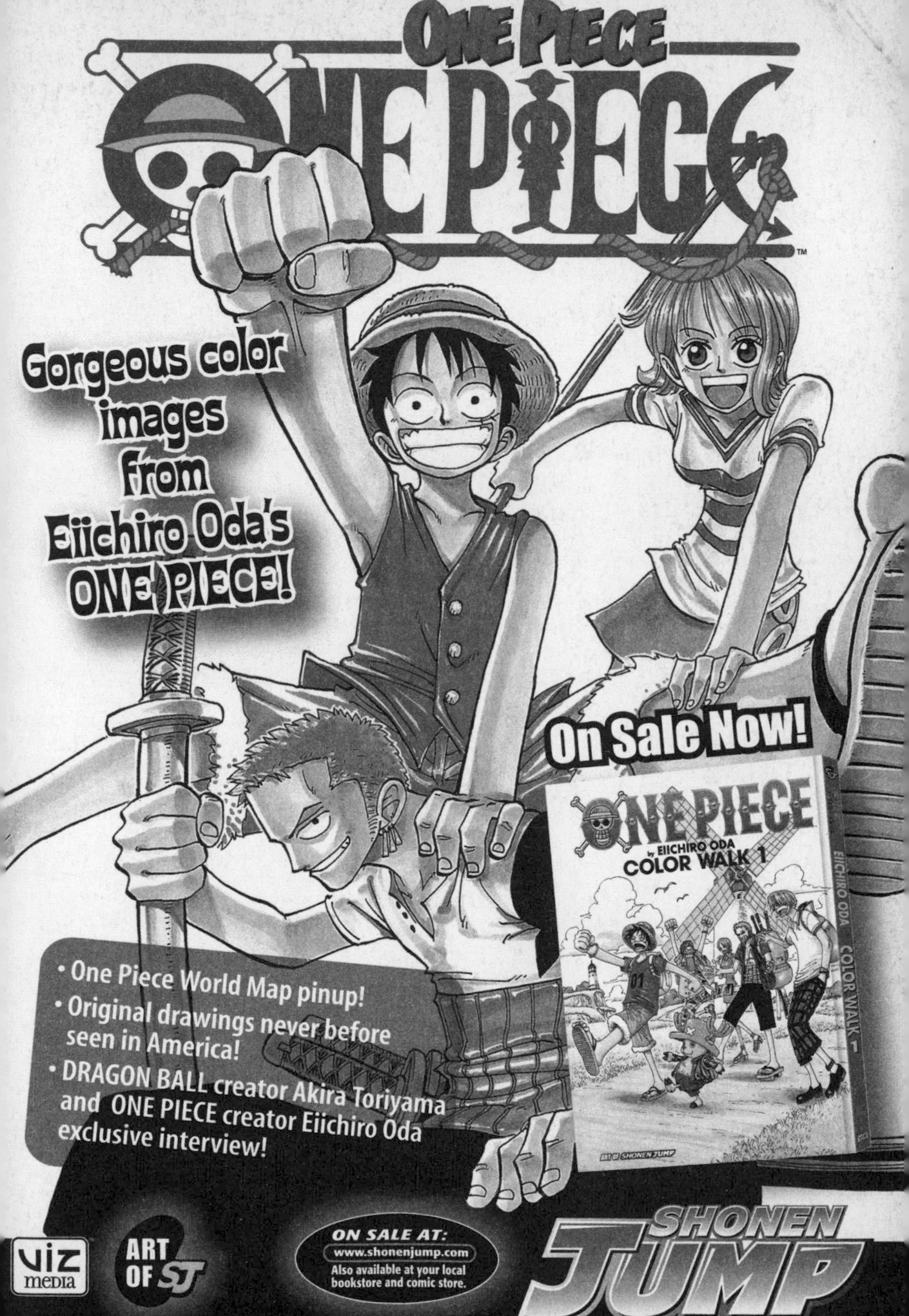
ONE PIECE
ONE PIECE™
Gorgeous color images from Eiichiro Oda's ONE PIECE!
On Sale Now!
ONE PIECE
by EIICHIRO ODA
COLOR WALK 1
EIICHIRO ODA
COLOR WALK 1
ART OF SHONEN JUMP
• One Piece World Map pinup!
• Original drawings never before seen in America!
• DRAGON BALL creator Akira Toriyama and ONE PIECE creator Eiichiro Oda exclusive interview!
viz media
ART OF SJ
ON SALE AT:
www.shonenjump.com
Also available at your local bookstore and comic store.
SHONEN JUMP

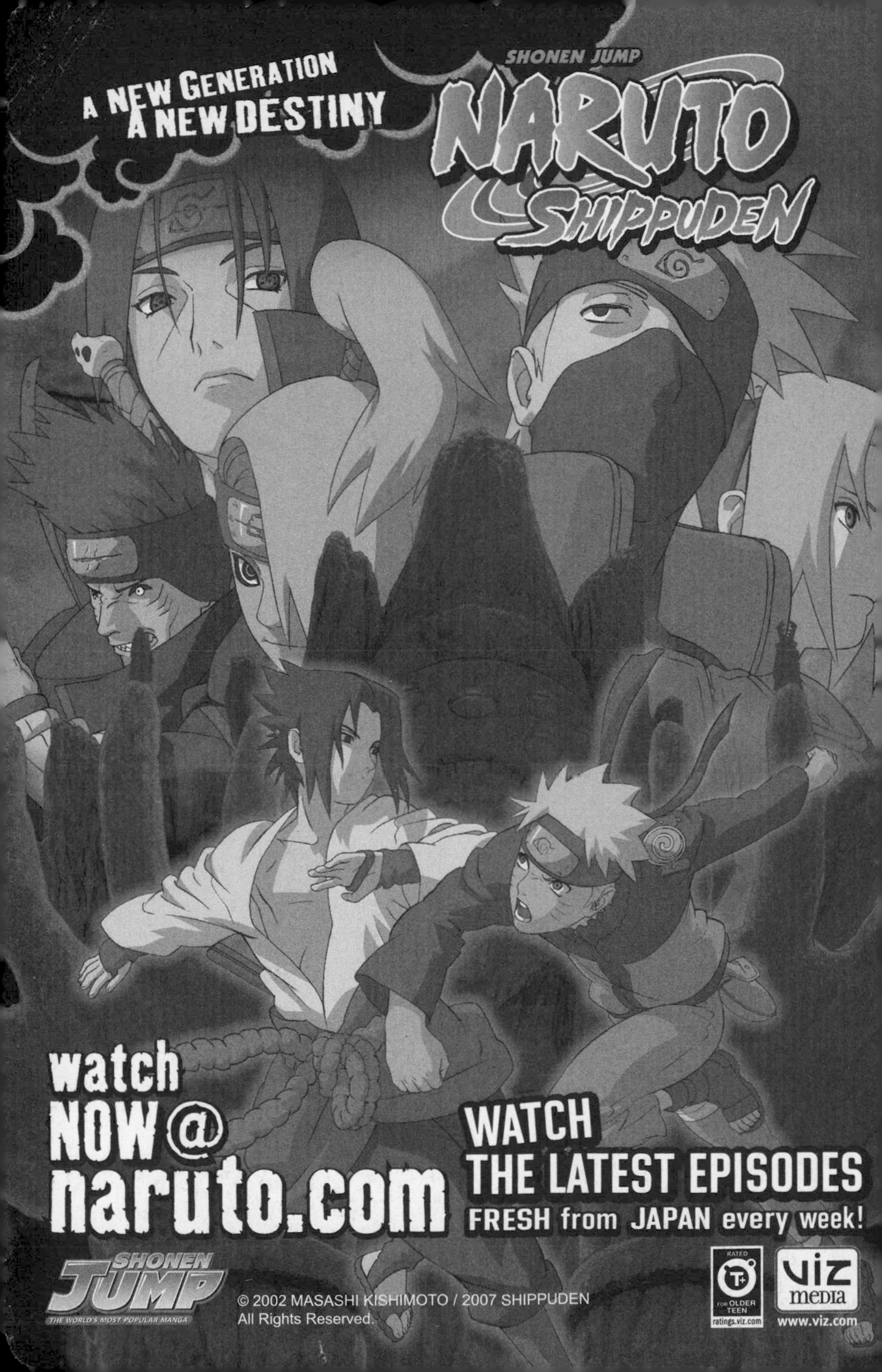

A NEW GENERATION
A NEW DESTINY
SHONEN JUMP
NARUTO
SHIPPUDEN
watch
NOW @
naruto.com
WATCH
THE LATEST EPISODES
FRESH from JAPAN every week!
SHONEN JUMP
THE WORLD'S MOST POPULAR MANGA
© 2002 MASASHI KISHIMOTO / 2007 SHIPPUDEN
All Rights Reserved.
RATED
T+
FOR OLDER TEEN
ratings.viz.com
viz media
www.viz.com

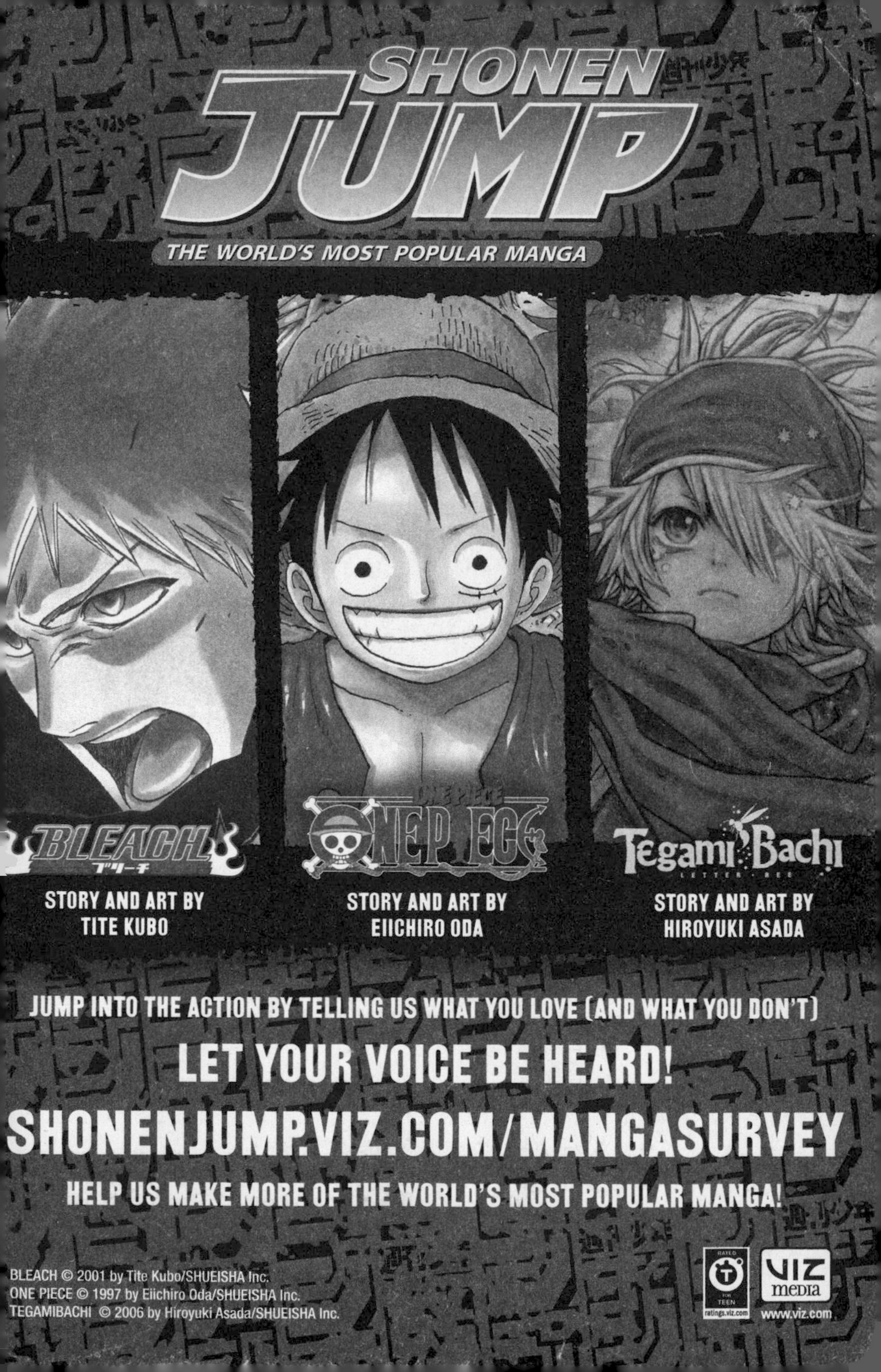
SHONEN JUMP
THE WORLD'S MOST POPULAR MANGA
BLEACH
ブリーチ
STORY AND ART BY
TITE KUBO
ONE PIECE
STORY AND ART BY
EIICHIRO ODA
Tegami Bachi
STORY AND ART BY
HIROYUKI ASADA
JUMP INTO THE ACTION BY TELLING US WHAT YOU LOVE (AND WHAT YOU DON'T)
LET YOUR VOICE BE HEARD!
SHONENJUMP.VIZ.COM/MANGASURVEY
HELP US MAKE MORE OF THE WORLD'S MOST POPULAR MANGA!
BLEACH © 2001 by Tite Kubo/SHUEISHA Inc.
ONE PIECE © 1997 by Eiichiro Oda/SHUEISHA Inc.
TEGAMIBACHI © 2006 by Hiroyuki Asada/SHUEISHA Inc.
RATED T FOR TEEN
ratings.viz.com
VIZ media
www.viz.com